BUM BAGS AND FANNY PACKS

England and America are two countries separated by the same language.
—GEORGE BERNARD SHAW

England and America are two countries separated by the Atlantic Ocean.
—EDDIE IZZARD

"The question is," said Alice, "whether you *can* make words mean so many different things."
"The question is," said Humpty Dumpty, "which is to be master—that's all."
—LEWIS CARROLL, *Through the Looking-Glass*

BUM BAGS
and
FANNY PACKS

– A –
BRITISH–AMERICAN
AMERICAN–*BRITISH*
DICTIONARY

JEREMY SMITH

CARROLL & GRAF PUBLISHERS
NEW YORK

BUM BAGS AND FANNY PACKS
A British-American American-British Dictionary

Carroll & Graf Publishers
An Imprint of Avalon Publishing Group Inc.
245 West 17th Street
11th Floor
New York, NY 10011

AVALON

Library of Congress Cataloging-in-Publication Data is available.

US dialect map reproduced with permission from Ann Arbor Press.
UK dialect map reproduced with kind permission from Peter Trudgill.
State information reproduced with kind permission from Bob Akerley at netstate.com.
Area Code tables reproduced with kind permission from Bennet Yee.
How to tell if you're American/English reproduced with kind permission from Mark Rosenfelder.
County information reproduced with kind permission from Jonathan Rawle.

ISBN-13: 978-0-78671-702-6
ISBN-10: 0-7867-1702-5

9 8 7 6 5 4 3 2 1

INTERIOR DESIGN BY PAULINE NEUWIRTH, NEUWIRTH & ASSOCIATES, INC.

Printed in the United States of America
Distributed by Publishers Group West

— Contents —

CONTENTS

— List of Tables —

— *List of Figures* —

— Acknowledgements —

THIS BOOK STARTED life as an online document at the same time as the web, where it has received a steady stream of feedback ever since. Thanks to all those thousands of surfers the world over. It works. It was also posted to the alt.usage.english newsgroup to solicit feedback, where it remains as one of their references. These guys are like word Ninjas. Cheers! That works, too.

General merciless needling was gratefully endured from Bob Andersen, Jim Collier, Richard Foster, Jeffrey Grass, Frank Griswold, Lainie Howard, Mark Irons, Vinnie Lo, Chris Lowry, Włodek Mier-Jędrzejowicz, Jen Neitzel, Michael Papadopoulos, Nick Reid, Frank Wales, Gene Weast, Trish Weber, and Vladimir I Yefriemov (especially our pronunciation discussions).

Especial thanks to Dan Tilque for help with the spelling list, Roger Weaver and Susan Christie who reviewed early drafts, Peter E Fox, David Spry, James Cloninger, and John & Alison Southern and their friends down at the pub, for significant vocabulary additions, and especially Mark S Brader, who went through everything—twice—and contributed much of the stuff I know and used to care nothing about—politics.

Thanks to my agent Rita Rosenkranz and editor Keith Wallman of Carroll & Graf for seeing in this work a 'real' book.

Any errors that slup in are clearly file transfers garbled in transmission.

— Obligatory Humour —

In the US . . .

An English exchange student asks someone "do you have a *rubber*." Taken aback, she says, "but I don't even know you." A bit confused, he assures her, "I'll only be a minute. I'll bring it right back."

When I was in *LAX* I asked an attendant for the toilet. He indicated where a *restroom* was. After half an hour I finally went to the *bathroom*, which I had discovered whilst diligently searching for the room full of couches.

A lady from the UK went for breakfast upon arriving in the US. She ordered fried eggs and was asked "how would you like your eggs?" She was perplexed and suggested "Cooked?"

A friend visiting me in California, after complaining about being *deplane*d instead of being allowed to *disembark*, saw a sign announcing 'Happy hour 4–6 p.m.' and said "Oh, everything here really is twice as big."

In the UK . . .

Three young American women go out for a night on the town. They regret wearing skirts as it's a bit cooler than expected. In the pub one says to the others, "I wish I'd worn my *pants*," and suddenly they began getting a lot of attention from the *lads*.

An American friend worked in an English pub one summer. A local ordered a *light and bitter* and my friend gave him a pint of bitter and some matches.

Another American friend was taken aback when she was invited to "go down to the *bloody pub* and get *pissed*."

In Piccadilly Circus, London, one of the *dossers* (a *panhandler*) asked an American tourist, "Can I *pinch* a *fag, mate?*"

An American, whose husband was stationed in England, got up early one morning to find out if the milkman could explain the small holes in the foil tops on the milk bottles, and the missing portions of cream. Without blinking, he suggested, "Must be yer tits, ma'am."

An American visiting English friends asked the missus how her new job was. He was very confused as she brightly told him "it's a really good *screw!*"

An American lady on the side of the road became very concerned when the nice Englishman calls out from under her car, "I can't quite see where the petrol's leaking out. Would you hand me a *torch*."

— *Introduction* —

THIS DICTIONARY IS for use by travellers, armchair, virtual, or otherwise. It provides a fun, handy reference for the ***Briton*** in America and the American in Britain. Americans will encounter British English whilst travelling in Britain, listening to a Briton anywhere, watching TV or a movie, listening to the radio, reading books, whilst surfing the web, and so on. And likewise will Britons encounter American English.

The dictionary has two halves: American to British, where the explanation and definitions of American words are in British, and British to American, where British words are explained in American terminology and spellings.

The definitions in this dictionary concentrate on the differences in American and British English, such as a different word for the same thing, or the same word used for different things. English sounds different and is spelt differently and also means different things, depending on which 'English' speaking country you are in.

The discussions in the sections and tables following give some perspectives on English, which will enlighten many, since in my experience, many Americans are clueless about British mores and many Britons are ignorant of the American way of life. Cluelessness notwithstanding, the American fascination with things British (tennis, Royal Family, ***football***, Beatles, history) is not reciprocated, though many Americanisms are considered hip in Britain, facilitated by the wide reach of US media. However, due to American insularity, knowledge of British English in America is less common than the reverse.

Whilst reading any part of this book, if any word looks odd (spelling, unfamiliar word, strange usage) look it up either in the dictionary or in one of the many tables. Throughout the work, all words that are *italic* are entries that can be looked up in the main dictionary in the *American → British* section, and

words that are **bold-italic** are entries that can be looked up in the *British* →
American section.

America, US, and *USA* refer to America and things American; ***Britain***, ***GB***,
and ***UK*** are used throughout in the informal sense to include the ***UK*** generally and things British.

Language can be broken down into many components, such as grammar,
vocabulary, and pronunciation, and also the written form with its symbols,
spelling, and punctuation. American and British have differences in each of
these components (though actually relatively few), and they make sense
when examined separately, but form a surprisingly bewildering, and sometimes amusing whole in everyday speech and writing. Furthermore, a difference will often be subtle enough that it's perceived but the reason remains
obscure. An American friend of mine remarked after a month in Britain, "At
first it seemed that I couldn't understand anything but I'm getting better!"

The dictionary makes no attempt to be formal, and in some instances is
tongue-in-cheek. However, every attempt has been made to ensure accuracy.
Again, the purpose is to aid understanding and communication, not to define.
For more formal treatments on any item consult *regular* reference books. Most
of the words in this lexicon actually occur in both American and British collegiate level dictionaries.

As you go through the dictionary you might find yourself saying, "Wait a
minute. I'm American, and I never say that!" or "I've lived in Britain all my
life and I've never heard it said that way?" or "this must be in the wrong section, that's a common word to me." There are many reasons for this, and these
are all touched on in the *Differences* section.

PARENTAL ADVISORY—EXPLICIT LYRICS

Nasty 'orrible stuff follows: There are plenty of 'street terms' and colourful
entries throughout the dictionary, included to further understanding. Differences occur especially in the dynamic areas of language, of which slang and
swear words are a major part, and again these are all expounded in the *Differences* section.

WHAT THIS DICTIONARY IS

➤ **reference:** This dictionary is intended to be used by Americans translating British, and Britons translating American. A word may have many
meanings but only words with differences are noted, with little or no indication of the quantity or kind of other meanings.

WHAT THIS DICTIONARY ISN'T

➤ **definitions:** This dictionary doesn't intend to define words. Where possible, only a synonym is given, because a word or phrase in your own language, with all its connotations, conveys so much more than a dry definition.

➤ **translations:** It would be futile to attempt to construct Americanisms or Britishisms using this dictionary. Although there are notes on the various types of differences there is no formal grammar or tutorial. Such things actually exist; consider actors studying for cross-cultural characters or linguists analysing dialects. Look through the references for books on particular topics.

   However, for those in the business of transatlantically translating novels, papers, and such, this dictionary serves as an excellent reference. There are some notes on this at the end of the *Differences* section.

➤ **slang:** This is not a slang dictionary, but it does contain a lot of slang, amongst other things. It is primarily a list of differences, and much slang falls into that list.

SECTIONS

The following notes briefly describe the sections or articles found in this book.

How to Use This Dictionary

This section describes the structure of the entries, and explains how to use the dictionary. It includes an annotated list of abbreviations used, and a pronunciation key, which includes the equivalent IPA symbols, since they are used in some of the articles, such as *Pronunciation*.

The Dictionary

The lexicons themselves, *American to British* and *British to American,* comprise the bulk of the dictionary.

Differences

This is a general article about the differences between American and British English. It touches on all the reasons there are differences: culture, vocabulary, usage, spelling, punctuation, and so on, although notes on accents, dialects, and pronunciation merit their own sections.

Accents and Dialects

This section includes maps of dialect regions in the States and Britain.

American & British Pronunciation Differences

This is a special article on pronunciation. It details each phoneme that is different, and includes phonetic charts.

American & British Spelling Differences

A list of 500 differently spelt words in over 30 categories.

History

American and British started to diverge almost 400 years ago, when the first British speaking settlers landed in Jamestown, Virginia, in 1607. Despite that, we go back almost 4 billion years, to the origins of life on this planet, to unravel some interesting aspects of this divergence.

This section gives the complete but brief history of the English language. It includes a bit of the anthropology of the original Germanic tribes, and their travelling companions the Celts. It also includes a brief but concise history of language by describing its evolution, as best known. The purpose of this section is to provide a complete context of language, a backdrop in which everything else comes into focus. The origins of the alphabet, next, is part of this context.

Alphabet

Inspired by some exciting recent archaeological excavations, we chart many letters of our alphabet from their possible hieroglyphic origins in ancient Egypt.

Tables

See the list of tables following the *Contents* for a complete list. There are tables of American things (like lists of the presidents), of British things (such as lists of Kings and Queens), American/British comparisons (such as weights and measures), and the special table mentioned above—American and British Spelling Differences.

How to Tell If You're American/English

These two contributions augment the notes on culture differences, and provide a pithy surprising self-referential look at our lives. See their web pages to compare additional nationalities.

References

In recent years, there have been a number of excellent books, by experts, on language in general and English in particular, that answer many questions and clarify misconceptions. These are listed, with annotations, in the *References* section (which closes the dictionary), along with all the other materials referred to in the other sections.

— How to Use This Dictionary —

FORMAT OF ENTRIES

word, variant /pronunciation/ [source or note] (class) qualifier part-of-speech :
meaning, definition, or equivalent word or phrase, 'idiom,' "example of usage," syn.
synonym, synonym, ant. antonym.

word, variant—word or phrase in bold. Any variants or alternatives are
separated by commas. Phrases are shown 'as is' (***the trots***) and not recast
(***trots, the***), and words such as 'the' are ignored for sorting purposes.

/pronunciation/—pronunciation is indicated as necessary. The pronunciation
key is found on the page immediately in front of the dictionary proper.

[source or note]—the square brackets indicate gratuitous notes—they are
unnecessary but provide the original word derivation or source, or some historical notes. For instance [region] means it originally derived from that
region, whereas (region) means it's only used in that region.

(class)—class indicates the kind of word, such as military, cooking, auto-
motive. Also, the parentheses may contain additional notes, or indicate in
which region the word is encountered. Occasional other English variety
words are included, which are indicated here, such as (Aus).

qualifier—there are over 30 qualifiers, such as abbr, expr, usage. Since they
are mostly abbreviated they are all listed in the table of abbreviations, page
10. (See note about usage below.)

part-of-speech—there are over a dozen parts-of-speech, such as n, adj, adv.
Since they are abbreviated they are all listed in the table of abbreviations,
page 10.

:—the ***pond***. The colon separates the word (and all of its various qualifiers),
from the meaning (with its accompanying notes). Furthermore, everything
left of the colon is in one language (say, American) and everything to the
right is in the other (British).

meaning, definition, or equivalent word or phrase—where possible, the word is explained using an equivalent synonym (*gnarly, grotty*), otherwise a definition or expository note.

'idiom'—phrases in single quotes are slogans, cliches, common terms and idioms, and also inscriptions (as in road signs, etc.).

"example of usage"—phrases in double quotes are samples of speech or writing.

[insertions]—same as above, gratuitous notes, source, etc., but also insertions in quotes.

syn. synonym, synonym—synonyms are given to clarify any explanation, and are employed as much as possible. (ant. antonyms are occasionally given.)

Well, that's the theory, anyway. Most of the parts are optional. The minimal entry consists of a word and its part-of-speech; *Arkansas* originally won the minimalist award in this dictionary—its only purpose being to indicate its pronunciation.

The usage qualifier is a kind of catch-all, indicating one of the following between American and British–

➤ a word is used with very different frequency (eg, a lot in one place, hardly at all in the other) (*ocean,* **sea**);

➤ an alternative word is used, and in some cases they could be transparently switched (*normal,* **regular**);

➤ or they could be switched but noticeably (*spool,* **reel**);

➤ a word has a different nuance of meaning (*rude,* **rude**);

➤ a switchable word isn't (*lawyer,* **solicitor**);

➤ an existing word is co-opted for a novel meaning (*heinous,* **brilliant**).

As everywhere else in this book, *italic* or ***bold-italic*** words, especially synonyms (and antonyms), are entries in the *American* or **British** section that may be referred to.

Words with numerous meanings are given separate entries (*check,* **pip**) rather than as numbered subentries under one entry.

The form of words are listed as they might be found in a novel (*band-aid,* ***hoover***), with the full form, along with caps or propriety marks ® ™ if any, accompanying as a parenthetical note.

The plural is given if its usage is more common (***headlamps***).

Care has been taken to ensure that spellings are correct, so hopefully implicit spelling variations (***nutcase***, nut case) indicate valid alternatives.

Occasionally, two or more words will be highlighted, and they actually reference the two separate words (*willy welly*) rather than a whole phrase (*screaming meemies*).

The entries show meanings peculiar to the particular country. They don't allude to other meanings, if any. For instance, *chill* has a dozen meanings, but just its particular American common usage meaning is listed. Also, only significant differences are noted. Insubstantial differences, such as accent, are not noted unless they have some interesting peculiarity.

The focus is on deciphering any strange word, and therefore regional synonyms, which embody a word's essence, and copious cross-referencing and alternate spellings, are given, rather than definitions and etymologies. The *Differences* section expounds on the nature of the differences, which clarifies why some entries are included and some are not.

Occasionally I have indicated levels of words as {+} positive or complimentary, (grandma compliant) {0} neutral, (mum approved) {-} negative or disparaging, (but vicar friendly) {- -} very negative or contemptuous, (though tolerated by understanding coworkers) {- - -} extremely negative and often offensive, (but ok with the *mate*s).

REFERENCE ENTRIES

Some words have so many synonyms (e.g. *bathroom,* **toilet**) that they are given as a list. And some ordinary words have been co-opted to serve as an anchor for a list, as indicated below in curly braces, such as {*cheat*} and {*puke*}. So, to find all the American synonyms for *drunk* look it up in the American section. Here is a list of all the reference (thesaurus) entries—the numbers indicate how many synonyms are listed (last time I looked).

US *syn* (*syn*)	UK *syn* (*syn*)
barf 12	{*puke*}5
bathroom 15	**toilet** 26
{*breasts*}7	{*breasts*}11
butt 6	**bum** 5
{*bye*} 6	{*bye*} 5
{*cheat*}8 (1)	
cool 8 (1), *bitchin'* 5 (2), *fresh* 5 (2), *neat* 5 (2), *rad* 7 (2), *sweet* 5 (2), *wow* 24	**brill** 1 (4)

US *syn* (*syn*)	UK *syn* (*syn*)
{*crazy*}7	{*crazy*}26
{*darn*}29	{*darn*}34
doodad 15	
{*drunk*}15	{*drunk*}29
dude 22	*bloke* 26
dude (term of address) 6	*mate* (term of address) 14
flip 5 (1)	
gabfest 5	
{*gay*}5	{*queer*}14
{*idiot*}10	{*idiot*} 37
jackalope 9 (1)	
panties in a ruffle 4 (1)	
{*penis*}15	{*penis*}16
{*sex*}10	{*sex*} 14
slimers 4	
{*vagina*} 12	{*vagina*} 7
	biffin 5
	dingleberries 6
	johnny 5 (1)
	ltd 7 (1)
	made redundant 7
	{*money*} 14
	pants 6 (3)
	{*police*}16
	{*pregnant*} 9
	scrubber 7
	{*tired out*} 9
	twig 8

— *Abbreviations Used* —
in This Dictionary

(look in main dictionary for abbr. not appearing here, e.g. *G B*, *US*, *UK*)

~	approximately	~grade 8 means approximately grade 8
abbr	abbreviation	
acr	acronym	a sayable kind of abbreviation like NATO and radar, but not BBC, bfd, or D.C.
adj	adjective	modifies (describes or limits) noun and pronouns (and gerunds—the -ing words 'he escaped by *swimming* rapidly')
adv	adverb	how? when? where? why? of a verb (ran *quickly*), adjective (*very* green), or adverb (*quite honestly*). (slowly, quickly, ill, well, very, too), adj + ly = adv (e.g. rare, honest; rarely, honestly)
Afr	African	
alt	alternative	alternative with equal distribution
ant	antonym	
arch	archaic	used to indicate ancient words still used
Aus	Australian	
bsl	backslang	'boy' becomes 'yob'
cf	compare	L. *confer*
col	colloquial	informal conversation
conj	conjunction	connectors: and, or, but, neither, nor, for, when
contr	contraction	
crsl	Cockney rsl.	
csl	Cockney slang	
dated	dated	refers to a defunct term, though still pops up in books, movies, and in jokes, etc.

derog	derogatory	intentionally offensive
dial	dialect	
echoic	echoic	word sounds like what it means (yada yada, poo poo), but not necessarily onomatopoeic
esp	especially	
euph	euphemism	vicar friendly alternative
excl	exclamation	
expr	expression	a string of elements analyzed as a unit, such as a sentence, or an idiom
Fr	French	
gesture	gesture	
Hindi	Hindi	spoken mainly in N. Central India, or its dialect Hindustani, influenced by Persian and spoken also in Pakistan
hist	historical	
idiom	idiom	fixed or frozen expression ('kick the bucket' = die). Idioms are not indicated in this dictionary, but are lumped into the more general 'expr.'
imp	imperative	
inf	informal	
intj	interjection	greeting, response, or exclamation, which may be followed by !
Ir	Irish	
jargon	jargon	
joc	jocular	indicates word used mostly for its humorous effect
L	Latin	
low	low	substandard usage
n	noun	word naming person, place, thing, quality, action, path, measurement in space or time, question, category, event, abstract concept, or no meaning
N	Northern	
num	number	
obs	obsolete	indicates a word no longer used
obsc	obscene	
offen	offensive	see derog. above
orig	original(ly)	
pl	plural	

pp	past participle	
pr	pronunciation	
prefix	prefix	
prep	preposition	What the rabbit does in relation to the table (*the rabbit jumps* on, between, because of, to, by, before, around, above, with, under, *in back of,* beneath, below, *the table*)
pron	pronoun	I, me, my, mine, myself; they, you, him, her, it, this, these; who, whose, whom; which, that, one, ones, one's; everybody, anyone
punc	punctuation	
qv	which see	L. *quod vide,* in cross reference
regional	regional	word used only in some region, not nationally
rsl	rhyming slang	
Scot	Scottish	
sl	slang	
sp	spelling	
Sp	Spanish	
suff	suffix	
symb	symbol	₵ # $ % ¢ d p £ s in various combinations
syn	synonym	or, synonymous with
trad	traditional	
usage	usage	indicates grammatical usage and usage frequency
usu	usually	
v	verb	word expressing action, being or occurrence
var	variant	prefixed to word markedly less common
vi	verb intransitive	does not take object, "The delegates met," "Shirley reads"
viz	L *videlicet*	namely, in other words
vt	verb transitive	requires object, "he met his fate," "Shirley reads poetry"
vs	versus	as opposed to, in contrast with
vulg	vulgar	

– *Pronunciation Key* –

		Vowels			Consonants			
IPA	/ /	short vowel	IPA	/ /	unvoiced	IPA	/ /	voiced
a		French _ami_	p	p	poopoo, slop, papa	b	b	baby, bib
æ	a	back, that	t	t	titty, tat	d	d	dada, did
ɑ	ah	ah, oompa, bard	k	k	kaka, clock	g	g	gaga, got, big
ɛ	e	less, men	s	s	sissy, sauce, pass	z	z	buzz
ə	ə	America (schwa)	ʃ	sh	shush, shock, station	ʒ	zh	fusion, beige
e			tʃ	ch	chichi, church	dʒ	j	geegee, judge
ɪ	i	trip, hit	θ	th	thick, ether	ð	dh	these thither, either
ɒ	o	cot, top	f	f	foofoo, fix, rough	v	v	view
ʌ	uh	cup, some	ʔ	?	honor, uh oh (glottal stop)	l	l	la la, lily
o		French _beau_	x	kh	Scottish loch,	m	m	mama, mother, grim
ʊ	u	put, foot	ç		German _ich_	n	n	nana, known
		long vowel		ll	Welsh _llan_	r	r	red, carry
ɑ:	ar	far, mark		t!	Tsk-tsk, tut-tut /t! t!/	ŋ	ng	ping
ɜ:	er	urge, her, bird		:	(lengthens vowel)	w	w	wee wee, way
i:	ee	easy, ski		( )	(present sometimes)	j	y	ya-ya, yet
ɔ:	or	more, door, bawd			/wes(t)minstə/	h	h	hee hee, hi
u:	oo	loot, through				hw	hw	whilst
		diphthongs						
ei	ay	ache, rain, prey						
aɪ	ie	eye, life, sky						
ɔi	oy	boy, coin						
ɑu, aʊ	ow	out, how						

13

Vowels					Consonants			
IPA	//	short vowel	IPA	//	unvoiced	IPA	//	voiced
ou, əʊ	oh	fl<u>ow</u>, s<u>ew</u>						
ɪə	ea	id<u>ea</u>, d<u>ee</u>r, f<u>ie</u>rce						
ɛə	air	<u>ae</u>rate, th<u>ei</u>r, c<u>are</u>						

Notes:

1. The / / column are the phonemes /fohneems/ as used in this dictionary.
2. The r in the vowel samples, even if underlined, is not pronounced
3. To make a Welsh 'll' put your tongue like you're making an 'l' and then blow.
4. To make the /t!/ sound say 't' without voicing, but suck instead of blow.
5. **p t** and **k** obstruct the air stream.
6. **l m n** and **r** are vowel-like consonants.
7. The **hw** sound in wh- words is pronounced by Scots, Irish, Welsh, N English and purists.

Mad dogs and Englishmen go out in the midday sun.
—NOEL COWARD

The English don't die, they just become discreet.
—HENRY NORMAL

— # —

! punc : *exclamation mark.*
' ` ´ ' punc cf : *inverted commas*, speech marks, quote marks.
" '' " punc cf : *inverted commas*, speech marks, quote marks.
( ) punc cf : *brackets,* round brackets, *parentheses,* "put it in brackets."
[ ] punc : *square brackets.*
{ } punc : curly brackets, *braces.*
< > punc : angle brackets.
« » punc : French brackets, speech marks.
. cf punc : *full stop, full point.*
/ cf punc : stroke, (solidus).
symb : hash, hash mark, "press the hash key," symbol for number, "ticket #3."
-a cf alt suff : a number of words that are spelled ending in –er are informally spelt with –a instead, because the southern non-rhotic accent doesn't pronounce the 'r': *botta, bovva, wotcha.*
-berry /bəri/ /bri/ suff : /beri/ the e of –berry, commonly a schwa (ə), often becomes glossed over, noticeable in many common words: strawberries /strorbrees/, elderberry /elder b(ə)ri/ wine, billberry /bilbəri/.
-ers suff : frequently added to the first part of a word to form an informal version. Many start in the upper classes (started in Oxford in 19C), and many have entered the main stream. Good examples include *brekkers, champers, fresher, footer,* Honkers (Hong Kong), *pragger-wagger, preggers, rugger, shampers, soccer,*

starkers, Twickers, wagger pagger bagger, and perhaps *stingers,* and *roller.*
-ery suff : *noshery.*
- on toast suff : superlative.
-orama suff : alt. to verb doubling, compare *-fest.*
-ward adv : in some instances British distinguishes between –ward and –wards (backward, *backwards*) where –ward is directional and –wards is manner of movement (backward is moving towards the back whereas backwards is moving back first). This is less true of other directional adverbs (*afterwards* downwards eastwards *forwards* frontwards heavenwards homewards inwards leftwards northwards rearwards rightwards seawards skywards southwards upwards westwards) but the –wards form is quite common generally and such usage carries over into words like awkwards (adj) and *towards* (prep), "this chair tilts all the way forwards."
£ (a Latin L) symb : pound, symbol for pounds sterling. 1968 began the *decimalisation* of the British currency when a pound became 100 new pennies. Prior to that a pound was 20 shillings, a shilling twelve pence (pennies) and the smallest division of a penny was a farthing. It is written £/s/d, and £/s/- for even shillings (£9/14s/6d nine pounds, fourteen shillings and sixpence, £9/14s/- nine pounds, fourteen). From 1776 till WWII £1 fluctuated between $3-$5 (1864 peak of $12). Since WWII it has fluctuated around $2 when 1d was 1¢ (low of $1.04 in 1985). Hence, the

slang *dollar* for *5/-*, and *half a dollar* for *half a crown*, was accurate until the early 1970s. See table of British Money.

£1 symb : symbol for one pound note (green), first issued in 1928, new *note* issued in 1968, and reverting back to coins in 1983, which are gold colored nickel-brass, like a large double-fat *nickel*.

£2 symb : bi-metal £2 coins have been in circulation since1997, see *£1* and *sovereign*.

£5 symb : symbol for five pound note (blue, though, like the *tenner*s, for about 100 years until 1957, they used to be huge white sheets inscribed with gold filigree, large enough to wrap up plenty of *money* in).

£10 symb : symbol for ten pounds or ten pound note (brown).

£20 symb : symbol for twenty pounds or the twenty pound note (rainbow colors).

£sd /el es dee/ symb : 'pounds, shillings, and pence,' *money* in general, and the British monetary system in particular prior to *decimalisation* (4 *farthing*s = 2 *half-pennies* = 1 *penny*, 12 pence = 1 *shilling*, 2 shillings = 1 *florin*, 5 shillings = 1 *crown*, 20 shillings = 1 *pound* (*sovereign*), 21 shillings = 1 *guinea*). See *new pence*, and table of British Money.

¼d /fahdhing/ symb : symbol for a *farthing*, four to a *penny*, bronze, a little bigger than a *cent*, went out of circulation in 1956.

½d /haypnee/ symb : symbol for a *half-penny*, bronze, about the size of a large thin *quarter*, actually exactly 1 inch in diameter, in circulation until 1970.

½p symb : bronze, 1971–1984, a little smaller than a *dime*. Even though part of *decimalisation*, people still always wrote £1.98½, rather than £1.985.

1/-, **1s**, **12d** symb : symbol for shilling (12d), cupro-nickel, size of a small *quarter*, in circulation until 1990, equivalent to *5p*, syn. *bob*, shilling *bit*.

1d /penee/ symb : symbol for *penny*, bronze, the size of a *half dollar*, in circulation until 1970.

1p /wun pee/ /nyoo penee/ /penee/ symb : bronze, introduced in 1971, about the size of a *cent*.

2/- symb : symbol for two shillings, *florin*, cupro-nickel, like a squat *half dollar*, in circulation until 1992, equivalent to *10p*, syn. two bob, two shillings, two shilling bit, "do you have any two shillings?"

2/6d /too n siks/ symb : symbol for *half a crown*, two-and-six (pence), cupro-nickel, larger than a *half dollar*, in circulation until 1967.

2d /tuhpənts/ symb : *twopence*, (also symbol for half *groat*).

2p /too pee/ (/tuhpənts/) symb : bronze coin, introduced in 1971, about the same size as a *Susan B. Anthony dollar*.

3d /thrəpəns/ /threpəns/ /thruhpəns/ /thrupəns/ /frepəns/ symb : symbol for threepence, threepenny bit, silver (about size of a *dime*) until 1920, then 12-sided brass coin like a fat *nickel*, in circulation until 1970.

4d symb : symbol for *groat*.

5/- symb : symbol for crown, five shillings, equivalent to *25p*, the size of a *silver dollar*, minted commemoratively but still legal tender.

5p symb : cupro-nickel coin, 1968–1990, made exactly the same size, shape, and value, as the old *1/-* or *shilling*. A smaller one, still cupro-nickel and introduced in 1990, is the size of a squat *dime*.

6d /sikspents/ symb : symbol for *sixpence*, cupro-nickel, size of a *cent*, in circulation until 1967, syn. *tanner*.

10 Downing Street n : the *Prime Minister*'s home and office, like the *White House*.

10/- symb : symbol for (brown) ten shilling note, syn. *ten bob* note.

10/6d symb : ten-and-six, also half a *guinea* (see Mad Hatter's *topper*).

10p symb : cupro-nickel coin, 1968–1991, made exactly the same size, shape, and value, as the old *2/-*, two shilling, or *florin*. A smaller one, still cupro-nickel and introduced in 1992, is the size of a *quarter.*

11-plus, 11+ n : *eleven plus.*

20/- symb : alt. for £1 (green), pound, *pound sterling*, *sovereign*.

20p symb : seven-sided cupro-nickel coin introduced in 1982, about the size of a thin *nickel.*

21/- symb : symbol for *guinea*, twenty-one *shillings*.

25p symb : like the *crowns* (*5/-*), these are minted commemoratively, the standard version being cupro-nickel, slightly larger than a *silver dollar.*

50p symb : seven-sided cupro-nickel coin introduced in 1969, about the size of a *half dollar.*

100 (telephone) num : operator, like *0.*

100p symb : *£1* is 100 (new) *pence.*

112 (telephone) num : see *999.*

192 (telephone) num : *directory inquiries*, *information.*

240d symb : *£1* is 240 (old) *pennies.*

999 (telephone) num : police, fire, and ambulance number, like *911*. (European standard number is *112*, also available in Britain nowadays.)

— a —

A4 n : standard paper size in Britain and Europe (21.0 x 29.7cm or about 8¼ x 11¾") equivalent to *letter.* See also *foolscap.*

abattoir n : slaughterhouse.

abdabs echoic n : incoherent hysterical babble, see *screaming abdabs.*

Abominable Snowman n : *yeti*, syn. *sasquatch, bigfoot.*

abroad n : continent of Europe (typically, but could be anywhere), "we're going on holiday abroad." [A kid, upon seeing a *GB* sticker on a car, said, "Oh look, they're Going 'Broad."]

abseil v : *rappel.*

abso-bloody-lutely intj : absolutely absolutely.

account card n : *charge card.*

accumulator n : (betting) parlay.

accumulator n : car battery, storage battery/cell (rechargeable electric cell).

ace intj adj : *excellent, awesome.*

accommodation n : *accommodations*, lodgings, *digs.*

ackers [Egyptian, *akka*, one piastre] n : pound notes or *money* in general.

acushla /ekushlah/ [Irish äcuisle O pulse (of my heart)] n : darling.

Adam and Eve crsl v : believe, usu. 'would you Adam and Eve it.'

advert inf n : used to refer both to TV *commercial*s and ads in magazines and newspapers, syn. ad, "I'm sick of the adverts on the *telly.*"

advocate (Scot) n : *barrister*, *lawyer.*

adze sp n : *adz.*

aerial n : *antenna.*

aeroplane sp n : *airplane.*

afters n : *dessert, pudding, sweet.* It's quite customary to have *dessert* following a main meal.

afterwards adv : *afterward*, see *-ward.*

Aga® /ahgə/ n : *stove* (Swedish design), notional emblem of comfortable middle class coziness, esp. in a semi-rural setting, hence Aga saga, a popular novel genre of family drama within that. 'Four stages of life—lager—Aga—saga—gaga.'

aggro sl n : aggression, but often in reference to street violence, syn. *bother*, *bovva*, also aggravation, annoyance, frustration.

agony aunt n : *advice columnist* (such as Ann Landers and Dear Abby).

airbrick n : perforated brick, to facilitate ventilation in building.

air gun n : *BB gun.*

airing cupboard n : linen *closet,* but with slats instead of shelves, and above or near the house's heat source, for drying and warming sheets, towels, etc.

A levels n : *GCE* advanced level, state exams taken in major subjects at the end of *sixth form* (age about 18) and usu. prerequisite for *college,* see *O levels, AS levels.* "It's amazing what you can do with an E in A-level art, twisted imagination and a chainsaw."—Damien Hirst.

all right /or(w)iet/ [the /w/ would become a pronounced r in some areas] intj : general purpose greeting, like *howdy,* muttered to get attention as when trying to get through a crowd with a heavy load, to agree, to disagree, or as an alt. to a grunt or hmm, or just to say *hi.*

all the rest! excl intj : response to an apparent *BS,* "it only cost a few quid—and all the rest!"

Alsatian (dog) n : *German shepherd.*

alternative usage adj : *alternate,* "every effort will be made to find a suitable alternative speaker."

aluminium sp n : *aluminum.*

aluminium miner sl n : down and out person shambling along with a grocery cart full of recyclables.

American muffin col n : *English muffin, muffin.*

amusement arcade n : games arcade.

Anadin n : pain killer, like Tylenol or Advil, originally just aspirin but now with *paracetamol* and ibuprofen versions. Well known slogan—'Nothing acts faster than Anadin.'

anaesthetist, anesthetist cf n : *anesthesiologist.*

analyse sp v : *analyze.*

ancient lights n : (law) if a window has been unobstructed for at least 20 years then it can be declared that its light may never be obstructed (by building, etc). Occasionally you'll see such a sign *post*ed over a window, declaring the precedent.

and all col expr intj : as well, "I've got three an' all."

ankle biter n : *sprog, rug rat,* also *wannabe,* esp. *Sloane wannabe,* see *Sloane Rangese.*

anorak n : *parka.*

anorak joc, mildly derog n : originally (early 1990s) a bit of a nerd, but now (1999) association of wearer is of *trainspotter,* geek, pervert, or obsessive-compulsive activist, "Before I get inundated by the anoraks telling me how to send quick replies to e-mails . . .," syn *granola, crunchie.*

answerphone n : answering machine.

anticlockwise adv adj : *counterclockwise.*

anti-social behaviour orders n : *restraining order,* see *ASBOs.*

anyroad expr adv : anyway, "anyroad, as I was saying," syn. *anyhoo.*

apple [apple's core—*score*] rsl n : *£20.*

Apple Mac (computer) usage n : *Macintosh.*

apples and pairs crsl n : stairs.

archer sl n : £2000.

argy-bargy /arjee barjee/ n : a lively discussion with confrontational overtones.

Aristotle crsl n : bottle, also *arse* (see *bottle*).

A-road n : numbered main road, *highway,* see *B-road.,* "the A4 is the Bath Road, but there are still parts of the old Bath road left."

arrows n : darts, "*fancy* a game of arrows?"

arse n : *ass,* "she fell on her arse," "I'm gonna kick your arse!" "He's a right arse," "Stop arseing around."

arsehole n : *asshole.*

arse over tit adj : fall, *snafu,* recto-cranial inversion.

arterial road n : main road in a road system, usu. an *A-road*, else a *trunk road*, "the Southend Arterial Road is the A127."

artex n v : ceiling texture, a textured finish commonly applied to ceilings.

artic abbr n : *articulated lorry*, syn. *semi.*

articulated lorry n : *trailer truck, tractor-trailer, semi.*

ASBOs /azbohz/ [anti-social behaviour orders] acr n : like *restraining order* but extends to prohibiting certain behaviors or going on particular streets, etc.

Asian cf n : person from India, Pakistan, etc., cf. *oriental.*

AS Level n : (advanced subsidiary level) a recently introduced official test after the first year of *sixth form*, hated by students as it introduces unnecessary stress to an otherwise clear two year study course for *A levels.*

assessor (insurance) n : *adjustor.*

assistant n : *shop assistant, sales clerk.*

ate /et/ (heard only) v : in many SE speakers, esp. Cockney, '/i et mi (cake)/' (see *me*).

A to Z /ay too zed/ n : *The* original atlas and guide to the streets of London.

aubergine n : *eggplant.*

au fait /oh fay/ adj : familiar or conversant, "is she *au fait* with . . ."

Auld Reekie n : Edinburgh.

aunt intj : see *my sainted aunt.*

auntie (usu of a car) adj : eccentric, individual, conservative, and somehow everlasting.

auntie intj : mock surprise, used when spotting a small blemish (for instance, an improperly cleaned dish, as if by auntie with fading eyesight), "auntie!"

Auntie BBC n : The BBC, also known as Auntie or Auntie *Beeb.*

auntie's coming, aunty's round n : that time of the month, "sorry, I can't, auntie's coming," syn. *painters are in.*

Aunt Sally [from a carnival game where the target is Aunt Sally's pipe] n : scapegoat, either unfairly so, or contrived.

au pair /oh pair/ n : foreign girl exchanging housework for room and board in order to be exposed to the language.

autocue [Autocue®] n : *teleprompter.*

autumn n : *fall.*

avocado pear n : avocado. See also *pit, stone.*

axe sp n : *ax* or axe.

aye, ay [Scot] intj : yes.

— b —

b&b n : Bed and Breakfast.

baby marrow n : *courgette.*

baby's arm (leg) n : strawberry filled pastry, *roly-poly*, syn. *dead man's arm.*

baby's dummy n : *pacifier.*

backwards adv : backward means moving to the back, and both backward and backwards mean moving back-first, although backwards is more common, "fell over backwards." See *forwards* and *-ward.*

badge n : *pin.*

bag n : *purse.*

bag v intj : put *dibs* on, "bags! (I that)," "bags not!," "that's bagged," see also *quis, ego.*

Bakewell tart (pudding) n : individual jam tart filled with almond paste.

bakshee [Hindi *bakšiš* gift] sl n : free, *buckshee.*

balaclava, balaclava helmet n : woolen cap covering head and neck with hole for face or eyes (popular with children playing in the snow and terrorists).

ballocking n : telling off, severe reprimand.

ballocks vulg sl intj : alt. sp. for *bollocks*, syn. *bullshit, balls.*

balls intj : testicles, but in this sense used exactly like *bullshit,* syn. *bollocks.*

balls up sl adj : screw-up.

bally sl euph adj : *bloody*, syn. darned, "bally colonials."

balsa wood n : strong but very light wood used in model making, and occasionally used by implication to describe something as insubstantial.

banger sl n : loud or explosive firecracker, syn. m80, cherry bomb. (See also *old banger, penny banger*).

bangers sl n : *sausages.*

bangers and mash n : sausage and mashed potatoes.

bank holiday n : banks are officially closed, legal holiday, equivalent to a national or federal holiday. There are actually only four bank holidays, but common usage also includes the two public holidays and the two holidays by Royal proclamation, see table of British Holidays.

banknote n : *bill, note.*

bap (N dial) n : hamburger buns, syn. roll, bun, cob, bannock (also in pl. sl. *breasts*).

Bard, Bard of Avon n : William Shakespeare.

bargee n : *bargeman.*

barge pole n : *ten-foot pole,* in full, I wouldn't touch it with a barge pole, or as my botany professor once emphasized, "I wouldn't touch it with a forty-foot plastic sterilised barge pole."

barking [barking mad] n : *crazy,* stark raving *bonkers.*

barmy sl adj : soft in the head, *crazy,* stupid, "yer barmy *git.*"

barnet crsl [Barnet Fair] n : hair, "has chopped off his spikey barnet cos it was wilting."

barney sl n : (public) scuffle, brouhaha, "there was a bit of a barney down at the *local.*"

bar of chocolate n : *candy bar.*

barrister n : *lawyer.*

barrow n : *hand truck.*

barse sl n : (usu. male) *biffin*, choad.

bart abbr n : baronet (found tacked on a name, as Sir John Jones, Bart), hereditary Sir, but not a Peer (see *Lords*).

bash inf n : attempt, to give it a stab, "who wants to give it a bash?" "I'll have a bash at it."

bash up col v : to thrash, to beat up (somebody), "somebody at the pub got bashed up."

basil /bazəl/ n : /bayzəl/ (both *herb* and person's name).

basin usage n : *bathroom sink.*

basin usage n : cooking bowl.

bastard (Aus) offen sl n : common Australian deprecation, "six-fingered inbred bastard."

bat (ping pong) n : *paddle.*

bate (also **bait**) sl n : a rage, "He's in a batey mood this week."

bath n : *bathtub.*

bath vi vt : to take a bath, and to bathe.

Bath bun n : spiced currant bun, often *frost*ed.

bathing costume n : bathing suit, *swimming costume, swimsuit.*

Battenberg cake [German town] n : square four-checkered pink and yellow sponge cake *frost*ed entirely in *marzipan*.

batty adj : *crazy.*

batty boy sl n : gay lad.

beak sl n : magistrate, judge.

bean cf expr n : nothing, and particularly no *money*, in expr. like, "don't have a bean," syn. *now't.*

beanfeast col n : a good time.

bean flicker sl n : lesbian.

beano sl n : *beanfeast*, party, celebration.

The Beano n : a popular children's *comic*, along with its sister, *The Dandy*, dating back to the 40s. The strips included Denis the Menace and Gnasher, Minni the

Minx, Desperate Dan, Beryl the Peril, Roger the Dodger, Calamity James, Smasher, and Korky the Cat. Also, Pansy Potter, Big Eggo, Keyhole Kate, Hungry Horace and Freddie the Fearless Fly. The style is similar to Betty Boop.

beans (food) n : this usu. means Heinz Baked Beans, see *beans on toast*, *English breakfast*. (Baked bean crsl. Queen.)

beans on toast n : Heinz Baked Beans warmed in a pan and poured over hot (buttered) toast, the staple of poor starving artists and other similarly underprivileged groups, but also a popular snack and part of many meals, see *toast and dripping*, *cheese on toast*, *Welsh rabbit*.

beat adj : tired, exhausted.

beat somebody hollow expr v : defeat, *beat the pants off somebody*.

beck (Northern) n : brook.

bedder col n : housekeeping in *college* dorms.

bedlam [London hospital of St Mary of Bethlehem—the world's first loony bin] n : mayhem.

bedsit n : *studio apartment*, studio flat, "it led back to his sordid little bedsit."

Beeb col n : The BBC, "let's see what's on the Beeb."

beefburger n : hamburger.

Beefeater n : Yeoman of the Guard.

beer n : Commercial beer brewers in the UK supply basic kinds of beer, such as light ale, bitter ale, brown ale, mild ale, stout ale, and lager. These are served in *pub*s singly or in popular mixes, such as *light and bitter*, *brown and mild*, *shandy*, *lager top*, *lager shandy*, and *lager and lime*. See *free house*, *gnat's piss*.

beer garden n : the usu. grassed area around some *pub*s with tables and chairs where patrons can sit with their drinks, kids can play, etc.

beer mat n : *coaster*.

bee's knees expr n : the best, "she's the bee's knees."

beetroot n : *beet*.

behove vt : *behoove*.

Belgian chicory (salad) n : *endive*, Belgian endive, witloof.

Belisha beacon /bel<u>ee</u>shə/ /bl<u>ee</u>shə/ n : flashing orange globe on pole by *zebra crossing*s, "when she said she loved him in front of his friends, he lit up light a Belisha beacon."

bell (telephone) col n : *call*, syn. *ring*, *tinkle*, "give us a bell."

bell end [tip of *penis*] sl n : fool, *git*.

belt v : dash.

belt up sl imp vt : shut up.

bender n : *hoser, wanker* (compare Aus. banana bender), also gay person.

Benny n : simpleton, *stoopid, (yokel)*.

bent adj : gay, "bent as a three-pound *note*," "bent as a nine-*bob note*."

bent adj : dishonest, corrupt, "a bent *copper*."

berk [rsl Berkeley or *Berkshire* hunt] n : annoying or inept person, *idiot*, boor, see *grumble*.

Berkshire /bahkshə/ n : one of the *Home Counties*.

bespoke [pp of bespeak] adj : custom-made, bespoke tailor = tailor making fitted clothes, see *Savile Row*.

best of British luck expr intj : more potent invocation of 'best of luck.'

beta /beetə/ n : /baydə/ β, the second letter of the Greek alphabet. Similarly, zeta ζ/zeetə/, and sometimes the prefix *meta-* /meetə/.

bevvy csl n : drink, "a few swift bevvies."

biccies /bikees/ col n : *biscuit*s.

biffin n : a deep red cooking apple.

biffin sl n : also biffon, perineum, syn. *choad, barse*, chin rest (usu. female), Finsbury bridge (male), niffkins bridge.

big dipper cf n : roller coaster.

big girl's blouse [N] sl expr n : *wuss*, "England batted like a big girl's blouse."

big wheel n : *Ferris wheel.*

bilberry n : basically a wild European blueberry, *Vaccinium myrtillus, blaeberry*, whortleberry (also called *huckleberry*).

bilge sl n : *BS.*

bill (restaurant) usage n : *check.*

Bill expr n : the Bill, *Old Bill* = the police.

billiards n : popular game in UK [introduced from Belgium in 1930s], as *pool* is in US, though supplanted by *snooker* in *pub*s.

Billingsgate n : violent invective (from the scolding of fish-women in the market).

billion cf n : was a million million. Starting with academe, the GB billion 10^{12} is more and more being replaced by the US *billion* 10^9 (and likewise *trillion*), see table 10, Number Denominations.

billy-oh /bileeoh/ sl n : strongly, very much, *gangbusters,* "he ran like billy-oh."

bin n : *trash can,* waste bin, *waste paper basket.*

bin vt : throw out, dispose, abandon, syn. junk, *can,* "you should bin it," "it's been binned."

bingo wings n : flabby underarms, esp. on female senior citizens frequenting bingo halls.

bin-liner n : *trash can* liner.

binman regional n : *dustman.*

bint dated sl n : girl, allusion to slag, prostitute.

bird sl n : young woman syn. *babe, chick, broad, cute* young thang.

bird crsl [bird lime, time] n : prison, doing bird = doing time in prison.

biro (Biro®) n : ball point pen.

biscuit (sweet) cf n : basically a small *cookie,* but with the texture of a sweet cracker, or the sandwich part of an Oreo cookie (the part around the filling), or a shortbread cookie. Of course, there are a

zillion varieties, with all the usual chocolate, creme filling, etc.

biscuit (unsweetened or *savoury*) n : *cracker.*

bish sl n : *cock-up*.

Bisto n : gravy powder, a British staple, like *Bovril, Marmite*, and *OXO* cubes, since 1908.

bit col n : small amount but often as ironic understatement, "bit of a cock-up," syn. *spot.*

bit n : coin when used with its value: threepenny bit, sixpenny bit, two shilling bit, as opposed to *note*.

bit of all right inf n : anything fantastic, but usu. a women, "that's a bit of all right," syn. *babe.*

bit off col adj : unseemly, *off-color,* "that was a bit off," also off color (unwell).

bitter n : see *beer.*

bitumen (Aus) col n : [asphalt] tarred road.

blackbird n cf : *Turdus merula,* along with the *thrush,* a common bird of lawns and hedgerows. It is a close cousin of the American *robin* but is all black with a yellow bill (females are brown), and both are actually thrushes.

blackcurrant n : *Ribes nigrum* (cousin of redcurrant bush *Ribes rubrum*), a very tangy berry, high in vitamin C, used in *jam,* candy, ice cream and cordial (*Ribena*), as grape flavoring is used in the US, see *grape jelly.*

blackeye bean n : *cowpea,* blackeye pea.

blackleg n : (in a strike) *scab.*

Black Maria n : prison van, patrol wagon, paddy wagon.

black or white (coffee, also tea) v : *with or without* (milk).

black pudding n : spiced blood sausage. (Clean and wash one sheep's stomach inside and out. Mix in a bowl 8 oz. suet, 2 chopped onions, 8 oz. oatmeal, 1 pint sheep's or pig's blood. Place in stomach bag, sew ends, and boil gently for 2½ hours. Prick bags to prevent bursting.— *Handbook to the Outer Hebrides,* written by local experts.)

black spot (road) n : notoriously bad junction or section of road.

blaeberry /blaybəri/ (Scot) n : *bilberry*.

blag col sl v : plot to get something (for free).

blag sl n v : robbery, rob, esp. with violence.

blart sl n : *vagina*, also *totty*.

blast intj : heck! "damn and blast it!"

blasted adj : damned, "the blasted weather."

blazes intj : heck! "where the blazes is she!"

bleeder n : in reference to a particularly trying person (and sometimes thing or situation), "who the hell's that bleeder," "bloody bleeder."

bleeding sl adj : alt. to *bloody*, by some a stronger swearword, "bleedin' *idiot*."

blighter inf n : irritating person, "cheeky blighter."

blighty sl n : the *British Isles*.

blimey sl intj : syn. jeez, see *cor blimey*, *gorblimey*.

blinkers n : *blinders*.

blinkers (car) n : *indicators*, *turn signal*, turn lights.

blinking sl adj adv : damned, euphemism for *bloody* (as an intensifier), "blinking *idiot*."

blither v **blithering** adj : blather, irritating, "blithering *idiot*."

blockboard n : *veneer* (plywood).

block of flats n : *apartment building*.

bloke n : fellow, cf. *dude* (see also *mate*) syn. {+} *lad*, {0} *chap*, bloke {-} *nit, nitwit, berk, twit*, clown, *twat*, twot, *div, dimwit*, {- -} *creep, twerp, prat, pillock, egit, bender, tosser* {- - -} *bugger, git*, fuckwit [Aus], *flid*, *bloody Queenslander, wanker*. Bloke is never used as a term of address '*hello bloke,' only as a reference, 'this bloke,' 'that bloke,' 'some blokes.'

the bloke col n : foreman, boss, the *gaffer*.

bloody intj adj : generic English swearword, ranging in intensity from impolite to as strong as fuck; used in all the same places as fuck but with not as strong a connotation. For example, like fuck, it is used as tmesis for emphasis and other effects, *abso-bloody-lutely*, 'not bloody likely,' "this is bloody good." [Known in Australia as the Australian adjective—kinda like motherfucker in some places in America.]

bloody hell /bluhdee el/ intj : general, all-purpose expletive, see *bloody*.

bloody-minded col adj : willfully obstinate, cantankerous, *butthead*.

bloody Queenslander (Aus) sl n : the ultimate insult.

bloomer sl n : *blooper.*

bloomers n : woman's baggy *knickers*.

blooming adj : euphemism for bloody (as an intensifier), "bloomin' *idiot*."

blotto sl adj : out of it (as in *drunk*).

blowed expr intj : usu. 'I'll be blowed,' syn. 'I'll be damned,' 'I'll be *dipped.'*

blower inf n : telephone, "get her on the blower," "he could hardly spit the words out on the *mobile* blower."

blow off vi : fart, "who blew off!"

blow the gaff expr v : syn. spill the beans.

bludger [Aus] n : scrounger.

blue n : person representing university in sport, esp. Oxford or Cambridge. A bit similar to a school *letter* for athletics.

bluebottle [indigo colour of uniform, crsl bottle & stopper *copper*] inf n : uniformed policeman.

boat race crsl n : face.

bob n : *shilling*, "lend me a bob, *mate*." (See a *couple of bob, ten bob*.)

bobbin usage n : *reel*, syn. *spool*.

bobble n : pom-pom.

bobble hat n : wooly hat with pom-pom on top. Waldo (*Where's Waldo*) wears a red and white striped bobble hat.

bobby inf n : policeman, syn. cop, *copper.*

Bob's your uncle expr intj : presto!, bingo!, voilà, there you have it, expression added to an explanation of something easily attainable, similar to 'there you are!' or 'piece of cake,' "do <this>, <this>, and then <this>, and Bob's your uncle!." [Most likely from A.J. Balfour's seemingly dubious and nepotic 1886 appointment to the post of Chief Secretary of Ireland by Prime Minister Lord Robert, Marquis of Salisbury—his Uncle Bob.]

bod [mil. body] inf n : person, "get six bods over to the house."

bodge n v : *kludge,* "the wiring is a temporary bodge to leave a *socket* live in the living room," also *botch.*

boffin n : research scientist usu. renowned as a genius, syn. Einstein, "ask Clive. He's a bit of a boffin."

bog sl n : *bathroom, restroom,* hence public bogs, *bog paper.*

bogey n : *booger.*

bogie n : wheeled truck for carrying rubble, coal, etc., or undercarriage of kind of rail car.

bog paper sl n : toilet paper, *loo paper, tp.*

bog roll sl n : toilet roll, *loo roll.*

bog-trotter n : generally deprecating term alluding to bathroom fetish or affliction with diarrhoea or some such, also derog. sl. for Irishman.

boiled sweets n : *hard candy.*

boiler suit n : *overalls.*

bollocking n : telling off, severe reprimand, *rocket,* "he gave me a right bollocking."

bollocks vulg sl n intj : popular and versatile swear word, testicles, syn. *balls,* "kick him in the bollocks," crap, *bullshit,* "what a load of bollocks," *screw-up,* "a complete bollocks."

boloney sp n : *baloney.*

bolshie, bolshy /bolshee/ and /bulshee/ [Bolshevik] n : *ornery, stroppy.*

bolter n : *Sloane* marital partner that runs off with (foreign) lover, see *Sloane Rangese.*

bomb cf n : great success, (see *costs a bomb*), "that party was a bomb."

bonce sl n : head, "I banged me bonce."

Bonfire Night n : *Guy Fawkes Night, November 5th.*

bonk cf v : to hit or bump into, also to have *sex.*

bonkers adj : *crazy,* "he's stark raving bonkers."

bonnet (car) n : *hood.*

bonzer sl (Aus) adj : excellent, *awesome, rad.*

boob n v : *blooper,* also *twit.*

boob tube (clothing) cf col n : tube top.

book v : *make reservation* (hotel, train, flight), "I booked a room."

book in v : *check in.*

booking office (train) n : ticket office.

bookstall n : *newsstand.*

boost (salary) v : *hike, rise.*

boot (car) n : trunk, or rear deck.

bootie sl n : a *marine.*

bootlace n : shoelace.

boot sale n : *car boot sale.*

boozer n : *bar, pub.*

booze-up n : festive occasion whose main activity is getting *sloshed.*

bop, bopping v : dance (to pop music), gad about, "Diana's bopping around in the kitchen."

Bo Peep crsl n : sleep.

boracic [*boracic lint skint*] crsl adj : broke.

Borstal hist n : now detention centre, *juvy, reform school.*

bortsch (also **borsch**) sp n : *borscht* or *borsch.*

bosh [Turkish] adj : nonsense.

boss-eyed col adj : having only one good eye, cross-eyed.

botch n v : bungle, *screw-up.*

botch-up n : total *screw-up.*

bother /bothə/ /hovə/ /bovah/ n : trouble, usu. in reference to street violence but also any kind of irritation or nuisance, syn. *aggro*.

botter sl n : *rear-ender*.

bottle /boʔl/ [from crsl 'bottle and glass' arse] adj : of a person, guts, nerve, usu. in an admirable way, of a thing, good, "any bottle?" "he lost his bottle."

bottle out v : loose one's nerve, chicken out.

bottom n : *butt*. (See *front bottom*.)

Bovril n : savory hot drink (around since 1874), and the kind of thing likely to be in the thermos of anyone out on a cold day for any length of time. Shackleton had it on his epic voyage in 1914, and it's been a favorite at football matches, "in the days when drinking at *football* matches was as common as a half-time pie and Bovril." See *Bisto*, *Marmite*, and *OXO*.

bovva, bovver [from its pronunciation] n : *bother*, "a spot of bovva?"

bowler (cricket) n : equivalent to baseball *pitcher*.

bowler hat n : *derby*.

the box col n : the *telly*, syn the *tube*.

box n : *cup* (genital protector in sports).

Boxing Day [from the practise of leaving out a Christmas box (gift) for tradesmen at Christmas, and other traditions going back in history] n : December 26th (St. Stephen's Day), day after Christmas (see table of British Holidays), national holiday.

box junction n : area of busy road *intersection* marked with a diagonal grid of yellow lines that cars may not pause in, to prevent gridlock.

box room n : *lumber room* or large *cupboard* in a house, usu. windowless.

box shifting n : discount selling.

boxty [Irish] n : flour and potato pancake, 'Boxty on the griddle, boxty in the pan, If you can't make boxty, you'll never get your man.'

brace brackets punc n : *braces, { }*.

braces cf n : *suspenders*.

brackets punc n : *parentheses, ( )*.

brain wave n : *brainstorm,* as in sudden bright idea.

brass inf n : *money*.

brass monkey weather expr adj n : (very) cold, "brrrr! it's brass monkeys, *innit?*," syn. *taters*, (from 'it's cold enough to freeze the balls off a brass monkey').

brassed off adj : *pissed off*.

brass knobs on expr adv : in style, added to any expression as emphasis, "same to you with brass knobs on."

brawn n : jellied meat product, usu. tinned, *headcheese*.

bread [crsl bread & honey] n : *money*.

bread pudding n : dessert made from layers of toast and raisins baked in milk [no kidding!]. Bread & butter *pudding* is layers of buttered bread, currants, sultanas, eggs and milk, with grated nutmeg. Another variation is crumbled bread, suet, currants and spices, baked and eaten cold. See *queen's pudding*.

break (school) n : *recess*.

break time n : *break*.

break up vi : end of school term, "we're breaking up today," "they don't break up until next week."

breasts cf n : syn. tits, *knockers*, *Bristol's*, boobs, *charlies*, threepennies [rsl: *3d* bit], chudleighs, lotties, norks (Aus), [whopping:] Norma Stits (Snockers), Gert *Stonkers*.

brekkers n : breakfast.

brick [contr shit a brick] sl v : extreme anxiousness, syn. sweat, sweat it, "he was caught; now he's brickin' it."

brick sl n : dense person, "thick as a brick," also generous and loyal person, "he's a real brick."

bridge roll n : *hot dog* roll.
bridleway n : bridle path, *trail*.
brill [brilliant] col adj intj : syn. *safe*, *cool*, *awesome!*, *excellent!*, *sweet*.
brilliant intj adj : full form of *brill*.
briny n : the sea.
Bristol's crsl [Bristol City] n : *breasts*, syn. *knockers*, *ta-tas*.
Brit n : person from *Britain*, *Limey*, *Pom*, *Sassanach*, see *Briton*.
Britain n : *Great Britain* but often used loosely meaning *UK*, also *England* (by some *English*). [The part-Welsh Tudors gained the English throne in 1485 and in the Act of Union of 1536 united Wales with England, with many Welsh people favoring Britain as a name for the union. Historian Norman Davies points out that a unified British state was first proposed in 1604 and realized in 1654 (see *Great Britain*), launched on a continuous career in 1707 (see *Great Britain already*), reached its greatest extent in 1801 (see *United Kingdom*), and began to disintegrate in 1922 (Irish Free State proclaimed, see *United Kingdom* again).]
British Commonwealth n : former name (prior to 1949) of the *Commonwealth*.
British Isles n : the geographical islands comprising *Great Britain* (8th largest island in the world), Ireland (20th), Channel Islands, and the Isle of Man.
British Rail tea n : simply dreadful hot strong bitter tea. Institutional *tea* is too many industrial-strength teabags steeped too long in large pots with unnaturally scalding-hot water, served with milk and sugar cubes (one lump or two?). This is British Rail tea or *railway tea*, although an alternative mode of preparation, for a single cup, is to stir milk sugar teabag and super-heated water, for that uniquely generic taste, available at less fine station *cafe*s and on the train. Can use to develop

film in a pinch. [British Rail (was British Railways) was privatized in the late 1990s.]
British Summer Time n : *summer time*, syn. *daylight saving time*.
Briton n : person from Britain, though it is rarely used for an individual, who would be called a 'person from Britain,' 'British person,' or *Brit*. Where used, it is usu. more indirectly, "three Britons were on the plane."
Brixton briefcase n : boombox, ghetto blaster. [Brixton in SE London with high population of West Indians.]
B-road n : numbered minor road, see *A-road*.
broad bean n : *fava bean Vicia faba*.
brolly n : umbrella.
bronze sl n : non-silver coins (esp. *old money*).
brothel creepers n : quiet thick soled shoes or ironically, large clodhoppers.
brown and mild n : (usu. a *pint* of) half brown ale and half mild ale, see *beer*.
browned off expr adj : fed up, despondent.
brown trout sl n : turd, see *white mice*.
Brummie /brumee/, **Brum** [contr. of Brummagem /broomijum/ (Birmingham)] n : person from Birmingham.
BSc abbr n : *BS*.
BSE abbr n : British Stamp of Excellence, on beef, etc., (just kidding!!!), bovine spongiform encephalopathy—mad cow disease.
BT abbr n : British Telecom.
bubble and squeak n : fried leftover cabbage and potatoes.
buck rabbit n : *Welsh rabbit* with a poached egg on top.
buckshee [corruption of Hindi backsheesh] n : free, *bakshee*.
budge up inf v : shift over (so I can have a seat), see also *bum shuffle*.
budgie usage n : budgerigar [Australian

parakeet], Britain's most popular pet behind cat and dog (although rabbits are coming on strong, and we're discounting goldfish).

buffet /bufay/ n : snack stand, common in *railway stations*.

buffet car /bufay/ (train) n : the *railway coach* serving snacks, etc, "there's no buffet car on this train."

bugger sl n v : *bloke*, "silly old bugger," to *screw*, cheat, ream, "I've been buggered!"

bugger, bugger it intj : *darn*, darn it, syn. fuck.

bugger all n : nothing, "he gave me bugger all for the half hour," syn. fuck all.

buggered, buggered out sl adj : tired, tired out, syn. *knackered, fagged out*.

bugger off imp v : scram, get lost.

bugger up sl v : to screw up.

buggery n : sodomy.

buggy cf n : two-wheeled buggy.

builder n : *construction worker*. In the general (socio-economic) scale of things, a builder is a solid point in the working classes (for the purposes of jokes, stories, etc.), a clear cut above the *dustman*, but below the *chippie*.

builder's cleavage n : *plumber's crack, butt crack*.

building site n : *construction site*.

building society n : equivalent to *savings and loan* company.

bullrush, bulrush cf n : *cattail Typha latifolia* or genus *Typhaceae* generally.

bullseye sl n : £50.

bully dated adj intj : splendid, jolly good.

bum cf n : *butt*, buttocks, syn. *arse, Khyber, jacksie*. See also *up the bum*.

bum v : cadge, scrounge, "he's always bummin' *fags*."

bum bag col n : *fanny pack*. (see *fanny*.)

bumf [military] n : bureaucratic paperwork, marketing collateral, or any intervenient documentation, from bum-fodder = toilet paper [German bumfodden = toilet paper].

bum fluff n : pubescent beard.

bummer cf n : *rear-ender*, also a general term of address like *bugger*, "get off me you bummer."

bump n : the male groin bulge, syn. *wad, packet*, "she was looking at Mick's bump."

bum shuffle imp v : a row of people shifting along a seat to make room for one more, syn. scoot over, *budge up*, "we have to bum shuffle, Ted's arrived."

bum-sucker sl n : *toady*, syn. *brown-noser*.

bundle sl n : fight or general brawl.

bung sl v : lob, throw carelessly, casually toss, "I'll bung it in the *post* on Monday," also n. a bribe, "he bunged him a few *quid*," "he asked for a bung."

bun in the oven expr n : *pregnant*, "she has a bun in the oven."

bunk, bunk off, do a bunk sl v : to play truant, to sneak off without telling anyone, to make a hasty exit, "he did a bunk," "I'm gonna bunk school today," "bunk the *tube* to Archway [tube station in N. London]."

bunk up sl v : to have *sex*, syn. shack up, *screw*.

bunny sl n v: *rabbit, talk*.

bun penny n : a Queen Victoria *penny* bearing her portrait with her hair done up in a bun (1860–1874), and found occasionally in one's change even up till *decimalisation*.

buoy /boy/ n : /booee/.

burgle v : *burglarize*.

burpers col n : radishes.

business centre n : *downtown*, see *city centre*.

busker (hence v **busk, busking**) n : person playing music for *money* in a public place, lots in the *tube* stations.

busy Lizzie (flower) n : *Impatiens, impatience*.

butch sl adj : usu. in ref. to women, syn. *macho.*

butcher n : inept *chippy*, "is he a butcher or a chippy."

butcher's [butcher's hook] crsl v : look, get a load of, *check out*, "let's go take a butcher's." See also *gander, squiz, recce, squint, flash, mince, shufti.*

butt cf n : large wooden cask, as in rain butt, the large barrel under the gutter to collect rain water. 'The Butts,' a location in some old towns (like 'The Green,' 'The Common,' 'The Plaza'), refers to the place where archery was practiced, using the round end of the butt as the target.

butter bean n : *lima bean.*

buttonhole n : corsage, *boutonniere.*

butty col n : (bread & butter) *sandwich*, see *chip butty* and *jam butty.*

buzzard cf n : *Butea* hawks.

buzz off imp v : scram, *beat it.*

bye cf intj : syn. *ta-ta, tally-ho, toodle-pip, cheerio, pip-pip, TTFN.*

by-law n : *ordinance.*

— **C** —

cabinet cf n : committee of senior ministers who control government policy.

Cabinet Minister cf n : member of the *Cabinet*, chosen by the *Prime Minister* (must be member of the *Commons* or the *Lords*).

cack n : crap, "that's a lot of cack."

cack-handed adj : clumsy.

cad n : syn. *asshole.*

cafe, caff /kaf/ sl n : café, *diner*, "let's go down the caff."

cake hole sl n : mouth, "watch yer cake hole!"

call-box n : *phone booth, kiosk.*

calling card n : *visiting card.*

calling line identification n : *caller ID.*

candy floss n : *cotton candy.*

caned /kaynd/ adj : stoned.

Cantabrigian /kantabrijian/ n : a person from Cambridge, also the university, (also a person from Cambridge, Mass.).

capsicum usage n : green and red (and yellow) peppers, *bell pepper*, "get some capsicums at the supermarket."

Captain Hook crsl n : book.

car (train) n : specific *railway coach* as in dining car, baggage car, etc.

caravan cf n : *trailer.*

caravan site n : *trailer park.*

car boot sale n : *boot sale*, impromptu flea market out of car *boot*s, akin to *garage sale* or *yard sale* [since 1980s].

carborundum® n : whetstone.

car crash n : *car wreck.*

cardphone n : phone, usu. in *kiosk*, usable only with a *phonecard.*

caretaker n : *janitor.*

carney adj : maliciously cunning, "a carney sod."

carnival n : parade to raise *money*, or merely for advertising.

car park n : *parking lot.*

carpet sl n : £3.

carragheen, carrageen n : Irish moss (*Chondrus crispus*) prepared in Ireland as a porridge, stew or (by stewing in milk) extract (which sets like *Jell-O*), and eaten as food or to sooth the stomach (esp. the morning after).

carriageway n : *pavement.*

carrier n : *carrier bag*, "keep this carrier away from babies and children."

carrier bag n : plastic carry *bag* (for groceries, household).

carry the can expr v : take the blame (for something), assume responsibility, "he always ends up carrying the can."

carsey /kahzee/ n : alt. sp. for *karsey*. [Italian *casa*, house, referring also to brothel.]

cashpoint (Cashpoint™) n : *ATM, hole in the wall,* cash dispenser.

caster sugar n : granulated sugar.

cat sl adj : catastrophic.

cat lick sl n adj : catholic.

catalyse sp v : *catalyze.*

catapult n : *slingshot.*

Catherine wheel n : cart wheel, "turn Catherine wheels."

Catherine wheel n : rotating firework.

cattle grid n : *cattle guard, Texas gate.*

catty abbr n : *catapult,* "trusty catty."

caustic soda n : *lye.*

cavalier (schoolboy) n : uncircumcised, "are you a *roundhead* or a cavalier."

ceilidh [Gaelic visit] /kaylay/ /kayli/ [Scot] n : anything from a house party or concert to a dance or an informal traditional dance.

central (or **centre**) **reservation** (road) n : *median* strip or divider.

centre sp n : *center.* See *city centre, business centre, central reservation.*

cha, char /chah/ col n : *tea,* "fancy a *cuppa* char?"

chad n : see *Mr Chad.*

chalk expr adj : see *like chalk and cheese.*

chalk figure n : *hill figure.*

Chalmondley /chuhmlee/ n : see *Cholmondeley.*

champers /shampers/ inf n : champagne (see also *shampers*).

change (car gears) v : *shift.*

channel-hopping v : *channel surfing.*

chap n : fellow, syn. *guy, bloke.*

char [contr] /chah/ n : char lady, "she went out charring to help out the family finances."

charge card cf n : *store* credit card, payable in full at the end of each month.

charlie sl n : *twit.*

charlies sl n : *breasts.*

Charlie's dead intj : your slip or knickers are showing.

chartered accountant n : *CPA.*

chartered surveyor n : licensed surveyor.

chat up v : *hit on, pick-up.*

chat up line n : *pick up line.*

chav n : Britain's burgeoning peasant underclass, but with a certain *council* chic, ghetto fabulous, see *crusty, townie, council,* syn. ned (Scot), skanger (Ir), yarko (*East Anglia*).

cheap usage n : *inexpensive.*

cheap and nasty expr adj : syn. *Mickey Mouse,* made in *Hong Kong.*

Chequers (Chequers Court, a mansion in Buckinghamshire) n : country residence of the *prime minister* (cf. *Camp David*).

cheeky adj : impudent, syn. ballsy, smartass.

cheerio intj : bye-bye, *ta-ta.*

cheers intj : a toast to your good health (when drinking), but also, depending on context, thanks, ok, best wishes, *you're welcome,* goodbye, *no problem,* and nothing in particular, kinda like OK.

cheese and rice crsl n : Jesus Christ.

cheesed off expr adj : bored, fed up, *teed off,* exasperated.

cheese on toast n : cheese melted on toast (*open-face*), another staple like *beans on toast.*

Chelsea unwinder n : cinnamon roll.

chemist n : *druggist, pharmacist.*

chemist, chemist's n : *drugstore, pharmacy,* "you can get those at the chemist's."

cheque sp n : *check.*

Chiantishire joc n : Tuscany, so named because so many English have made their (*holiday*) homes there.

chicken tikka masala n : tandoori style mild chicken curry with fluorescent red-orange sauce, ousting fish and chips as the nation's most popular dish.

chickpea n : *garbanzo,* also called common or yellow gram.

chicory (salad) n : *endive,* Belgian endive, witloof.

chillum [Jamaican *pipe*] n : large funnel shaped *joint*, or one made from a tube of clay, wood, or even a hollowed out carrot.

chimney stack n : part of chimney above roof.

china crsl [china plate] n : *mate*, "'ello me ol' china."

Chinese (beer) n : lager *bitter*.

Chinese burn n : *Indian burn.*

Chinese gooseberry n : *kiwi fruit.*

chinless wonder col n : ineffectual usu. upper class person.

chinwag inf v : chat, *gabfest.*

chip butty n : bread & butter *sandwich* made with *chips*, quite popular esp. after a few beers (real cholesterol special).

chipolata n : small sausage, bit like a small *wiener,* found down at the *chippy.*

chippy [from chip on shoulder] adj : resentful.

chippy, chippie inf n : carpenter, esp. on a *construction site* (see also *butcher, sparky*). Also a purveyor of fish and chips.

chips cf n : *French fries,* only larger and greasier.

chiropodist n : *podiatrist.*

chirpy inf adj : peppy, cheerful and lively.

chivvy v : to hurry along.

choccy biccies /chokee bikees/ joc inf n : scrumptious chocolate *biscuits*, equivalent to chocolate chip cookies. Mention chocolate *biscuits* to an American and they'll probably cringe, but the *Arkansas* golfer John Daly starts the day with his *mamma's biscuits* and chocolate gravy.

choc-ice n : chocolate covered ice cream bar.

chock-a-block adj : completely full, syn. *chock-full.*

chock-full adj : completely full.

chocolate teapot sl n : useless, 'as useful as a chocolate teapot.'

choked adj : speechless with emotion.

Cholmondeley, Cholmondesley /chuhm-lee/ n : a last name famous for its surprising pronunciation, as are Beauchamp /(beecham)/, Cockburn /kohbern/, *Featherstonehaugh*, Menzies /mingis/, and Woolfhardisworthy /(woolsey)/.

chopper sl n : *penis.*

chrimbo, also **chrimble** sl n : alt. sp. *crimbo, crimble.*

Christian name n : *first name, given name,* see *surname.*

Christmas cake n : like a rich fruitcake *frosted* with *marzipan* and *icing*.

Christmas cracker [introduced in 1847] n : fire cracker, traditional Christmas party favor containing paper party hat and a fortune cookie-like message. Occasionally used to describe something that's too brief, "He came like a Christmas cracker."

Christmas pudding n : traditionally, a bowling ball-shaped rich fruitcake-like steamed suet *pudding* featuring dried fruit, served flambé with a sprig of holly. See *plum pudding*.

chuck n : generic term of address, syn. *mate*, "'ello chuck."

chuddies (Hindi underpants) sl n : *pants*, "kiss my chuddies."

chuffed adj : pleased, enthused, syn. *stoked,* psyched.

chuftie (N) sl n : *vagina*, chuftie-plug = tampon, see *white mice*.

chumley n : see *Cholmondesley*.

chunder [Aus] /chuhndah/ v : throw up.

Chunnel n : Channel Tunnel, 31 miles from Folkstone to Calais, but serviced by passenger train (Eurostar) that goes from London to Paris (3 hours) or Brussels.

chunter col v : grumble, mutter.

CID abbr n : Criminal Investigation Department, and the plain clothes police detectives who work there.

cider cf n : alcoholic drink made from fermented apple juice, usually *fizzy* but available still, "Whitfield Diffie and Ellis discussed . . . how rats in the barrel improve the taste of cider," see *scrumpy*.

cinema n : movie theatre.

circle (theatre) n : *balcony*.

City cf n : the City is London's original Roman walled town, and today's financial district, with the *East End* to the east, and the *West End* to the west. There are about 60 *town*s in the UK using the title City, either by (historical) charter, or importance commercially, industrially, or as a see. The idea that a British city must contain a cathedral is partially true. (And a hamlet is a village without a church.)

city centre n adj : *downtown*.

claggy [Geordie] adj : filthy, syn. *grody, crusty*.

clanger inf n : blunder, syn. *blooper;* expr. 'drop a clanger' = faux pas.

clapped out inf adj : of a person or machine (esp. a car), worn out, marginally functional, syn. *knackered*, rust bucket, beat-up.

clarts [Geordie] n : clods of earth, hence clarty = muddy, filthy. 'all clarted-up' = made-up (women).

class (school) n : *grade*, syn. *form*.

clear off!, clear out! inf imp v : go away! syn. *beat it!*.

cleg n : horsefly.

clerk /klahk/ n : /klerk/. There are numerous words spelled with '-er-' but pronounced /ah/, notably *Derby*, *Berkshire*, *Hertfordshire*.

click inf vi : realize, flash of understanding, the moment of getting a *clue,* syn. catch-on, *cotton*, cotton-on, *twig*, *tumble*.

cling film, clingfilm n : *Saran Wrap,* plastic foil (Aus).

clink sl n : prison.

clinker cf n : something outstanding.

clique /kleek/ n : /klik/.

cloakroom n : *bathroom,* also *checkroom*.

clobber [Yiddish] sl n : clothing, gear, *kit*.

clock sl n : face.

clock v : to notice.

clock up v : to attain.

clockwork adj : *windup,* "clockwork toy," "clockwork radio."

close /klohs/ n : small quiet dead-end residential street, cf. *cul-de-sac*, *mews*, *drive*, *blvd*, *road*, *street*.

clot inf n : clumsy person, *klutz,* fool.

clothes-peg n : *clothespin, peg*.

clotted cream n : really thick rich cream used like butter on pastries, scones, etc., and mostly associated with the SW, see *Devonshire cream*.

clout usage v : hit, slap, clip.

Cluedo (game) n : *Clue.*

coach (train) n : car, *railway coach,* but dining car, baggage car, etc.

coach n : generic term for commercial bus service, such as Greyhound, "Are you coming by train or coach?"

coaster n : coastwise boat or ship.

cob n : foul mood, "He's got a cob on."

cobblers crsl [*cobbler's awls balls*] n intj : rubbish, nonsense, "what a load of old cobblers."

cock col n : *mate*, "'ello, cock!," "hello *me* old cock."

cock sl n : nonsense, "what a load of cock!"

cock n : *rooster.*

cock a snook v gesture : show contempt, thumb ones nose, "maybe it's just his [Eric Idle's] way of cocking a snook at the whole crazy world."

cock cheese sl n : *headcheese, knob cheese*.

cockles n : an edible bivalve *mollusk* popular in *seaside* towns as a snack (served raw with vinegar, and a bit of bread & butter), esp. in the *pub*s. "Cockles and mussels, alive, alive oh."

Cockney n adj : person born within the sound of Bow /boh/ Bells, *City* of London, syn. *east ender*.

cock-up n (**cock up** v) : *screw-up*.

cocoa expr intj : see *I should cocoa*.

codger inf n : old man.

codswallop sl n : *hogwash*, twaddle, "wot a load of cods."

co-inkydinky n : coincidence.

coley n : kinds of food fish such as pollack (saithe) or *rock-salmon*.

collar stiffener n : *collar stay*.

collar stud n : *collar button*.

college n : university.

collywobbles sl n : nervousness, butterflies in the stomach.

the Colonies col n : America.

colour sp n : *color*. See also *-or, -our*.

colours n : athletic award at some *school*s and *college*s, signified with a ribbon (or uniform), 'Cambridge Blue,' 'Crusaders' Colours.'

colour supplement n : color magazine included with the Sunday paper.

come the raw prawn (Aus) expr v : attempt to cheat or trick, usu. used as an accusation, "don't come the raw prawn."

comfy contr adj : comfortable.

comic cf n : comic book, strip cartoons.

commercial traveller n : *traveling salesperson*.

commissioner for oaths n : *notary public*.

the Commons n : the *House of Commons*.

the Commonwealth n : international association of the *UK* and the majority of its former colonies (53 as of 2003), formerly called the *British Commonwealth*.

compère n : *emcee, MC*.

complection sp n : not yet an official spelling of complexion.

concession n : discount.

confused usage cf v : perplexed, disconcerted.

conk sl n : nose, syn. *hooter*, neb.

conker inf n : *buckeye*, horse chestnut.

conkers n : children take turns bashing a threaded *conker* with their own to try and break it, "want a game of conkers."

conscription n : *draft*.

constitution cf n : The *UK* has no single constitutional document, but does have a number of Acts of *Parliament* that serve a constitutional function. Other constitutional matters are based on tradition alone. In either case, *Parliament* has the power to amend the constitution by itself, so rights for the people are guaranteed only by tradition and not by the constitution.

the Continent n : mainland Europe as opposed to the *British Isles*, "we're going to the Continent this summer."

continental breakfast n : unlike *English breakfast*, this is an espresso and roll, or the interpretation du jour.

convenience n : *lavatory*, bathroom, esp. *public convenience*.

convoy col n : mobile hippy commune.

cooker n : *stove*, "the *flat* has an electric cooker, but I prefer gas cookers."

cookie cf n : the *cookie* is now marketed in Britain but colloquially refers to the *chocolate chip cookie*.

coon cf offen sl n : black person, syn. *wog*, nigger.

cop expr n : use, in negative as in 'no cop,' 'not much cop' = useless, disappointing, "rivals are not much cop."

cop it expr v : get into trouble, "I'm going to cop it now."

copper inf n : *police*man, syn. *Mr. Plod*.

copper n : *penny*.

coppers n : pennies, *money*, "I can spare a few coppers."

coppice n : thicket, copse.

cor [contr *cor blimey*] intj : syn. *wow*, gee.

cor blimey sl adj : down to earth and all

business, "he wears cor blimey trousers," see also syn. *gorblimey*.

cor blimey! [contr God blind me!] intj : [the quintessential Cockney exclamation] syn. jeeze!, *gorblimey*.

coriander n : *cilantro.*

corker sl n : astonishing person or thing, "she's a corker."

corking sl adj : astonishing.

corn cf n : generic term for small grain cereals (barley, wheat, oats, rye, etc.), though a field of corn is usu. wheat (in England & Wales, or oats in Scotland); corn-on-the-cob type corn is called *maize*.

corner shop n : *convenience store,* see *newsagent.*

cornet (in full **ice cream cornet**) n : *ice cream cone.*

cornflour n : *cornstarch.*

Cornish pasty /pastee/ n : seasoned meat and vegetables baked in pastry shell that's pinched closed.

cosh n v : bludgeon, club.

cos lettuce n : *romaine lettuce.*

costs a bomb expr v : expensive.

cot cf n : baby's *crib.*

cottage pie n : a baked dish of *minced meat* topped with mashed potato.

cottaging v : solicitation for, and gay sex in public *loo*s [cottage sl. public *loo*], "No camping or cottaging."

cotton (sewing) n : *thread.*

cotton inf v : realize, syn. *twig, tumble, suss.*

cotton wool n : *cotton, cotton balls.*

couch grass /kooch/ n : *crab grass.*

council derog adj : *trailer trash, chav* (see *council flat, council house facelift*).

council estate n : *housing project.*

council house, council flat n : rented house or *flat* owned by local council, often in *council estate*.

council house facelift n : also Croydon facelift, hair tied back in a very tight bun,

but usu. in derog. reference to lower-class (young) women, equivalent to *trailer trash*.

council tax n : nasty, compulsory property tax, even if only renting, which replaced the *poll tax*, (formerly, the *rates*).

counterpane n : *bedspread.*

countryside n : the pastoral splendor of the famous English countryside.

couple of bob expr n : some *money*, "I bet that set you back a couple o' *bob*."

courgettes n : *zucchini, baby marrow*.

course usage n : class, *program,* "postgrad course," "she's following a course in antiques when she retires."

courtesy /kertəsee/ or /kortəsee/ n : /kertəsee/.

court shoes n : *pumps.*

Coventry, send to expr v : ostracize, shun.

cow derog sl n : irritating woman, "silly old cow," syn. bitch.

cow gum n : *rubber cement.*

coypu n : *nutria (Myocastor coypus).*

crack [Ir *craic*] sl n : good time, good conversation, interesting encounter, hence 'what's the crack' (*what's up,* what's *going down?*), 'where's the crack' (where's the action).

cracked in the right place expr n : supposed *idiot* who nonetheless looks after his own interests adroitly.

cracker n : *Christmas cracker*.

crackers sl adj : *crazy,* insane.

cracking adj : excellent.

cranial fins sl n : ears.

cranky cf adj : eccentric.

crash n : *car crash, wreck.*

cravat n : *ascot.*

crayfish n : *crawfish, crawdad.*

crazy cf adj : syn. *barking, barmy, nutty, very silly, mad, dotty, potty, wango dingo, nut case, nutter, mental, bonkers, off your trolley,* round the bend, *round the twist,* up the pole, *scatty*, meshuga, *batty*, *loopy*, *crackers*, loony, *out me head*, *do lally tap*, Lakes of Kilarney.

cream cracker n : *soda cracker,* usu. eaten with cheese.

cream crackered rsl adj : *knackered.*

cream tea n : *tea* and *scones* with *clotted cream* and *jam.*

cream up v : apply sun tan lotion.

create sl v : kick up a fuss, "she doesn't *half* create" = kick up a hell of a fuss.

creche n : day nursery, day care.

creek cf n : the part of a stream, river, inlet or estuary affected by tides.

creep n : obnoxious or servile person, syn. *fink, hoser.*

crematorium n : crematory.

creps csl n : flash *trainers.*

cricket n : see *not cricket.*

crikey intj : expressing astonishment, syn. jeeze.

crimbo, also **crimble** sl n : Christmas, "this years crimbo CD," "merry crimbo."

Crimplene n : synthetic polyester used as fiber and also the fabric made from it, syn. *Terylene*, Dacron.

cripes intj : syn. whoa!, criminy.

crispies inf n : *money.*

crisps n : *potato chips* (also corn *chips*).

crock cf inf n v : usu. old crock, decrepit old person (or thing, like a car), usu. crock up, to wreck.

crocodile n : a line of walking school children, one or usu. two abreast.

cropper inf n : usu. 'come a cropper,' victim of a disaster, "He came a *right* cropper," but "poor cropper."

cross adj : angry, *mad,* "I was so cross with him," "it made me cross."

crossroads usage n : *intersection.*

crown n : see *5/-.*

crumble n : kinds of fruit (or vegetable) pies with a crumbly topping made from flour

and fat rolled to be like breadcrumbs, 'rhubarb crumble,' cf. *buckle.*

crumbs intj : syn. *crikey,* gosh.

crumpet (food) n : similar to an *English muffin,* prepared from eggless batter (rather than dough as in a *muffin*), risen with yeast, and cooked on a griddle, served toasted and buttered (yum!).

crumpet n : woman as *sex,* 'bit of crumpet' = 'a piece of ass,' "lovely bit of crumpet."

Crunchie (candy bar) n : similar to Butterfingers.

crushing bore expr n : mercilessly boring person or situation.

crustie n : homeless person, usu. young, dreadlocks, begging, dog on leash.

crusty adj : (same meaning as in the US) grungy, *grotty.*

crutch cf n : *crotch,* "kick him in the crutch!"

CTM abbr n : *chicken tikka masala.*

cuckoo n : well-known bird throughout Europe both for its distinctive Spring 'cukoo' call echoing from the woods, a harbinger of warm weather, and inspiration for the cuckoo clock sound, and also for its parasitic habit of laying its one large egg in the nest of a smaller bird, which then hatches and kicks out any eggs and nestlings and feeds voraciously from its diminutive foster parents. The *cowbird* in the US is similarly parasitic.

cuddle [and kiss–miss] crsl n : girl, *bird.*

cul-de-sac n : usu. sign–*dead end,* not a through street, "she lives on a cul-de-sac."

cupboard n : *closet,* 'a skeleton in the cupboard.'

cuppa col n : a cup of *tea,* "fancy a cuppa?"

curate's egg n : something part good and part bad. From cartoon in *Punch* 1895—at breakfast—Bishop: "I'm afraid you've got a bad egg, Mr Jones." Curate: "Oh no, I assure you! Parts of it are excellent!"

curly wurly (candy bar) n : *marathon bar* (now defunct).

currant bun crsl n : sun.

current account (banking) n : *checking account.*

curriculum vitae n : *résumé,* resume.

curtains n : *drapes.*

custard cf n : made with milk and fine corn flour, this popular thin, yellow, sweet dessert is eaten hot like soup, or over other desserts (cake or pie), or chilled so that it sets. The French consider it to be the only sauce the English are capable of making.

custard and jelly crsl n : *telly.*

custard apple n : *cherimoya,* sweetsop, *sugar apple, Annona* sp.

cutthroat, cut-throat razor n : *straight razor,* (see *Sweeney Todd*).

cv abbr n : *curriculum vitae.*

cwm /koom/ [Welsh] n : valley.

– d –

d n : symbol for *old penny,* see *p,* and table of British Money.

dab hand n : adroit or adept person, "he's a dab hand with a saw."

dabs n : small fish sautéed whole.

daft inf adj : daffy, wappy, foolish "daft *ha'p'orth*" /daft haypəth/, 'daft as a brush.'

dags (NZ) sl n : dried *jubnuts,* hence "rattle your dags"–get a move on, see *dingleberries.* Also, dag means *mate,* good guy, all right *bloke.*

dahlia /dayleeə/ n : /dahleeə/.

daisy roots, daisies crsl n : boots.

damn your eyes expr intj : damn you.

damp squib n : ineffective firecracker, and hence anything underwhelming.

dandelion clock n : seed-head of a dandelion.

The Dandy n : a sister comic book to *The Beano.*

darbies sl n : handcuffs.

darn cf intj : exclamation of surprize, annoyance, syn. {++} *brill, safe* {+} *cor* {0} *crumbs, Gordon Bennet, all right, lumme, och* {-} drat, fudge, *bally, cripes, blazes, crikey, blast* {—} damn, *blimey, cor blimey, gorblimey, stuff* it, *knickers, rollocks, flip* {—} *bleeding* heck, bleedin' Ada, *bollocks, feck, fucklesticks,* fuckle-doodle-doo, *sod* (it), *bugger* (it), *bloody hell, bloody,* fuck, (and the rest).

data /dahtə/ n : /daydə/.

dead beat cf adj : really *beat.*

dead man's arm n : strawberry filled pastry, syn. *baby's arm.*

dear usage adj : *expensive.*

death duty n : *death tax, estate tax.* Death duty became capital transfer tax in 1975 and inheritance tax in 1986.

decimalisation (see table of British Money) n : the changeover from *£sd* to decimal currency (100 new pence, or 100*p* = *£1*), initiated with introduction of the *5p* and *10p* coins in 1968, the *50p* in 1969 and completed by 15th February 1971, the official start date, with the *½p, 1p,* and *2p.* The *20p* coin came out in 1982, and the *£1* coin in 1983. The changeover period was originally scheduled to last a year though the old currency stopped being used in about half that time. The *5p* and *10p* coins were the same size and value as the old *1/-* and *2/-* coins, and served to gently introduce the new decimal currency when it came out in 1968. The old coins remained in circulation long after decimalisation, perhaps for the same reason (much to the confusion of visitors). They were finally withdrawn about a year after new, smaller *5p* and *10p* coins were issued in 1990 and 1992.

decorator n : *paper hanger.*

deerstalker n : Sherlock Holmes hat, cap peaked front and back, ear flaps tied up or down.

def [definitive] adj : syn. *awesome!, rad.*

defence sp n : *defense.*

degree n : bachelor's is graded: fail [F], pass [E], honours; honours are third class [D], lower second (2:2) [C], upper second (2:1) [B], first class [A], and 'starred first' [A+] indicating exceptional merit.

dekko [Hindi, Romany] v : look, glance, syn. get a load of.

demerara n : demerara sugar is a golden brown crystal sugar, popular in cakes and biscuits, and can be substituted with turbinado sugar.

depot /depoh/ cf n : service or storage buildings for buses or trains.

depressive n : *downer.*

The Derby /dahbi/ n : annual horse race at Epson *Downs* in Surrey, syn. *Kentucky Derby.*

derv n : *diesel* fuel.

Devonshire cream n : *clotted cream* from Devon (and Cornwall).

DfT (was *DTLR*) n abbr : Department for Transport, *DOT.*

dialing code n : *area code.*

diamanté n : *rhinestone.*

diarrhoea sp n : *diarrhea,* syn Aztec two-step, the *squirts,* the *squits,* the *trots,* see also *bog trotter.*

diary cf n : small *engagement calendar, day planner,* agenda, *appointment book,* or *date book.* Also personal *journal,* as in Bridget Jones' Diary.

dibber n : *dibble.*

dicey adj : *risky.*

dicky sl adj : unsound, syn. *dodgy, flaky,* "the kids are at home in bed with dicky tummies."

dicky bird crsl n : word.

diddle cf inf v : swindle.

diddums intj : mildly sarcastic commiseration said to over-reacting hurt person, esp. children, syn. *'aw shucks.'*

diddyman n : small man.

digestive biscuits n : dangerously addictive drug with no known remedy. Actually, it's just a semi-sweet wholemeal *biscuit,* and you can sometimes get them at Safeway, but they probably epitomize what any British person thinks of as a *biscuit,* and for those addicts, a cup of tea and biscuits ends up being as many cups of tea required to consume the whole packet. (So there!) "What's Your favourite *biscuit*?" "It's got to be the Chocolate Digestive, plain or milk. Unsurpassable in the biscuit world."— Noel Gallagher, Oasis.

digger sl n : Australian.

digs n : lodgings.

dim col adj : dim-witted, "he's a bit dim."

dimwit col n : general denigrating term, syn. dillweed, hosehead.

din-dins joc n : dinner.

dingleberries sl n : *clingons,* see *jubnuts* for the idea, syn. dangleberries, *bum*-tags, clagnuts (N), *dags,* clinkers, fartleberries.

dinkum [Aus, NZ] adj : genuine, right, ok, usu. 'fair dinkum.'

dinky cf inf adj : tiny, also nifty.

dinner n : usu. dinner but sometimes lunch; normally folks have breakfast, lunch, and dinner, but some folks have breakfast, dinner, and tea (see *tea* and **high tea**).

dinner jacket n : *tuxedo.*

directory enquiries (telephone) n: *information,* "ring directory inquiries," (dial *192*). Phone companies now use enquiries, but the common spelling in print is inquiries.

dirty weekend n : going away for a surreptitious weekend fling, the classic being the boss and his secretary, syn. ski week-end, cf. *funch*.

disc sp n : all computer related disks, apart from floppy disks.

disembark (from a plane) v : *deplane, debark*.

dish the dirt expr v : *bad-mouth*.

div [from deviant?] n : silly or stupid person, syn. *wienie*.

diversion usage n : *detour* (road sign/instruction).

DIY abbr n : Do-It-Yourself, a DIY shop is equivalent to Home Depot or a hardware store (like the now defunct Builders Emporium).

do usage v : *take* (*course*, class).

docile /dohsiel/ adj : /dos-l/.

doctor's spatula n : *tongue depressor.*

doddle n : push-over, piece of cake.

dodgems n : bumper cars.

dodgy adj : *flaky*, tricky.

dog and bone crsl n : phone.

dog-end n : cigarette butt.

the dogs inf n : greyhound racing.

dog's ballocks sl expr n : the best, the *bee's knees*, syn. *dope, awesome*, mutt's nuts, dog's danglies, "this is the dog's bal-locks."

dogsbody n : *gofer*, drudge, general errand boy, *tea boy*.

dog's breakfast (or **dinner**) inf n : mess, bungled situation (though 'like a dogs dinner' means arranged, dressed well, usu. ostentatiously).

dole n : government unemployment bene-fits, hence 'on the dole.'

dollar sl n : five shilling piece, *5/-*, five *bob*, *25p*.

dong sl n : *penis*, syn. *ding-a-ling*.

donkey's years inf n : long time, but often used to dramatize anything beyond the recent past, syn. *coon's age*, dog's age, "I haven't seen you in donkey's."

don't let's usage v : *let's don't.*

doobrie n : *dubry*.

doofer csl n : half-smoked cigarette saved for (do for) later, see *ron*.

doolally (sometimes n *doolally tap*) col adj : *crazy*, "she's a bit doolally."

do one's nut sl expr v : to throw a fit, *having a BIG cow*, throwing a *wobbly*, "he did his nut."

dope cf sl n : refers often to marijuana and hash rather than drugs in general.

Doris n : proverbial dumb blonde secretary.

Doris trap n : domesticated distant cousin of the Kite-eating Tree that lays in wait for *Doris*es (in places like loose floor boards), see *treacle well*, gotcha, *pratfall*.

dosh sl n : cash, *money*.

doss sl v : sleep, bum around.

dosser n : *transient, bum.*

doss house n : *flophouse*, half-way house, shelter.

DTLR n abbr : Department for Transport, Local Government and the Regions, now *DfT*.

dotty adj : slightly touched.

double-barrelled adj : a two-part *surname* joined by a hyphen, 'Robert Baden-Powell,' occasionally without, 'John Maynard Smith.'

double Dutch n : *gobbledygook.*

Downing Street n : see *10 Downing Street*.

Downs n : undulating chalk and limestone uplands; 'the Downs' refer to both the North Downs, which are mostly in Kent, and the South Downs, which are mostly in Sussex and Surrey.

down the pan expr adj : *down the tubes.*

drain (indoors) n : *sewer pipe, soil pipe.* (Also, the Waterloo & City line is known as the Drain. It has just one stop, and is the second oldest *tube* line, 1898.)

draper n : *dry goods store*, dealer in fabrics and sewing supplies.

draught (air currents, and drawing of liquids, only. Not, for instance, bank drafts, etc.) sp n : *draft.*

draught excluder n : *weather stripping.*

draughts /drahfts/ (the board game) n : *checkers.*

draughtsman sp n : draftsperson.

drawing pin n : *thumb tack.*

dress circle (theatre) n : *mezzanine.*

dressing gown n : *bath robe.*

dribble v : *drool.*

drily sp adj : dryly.

dripping n : fat saved from roasted meat used as savory butter, *toast and dripping* being a popular snack.

drive n : common designation for small residential street, see *mews, close,* blvd, *road,* street.

driving-licence n : *driver's license.*

dropsy sl n : tip, bribe, "It's *crackers* to slip a *rozzer* the dropsy in snide" (snide here probably means counterfeit money).

druggist n : *chemist.*

drunk cf adj : syn. {-} *tiddly,* tipsy, *half-cut, squiffy,* half-seas-over{- -} *pissed, sloshed,* tight, *plastered,* bottled, *mullered,* elephant's (trunk), boozed, *wellied, sozzled, stocious* {- - -} pissed as a newt, newted, leathered, *pickled,* banjo'd, *jar*'d, palatic [Ir], blind drunk, *paralytic, blotto,* trolleyed, *rat-arsed, stonkered.*

dual carriageway n : *divided highway.*

dubrie, dubry, doobrie sl n : rubbish or stuff, "what's all this dubries?" "pack all the dubrie-wallah and let's go!"

duck, ducks n : term of address or endearment, often to children, "hello duck," "hello ducky." Also see *ducky.*

duck v : *dunk* (someone under the water as a joke).

ducky sl adj : gay person, "he's a bit ducky, isn't he?"

duds n : clothes.

duff sl adj : no good, useless, broken.

duffer usage sl n : person of mediocre abilities, "who's that old duffer?"

duff up sl vt : beat up.

dummy n : *pacifier,* [German *sauger*].

dungarees n : *overalls, farmer john* style—*pants* with bib and shoulder straps, see *boiler suit.*

dunny [Aus] sl n : outhouse, syn. *bog.*

durex [from Durex™ brand of condoms] n : condom, syn. *johnny* (In Aus. Durex™ is a brand of *sellotape* or *Scotch tape*).

dustbin n : *garbage can, trash can.*

dustbin bag n : *trash bag.*

dustbin lorry n : *dustcart.*

dustbin man n : *dustman.*

dustcart n : *garbage truck.*

dustman n : *trash man, garbage man.*

duty /dyootee/ or /jootee/ n : /dootee/.

duvet /doovay/ n : *quilt,* down *comforter, eiderdown.*

DVLA abbr n : Driver and Vehicle Licensing Agency, the agency in Swansea Wales that issues *driving-licence*s, syn. *DMV.* Actual driving tests are conducted out of DSA locations (Driving Standards Agency).

dynamo (car) n : *generator.*

— e —

earhole /ear-ohl/ v : to buttonhole someone. See expr *on the earhole.*

earth (electrical) n : *ground,* 'earth wire,' 'earth leakage unit.'

earthed (electric current) v : *ground*ed.

East Anglia n : England's eastern counties that form the characteristic rounded bump in the south-east, see map at table 14, Counties.

East End n : London east of the *City* as far as the River Lea.

east ender n : person from the *East End*, *Cockney*.

EC n : European Community, an economical institution.

Eccles cakes [Eccles—town in Lancashire] n : fancy currant cakes.

economy, economy class (flying) n : *coach*.

edgeways adv : *edgewise*.

eejit, egit /eejit/ n : *idiot* [Irish pronunciation of *idiot*], "heathen egit."

eff [euph fuck] v : eff & blind = swear, see *effing*, *xxxx*.

effing [euph fucking] v adj : "he's always effing and *bleeding*," "effin' idiot."

egg custard n : *custard*.

egg flip n : *eggnog*.

eiderdown n : *comforter.*

eidetic memory n : photographic memory.

eighteen [pence] crsl n : sense.

eisteddfod /iestethvod/ /iestedfəd/ [Welsh] n : competitive arts festival.

elastic band n : *rubber band.*

Elastoplast [Elastoplast®] n : *band-aid.*

elections cf n : general elections for *Parliament* have no fixed schedule, and are usu. called whenever the governing party feels it has the best chance, up to a limit of about five years since the last one. The campaign period starts when the election is called and lasts about a month. Elections for local offices are completely separate.

electric cooker n : *range.*

electric fire n : *electric heater* with incandescent element.

electrics n : electrical equipment, wiring.

electron card n : *ATM* card.

electronic post n : email.

elementary school cf n : same as in US, *grade school,* but see *primary school.*

eleven plus hist n : test perpetrated upon unwitting eleven-year olds to decide who went to *grammar school* and who did not.

elevenses n : mid-morning *tea break.*

elk cf n : *moose.*

Emerald Isle (poetic) n : Ireland.

emmet [dial ant] n : disparaging term for tourists to the SW–Devon and Cornwall—because they invade in the summer like an army of ants. (See also *grockle*.)

em rule punc n : em dash, long dash (see punctuation in Differences section).

emulsion paint n : *latex paint.*

endive n : *chicory.*

endorsement n : the point on your *driver's license* from a traffic *ticket.*

engaged, engaged tone (phone) adj : busy, *busy signal.*

England, English n adj : often used where *Britain*, British is meant, esp. by (careless or ignorant) Americans or (careless or arrogant) English people (as opposed to Scottish, Welsh, and Northern Irish). For instance, this dictionary started life as the *Dictionary of American and English Usage.*

English breakfast n : as served in B&Bs, hotels, etc. is quite a substantial meal composed of some of *beans*, fried tomatoes, sausages, bacon, *black pudding*, fried eggs, and toast and marmalade, and of course, *tea*. Quite a contrast to *continental breakfast.*

enquire usage v : *inquire.*

en rule punc n : en dash, cf. *em rule*.

entered (goods bought) v : *charged,* **put down**.

entrée cf n : starter, first course.

entryphone ® n : intercom on front door.

escape road (road) n : *runaway ramp.*

Esq cf abbr [Esquire] n : letters after name for formal address (rather than Mr. before name) where there would otherwise be none.

Essex girl n : dumb blonde, "A group of Essex girls went to a Dagenham disco to dance the night away around their *hand-bags*."

estate agent n : *Realtor,* real-estate agent.

estate car n : *station wagon.*

Estuary English n : the name given to the late 20 C accent which is the inevitable assimilation by Standard English of the *Cockney* accent, in the London and surrounding (Kent & Thames Estuary) areas, cf. *Mockney.* (Features include dropping h's (hat /at/), glottal stopping t's (bitter /bi?ə/), and pronouncing l like w at the end of a syllable (milk /miuk/).)

Europe n : includes *Britain*, but most British consider themselves British, not European, see *England*.

event expr usage adv : in the event = as it turns out, "I thought it was tomorrow, but in the event, I decided not to go anyway."

evidently cf usage adv : obviously.

exam n : *test,* esp. end of term or end of year tests, "my driving exam is on Monday."

exclamation mark punc n : *exclamation point (!).*

ex-directory (phone book) adj : *unlisted.*

exhaust pipe n : *tail pipe.*

expiry date n : *expiration date, sell-by date*. UK food items usu. have a date printed on the package, sometimes adjacent to a 'best before <date>.'

– f –

f v : see *eff, effing*.

face flannel n : *washcloth.*

facety [Jamaica] n : obnoxious, feisty, impudent, *rude*.

faff v : dither, *futz, diddle,* potter about uselessly, be indecisive, "I spent the day faffing about in my room."

faffer n : consummate *faff* artist, "he's a bit of an old faffer."

fag cf sl n : cigarette.

fag-end sl n : cigarette butt, syn. *dog-end*, also the end of something, as in "fag-end of the day."

fagged out, **fagged** adj : tired out, syn. *beat*.

faggot and mushy pea batch [Northern] n : meat ball in hamburger buns with *mushy peas* applied like gravy.

faggots cf n : meat balls. Real faggots contain pig offal–hearts, lungs, spleens and livers in particular–in addition to the usual pork, onions, apples, bread, herbs, salt and pepper, and then are baked.

fair n : school fair, syn. *fun fair, carnival, amusement park.*

fair dinkum [Aus] adj : honest, true, genuine, thorough, complete.

fairy cake n : small cupcake, usu. with *frosting*.

fancy usage v : to like or want, also specifically sexual attraction, "I fancy her," see *pull*.

fanny cf n : *vagina,* syn. *pussy.*

Fanny Adams n : nothing at all, see *sweet FA*.

Fanshaw n : spelling of *Featherstone-haugh* because of how it is pronounced /fanshor/. It can also be pronounced /fed-hestenhor/, /feerstenshor/, /festenhor/, /feesenhay/. Many place names (*Gloucester*) have suffered a similar fate.

Father Christmas usage n : *Santa, Santa Claus.*

farthing n : $^{1}\!/_{4}d$, coin of least value, "haven't got two brass farthings to rub together."

Featherstonehaugh /fanshor/ n : person's *surname*, see *Fanshaw, Cholmondesley*.

feck [Ir] sl intj : weak euph. for fuck.

feckless sl adj : ineffectual, *gormless*.

feel [feel fine] rsl n : £9.

fête n : village *fair*.

fibreboard n : *masonite*.

fiddle n v : dishonest scheme, swindle, "I think she's on the fiddle," 'fiddle the books.'

fig roll n : *fig Newton.*

fillet /filit/ n v: /filay/.

film n : *movie,* see *pictures.*

Filofax® n : *Daytimer®.*

filth sl expr n : 'the filth' = the *police.*

fire brigade n : *fire department.*

fire engine n : *fire truck.*

fireworks day n : *Guy Fawkes Day,* syn *4th July.*

first floor n : *second floor,* see *ground floor.*

first school n : school for children from 5 to 9 years old.

fish fingers n : *fish sticks.*

fish slice n : *spatula.*

fit expr adj : ready, "are you fit," "I'm fit, let's go," 'really fit' = good looking, '*quite* fit' = attractive, etc.

fitted (carpet) n : wall-to-wall.

fiver /fievə/ sl n : five pound note, *£5.*

fizzy drink n : carbonated soft drink, *soda, pop, coke.*

flaked out adj : tired out.

flannel n : *face flannel,* face cloth, wash cloth.

flannel inf n : deceiving flattery, evasive talk, syn. *BS,* "what a load of flannel."

flapjack cf n : sweet chewy pancake (think granola *brownie*) made from oats butter sugar and *golden syrup.*

flash usage v : to show rapidly, "give us a flash" (= give us a look).

flash Harry expr n : conspicuously well dressed person.

flash the Vs /veez/ v : make a *V-sign,* equivalent of *flipping the bird.*

flat n : *apartment.*

flautist /flortist/ sp n : /flootist/ *flutist.*

flea in his ear expr adv : chided, 'he went out with a flea in his ear.'

Fleet Street n : British journalism (many national newspapers being on Fleet Street in London), also the location of *Sweeney Todd*'s barber shop in the 18th century.

flex n : *electric cord,* twisted pair.

flibbertigibbet (sp varies) obs n : flighty gossiping woman.

flick-knife n : *switch blade, swish blade.*

flid [contraction of thalidomide] offen n : syn. *tard, spaz.*

flim [flimsy] n : five pound *note,* esp. from before the war (WWII), see *£5.*

flip, flipping sl v : "what the flipping heck was that?" sometimes used like a euph. for fuck, "flippin' *idiot,*" syn. *darn*ed.

flob v n : to spit, spittle, *yocker,* syn. to *gob.*

flog sl v : sell, often illicitly, also to steal, "Amazon.com was so successful flogging books online . . .", also to *slog.*

florin n : two *shilling* bit, *2/-.*

fluff usage n : *lint.*

fluid ounce cf n : 28.4 ml (smaller than a US *fluid ounce* by 1.2 ml), 20 to a *pint,* see table of measures.

flummox v : confuse, "I'm flummoxed."

flutter inf n : gamble, small bet (on the horses), "a bit of a flutter on the *gee-gees.*"

Flying Squad n : specifically, refers to *Scotland Yard*'s elite anti-crime unit, glamorized by the 1970s drama The *Sweeney.*

flyover (road or rail) n : *overpass.*

foolscap n : (traditional) paper size (12–13½ x 15–17"), or generally, a piece of writing paper, "take out a sheet of foolscap."

football cf n : *soccer.*

footer /fu?ə/ col n : *football.*

footpath n : *trail,* Public footpaths (surprisingly plentiful, some *quite* ancient) are so indicated in *ordinance survey maps* by a red-dotted line, and landowners in whose land they fall are required to allow right-of-way (but not maintenance), which is gleefully enforced by the locals.

forehead /forhed/ /forid/ n : /forhed/.

forename n : *first name, Christian name*, see *surname*.

for hire n : for *rent,* often as notice or sign on equipment.

form (school) n : *grade,* form 1 approximately equivalent to grade 6, etc., form 5 (~grade 10) last legal class, form 6, lower and upper (~grade 11 and 12) required prior to university, see *O* and *A levels.*

forsythia /forsietheeə/ n : /forsitheeə/.

forthcoming usage adj : *upcoming.*

fortnight [fourteen nights] n : two weeks.

forwards adv : forward means moving to the front, and both forward and forwards mean moving front-first, "gently plodding forwards," "genes are transmitted forwards from generation to generation." See *backwards* and *-ward.*

foul (pool, billiards, snooker) v : *scratch.*

foyer n : *lobby.*

Fred Bloggs n : name, like *Joe Blow,* given to a generic person, as in joke telling, story telling, etc. syn. *man on the Clapham bus.*

Fred Karno's [popular comedian noted for troupe of whimsical oddities and caricaturists] expr intj : mayhem, bedlam, "What in Fred Karno's is going on here?" syn. *tarnation.*

freefone, **freephone** [Freefone™] (phone) n adj : *toll-free,* "what's their freefone number?"

free house n : Most *pub*s are owned by a brewery, so when you order a *light and bitter* it will be Watneys or Courage or whatever, depending upon whose pub you're in. A free house is not so controlled and sells whatever it pleases.

Freepost n : *Business Reply Mail,* a scheme whereby anyone can write an address (or use a preprinted label), typically including freepost in all caps, usu. to a business in response to some promotion. (The business pays the *Royal Mail* a *licence* fee, and for each response.)

French bean n : *string bean.*

French letter n : *johnny.*

French toast n : buttered one side and toasted the other.

fresher n : college *freshman.*

Friesian [area in NW Netherlands] /freezhan/ n : the black and white *Holstein* cows.

frig sl vi vt : masturbate (esp. females), syn. kit-kat shuffle, as well as fuck, 'frigging in the rigging.'

frilly knickers n : racy *knickers* (from when frilly was racy).

fringe (hair) n : *bangs.*

fripperies n : knickknacks, trivialities.

frock usage n : woman's dress.

frog and toad crsl n : road, "I went down the frog and toad in me new *jam jar.*"

front bottom sl n : *fanny, minge.*

frontier n : national *border.*

frowsty adj (**frowst** n v) : frowzy, also musty.

fruit machine n : slot-machine, also *one-armed bandit.*

fry-up inf n : fried bacon, sausage, eggs, potatoes, and such.

fucklesticks joc intj : humorous version of fuck, syn. fuckle-doodle-doo, fuckory-duckory-dock.

full monty n : the whole thing.

full point punc n : *full stop.*

full stop punc n : *period, full point,* and also used as emphasis—"I'm not going, full stop!"

funeral director n : undertaker, *mortician.*

funfair n : *amusement park, carnival.*

fussed expr adj : see *not fussed.*

– g –

gabardine col n : raincoat, "gabardine *mac*."

gaffer n : boss, *the bloke*.

gaffer tape n : *duck tape, duct tape*.

gagging v : really desperate for something, syn. *jones*ing, 'gagging for it' = *horny*.

galoshes n : *rubbers*.

gamahuche /gamahoosh/ [N] sl v : oral *sex*, *muff diving, quimling*.

gammy adj : bad, "gammy leg."

gamp col n : umbrella, esp. the huge kind like you'd filch from a better hotel, syn. *brolly*.

gander n : glance, *check out*.

ganger, gangerman /gangə/ n : foreman of a gang of *navvies*.

gangway n : *aisle*.

gannet col n : glutton, syn. pig.

gaol, gaoler var sp n : *jail,* jailer.

garage /gərahj/ /garij/ n : /gərahzh/ *petrol station*, a *gas station* will often be referred to as a garage, even if there is no actual associated garage or *body shop*, "there's a garage on the corner."

garden cf n : *yard*.

garden [garden gate] rsl n : £8.

Garibaldi biscuits n : slightly soft rectangular biscuit with embedded currants, and hence known as the squashed fly biscuit.

gash sl adj : spare, extra, "gash copy."

gas mark n : gas mark 1 is 275°F (135°C) and increases 25°F (14°C) per mark up to gas mark 8 at 450°F (232°C). Two prior increments are gas mark ¼ at 225°F (107°C) (equivalent to mark E(conomy) or S(low)) and gas mark ½ at 250°F (121°C).

gaup /gorp/ col vi : gape, stare obtrusively, "what are you gauping at!"

gawp /gorp/ v : alt. sp. *gaup*.

gazump [Yiddish gezumph—swindle] v : raise house price after verbal agreement.

gazunder v : lower amount offered on house after verbal agreement, also (n. gazunda) chamber pot.

GB abbr n : *Great Britain*, colloquially GB refers to the *UK*. GB is often or also used, instead of *UK*, as a general British moniker such as the international insignia on cars and domain name on the internet.

GBH (*police* usage) abbr n : grievous bodily harm, "she gave me GBH in my ear."

GBP abbr n : Great British pounds (actually *UK* pounds), occasionally used to distinguish it from other currencies, similar to saying *USD* for US dollars.

GCE abbr n : General Certificate of Education.

GCSE abbr n : General Certificate of Secondary Education, the new name (1988) for *O levels*.

gearbox n : *transmission*.

gearing (business) v : *leverage*.

gear stick n : *gearshift,* gear lever.

gee-gee n : (child's word for) horse.

gee-gees inf n : horses (as in betting and racing).

geezer sl n : *bloke*, "there were a few geezers down at the *pub*," decrepit old man, "he was a bit of a geezer," *cool* guy, "what a geezer!"

gen n : info, "I think I have enough gen to make a go at it."

gentlemen n : common sign for *men's room*.

gents n : common sign for *men's room*.

Geordie n : person from Newcastle (Tyne and Wear), their language.

get cracking imp v : get on with it, *get your ass in gear.*

get knotted! imp v : jump in the lake!

get out your head expr v : get high, cf. *out me head*.

get stuffed! imp v : *take a hike*.

getting off at Clapham Junction expr v : coitus interruptus, "'His Lordship" I think, uses the phrase getting off at Clapham Junction, the last stop before Waterloo Station in London'—Leslie Thomas. Also, getting off at Redfern [Aus, Redfern is the last stop before Sydney Central], get off at Edge Hill [last station before Liverpool Lime Street, or even get out at Broadgreen, station before Edgehill], Haymarket [Edinburgh], Paisley [Glasgow], Gateshead [Newcastle], Marsh Lane [Leeds], etc. See **Vatican roulette**.

getting the vapours expr adj : getting *cross* or upset.

get your end away sl expr v : *sex*, "Buddha found enlightenment, George V got his end away."

geyser (gas) /geezer/ n : /giezer/ *water heater.*

gherkin n : small green *pickle.*

ghost train n : *fun house.*

gift voucher n : *gift certificate.*

giggle n : lark, harmless prank.

gilbo [Gilbert?] n : phlegm, syn. *loogie, flob*, green smoking oysters, see **green Gilbert**.

ginger beer n : sweet mildly-alcoholic cloudy ginger-flavored *fizzy drink*, popular home-made like American kids make lemonade.

ginger beer shandy n : *shandy* but made with *ginger beer* in place of *lemonade.*

ginormous sl adj : extra huge, enormous.

Girl Guide n : *Guide*, Girl Scout.

giro /jieroh/ n : government unemployment payment "I'm *skint* 'cos I forgot to cash *me* giro."

giropost n : Government banking service run by the Post Office.

gis (heard only) contr sl v : give us, "gis a *pint*a *bitter mate*" /gisə pi?ə bi?ə may?/.

gissit (heard only) contr csl v : give us it, commonly heard by children.

git n : stupid person, *jerk,* also nasty person, real bastard, " . . . and he's a lying git," "Americans have different ways of saying things. They say 'elevator,' we say 'lift' . . . they say 'president,' we say 'stupid psychopathic git'"—Alexi Sayle.

give a monkey's expr v : see *not give a monkey's.*

give it a rest v : shut up, quit (the *BS*).

given name n : *first name,* see **surname**.

give over regional col expr imp v : similar to 'give me a break,' but also means desist, "give over crying."

give way (road sign) imp v : *yield*. Most British minor road *junction*s are guided by give way (*yield*) signs, as opposed to *stop signs.*

glandular fever n : *mononucleosis.*

glossy, glossy magazine col n : *slick,* upscale magazine (glossy ads and pictures).

Gloucester /glostə/ n : a town in England, like so many, whose pronunciation is much abbreviated from its spelling. Others include Beaulieu ('Bewly'), Bicester /bistə/, Cirencester /sisitə/ by the locals, Leicester /lestə/, Leominster /lemstə/, Worcester /wustə/, Wymondham /Windəm/. Towns ending in '-ham' and '-mouth' are usu. pronounced /əm/ and /məth/: Clapham /klapəm/, Weymouth /waymeth/, and counties '-shire' are /shə/: **Berkshire, Hants, Hertfordshire**, Herefordshire /herifədshə/, **Worcs** /works/ or /wustəshə/. See also **Cholmondesley**.

GmbH [German] abbr adj : Gesellschaft mit beschränkter Haftung—incorporated, limited liability company.

gnat's piss n : weak, or otherwise horrid *tea* or *beer*, syn. horse piss, "what's this! Gnat's?"

gob n : mouth, syn. *cake hole, laughing gear, north and south*, "shut yer gob."

(Hence, words like **gobshite** and **gobsmacked**.)

gob n v : spit, syn. *flob*, *yocker*.

gobshite n : pernicious blabbermouth, blatherskite, (see *shite*).

gobsmacked [N] sl n : astonished, astounded.

gobstopper n : jawbreaker, *hard candy*, syn. all day *sucker*, sour ball.

go commando expr v : eschew underwear. See *bravo*.

god bothering expr v : fervent religious grovelling, syn. bible thumping.

godfors crsl [god forbids] n : kids, see *saucepan lids*.

goggle-box col n : *TV* set.

golden elbow n : 'conveniently' retired with a good pension.

golden syrup n : honey-like syrup [made in cane sugar processing like *molasses*] used as honey substitute and in cooking (imparts mild *treacle* flavor), corn syrup substitute.

gold top n : bottle of unpasteurized milk with a gold top (see *milk top*) indicating rich milk about equivalent to 5% fat milk, see *silver top*.

golliwog n : like a pickaninny doll.

golliwog badge n : very popular golliwog-style *pin* available by redeeming coupons from Robertson Jam Co (their logo).

gone for a Burton expr adj : said when someone or something is inexplicably absent, lost, missing, or (thought) destroyed.

gong col n : medal.

The Good Life (TV show) n : *Good Neighbors*.

the goods n : a true *Sloane* seen as a potential mate.

goods train n : freight train.

goods truck (railroad) n : *freight car*.

goods van (railroad) n : *freight car*.

goolies n : *balls*, syn. *nuts*.

goon sl n : *stoopid* or playful person.

gooseberry n : odd man out as in the third person on a *date*, 'playing gooseberry.'

goosegog /guzgog/ col n : gooseberry.

goose pimples n : *goose bumps*.

gor contr excl intj : *gorblimey*.

gora [Indian] n : white person.

gorblimey adj : descriptive of a working class person or his condition, 'My old man's a dustman, He wears a dustman's hat, He wears gorblimey trousers, And he lives in a *council flat*,' gorblimey = *cor blimey*.

gorblimey! [contr God, blind me!] excl intj : see *cor blimey*.

Gordon Bennett [founder of NY Herald, son sent Stanley to find Livingstone] intj : uttered in surprise, "Gordon Bennet! Fancy bumping into you here!" syn. '*stone the crows*.'

gormless adj : *dork*, foolish, lacking sense.

government n : includes the sense of an *administration*, "the Blair government."

graft n v : *slog*, work *real* hard, syn. *ass in gear*.

grammar school n : selective state *secondary school*, and historically, preparatory for university, as opposed to *secondary modern*, see *eleven plus*.

gramophone n : *phonograph*.

grand cf sl n : £1000.

grass v (**grass**, **grasser** n) : informer, syn. *fink*.

grease-proof paper n : *wax paper*.

greaser sl n : (motorcycle) biker.

Great Britain n : Great Britain = England + Scotland + Wales (unofficially since 1603 when James VI of Scotland also became James I of England, officially since 1707 with the Act of Union with Scotland); colloquially *GB* refers to the *UK* (GB + N. Ireland). See *Britain*.

green beans cf n : *runner beans*.

green fingers n : *green thumb*.

greengage [Sir William Gage (1777–1864), botanist, introduced the plum from France] n : *green plum*.

green Gilbert sl n : *booger, bogey* (see *gilbo*).

greengrocer n : shopkeeper of fruit and vegetable store.

greengrocer's n : fruit and vegetable store.

grey sp adj : *gray*.

grill usage v : *broil*.

gripe water [Gripe Water®] n : carminative for baby colic.

grizzle v n : grouch, whine, whining person (usu. of small children).

groat n : *4d*, silver coin 1351–1662, fourpenny bit 1836–1856, small sum, "don't care a groat."

grockle n : tourist, day tripper, *holiday* maker, by southerners of northerners, islanders of mainlanders, but esp. by Cornish and Devonians of the rest, "particularly during the grockle/*emmet* open season."

grotty adj (back formation *grot* n adj) : unpleasant syn. *scuzzy, **crusty**, gnarly*.

ground floor n : *first floor*, (UK: ground, 1st, 2nd, 3rd . . . , US: 1st or ground, 2nd, 3rd, 4th . . .).

groundnut n : peanut.

groundsheet n : *ground cloth*.

grub n : food, "someone's *nick*ed me grub?"

gruel n v : punishment, punish.

grumble n : *whiner*.

grumble crsl n [grumble and grunt] : cunt.

grummet, grommet dated sl n : cunt.

grundies crsl [Bill Grundy's undies] n : *pants*.

guard (railway) n : *conductor*.

guard's van n : *caboose*.

gubbins n : foolish person, usu. self referential, "what a gubbins I am."

gubbins n : gadget syn. *widget*.

gubbins n : junk, *kit*, stuff.

Guide n : *Girl Scout, **Girl Guide***.

guillotine n : *paper cutter*.

guinea n : gold coin last minted in 1813, but still used to refer to *21/-* values (105% of £1), "make it guineas and we have a deal."

gumboots n : *rubber boots, **wellies***.

gummy adj : toothless.

gun dog n : *bird dog*.

gunge /gunzh/ n : gunk, crud, slime, indeterminate viscous yuck.

Gunpowder Plot n : the attempt by Guy Fawkes to blow up the Houses of Parliament in 1605, but he was caught and executed, commemorated as *Guy Fawkes Day*.

guv [contr governor] sl n : syn. boss, chief, the old man, also (deferential) term of address, " 'ello guv'nor," "***wotcha***, gov."

Guy Fawkes Day, Guy Fawkes Night n : *November 5th*, commemorates the *Gunpowder Plot* with fire works, like *July 4th*. Children used to dress up a 'guy' (like a scarecrow) and cart him around for *money*, with a cry of "***penny*** for the guy" with which they would buy fireworks. These would be *set off* in the evening around a bonfire with the guy sitting on top.

gypo /jipoh/ [Gypsy] sl n : syn. *white trash*, "you're such a gypo."

gypsy's [gypsy's kiss] crsl n : piss, "go for a gypsy's."

– h –

haberdashery cf n : *notions*, sundries.

hackney carriage n : taxi cab.

haggis [Scot] n : oatmeal, onions, and suet mixed with minced sheep's offal and boiled in its maw.

hair grip n : *bobby pin*.

hair lacquer n : *hair spray*.

hairpin n : *bobby pin.*
hairpin bend n : *hairpin corner* or *hairpin turn.* See also *zig-zag bend.*
hair slide n : *barrette.*
half expr adv : see *not half.*
half n : half a *pint* (of beer), "fancy a *quick half.*"
half a crown n : a value of *2/6d,* or the *half-crown* coin, larger than a *half dollar.*
half a dollar sl n : *half a crown, 2/6d,* (12½p), see *£.*
half-crown n : another way of saying and writing *half a crown.*
half-cut sl adj : *drunk.*
half-inch crsl v : *pinch,* steal.
halfpenny /haypnee/ /haypəns/ n : *½d.*
hamburger bar n : generic name for a hamburger joint.
hamper cf n : *gift basket,* usu. lidded, "my great aunt used to send us a hamper at Christmas," also picnic hamper. The traditional Christmas hamper contained a turkey, string of sausages, Christmas crackers, can of spam, mince pies, bottle of sherry, and a *Christmas pudding.*
Hampton crsl [Hampton Wick] n : dick.
handbag (lady's) n : *purse.*
handy shop n : *convenience store, corner shop.*
hang about csl imp v : wait a moment.
hanger n : a wood, esp. beech, on a steep hillside, esp. on the *Downs.*
hanky-panky cf n : sexual dalliance.
Hants. abbr n : Hampshire /hampshə/.
ha'p'orth /haypəth/ n : *halfpenny's* worth, but used in reference to any trifling amount, "he's not worth a ha'p'orth."
hard adj : tough, "he's acting hard."
hard case n : *tough guy,* tough.
hard case (NZ Aus) n : eccentric, funny person.
hard core n : the rubble used as back fill for roads, building foundations, etc.
hard lines col expr intj : hard luck.

hard shoulder n : the paved shoulder of a road as opposed to a *soft shoulder* such as a grass *verge.*
hard slog n : grimly admirable *slog,* such as a long day at work or a hard work out.
Harley Street n : most prestigious address in London for doctors.
Harry Potter and the Philosopher's Stone n : *Harry Potter and the Sorcerer's Stone.*
hauliers n : *haulers* (trucking).
have it away expr v : *sex.* 'What's the height of noise? Two skeletons having it away in a *biscuit* tin.'
have it off expr v : *sex,* "they were having it off in the bedroom."
have it up expr v : *sex.*
haver v : dither, hem and haw, (Scot) blather.
head boy/girl n : head *prefect,* cf. *valedictorian.*
headlamps n : headlights.
head waiter n : maître d.
Heath Robinson [cartoonist] adj : syn. *Rube Goldberg.*
hedgehog n : cute, shy, small insectivore covered in spines, hedgehogs are popular garden visitors, often encouraged by leaving out a saucer of milk. Beatrix Potter's Mrs. Tiggywinkle is a hedgehog. The European hedgehog is related to the South African hedgehog, popular in the US as a pet. They are unrelated to spiny echidnas (monotremes, Australasia) and porcupines (plant-eating rodent, New World), but all represent fine examples of convergent evolution. (Some implicate rutting hedgehogs in crop circle formation.)
helmet sl n : glans, top part of the *penis.*
hen party n : girls only party, esp. pre-wedding.
herb /herb/ n : /erb/ /herb/ (see also *homage*).

47

Herberts expr n : boys or men or even the children, a mild term often used with a touch of pride or annoyance, "get the Herberts out of the house!"

Hertfordshire /hahtfədshə/ n : one of the *Home Counties*.

hessian n : *burlap,* sack-cloth.

het up adj : flustered, agitated, "don't get het up about that silly old landlord!"

hic! intj : used (verbally and in writing) to indicate a drunken state.

highers n : in the Scottish school system, exams are Standard (equivalent to *GCSE*), Highers (equivalent to the new *AS level*), and Advanced Highers (equivalent to *A levels*), although most folks go to *college* with Highers for a four-year term with the first year covering the Advanced Highers level—equivalent to the American four-year system, "sitting highers in college," "I did seven O grades and six Highers."

high street n : *Main Street.*

high tea n : the main evening meal, which would include bread & butter, and tea, but in some cases where folks may usu. have tea in the late afternoon and their evening meal later, high tea would be when these two collide (like breakfast and lunch becoming *brunch*).

hill figure n : horse or man carved into side of chalk hill, syn. *chalk figure,* see *white horse* and *Long Man of Wilmington.*

hire cf v : *rent* (something), see *for hire,* "Alfie worked for a car hire firm."

hire purchase n : *installment plan,* finance (see the *never-never*).

hither and thither expr n : *hither and yon.*

hoarding n : *billboard.*

hob n : flat top of *cooker,* hot plate.

Hobson's choice expr n : choice between two unsatisfactory ones, or the choice between that offered and nothing, "Henry Ford's offered a Hobson's choice—the customer can have any color he wants so long as it's black."

hock n : white German Rhine wine, see *plonk.*

hock usage n : debt, usu. 'in hock' to bank, person, etc.

hockey cf n : field hockey.

hod n : bricklayer's open box on a pole for carrying bricks.

hogmanay n : Scottish New Year's Eve festivities.

hoick sl vi vt : spit, also to yank.

hole in the wall col n : *ATM* machine, cash machine, *cashpoint.*

holiday (see table of British Holidays) cf n : *vacation,* "they went on holiday," "they went on their holidays," "I'm on my holidays." Although holiday means vacation, public holidays are equivalent to US national holidays. *Bank holidays,* when banks are officially closed (two or three times a year) are usu. public holidays.

hols n : *holiday*s, "where are you going for your hols this year?"

homage /homij/ n : /ahmij/ /hahmij/ (see also *herb*).

Home Counties n : the counties closest to London: *Berkshire,* Buckinghamshire, *Hertfordshire,* Essex, Kent, Surrey (and Middlesex before it was absorbed by London, see table 14, Counties).

homely cf adj : (of a woman or a house) domestic, simple, pleasant, homey.

Hong Kong n : see *made in Hong Kong.*

hood n : *top,* of a *convertible,* or of a *pram.*

hoo-ha n : fuss, unmerited commotion, flap, "I dodged the usual hoo-ha."

hooky cf sl n : stolen, or of dubious provenance.

hooray Henry n : a male blessed with a little too much success, magnanimity, time, visibility, and audibility.

hooter sl n : nose, *conk*.

hooter n : car horn, also any kind of steam whistle such as on steam trains or the factory work bell.

hoover [Hoover®] n v : *vacuum cleaner, vacuum.*

hop about expr imp v : syn. get moving, *move your butt.*

Horlicks n : malted milky hot drink, a bit like ovaltine, but comes in a ready to mix powder, like cocoa. Also euph. for *bollocks*, "a complete Horlicks"—British foreign secretary Jack Straw 2003, in reference to the *dodgy* dossier.

hosiery n : light knitwear, esp. underwear.

hotchpotch n : *hodgepodge.*

hough n : hock.

houghmagandy /hokmagandi/ (NI Scot) n : screwing around.

house agent n : *Realtor.*

the House of Commons n : the elected part of *Parliament*, and the most powerful one. Currently (2003) there are 659 seats (in the sense of positions; the Commons chamber has only 427 actual chairs). The *King* or *Queen* is not allowed to enter the Commons chamber.

the House of Lords n : membership consists of Lords Temporal (peers, some appointed for life and others hereditary) and Lords Spiritual (various bishops and archbishops of the Church of England). In 1999 the number of hereditary peers eligible to sit in the Lords was reduced, so the life peers now form a majority.

Houses of Parliament n : like the *Capitol*. Houses of *Lords* and *Commons* regarded together.

house-train v : *housebreak, potty train.*

housewife /howswief/ /huhzif/ n : sewing kit, syn. ditty bag.

housing estate n : like a *subdivision*, a number of houses built together on a tract of land.

Hovis® n : generic brown bread dating back to 1890 (by name, 1866 by product), and supported by strong advertising, a famous line being 'Don't say brown, say Hovis.'

How do you do? expr intj : formal greeting like, How are you?

howler inf n : blunder.

how's your father expr intj : generic expression for anything rather left unexpressed (How about them *A's*?), also *bullshit* in answer to an impudent question, and sometimes with notable derision, ". . . and how's yer father," also *penis*, also *sex*, "the occasional bit of hows-your-father," 'Ten Bloody Marys and Ten Hows Your Fathers'—Elvis Costello and the Attractions.

h.p. abbr n : *hire purchase.*

HP Sauce® n : like *A1 Sauce*, a brown spicy sauce.

huddle v : to muddle together.

hum sl n v : stink.

humbug n : hard, mint flavored *candy*, "want a humbug?"

hump (road) n : *speed bump*, 'humps for 250 yds' (in front of a busy *roundabout*).

hump col v : carry (a heavy load).

the hump csl n : the blues, or a spate of depression or irritation, "it gives me the hump," 'take the hump' = take offense.

humpty csl euph adj : serious illness, "things are a bit humpty with him."

hundreds and thousands n : *sprinkles, spreckles, jimmies,* though hundreds and thousands tend to be silver (or gold) rather than multicolored.

hussy, huswife n : *housewife.*

hypermarket n : supermarket of unusual size.

– i –

ice n : snow cone, *sherbet,* sorbet, or ice cream.

ice lolly n : *popsicle.*

icing n : *frosting.*

icing sugar n : *confectionery sugar.*

identification parade (*police*) n : *lineup.*

idiot cf n : *egit*, prick, *wally*, dimbo, *prat*, dippy, *twerp*, *twit*, *nitwit*, *mug*, *nit*, *git*, *div*, *pranny*, prannet, *thicko*, dappy, twunt, *berk*, *nutter*, melon, *flid*, *spaz*, mophead, dippo, drip, *nesh*, headcase, *nelly*, *nutcase*, *pillock*, spasmo, *gooseberry*, *dimwit*, *bender*, *clot*, wankipants.

ill usage adj : injured, "the crash victims are seriously ill in hospital."

immersion heater, electric n : *water heater.*

impolder (also **empolder**) vt : reclaim from the sea (from the Dutch polder).

Indian col n : refers to Indian food (curry, etc), used in the same way as 'Chinese,' "fancy an Indian." Britain has a large Indian population, and lots of really good Indian restaurants. See *CTM*.

Indian ink n : black, indelible, drawing ink.

indicate (car) v : *signal.*

indicator n : *turn signal*, *blinkers*.

infant n : schoolchild between about 5 to 7 years of age (as well as its usu. meaning).

infant school, the infants n : school for children prior to *primary* or *first* school, about equivalent to *K*-1, see *infant.*

inglenook n : the nook at the side of a large fireplace, or the seat therein.

inky blue crsl n : flu, "a touch of the inky blue."

innit [isn't it] expr intj : a filler word, like 'like,' but usu. at the end of a sentence, "don't mind the mess, that's how I live, innit," "do you like me, innit," syn. *eh?*

irie adj : *good,* pleasing.

iron crsl (iron hoof) n : *poof*, "I know you're all irons, but I admire what you're doing."

inside lane cf n : *outside lane.*

inside leg n : *inseam,* "how long's your inside leg?" See *outside leg*.

interchange (road) n : main *junction* on motorway (see *intersection*).

interval n : *intermission* (*movie*s, plays, concerts).

in the club adj : in the pudding club, *pregnant*.

inverted commas punc n : *quotation marks,* ' ` ' ', " " ".

invigilator n (**invigilate** v) : *proctor,* monitor or supervisor during an examination.

IRA /ei ahr ay/ cf n : Irish Republican Army.

Irish moss n : *Chondrus crispus* dried *carageen*.

Irish stew n : lamb stew with onions, potatoes, etc. (not stewed leftovers).

ironmonger's n : *hardware store.*

I should cocoa joc csl expr n : I should hope so, but usu. used ironically or humorously.

– j –

jab n : *shot.*

jack n : see *on your jack*.

jackanory [children's TV storybook show 1965–1995] crsl n : story.

jacket potato n : baked potato, "What fillings would you like with your jacket?"

jack in inf v : to quit, "I told them to jack it in."

jacksie, jacksy sl n : *bum*, *butt*, "up your *jaxy*."

Jaffa cakes n : LU® Pim's orange fancy cookies (yummy).

jam n : *jelly,* preserves.

jam butty n : *jam sandwich*, also sl. for *panda car* which were white with a bright red day-glo strip along the side, "ram jam butty."

jammy col adj : lucky, "jammy bastard."

jam jar n : glass jelly jar, also crsl. car.

jam rag sl n : *sanitary towel* or tampon.

jam tart n : jelly pie, syn. *Bakewell tart*.

jar sl n : *pint* of *beer*, hence jar'd = *drunk*.

jaxy, jaxie alt sl n : *jacksie*.

jelly n : *Jell-O*.

jelly babies n : baby-shaped *gummi bears*, Dr Who's favorite snack, "care for a jelly baby?"

jemmy (short crowbar) n, vt : *jimmy*.

jerbil sp n : var. of gerbil.

Jerry sl n : person from Germany.

jig-a-jig n : the *sex* act, "hubbly bubbly, big fat lady, very good for jig-a-jig" (an offer made, with accompanying gestures, in an African port in the '50s or '60s).

jigger (*billiards*) col n : cue rest.

jiggered sl adj : *knackered*.

jiggery-pokery col n : *hanky-panky*.

Jimmy Riddle crsl v : piddle.

joanna crsl n : piano /pyanə/.

jobbing adj : freelance (actor, builder, worker).

jobsworth n : peon (petty official, minor bureaucrat) zealously upholding petty rules and regulations [sorry *mate*, it's more than my job's worth to . . .].

Jock sl n : Scotsman, *Scot*, *Lallan*.

Joe Bloggs n : the modern version—son of *Fred Bloggs*.

John Bull n : Englishman as personifying the nation, equivalent to *Uncle Sam*.

johnny n : condom, syn. *rubber*, *rubber johnny*, *durex*, *French letter*, *willy welly*, *remould*.

John Smith n : syn. *John Doe* (Jan Modaal (Dutch)).

John Thomas sl n : *Johnson*.

joined up writing n : *cursive* writing.

joiner n : skilled carpenter.

joinery n : woodwork, usu. fine.

joint (food) n : *roast*.

joint cf n : joints in the UK are usu. made

with tobacco, into which is crumbled the usual hash, or whatever form the *dope* comes in. Furthermore, it is usual to carefully glue a number of *skins* together (3-skin, 4-skin, 5-skin), resulting in a large cigar-sized joint.

jolly usage adj v adv : happy, encourage, very, 'jolly good.'

josser sl n : *butthead*, also *bloke*.

jostling throng n : crowd.

jotter n : notebook, notepad, exercise book, "get out your jotters . . . ."

jubnuts sl n : the clumps of manure-matted wool around a sheep's *butt*.

jug n : *pitcher*.

juggernaut n : very large truck, *semi*.

jumble sale n : rummage sale.

jumper cf n : *sweater*.

jump leads n : *jumper cables*.

junction (road) n : *intersection*, also *motorway* exit, typically numbered, "I'm getting off at junction 24."

junk n : *garbage*.

— k —

karsey, kharzi, karsy /kahzee/ csl n : *loo*, but perhaps more towards the sense of outhouse, shithouse [Italian *casa*, house, referring also to brothel.]

karsey nail csl n : the place to impale bits of paper for use as toilet paper, "stick it on the *carsey* nail when you've finished reading it" (see *bumf*).

Kate crsl [Kate Carney] n : Army.

kecks (N) n : *trousers*.

kedgeree n : European dish of fish, rice, eggs, etc. and hence the breakfast dish with *kipper*s, (Indian dish of rice, split pulse, onions, eggs, etc.).

keech, keek Scot sl n : shit, syn. (Ir) gick.

kerb (*sidewalk*) sp n : *curb*.

kerb-crawler n : person *kerb-crawling*,

usu. driving slowly around the red light district looking for action, and the action provider.

kerb-crawling v : soliciting, see *kerb-crawler*.

kerfuffle n : fuss, disturbance, commotion.

kettle n : often refers to an electric kettle, hence "turn on the kettle" rather than "put the kettle on." Either way, any reference to kettle usu. indicates it's times for a breather (*tea*!), "let's put the kettle on."

Khyber crsl [Khyber Pass] n : *arse*.

kieselguhr n : *diatomaceous earth*.

kife sl n : *crumpet*, chick.

King (political role of) n : see *Queen*.

King's Speech n : see *Queen's Speech*.

kiosk n : *phone booth, call-box*.

kip v : sleep, nap, also bed.

kipper n : smoked herring.

kirby-grip (also Kirbigrip®) n : *bobby pin*.

kit n : clothes, "where's me kit?" piece of equipment, "that computer is a nice bit of kit."

kludge /kluhj/ cf n : /klooj/ improvisational *botch* or *lash-up*, usu. referring to computer hardware or software.

knacker n : buyer of old horses for slaughter.

knackered [from *knacker*] adj : tired, dead tired, worn out, "I'm bloody knackered," also broken beyond repair, "that car's knackered," syn. *jiggered*.

knacker's yard n : *knacker*'s place of business.

knacks, knackers n : testicles, syn. *nuts, balls*, nads.

knee trembler csl n : screwing standing up, 'against the wall.'

knees-up inf n : dance, party.

Knickerbocker Glory n : kind of sundae in a tall glass.

knickers n : *panties*, lady's underwear, undies.

knickers sl n intj : rubbish, nonsense, crap, *pants*.

knickers in a twist expr adj : frustration over insurmountable trivialities, syn. *panties in a ruffle*, "Don't get your knickers in a twist."

knob sl n : *penis*.

knob, knobbing sl v : to have *sex*.

knob cheese sl n : *headcheese, cock cheese*.

knobs on expr adv : a slightly toned down 'with *brass knobs on*,' "yes, she told me, with knobs on."

knock usage inf v : criticize, make fun of, "stop knocking *Neasden*."

knock about expr v : hang out with.

knock back inf v : gulp down (a drink).

knockers sl n : tits.

knock for six expr v : also 'hit someone for six,' to shock or surprise.

knock up cf v : wake up call.

knock up, knock around v : practice warm up prior to game proper (tennis, etc.).

— l —

L n : learner, see *L plates*.

label usage v n : *tag*.

lad usage n : *dude,* boy, young man, 'the lads' is your *mate*s, see *real lad, laddish*.

ladder n : *run* in tights.

laddish adj : disapproving, of typical young men's behavior, see *real lad*.

ladies n : *ladies' room*.

ladies' fingers n : *okra,* bhindi, see *gumbo*.

lady, Lady Godiva rsl n : *fiver*, £5.

ladybird n : *ladybug*.

lady's handbag n : *purse*.

lag v : to insulate pipes or roof with lagging (insulating material).

lager and lime n : lager mixed with lime (Rose's lime juice) which, like *shandy*, is popular as a refreshing drink in hotter weather. ["British lager is an imitation continental beer drunk only by refined ladies, people with digestive ailments, tourists, and other weaklings."— *Muenchen Suddeusche Zeitung*, April 1976.]

lager shandy n : *shandy* made with lager instead of beer.

lager top n : lager topped with *lemonade* (or *bitter*).

laggy band col n : *elastic band*, *rubber band*.

Lallan n : (Scottish) lowlander, see *Scot*.

larder usage n : *pantry*.

lark n : a line of business or some activity, but now usu. disparaging, "what a lark!"

lashings n : lots of, abundance, "lashings of ice cream."

lash-up n v : thrown together, contrivance, "you can lash up [program] a computer game."

laughing gear n : mouth.

laundrette, launderette n : *laundromat*.

lav abbr n : *lavatory*.

lavatory n : *john, bathroom, restroom, porta-potty, toilet*.

lay-by (road) cf n : *pull-off*.

lay off! col excl imp v : cease, desist.

leader n : *concert master*.

leader, leading article (newspaper) n : *editorial*.

Leader of the Opposition n : leader of the *Opposition* party.

learned /lerned/ pr adj : educated.

learner, learner driver n : *student driver*.

learner plates n : *L plates*.

leave it out intj : be serious, you're kidding, get real.

leave off intj : give me a break.

leccy, lecky [abbr] n adj : electric, as in "has he paid the leccy bill?" but also in general to refer to the *mains* or *electrics*, "the leccy man," "leccy guitar," "leccy beach" (tanning salon).

lecturer n : *assistant professor*.

left luggage office (railroad) n : *baggage room, checkroom*.

leg it col v : walk or run (as opposed to bicycle or go in a car), "the car broke down so we had to leg it," "Leg it! Here comes the cops!"

leg over sl v : have *sex*, *screw*, "get a bit of leg over."

lemon (Aus) sl n : lesbian.

lemonade cf n : commercial lemon flavored carbonated soda, similar to 7-Up or Sprite, unless qualified as 'home made.'

lemon curd n : yellow paste made from lemons used as a spread on bread or toast. Tastes like *applesauce* but without any apples in it.

lergy n : see *lurgy*.

let v : *lease* or *rent* land, house, rooms, etc., (the sign 'To Let' = 'for rent.' A favorite prank is to replace the space with an i, esp. when the sign is 50' high on the side of a skyscraper).

let off steam expr v : blow off steam.

let off usage v : *set off*, "the kids are letting off *banger*s."

let off v : fart, "did you let off?"

letterbox n : *mail slot* (in door) or *mailbox*. See *pillar box*.

letterpress n : text in a book excluding illustrations.

level crossing (railroad) n : *grade crossing, railroad crossing*.

lever /leever/ n v : /lever/.

lido n : outdoor pool or beach recreation area.

lieutenant /lef tenənt/ (Army /lə tenənt/ Navy) cf n : /loo tenənt/ the British pr. arose possibly by 15th C misreading the u as v, which sometimes was pr. like f.

lifebuoy, lifebelt sp n : life buoy, *life ring*.

life-jacket n : *life preserver*.

life preserver cf n : *blackjack* (bludgeon).

Liffey water n : Guinness [the brewery is on the River Liffey, which flows through Dublin].

lift (car) n : *ride.*

lift n : *elevator.*

light and bitter n : (usu. a *pint* of) half light ale and half bitter ale, see *beer.*

light bulb cf n : UK light bulbs are pushed in with a half-twist.

lightning conductor n : *lightning rod.*

light switch cf n : in UK, up is off, down is on.

like chalk and cheese expr adj : emphasizing the complete difference between two people or things, like apples and oranges, "that's chalk and cheese."

Lilo® n : air bed.

Limey n : person from England, *Pom, Sassanach, Brit.*

limited company n : private *corporation,* see *ltd.*

line, railway line n : *tracks, railroad tracks.*

lino /lienoh/n : linoleum, syn. vinyl.

lip salve n : *chapstick.*

liquidiser, liquidizer n : *blender.*

liquorice sp n : *licorice.*

liquorice all-sorts n : enduring and popular *candy* featuring about a dozen standard forms around the licorice theme.

listed (building) adj : officially designated as historic.

liver sausage n : *liverwurst.*

Liverpudlian n : person from Liverpool, *Scouse.*

Llanfairpwllgwyngyllgogerychwyrndrobwllllantysiliogogogoch [Welsh *Parish (of) Mary (in a) hollow (of) white hazels fairly near the rapid whirlpool (with the) parish (of) Tysilio (at the) red cave*] /llan veir pooll gwin gill goh gə rux wurn droh booll llan tie silioh go go gox/ n : a Welsh village name contrived to be the longest British word.

loads n : lots, *buttload,* "loads of noise next-door."

loaf crsl [loaf of bread] n : head, "use your loaf."

local n : your most frequented or local *pub.*

lollipop n : *sucker,* also *popsicle.*

lollipop man n : *crossing guard.*

lolly n : *money,* cash, syn. dough.

lolly n : *popsicle, iced lolly.*

lombard acr n : lots of *money* but a real dick.

Long Man of Wilmington n : Iron Age 226'-high chalk hill carving of a man holding two poles, one of two such giants in Britain, the other being the 17th-century club-wielding 180' Cerne Abbas Giant or Rude Man (because of his giant phallus). Many such carvings are found around Britain, such as the Gog Magog Hills goddess in Cambridgeshire and *white horses.*

loo n : *bathroom,* syn. *john, bog.*

loofah usage n : bath sponge.

loo paper n : toilet paper, *tp, bog paper.*

loo roll n : toilet roll, *bog roll.*

the Lords n : the *House of Lords.*

lorry n : *truck,* see also expr. fell *off the back of a lorry.*

lost property n : *lost and found.*

loudhailer n : *bullhorn.*

lounge n : *living room.*

lounge bar n : *saloon bar,* see *pub.*

lounge suit n : business suit.

love n : see *luv.*

love bite n : *hickey.*

love juice col n : clear pubescent *spunk.*

L plates n : *learner plates,* large white sign with big red letter L, attached to rear (and front) of *learner driver*'s car. Driver must carry a *provisional licence.*

ltd [abbr] cf n : *limited company,* syn. *inc, plc, pty ltd, p/l, GmbH, SA, NV,* AG.

lucerne (also **lucern**) n : *alfalfa.*

ludo (game) n : *Parcheesi.*

lughole col n : ear, syn. cranial fins.

lugs abbr n : *lughole*s.

lumber room n : room in a household used for storage.

lumme /lumi/ [contr (lord) love me] intj : syn. *darn*, jeez, "oh, lumme, he's going to hit the tree."

lump o' lead crsl n : head.

lurgy /lergee/ [invented on *The Goon Show*] n : fabled, highly contagious, dreadful and terminal disease, "the dreaded lurgy," syn. *cooties*.

lush cf intj adj : fine, "she's lush," "I had a lush kebab last night."

luv (love) n : a familiar form of address, and informally, often so spelled, "*ta*, luv," "mornin,' luv," " 'ello luv."

— m —

mac, mack col n : raincoat.

mackintosh, macintosh n : raincoat.

mad cf adj : *crazy*, both insane, "I think he's mad," and excited, "I'm mad about the *flat*."

made in Hong Kong n : cheaply made knick-knack, *Mickey Mouse*, (but better than made in Taiwan).

Madeira cake n : *pound cake.*

made redundant euph v : *fired*, syn. *sacked*, discharged, let go, terminated, 'asked' to take 'early retirement,' letter of resignation is 'accepted,' (the contract 'expired' and wasn't 'renewed').

mag contr n : magazine, porno mag, *trash mag*, syn. *zine.*

Magdalen(e) /mordlin/ n : the pronunciation of Magdelen College, Oxford and Magdalene College, Cambridge.

mains n : household electricity, as opposed to batteries, "mains lighting," 'mains voltage.'

the mains n : central utility distribution network (gas, electricity, water, etc.), 'the gas mains,' 'water mains.'

maize n : *corn.*

majority cf n : larger number or part.

make (business) v : *turn,* as in make a profit.

malteasers (Mars chocolate *candy*) n : whoppers, malted milk balls.

man on the bus n : *man on the Clapham bus*, "Judged by the criteria of common sense and what the man on the bus calls science."

man on the Clapham bus [originally omnibus] n : man in the street, syn. *John Q. Public*, *Fred Bloggs*.

Mancunian n : person from Manchester.

mangelwurzel n : large coarse yellow-orange beet used for cattle fodder. Used as a jocular term, in the same way Dave Barry uses *rutabaga,* esp. when making fun of country folk (*hicks*).

mange-tout [French *eat all*] n : *snap pea,* sugar (snap) pea, snow pea.

mangle n : *wringer,* "This is the best moment of my life; since Granny caught her tits in the mangle"—Daley Thompson, British decathlon 1980 & 1984 gold medalist, on TV.

manky, (also **mankey**) adj : shaky, *flaky,* rotten, decrepit, *naff,* "Better than picking up the manky *Y-fronts*," mank it up = to *botch* it or screw something up.

manual (car) n : *stick shift.*

Marathon (*candy bar*) cf n : *Snickers,* although the Marathon, since 1990, is called Snickers in the UK as well.

marge col n : margarine.

marigolds [Marigold™] n : orange rubber gloves, "there's some marigolds under the sink."

marines cf n : Royal Marines.

marks (school) n : grades, "he gets good marks." (See also *gas mark*.)

Marks and Sparks col n : Marks & Spencer (Department Store), also written as M&S.

marmalade n : *jam* made from Seville oranges (which are bitter), popular on toast at breakfast.

marmalade-dropper col n : usu. in reference to a shocking or outrageous newspaper item (which you're reading during breakfast, and is so arresting that you forget the toast you're holding and the *marmalade* dripping from it), syn. muffin-choker, *coffee spitter.*

Marmite (marmite) /marmiet/ [Fr small pot] n : black savory paste made from spent brewer's yeast, that comes in a distinctive small black jar with a yellow lid. It's been around since 1902, and like other acquired tastes (*marmalade*, *lemon curd*, warm beer, and peanut butter in America) most people love it (popular on toast), but those that don't join the rest of the world and revile it, "We take intense satisfaction from the essential Britishness of the product and its lack of appeal for the majority of the world's population."—Tony Banks, 2002, "His favourite food is Marmite—every true British explorer loves it"—mother of Tom Avery. See *Vegemite*.

marquee cf n : large tent, erected for functions like garden parties, fairs, etc.

marrow [OE *maerg* = pith] n : *zucchini, squash.*

Mars bar (candy bar) n : *Milky Way.*

Mary, Mary Ann sl n : effeminate gay, particularly the submissive partner.

marzipan n : sweetened colored almond paste used as a cake *frosting.*

mash (Northern) col n : *tea.*

mash col n : mashed potatoes, see *pie & mash.*

match usage n : *game.*

mate n : friend, *buddy, pal.*

mate (term of address) n : cf *dude* (see also *bloke*) syn. {++} *ducky, love, pet,* {+} *luv, chuck,* old bean, *china,* {0} *mush,* chum, *mucker,* guv, guv'nor, squire, *duck, cock.*

material usage n : *fabric.*

maths n : *math.*

matlow, matlo, matelot /matloh/ sl n : sailor.

matron n : head nurse or ward nurse, see *sister.*

maundy money /morndi/ n : silver coins (specially minted for the occasion at *1d, 2d, 3d, 4d*) given to poor people, usu. in a ceremony in Westminster Abbey, on Maundy Thursday (Thursday before Easter) by the reigning monarch. The number of years in the present reign determines how many men and how many women receive a bounty (bag), which contains as many *pence* as the monarch's age.

mauve /mohv/ n : /mahv/ (rhymes with cause) or /mohv/.

max headroom (road sign) n : 'max clearance.'

McJob n : generic, low-pay, low-benefit, job, e.g. waitron.

MD abbr n : managing director, *CEO.*

me /mi/ pron : 'my' is often informally pronounced /mi/ and is frequently written as 'me' to indicate this, "I'm going out (of) me head," "where's me tea?" "she *ate* me cake."

mean cf adj : stingy.

meet usage v : *meet with.*

Melton Mowbray pie n : a kind of meat pie.

Member of Parliament n : like *Congressperson.* Used only to refer to members of the *Commons,* not the *Lords.*

mens n : *men's room.*

mental adj : *dumb, crazy,* often in a nervously challenging way, "you must be mental."

Mersey n adj : pertaining to Liverpool (and Merseyside) accent, people, culture, see *Scouse.*

mess about v : to play around.

metal n : road-metal, gravel for surfacing dirt roads, hence metalled road.

meths col n : *methylated spirits*, meths-drinker = so addicted *bum*.

methylated spirits n : methanol-denatured alcohol, also usu. colored purple to dissuade addicted *tramp*s.

metier n : *shtick*.

metre n : unit of measure, (meter is the measuring device).

mews n : cosy little urban street, or the *flats* on it, usu. formerly stables, see *cul-de-sac*, *close*, *drive*, blvd, *road*, street.

Mexican wave n : the *wave*, La ola (Germany), [enthusiastically adopted by Mexican *football* fans at the 1986 World Cup].

MI5 /em ie fiev/ abbr n : department of Military Intelligence concerned with national security, more or less equivalent to the *FBI*.

MI6 /em ie siks/ abbr n : espionage group in Military Intelligence (think 007, James Bond), more or less equivalent to the *CIA*.

miaow sp v n : meow.

mick expr v : see *take the micky*.

Mick offen n : Irishman, *Paddy*.

The Midlands n : inland counties of central England.

mif acr n : milk in first, "mif?" "are you a mif?" ant. *tif*. Some people make a cup of tea by pouring the milk in first and then the tea. If someone should make them a *cuppa* by pouring the tea in first their reaction ranges from quiet disdain to horror, and for many, such a sacrilege is a serious *religious issue*. Stories are rife of convalescing Grandma in her bedroom being brought up a cup of tea and *knowing* that the milk wasn't poured first, even though Granddaughter is intimately familiar with the *precise* quantities. In fact, the pioneering statistician R A Fisher confirmed this ability whilst developing 'statistical hypothesis testing.' There is a feeling by some that it is a regional thing; that there

tends to be, for instance, more mifs than *tif*s in the north and a higher concentration of *tif*s in the southeast. See also *tea*.

miking v : having an unauthorized rest or break, shirking, "having a mike."

milk float n : small electric vehicle for delivering milk around the neighborhood.

milk top n : the foil top (or cap) on milk bottles, "a pint of gold top, and two silver tops." Their color designates the kind of milk: gold—full milk, silver—lighter, red—low fat. As kids, you might stamp them flat as use them as game tokens.

Milky bar n : (candy bar) *Three Musketeers*.

mince n : *minced meat*.

mince v : look, see *minces*.

mince v : walk with affected delicacy, "mincing around," (see *strut*).

minced meat /mints(d) meet/ n : *hamburger meat,* ground beef, (plus all the allusions, "I'm going to make minced meat of him").

mincer n : *meat grinder.*

minces crsl [mince pies] n : eyes.

mind the gap imp v : an implacable recorded announcement, along with signs painted on the platform, necessary in some curved *tube* stations because the trains don't quite fit, and you have to step over a gap, quite big enough to fall into, to get on or off the train. The phrase is frequently co-opted, for instance by tourists visiting London and discovering a larger cultural gap than expected, as well as for titles of books, bands, projects, and such. New female recording dubbed Sonia (gets on yer nerves).

minerals n : mineral water.

ming /ming/ n v : a more acute, eye-watering, iridescent kind of *pong*, stink.

minge /minj/ sl n : *vagina*. (Animals that pee backwards are retromingent.)

minger n : /minjer/ really ugly woman, syn. swamp donkey, /minger/ smelly person.

mingy /minjee/ [mean and stingy] adj : miserly, also meager.

mini-break n : going away for the weekend, mini-*vacation*.

minicab n : car used as taxi, typically unlicensed.

minim n : half note, see Musical Table.

minor n : younger (or second) of two children, "Smith minor, report to the office."

minority government n : Although *Britain* has only two major political parties at present (Labour and Conservative), there are several others with enough support (Liberal, for instance at around 10%) to have some members in the *Commons*. It is possible for a party to govern without holding a majority of the seats by themselves, so long as they can attract enough support from other party members to win a majority on key votes. If not, a new general *election* is held.

The Mint n : The Royal Mint. The Mint mints coins of the realm and does this for many other countries, many of which are former colonies. (The Bank of England prints the paper money (cf. *BEP*), bank *note*s, likewise for many other countries.)

missis, missus sl joc n : the wife, the old lady, also informal term of address, syn. *ma'am*.

mix (beer) n : brown and *bitter*.

mobile n : *cellphone*.

mockney adj : of a Cockney wannabe, a person who aspires to be Cockney, esp. someone from upper classes trying to curry favor, cf. *Estuary English*.

moggy, moggie n : endearing term for cat (like calling your dog 'my old mutt'), otherwise a *manky* cat.

moke sl n : donkey.

mollusc sp n : *mollusk*.

momentarily cf adv : for a moment.

money n : *ackers*, *bob*, *brass*, *bread*, *coppers*, *crispies*, *dosh*, *lolly*, *moolah*, *oof*,

readies, *spond*, *spondulicks*, tosh.

money card n (telephone) : *calling card*, *phonecard*.

monkey sl n : £500.

month of Sundays [Ir, figure about 31 weeks] n : long long time, syn. *yonks*.

moo derog sl n : woman, see *cow*, "silly old moo."

moolah /moolah/ sl n : *money*.

moot cf usage adj : debatable, as in "that's a moot point" meaning 'that's a debatable point.'

MOT [Ministry of Transport] n : compulsory annual test of vehicle's roadworthiness, the certificate of which is displayed on the inside of the *windscreen* (in a similar manner to the required tags on the *license plate*s), "God knows how I got my MOT," see *street legal*.

motg abbr v : morally obliged to go (to some formal occasion, esp. if you are some VIP, *royal*, or person of distinction), see *Sloane Rangese*.

mother sl n : £9.

motorway n : *freeway, expressway*.

mould sp n v : *mold*.

moult sp n v : *molt*.

mouth and trousers csl expr adj : hot air, 'all mouth,' dude with a *'tude*, "he's all mouth and *trousers*," see *Monday morning quarterback*.

MP abbr n : *Member of Parliament*. As a title, used after the name, 'Winston Churchill, MP.'

Mr Chad n :——ooo-$^{(\text{O}_\text{U}\text{O})}$-ooo—— the graffiti of a little bald guy peaking over a brick wall often accompanied by 'wot no ___,' see *Kilroy*.

M-road n : *motorway*, the first being the M1, opened in 1959.

Mr Plod [from Mr. Plod the policeman in the children's stories of Enid Blyton] n : a policeman, or the *police* in general, "better nip off, here comes Mr. Plod."

MSc abbr n : *MS.*

muck n : manure, 'chicken muck,' 'pig's muck,' 'cow muck,' 'muck spreader.'

muck col n : crap, "why're you eating that muck?"

muck about, muck around col v : fool around, or *potter.*

mucker sl n : *mate.*

mudguard n : *fender.*

muesli n : like *granola*, but typically raw ingredients rather than toasted.

muesli col n : stereotypical environmentally conscious, *muesli*-eating (health conscious), ex-hippie but now professional, see *granola* and *crunchie.*

muffin cf n : similar to an *English muffin*, or a *crumpet* made from dough rather than batter, served toasted and buttered.

mug cf sl n : scapegoat, also fool or simpleton, see *muggins.*

muggins inf n : simpleton.

mug up v : study up.

mullered adj : *drunk* or stoned.

mum /mum/ col n : the person (mutually) designated to pour the tea at *tea*, "I'll be mum," "will you be mum?"

mum /mum/, **mummy** n : mom /mahm/, mommy.

mumblers sl n : women's bike shorts, (see the lips moving, but can't make out what they're saying), syn. *camel toes.*

mumchance adj : tongue-tied.

mummerset n : provincial accent, contrived or real, as used by actors.

mummy n : *mommy*, mamma, *momma.*

mumsy inf adj : disagreeably mother-like.

mung beans n : *bean sprouts.*

mush /mush/ [Romany] n : friend, "He's /mi/ mush," "*oi*, mush," "where's your mushtanger?" = where's your *mate*?

mush /mush/ sl n : face.

mushy peas [Northern] n : dish made from a kind of starchy pea cooked till the consistency of *porridge.*

muslin n : *cheese cloth.*

mustard cf n : English mustard is spicy hot, like a hot, non-fruity wasabi (horseradish).

mustard and cress n : *sprouts.*

muzzy inf adj : unclear.

my sainted aunt intj : exclamation of disbelief or surprise.

— n —

nacks n : see *knacks, knackers.*

nab usage v : *pinch, nick.*

naff adj intj : undesirable, tasteless, syn. *tacky, crusty, gnarly*, "it's a bit naff?"

naff all expr n : nothing, *sod all*, fuck all, *bugger all, sweet FA.*

naff off imp v : *piss off.*

nail varnish n : *nail polish*, nail enamel.

nan, nanny col n : grandma.

nang csl adj : *cool.*

napkin cf n : as well as table napkin, this also means *diaper* and *sanitary napkin; serviette* would be unambiguous.

nappy n : *diaper.*

Nappy Valley n : young couples with primary & preschool aged children, and the location they're migrating to, esp. the south London baby hinterlands around Kingston, Clapham, Balham and Wandworth Common (highest birth rate in Europe—2004).

nark sl n : informer, also bitter complainer—see following, cf. *narc.*

narked adj : annoyed, irritated, syn. pissed.

narky sl adj : irritable.

natter v : chit-chat, blab, bavardage.

navvy n : *construction worker*, unskilled laborer.

Neasden n : proverbial suburban, low-rent, forgetful place with a funny sounding name. (During the 1970s it was made such fun of (with the help of Monty

Python) that the locals instigated a national 'stop *knock*ing Neasden' campaign). England has no end of hamlets with funny names, like Barton in the Beans, Little Snoring, Middle Wallop, Steeple Bumpstead, Wigglesworth, and Wormelow Tump.

neat cf adj : *straight, straight-up;* a neat whiskey is a whiskey *straight.*

neat (Aus) adj : even, "three dollars neat, thanks."

neep n : turnip (Scot), swede (N), "neeps and *tatties.*"

nelly n : silly or effeminate person. See also expr. *not on your nelly.*

nervy cf adj : nervous or excitable.

nesh col n : *wimp.*

Nestlés /nes-ls/ n : /neslees/.

net curtains n : *sheers, underdrapes.*

nettles n : *stinging nettles.*

netty [*Geordie*] n : *bathroom,* often outhouse.

the never-never inf col n : *hire purchase,* also now used for credit cards, "it's spending on the never-never."

new pence n : generally—the new decimal currency (see *decimalisation*) where 100 new pence equals a pound (100p = *£1*) and the coins circulating are *1p, 2p, 5p,10p, 20p, 50p,* and the *sov* (*£1*), as opposed to the old *£sd* currency; and specifically the new pennies—coins were minted with 'new penny' or 'new pence' from introduction until 1981 when they now use just 'penny' or 'pence.'

newsagent n : newspaper store, but typically, like a *convenience store,* also carries candy and tobacco, "where's the nearest newsagents?"

NHS abbr n : National Health Service (universal health care, about equivalent to membership in an *HMO* such as Kaiser).

niche /neesh/ n : /nich/.

nick sl v : catch or arrest.

nick sl v : steal, "the wing mirrors had been nicked."

the nick sl n : jail.

nicker (pl nicker) sl n : *pound (£),* "it cost 'im twenty nicker."

nick off v : to steal away, *bunk off,* "she nicked off to Australia."

niff (adj **niffy**) n v : *pong,* stench, "bit of a niff," sniff, smell, "have a niff."

nightdress n : *nightgown.*

nimby acr n adj : Not In My Back Yard, e.g. *Chunnel* nimbys would be Kent residents who like the *Chunnel* idea, as long as development doesn't impact their land, view, residence, whatever. (Related political science acronyms: lulu—locally unacceptable land use, banana—build absolutely nothing anywhere near anything, *quango.*)

nine-bob note sl expr n : gay, *three dollar bill,* "he's as *queer* as a nine *bob* note," but also (originally) queer as in strange.

ninny n : foolish (*soppy,* wimpy) person.

nip v : to go nimbly, quickly, or briefly, "let's nip in(to) the *pub* (for a *quick one*)."

nip off n : take off.

nipper col n : young child.

Nissen hut n : like a *Quonset hut.*

nit n : *nitwit.*

nitwit n : fool, stupid person.

nob n : well-to-do person, rich, upper class, syn. *toff.*

nobble v : con, acquire underhandedly, tamper with.

no claims bonus n : *good-driver discount.*

noddle col n : head, syn *noodle.*

noddy n : buffoon, simpleton.

non-u [1954] adj : of language, dress, not upper class, see *u.*

the noo [Scot] n intj : now (the present moment), '*och aye* the noo' being seen as the stereotypical Scottish intj.

norks [Aus] sl n : *knockers,* "*cracking* pair of norks."

normal usage adj : *regular.*

north and south crsl n : mouth.

North Country n : northern England, Northumberland.

north of Watford euph n : where civilization ends. Watford is a town on the northwest of London (now merely a suburb) on a main thoroughfare to the north through a valley (The Watford Gap).

nosey parker n : busybody.

nosh (food) n : food.

nosh v : to eat.

noshery sl n : snack bar, syn. *eatery.*

nosh-up n : big meal or feast.

not cricket expr adj : of inappropriate behavior, not playing the game, no-no, not the thing to do, 'it's just not cricket.'

not done expr n : no-no.

note (banknote) n : *bill* when used with value: ten *shilling* note, five pound note, *nine-bob note*; see *bit*. They vary in size, being slightly larger with increasing value.

not fussed expr adj : not bothered (by something), I'm not fussed = I don't mind, syn, *no problem, no worries*.

not give a monkey's expr v : don't care, not give a rip, *not give a toss,* "I couldn't give a monkey's whether you like East-enders or not."

not give a toss expr v : don't care, not give a rip, "I don't give a *toss*."

not half sl expr adv : to an extreme degree, "not half bad" = extremely good, "he didn't half run" = he ran like *billy-oh*, "I wouldn't half love a *fag*."

not half! excl intj : yes! "not half, *mate*!"

noticeboard n : *bulletin board, pin board.*

no tipping (sign) imp v : *no dumping,* see *tip*.

not on your nelly [crsl Nelly Duff, puff, breath of life, life] excl intj : not on your life, not likely.

nought (also naught) /nort/ n : zero.

noughts and crosses n : *tic-tac-toe.*

November 5th n : 'Remember, remember, the 5th of November,' see *Guy Fawkes Day*.

no worries [Aus] expr intj : *no problem.*

nowt /nowt/ (Northern) n : nothing, "she's done nowt all day, just *sout* on *fanny*."

nuddy col euph adj : nude.

number plate n : *license plate.*

nut sl n : head. See also expr. *do one's nut.*

nutcase n : *crazy*, nuts, stupid.

nut chokers sl n : *tightie-whities.*

nutter n : nutcase, maniac, person with a fanatic streak "afro-wig-wearing nutter."

NV [naamloze vennootschap (nameless partnership)—Netherlands] adj : public corporation, syn. *ltd.*

— O —

oaf n : clumsy *idiot.*

OAP abbr n : *old age pensioner, senior citizen.*

och /okh/ [Scottish and Irish] intj : oh, ah.

och aye /okh ie/ [Sottish and Irish] excl intj : oh yes, ah yes.

ofay, offay adj : see *au fait.*

office block n : office building.

offie col abbr n : *off licence*.

off licence n : *liquor store, packy.*

off the back of a lorry expr adj : stolen, syn. *five-finger discount.*

off your trolley expr adj : of strange or singular behavior, slightly *whacked, crazy.*

oi, oy imp intj [hoy] : like 'hey!' but demanding rather than pleading. In its most extreme, it comes out as an arresting, sharp, guttural growl, not unlike a lion's growl that petrifies its prey. At the other end, say, "oi *mate*!," it's an 'excuse me' or 'watch out.' Heard in *football* chants, e.g. 'Oggy, oggy, oggy. Oi, oi, oi.'

oik n : an unpleasant youth.

old age pensioner n : *OAP*, *senior citizen.*
old banger sl n : decrepit old car, flivver.
Old Bill n : the *police*, syn. the law.
The Old Lady of Threadneedle Street n : Bank of England.
old money n : currency before *decimalisation*, also refers to wealth that's been in a family for many, many generations, for instance with royalty or landowners.
old penny n : the *penny* before *decimalisation*.
O levels n : *GCE* ordinary level, state exams taken in each subject at the end of fifth *form* (age about 16), now called *GCSE*s, see *A levels*.
on about v : talking about, "whaddya on about?"
oncer /wunsə/ dated sl n : one pound *note*.
one-off adj n : only one instance of (event or product), one-shot.
on heat v : *in heat.*
On Her Majesty's Service (on envelopes) adj : equivalent to *Official Business*.
ont [North] n : on the, "I were *sout* ont bus."
on the cards expr n : *in the cards.*
on the earhole expr adj : down on [his] luck, schnorrer.
on your jack crsl [Jack Jones] n : on your own.
oof sl n : *money.*
oofy sl adj : monied, also expensive, syn, *spendy.*
open adj : open *sandwich* = *open-face* sandwich.
opening hours, opening times n : business hours.
opening time n : when the *pub*s open, "when's opening time?"
opposite usage prep : *across from.*
the Opposition n : the largest party other than the one forming the present *government*, usu. the one with the second-most seats in the *Commons*.
orbital (road) n : major *ring road* (e.g. M25

around London).
ordinance survey map n : the entire British Isles has been mapped since the mid-1800s with a famous set of one-inch-to-the-mile maps.
ordinary usage adj : *regular, normal.*
ordinary shares n : *common stock.*
oriental cf adj n : an object or person from China, Thailand, etc. (See *Asian*.)
orientate v : to orient.
ott abbr adj : over the top, too much.
OU abbr n : Open University.
out me head col expr adj : 'going out of my head' means going *crazy*, 'getting out of my head' means getting high.
outside lane cf n : *inside lane,* lane closest to *median divider,* i.e. the fast (rightmost) lane.
outside leg n : *outseam,* (see *inside leg*.)
outwith (Scot) prep : outside, beyond, "the golfer finished outwith the leading 38," "land outwith the urban area."
oven cloth n : *pot holder.*
overall n : loose, light, long jacket used while working (painting, cleaning, etc.).
overalls cf n : *boiler suit*, coveralls.
overheads n : *overhead* (running costs).
overtake (traffic) usage v : *pass.*
over the moon expr adj : extremely happy, "I'm not exactly over the moon about it."
owner-occupied flat n : *condominium.*
Oxbridge n : Oxford and Cambridge Universities, and being the most regarded, somewhat like *Ivy League.* See also *redbrick.*
OXO (OXO®) [oxen] n : OXO cubes are savory bullion cubes, and have been around since about 1900. See also *Bisto, Bovril,* and *Marmite.*
Oxon abbr n : Oxfordshire, see table 14, Counties.
oxter [Ir Sc] dial n : armpit, "I'm going to miss several opportunities to shave the oxters."

oy imp intj : sp. var. of *oi*.

oz cf n : ounce, see *fifth*, *fluid ounce*, *pint*.

– p –

p /pee/ n : symbol for *new pence*, see *d*, and table of British Money.

pack n : *deck* (of cards).

packed lunch n : *sack lunch, brown bag lunch*.

packet n : a pile of *money*, "costs a packet." (See also *bump*.)

pack it in col usage v : quit, stop, "let's pack it in for the night."

pack of cards usage n : *deck* of cards.

Paddy n : Irishman, syn. *Mick*.

pageboy (wedding) n : *page*.

pah intj : *pshaw*.

painters are in expr n : menstruating, syn. have the painters in, painters and decorators are in, *aunty's round*.

Paki offen n [Pakistanis] : any Asian from the Indian continent, even if via E. Africa.

PAL n : brand of dog food, like *chum*. A famous TV ad showed a *tramp* hungrily eyeing a can of PAL he was opening, spoon some out, smell it lovingly, and as the voice over said "believe it or not, Pal is for dogs" he fed it to his cute puppy, which was sitting next to him all along.

Palace of Westminster n : another name for the *Houses of Parliament*. Like the *Capitol*.

palari n : see *polari*.

palaver n : commotion.

pancake n : crêpe.

Pancake Day n : Shrove Tuesday, day before Ash Wednesday (same day as Mardi Gras or Fat Tuesday), and yes, we eat *pancake*s, with sugar and lemon juice, though they're more like crêpes.

panda car n : *police* car, the basic utilitarian, non-emergency, low speed, high-profile, around town variety, generally white in color with a brightly colored (day-glo) stripe around the middle, see *jam butty*.

panel-beater n : auto body repairman.

pantechnicon n : *moving van*.

panto n : pantomime.

pantomime n : Christmastime theatre in Victorian tradition of popular fairytales, slapstick & farce, singing & dancing, stock characters, cross-dressing and audience participation.

pantomime n : farcical situation, "it's the *Commons* panto."

pants cf n : underwear, syn. *shorts, briefs, boxer shorts, Y-fronts, knickers, trollies, chuddies*, unthinkables, nasties, nut chokers. (See also adj. *pants*.)

pants sl adj : crap, *piss poor*, syn. *knickers*, "it's pants!," "that was pants!"

papier-mâché /papiay mashay/ n : /payper mashay/.

paracetamol /paraseetəmol/ n : mild pain relieving drug (acetaminophen), available over the counter like Tylenol & Excedrin (acetaminophen), aspirin, or Advil (ibuprofen). 'Why can't you find aspirin in the jungle? Cos paracetamol.'

paraffin n : *kerosene*.

paraffin wax n : *paraffin*.

paralytic adj : blind *drunk*.

park the leopard col sl v : puke, (many forms—park a tiger, park the custard).

parkway cf n : *railway station* on the edge of town with extensive parking, to facilitate commuting. Eg. Bristol Parkway, Alfreton & Mansfield Parkway, Didcot Parkway.

parky (weather) adj : chilly, "it's a mite parky" (of sharp biting windy weather).

Parliament n : like *Congress*. Comprises the *House of Commons*, the *House of Lords*, and the Crown (*King* or *Queen*).

parlour usage n : (sp. parlor) *sitting room*

or front room or *living room* or *den.*

parson's nose n : the piece of a fowl's rump where the tail feathers stuck in.

pash n v : kiss, 'pash and dash.'

passing note (music) n : *passing tone.*

pass wind v : fart, pass gas, break wind.

pastille n : small fruit *candy,* sometimes medicated.

pasty /pastee/ n : small savory pie, see *Cornish pasty.*

patience (card game) n : *solitaire.*

pavement cf n : *sidewalk.*

pawky [Scot] adj : dryly humorous, canny.

pawpaw n : *papaya.*

payment card n : *debit card.*

pearlies n : refers to the pearly kings and queens and their glittering dress, which is covered in pearl or mother of pearl buttons. They are London costermongers, and are seen in parades, at charities, and such.

pear-shaped expr adj : fiasco, or of a project that, through no fault of anyone, becomes a disaster, "Ukraine's Orange Revolution starts to go all pear-shaped."

pease pudding, pease porridge n : baked split peas (originally the Carlin pea) flavored with ham (and eggs).

pebble dash n v : exterior wall finish (pebbles embedded in mortar), often the first step in trendifying one's house.

pecker cf n : courage, spirit, "keep your pecker up," also sl. nose, "wot a honkin' pecker."

peckish adj : a little hungry, snackish.

pedestrian crossing n : *crosswalk.*

pedlar alt sp n : peddler (of things or opinions).

peepbo excl intj : *peekaboo* (game with babies).

peg n : *clothespin, clothes-peg.* Also a *shot* or a measure of wine.

peg away, peg along v : persist (at some task).

peg it col v : *leg it.*

pelican crossing n : button controlled *crosswalk, pedestrian crossing, zebra crossing,* by means of flashing green walking man or red standing man (equivalent to the walk/don't walk sign) with or without beeps.

pelmet n : *valance* (hides curtain rod), also pelmet skirt—very short mini-skirt (wide belt).

pelting down expr vi : raining cats and dogs.

pence suff n : pl. of *penny,* when referring by value (*sixpence* worth) rather then a number of coins (six pennies) or coin value (ten pence).

penis cf n : syn. *willy, chopper,* prick, *todger,* tadger, tool, cock, *bell end,* wang, *Hampton,* whanger, *dong,* dongler, *John Thomas, wee wee, knob, plonker.*

penn'orth /penəth/ contr n : an (old) *penny's* worth.

penny cf n : primary sub-unit of British currency like the cent is to the dollar, though referring to either old or new pennies (see *decimalisation*), syn. *copper.*

penny banger sl n : the smallest or cheapest firecracker, but still (hopefully) with a loud pop (see *damp squib*).

the penny drops expr v : to realize, syn. *twig,* "her face lit up when the penny dropped."

penny house n : *bathroom,* see *spend a penny.*

period drama sl n : *pms, muff* huff.

perisher col n : exasperatingly inevitable person, esp. child, "why you little perisher!"

personal call (phone) n : *person to person.*

perspex n : plastic sheet, like *plexiglass.*

perv mag [perverted magazine] n : porno *mag,* jazz *mag.*

pet n : term of endearment.

Pete crsl [DJ Pete Tong] adj : wrong, "it's

all gone a bit Pete."

petit pois n : small green peas.

petrol, petroleum n : *gas, gasoline*.

petrol station n : *gas station, garage*.

phoar /fwuah/ sp intj : *wow, yowser,* whoa!

phonecard n : credit card sized plastic card for use with *cardphone*.

pickaxe n : *pick*.

pickled adj : *drunk*.

pickles cf n : jar of chutney-like sauce, popular in cheese *sandwiches*, Branston Pickle (brand).

picture rail n : the molding around a room about one foot below the ceiling which, in some places, is actually used to hang pictures from.

the pictures n : the flicks, the *movies*, "what's on at the pictures?"

pie and mash n : traditional *East End* favorite, minced beef and mashed potato pie with liquor (or green gravy—parsley sauce), often accompanied with jellied eels.

pig's ear expr n : *screw-up, balls up*, "you made a pig's ear of that, then!" also crsl. beer.

piffle n : nonsense.

pig inf n : something difficult or unpleasant, "it's a pig of a journey in a Citroën."

pigsty n : *pigpen*.

pigtails n : *braids*.

pikey derog sl adj n : scruffy, ill-bred, [originally from] gypsy or person living like a gypsy, see *gypo* [Brad Pitt in *Snatch* was a Pikey].

pile of pants sl n : load of crap, *pants, knickers*, "this is a pile of pants."

pillar box n : *mailbox*, the GB pillar boxes are over 6' tall, made of cast iron and painted bright post office red.

pillock n : *idiot*, irritating person, "you daft pillock!"

pinafore n : *jumper.*

pinch v : steal.

ping pong crsl adj : strong.

pint n : pint of *beer*; the imperial pint is 20 fl oz, which are a tad smaller than US fl *oz* (only 16 of which make an American *pint*, see *fluid ounce*), hence is more than 20% larger than a US *pint*, see table of measures.

pinta /pientə/ n : pint of milk, from a very successful advertising campaign: 'drinka pinta milka day,' "stop the milkman and get an extra pinta."

pip n : small hard seed of grape, cherry, apple, orange, pear, etc, see also *stone*.

pip n : tone or beep, as in an answering machine or the time signal, "at the pip the time will be . . . ."

pip sl n : irritation, exasperation, "He gives me the pip."

pip n : *star* indicating rank: one pip for a Major-General, two for a Lieutenant-General, and three for a General.

pip v : narrowly defeat, "he was pipped at the post," "we were pipped to the *post*."

pip-pip excl intj : bye-bye.

piss artist n : irritating person, esp. one who becomes so when inebriated.

pissed cf adj : *drunk*.

pissed off adj : *pissed,* annoyed, agitated, irritated.

pissing around expr v : diddling about, *mucking around*.

piss off imp v : scram, *beat it.*

piss poor adj : useless.

piss take sl vi : to tease, ridicule, *take the piss*.

piss-up n : drinking party, syn. *booze-up, slosh-up*.

pissy adj : *stroppy,* pms-y, "he's in a really pissy mood."

pitch n : playing *field*, 'cricket pitch,' 'football pitch.'

p/l [Aus] n : *pty ltd*.

plaid /plad/ [Scot] n : the material from which tartans are made.

plait /plat/ v : *braid.*

plaits /plats/ n : *braids.*

plant n : construction equipment, machines and vehicles, 'plant for hire,' sign: 'Heavy Plant Crossing.'

plaster n v : bandage, syn. *band-aid, Elastoplast*, see *sticking-plaster*, "plaster that wound."

plaster board n : *sheet rock.*

plastered sl adj : *drunk.*

plasticine [Plasticine®] n : *play-doh.*

plates crsl [plates of meat] n : feet.

plates and dishes joc crsl n : the *missis.*

plc n : public limited company, syn. *inc, ltd.*

plimmies n : *plimsolls*, syn. *tennies, trainers.*

plimsolls, plimsoles n : *sneakers*, syn. *tennis shoes, trainers.*

plod col n : policeman, see *Mr. Plod.*

plonk n : cheap table wine.

plonk down v : *plunk down*, drop down, as in plop down wearily into a chair, or plonk down *money*–finally succumb to payment.

plonker [euph for *penis*] n : dickhead, *idiot*, fool, *wally.*

the Plough n : the *Big Dipper* [part of the constellation of the Great Bear].

ploughman's lunch n : *pub* lunch consisting of hunk of bread & cheese and a *pint*, "let's just get a ploughman's."

plover's eggs n : a delicacy, like quail eggs.

plum duff [duff = dough] **plum pudding** n : steamed suet *pudding* with raisins (contains no plums), syn. *spotted dick, Christmas pudding.*

plus-fours n : *knickers.*

PM abbr n : *prime minister.*

PMQs abbr n : *prime minister*'s questions, a half hour session every Wednesday when *MP*s get to ask the *PM* questions; now televised.

pmt [premenstrual tension] n : *pms.*

pneumatic drill n : *jackhammer.*

pocket money n : (children's) weekly *allowance.*

podgy adj : pudgy.

point (electrical) n : *power point.*

points (railway) n : *switch.*

poke (*sex*) sl v n : *screw,* "good for a poke."

poke n : oomph, "does it have any poke?" (of a car).

polari n : formerly theatrical slang, now gay slang, intermixed with Cockney, etc.

police n : syn. *bluebottle, bobby,* bubbies, busies, cop, *copper,* the *filth, Mr. Plod, Old Bill,* peeler (NI), *rozzer, scuffers, the Bill, The Sweeney,* the *bronze,* titheads. See also *CID, panda car,* Scotland Yard, z-car, sleeping policeman.

poll tax n : nasty horrible 'person' tax, also known as community charge, introduced in April 1990, and replaced by *council tax* in April 1993.

Polo mint® n : strong mint candy in the same shape as *lifesavers.*

Polyfilla n : like *spackle,* plaster.

Pom, Pommy, Pommie [Aus, contr pomegranate rsl Jimmy Grant rsl immigrant] n : English person, syn. *Limey, Sassanach, Brit,* "Pommy bastard."

Pomfret-cake /pomfrit/ n : *Pontefract-cake.*

Pompey n : Portsmouth (major port and navel base on the south coast).

ponce [N] n : pimp, or simply an unpleasant parasite.

ponce n : gay or affected person, show off, fop.

pond, also **the Herring Pond** n : Atlantic Ocean, "across the pond."

pong (adj **pongy**) n v : reek, stench.

pongo n : soldier, also (Aus/NZ) Englishman.

Pontefract-cake /pomfrit/ n : flat round strong licorice candy, (originally from Pontefract, was Pomfret, Yorkshire).

pontoon (card game) n : *twenty-one, blackjack.*

pony (racing) sl n : £25.

poof, poofta, poofter n : gay.

the pools n : national betting on football matches, syn. the lottery.

poozling (NZ) v : see *totting*.

poplar cf (tree) n : *cottonwood*.

popper inf n : *snap*, *press stud*.

poppet n : term of endearment, syn. honey, *sweetie*.

pop your clogs joc expr v : die (see *cool*).

porkies crsl [pork pies] n : lies.

porridge n : *oatmeal*.

porridge crsl [borage (→ porridge) and thyme, doing time] n : jail.

portaloo (Portaloo™) col n : *portapotty, portapot*, syn *turdis*.

porter n : *doorman*.

posh usage adj : *swish*, upscale.

post cf n v : *mail*.

postbag n : *mailbag*.

postbox n : *letter-box*.

postcode, postal code n : like *zip code*, but comprised of two groups of three letters and numbers; Britain LLN NLL; Canada LNL NLN.

postgraduate cf adj n : college *graduate*.

postgraduate degree n : *graduate degree* (masters or PhD).

postie col n : *postman*, "has the postie been (round)?"

postman n : *mailman*.

postman's knock n : pubescent children's game: They take turns in a closet and the rest take turns to pretend to be a postman knocking, and then enter and kiss for some specified time.

poteen, potheen /putcheen/ [Ir] n : strong illicitly made Irish liquor, from potatoes, syn. *moonshine, hooch*.

pot plant cf n : houseplant.

potter v : *putter*, "he's pottering about in the garden shed."

potty adj : silly, *crazy*, slightly soft in the head.

pouf, pouffe n : *ottoman*, Moroccan leather-covered low seat–like a large marshmallow–popular as a footstool.

pound [because it once equaled a pound of silver] n : see £1, *sterling*, *sovereign*, syn. *quid*.

power point n : electrical *outlet*, *socket*.

pragger-wagger n : Prince of Wales, see –*er*.

pram [perambulator] n : *baby carriage, baby buggy*.

prang vt n : *fender bender*.

pranny n : *prat*, also *vagina*.

praps contr adv : perhaps, whatever.

prat, pratt derog n : *twit*, also *vagina*.

prawn n : shrimp. See *come the raw prawn*.

precinct cf n : see *shopping precinct*.

prefab [prefabricated] n : a style of house considered by some to be inferior, and hence reflecting on their occupants or the neighborhood.

prefect (school) n : in many *private school*s a cadre of senior students are assigned monitor duties, usu. signified by a prefect badge and/or different colored jacket. Although a potentially despicable position, from the point of view of other students, they are typically drawn from the better students who have natural leadership abilities, and garner a mutual respect. "Quick! Down here. A prefect's coming." See *head boy/girl*.

preggers adj : *pregnant*.

pregnant adj : in the family way, in the club, *preggers*, a *bun in the oven*, *in the (puddin') club*, *up the spout*, up the duff, up the poke, up the stick.

prep school [preparatory] n : *private school* for kids up to 11 or 13.

presently cf adv : in a moment, shortly, "the *sprouts* will be done presently."

press stud n : *snap*, *popper*.

primary school cf n : school for children esp. under the age of 11, *grade school.*

prime minister n : head of *government* (not state, see *Queen*), not elected directly; the leader of the party that controls the *House of Commons* becomes prime minister. (Formally, the *King* or *Queen* proposes that person as *PM* to the *Commons*; but anyone else who was proposed would be promptly rejected.) If the *PM* dies or resigns, the party chooses a new leader, who becomes *PM*.

prime minister's questions n : see *PMQs*. [Scotland & Wales: First Ministers Questions, Canada: Question Period, Aus & NZ: Question Time.]

prise (or **prize**) **open** v : *pry open.*

private school cf n : independent school supported wholly by fees of the students (no government support), see *public school.*

proctor cf n : officer at certain universities having mainly disciplinary functions.

produce /prod(y)oos/ n : /prohdoos/ fruits and vegetables.

professor n : *full professor.*

programme sp n v : *program,* course (but computer program is same).

promenade n : *boardwalk.*

propelling pencil n : *mechanical pencil.*

proper usage intj adj : cool, awesome, wicked, good, also very, "this food is proper tasty."

properly usage adv : to the extreme, "we saw some properly big fat awesome bands," "until it births properly big."

proud usage adj : raised above surrounding area, "the wound is proud."

provisional licence n : *driver's permit.*

pseud n : *flake, trendy,* person badly disguising lack of coolness.

PT (school) n : physical training, Egyptian PT = sleeping.

pty ltd [Aus] n : proprietary limited company, syn. *inc, ltd, plc.*

pub n : *bar.* Pubs in *GB* usu. have two sections: the *public bar* (bar stools, sawdust on floor, billiard tables, darts), and the *lounge bar* or *saloon bar* (*posh*er section, leather couches, tables). It is not uncommon, esp. in less urban areas, to also have a *beer garden.* Hours traditionally were 11am–3pm, then 5pm–11pm. It's not unusual for pubs to have quite substantial lunch menus. Pubs are social places rather than meat markets or refuges for the lonely and the lost. See *publican, beer, free house, pint, half, bar.*

publican n : *pub* proprietor.

public bar n : the least expensive bar in a *pub,* which see.

public convenience n : public *restrooms, comfort station.,* commonly indicated with *gents, gentlemen, ladies.*

public prosecutor n : *district attorney.*

public school cf n : a kind of *private school,* often boarding, providing secondary education, usu. *college* preparatory, the foremost being the 'Seven Public Schools' (Eton, Harrow, Winchester, Westminster, Charterhouse, Rugby, and Shrewsbury). Originally public in the normal sense, and traditionally preparatory for (esp.) *Oxbridge* and public service.

pud /pud/ cf n : *pudding,* "what's for pud?"

pudding n : *dessert,* "what's for pudding!" "how can you have any pudding if you don't eat your meat"—Pink Floyd.

pudding n : traditionally, a cake-like dessert but steamed rather than baked (*roly-poly, plum duff,* sponge pudding, *Christmas pudding*), and extended to savory pie (steak & kidney pudding, *Yorkshire pudding,* though *black pudding, pease pudding*), tarts (treacle pudding), and other kinds of desserts (*bread pudding,* rice pudding).

puke n v : cf. *barf,* syn. *sick, chunder,* spiff your biscuits, *park the leopard,* Wallace (and Gromit).

pukka /puhka/ adj : wicked! as in mighty fine.

pull v : *pick up, chat up,* "he's going to pull a girl at the party," "going on the pull," also to *snog.*

pull-in n : *road* side *cafe* esp. for *lorry* drivers, syn. *transport café, truck stop.*

Pullman cf n : deluxe train car (or train), "can we go on the Pullman carriage?"

pull round v : regaining one's health.

pull your socks up expr v : pull yourself together, get a grip.

pump (Scot) v : fart.

pumps cf n : *tennis shoes, sneakers, plimsoles.*

puncture outfit (bicycles) n : *patch kit.*

punnet n : small ½ pint fruit basket.

punt col n v : bet, gamble.

punt n : Irish pound.

punter col n : gambler, hence client, customer, member of audience, "look at all those lovely punters (with their big fat wallets)."

punter sl n : *john* (male client of a prostitute).

pupil n : students at *school* tend to be referred to as pupils, and at university, as students.

purse cf n : *coin purse* or *change purse.*

put through (telephone) v : *connect.*

putty cf usage n : usu. refers to window putty rather than a general putty.

push bike col n : bicycle.

pushchair n : *stroller.*

put a sock in it expr v : shut up.

put down (goods bought) v : *charged, entered.*

– q –

quango [*qu*asi-*a*utonomous *non*-governmental *o*rganisation] n : semi-public co-op, appointed by the government, for some activity or project, but works independently.

quart cf n : a British quart is slightly more than a liter (1.136523 l), see *pint,* and table 8, Measures.

quay /kee/ n : wharf, pier, dock.

Queen (political role of) n : Although all actions of the *government* are made in her name as Head of State, the (King or) Queen does not normally take an active part in politics; her position is a ceremonial one. Legislation once passed by the *Commons* and the *Lords* requires her assent to be enacted, but this is always given. The one situation when she may exercise actual power is when a *minority government* loses the support of the *Commons*: it is her decision whether there is a new general election at once, or whether another party can try to form a *minority government* instead. The Queen is also the Queen of Canada and about a dozen other countries, and the head of the *Commonwealth*; these are now all considered separate offices.

queen's pudding n : fancy *bread pudding,* baked also with *jam* and meringue, and can contain booze (hence like poorman's trifle–but bread instead of sponge cake and meringue instead of whipped cream).

Queen's Speech n : like the *State of the Union* address. Traditionally, at the start of each annual session of *Parliament,* the *King* would enter the *House of Lords* chamber and describe what legislation he wanted passed. Now the *Queen* still delivers such a speech, but it's written by the governing party and forms a declaration of its legislative intentions. Also often refers to her Christmas message.

queer n : cf. *gay,* syn. *bent*, fairy, *batty boy*, *bender*, *botter iron*, *ducky*, *ponce*, Nancy boy, pansy, *poof*, *poofta*, quean, shirtlifter, *willy* woofter.

queer street sl n : bankruptcy.

queue n : *line.*

queue v : stand in *line, line up,* an inevitable ritual encountered in any journey.

queue up imp v : *line up.*

quick half n : a quick *half pint.*

quick one n : a quick *pint.*

quid (pl quid) n : *£1*, one *pound sterling*, same as *buck* for *dollar.* (Also sl. for £1000 and £1,000,000.)

quids in inf expr adj : flush, out ahead, financially.

quieten v : quiet, settle, settle down.

quilt n : *comforter*, *duvet*.

quimling, quimle n v : cunnilingus, and general stimulation, syn. *muff diving, gamahuche*.

quis, ego /kwiz egoh/ [L who? I!] excl pron : A person (usu. school kids) announces something for free with "quis!" and the first person to say "ego!" gets it.

quite cf usage adv : slightly, e.g. "I quite like you" = "I like you a little," 'quite good' = mediocre, acceptable, "quite ill" = a bit off color, although 'he's quite *fit'* could mean he's *hot.*

quod sl n : jail.

— r —

rabbit [crsl rabbit and pork–talk] v : talk incessantly, jabber (cf. *motor mouth*), "she does rabbit on."

RAC abbr n : Royal Automobile Club, syn. AAA.

radio [rental] rsl adj : *mental*.

RAF abbr n : Royal Air Force, syn. *USAF.*

rag derog n : newspaper, magazine, comic books, etc., syn. *mag*, see *trash rag*.

rag v : tease.

rag and bone man n : itinerant junk man, in the old days he'd wander the streets with his (horse-drawn) cart calling out for 'any old iron.'

rag-tag and bobtail [the two main animal characters in a children's TV show] n : riff-raff, the dense unwashed masses.

rag week n : fund (hell) raising program by students including *college* newspaper, stunts, parades and entertainment, syn. *rush* week.

railway n : *railroad.*

railway coach, railway carriage n : *railroad car* or rail car.

railway line n : *railroad tracks.*

railway station n : *train station.*

railway tea n : *British Rail tea*, equivalent to *truck stop* coffee.

railway ticket n : train ticket.

rambler n : hiker.

ram raid v : breaking into and *burglariz*ing a *store* by means of crashing a car into it.

randy adj : *horny.*

Ranger n : senior *Guide.*

rapeseed oil n : *canola* oil.

raspberry [orig crsl raspberry tart = fart] n : blown derisive, syn. *razz, Bronx cheer.*

rat-arsed sl adj : *drunk*.

the rates n : kind of property tax, but replaced by *council tax* (via the *poll tax*).

rave up n : wild party.

Rawlplug® (often heard as 'raw plug') n : *screw anchor*, plastic plug used for holding screws in masonry.

raw prawn (Aus) expr n : see *don't come the raw prawn*.

RE abbr n : religious education, *RI*, *RS*.

read v : study (at university), "I read botany at London," syn. *major.*

reader n : *associate professor*, researcher.

readies n : cash, *money*, syn. *dosh*, tosh.

real lad n : a term of admiration, a guy considered blessed of all good male attributes, he can *pull birds* with ease, equivalent to real *guy, hunk, cool dude,* "he's a real lad."

really cf adv : usu. a response indicating surprise, disbelief, or disinterest.

rear-ender derog sl n : gay guy, syn. *up the bum.*

recce /rekee/ [reconnaissance] n v : *check out, scope* out, recon (mission), "I'm going to recce that new place tomorrow," "I did a recce yesterday," cf. *recon.*

reception (hotel) n : *front desk.*

Red Arrows n : *RAF* crack exhibition flying team, syn. *Blue Angels, Thunderbirds.*

redbrick adj : (originally pejorative) newer university, see *Oxbridge.*

redundant adj : to be *made redundant* is to be laid off.

reel usage n : *spool, bobbin,* "reel of *cotton.*"

register (*school*) usage n : usu. call/take the register, roll-call.

registration number n : *license plate number.*

religious issues cf n : *MIF* or *TIF*, Man United vs. Spurs, Corrie vs. EastEnders, Celtic vs. Rangers, BBC vs. ITV, driver or cyclist, petrol vs. diesel, cash or credit, buy or rent, North vs. South (of *Watford*), protestant vs. catholic, Labour vs. *Tory.*

remould (*tyre*) n : *retread.*

removal man n : moving man.

removals v : moving (house, etc.), hence removals van, *removal man*, etc.

repeat n v : to re-taste food as a result of burping or indigestion, "urgh, I've got egg repeats."

rest v : see *give it a rest, all the rest.*

return ticket n : *round-trip ticket,* "two returns to London, please."

reverse usage (car) v : *back up.*

reverse charges, reverse charges call v n : *call collect, collect call.*

reversing lights n : *backup lights.*

revise, revising v : study, studying, esp. prior to tests, syn. cramming, *swot*ting.

rhubarb cf sl intj n : *codswallop,* also word salad as used by actors in crowd scene enacting conversation.

RI abbr n : religious instruction, *RE, RS.*

Ribena n : *blackcurrant* cordial, popular drink and cocktail addition (*rum and black,* vodka & black, Pernod & black, snakebite & black).

Ridings of Yorkshire [third thing] n : England's largest county comprised the East Riding, West Riding and North Riding, see table 14, Counties.

right (emphasizer) expr adj : real, "he's a right *charlie,*" "right *twit,*" "right *git.*"

right charlie expr n : dunce.

right git expr n : esp. annoying person.

right one col n : *twit.*

ring, ring up v : *call,* phone, syn. *tinkle, bell,* buzz, "ring you tomorrow," 'ring around' (*call* a *bunch* of people).

ring back v : *call* back.

ring in v : to *call* in (to work).

ring off v : hang up (phone).

ring road n : *beltway.*

rise n : pay *raise.*

road usage n : *street,* cf. *cul-de-sac, close, drive, blvd, mews.*

roadworks n : *construction.*

robin cf n : this bird of legend, due to its cheeky but endearing character, is found all over the UK–a small (5½"), red-breasted chat-thrush *Erithacus rubecula* resembling a warbler.

rock n : originally a 12" long 1" thick, mint candy cane, white with pink outside, found in the beach-side stalls of coastal tourist towns with the name of the town embedded in clear red candy all the way through its length, e.g. Southend rock,

Brighton rock, Blackpool rock. These days they come in various sizes, colors, and patterns, including swirled like Christmas candy canes.

rock usage cf n : large boulder.

rock-eel, rock-salmon n : dogfish, catfish. [They were renamed these to make them sound more appetizing, and it apparently has worked wonders.]

rocket (green leafy vegetable) n : *arugula.*

rocket n : spirited rebuke or telling off, syn. *bollocking, bawl out, chew out.*

Rods col contr n : Harrods (the department store in the *West End*).

roger sl v : *screw (sex),* "Roger the cabin boy."

roller col n : Rolls-Royce car.

rollocking euph v : *bollocking.*

rollocks [perhaps from *Jack Rollock's Adventures*] euph intj : *bollocks.*

Rolo® /roh loh/ n : a roll of caramel-filled chocolates, "want a Rolo?"

roly-poly, jam roly-poly, roly-poly pudding n : suet pastry *pudding,* often served with *jam,* made into a roll.

ron contr col n : later on, see *doofer,* "save it for ron."

ronson (Ronson lighter) crsl n : *butt,* "up your ronson!"

root v : search, rummage, "A sophisticated programme then rooted through a huge depository of text, images."

root for v : *buck for.*

rootle v : rummage around, *root.*

ropy, ropey col adj : poor in quality, *dodgy, flaky,* also, forming gelatinous threads, "ropey this morning" (dentist, of viscous spit).

rosy [Rosy Lee] crsl n : *tea.*

rot col n : rubbish, nonsense.

roundabout (road) n : *traffic circle.* Conceptually, replacing a four way stop with a four way *yield,* and traffic in the inter-section moves in a circular fashion. To enter the fray you do yield to traffic already there, but if there is none, you can sail on through. The actual circle is much larger than imagined, judging by the small experimental ones seen in various American towns. [Gyratory circuses were renamed roundabout by American Rearsall Smith of the BBC Advisory Committee on Spoken English in the 1920s.] Also, merry-go-round, *carousel,* and also 'see-saws, swings, and round-abouts' in the children's playground.

round brackets punc n : *brackets, ( ).*

rounders n : a baseball-like game, though less formal, popular at *schools* and as exercise or recreation.

roundhead (schoolboy) n : circumcised, see *cavalier,* syn. yiddled whanger.

round the houses crsl n : trousers, also a futile mission or endeavour.

round the twist col sl expr adj : round the bend.

row usage n : argument, disturbance, or fight, usu. domestic, "they're having a row," "row erupts in *Commons.*"

royal n : any member of the royal family, "there might be some royals there."

Royal Mail n : equivalent to *Postal Service.*

rozzer [Hebrew *chazer* pig] sl n : policeman.

RS abbr n : religious studies, *RE, RI.*

rubber cf n : *eraser.*

rubber johnny n : *rubber, johnny, condom.*

rubbish n : *trash, garbage,* also nonsense, *bullshit.*

rubbish adj : crap, "they gave us a rubbish breakfast."

rubbish v : to *bad-mouth, slate.*

rubbish bags n : *trash bags, garbage bags.*

rubbish tip n : *garbage dump.*

rubbishy adj : trashy.

rucksack n : camping *backpack,* also school *backpack.*

ruddy col adj : *bloody,* "around and around went the ruddy great wheel."

rude cf usage adj : indecent, lewd.

rugger col n : rugby.

rum adj : odd, curious, queer, "it's a rum do."

rum and black (drink) n : rum and *Ribena.*

rumble col n : *barney,* fight.

rumbled v : found out.

rumble strips n : set of raised strips in road serving as an audible caution sign.

rumbustious adj : *rambunctious.*

rumpy pumpy sl v : *sex,* syn. *hootchycootchy.*

runner bean n : *green bean,* scarlet runner, *pole bean.*

run-up n : period just before action or event.

— S —

SA [French Société Anonyme] n : corporation, syn. *inc, ltd.*

sachet usage n : packet (as in the small paper or plastic ones at fast food places containing things like instant coffee, *ketchup* and so on).

sack n v : *fire* (from a job), *can,* *made redundant,* "he got the sack," "I'll give him the sack," "he was sacked."

sack barrow n : *hand truck,* dolly.

safe col adj intj : syn. *brill, cool.*

salad onion n : *green onion, spring onion.*

saloon bar n : like the *lounge bar,* the better or more comfortable bar than the *public bar,* see *pub.*

saloon car n : *sedan car.*

salt beef n : *corned beef.*

sandpit n : *sandbox.*

sandwich cf n : a sandwich is assumed to have the bread buttered, in addition to the contents, if any, see *butty, chip butty,*

jam butty, **sarnie,** "well, did you want bacon, lettuce, or tomato?"

sandwich course n : college course including periods of practical experience, hence sandwich student.

sanitary towel n : *sanitary napkin.*

sapper n : private in the Royal Engineers [from a person who digs saps (trenches)].

sarky sl adj : sarcastic.

sarnie n : *sandwich.*

Sassenach [Scottish and Pictish] joc derog n : Saxon folk south of Hadrian's Wall (English people, syn. *Limey, Pom, Brit*).

sat regional pp v : seated or sitting, "I've been sat here all day," see *sout.*

satchel n : child's or student's school bag, shoulder bag, often *backpack.* See also *rucksack.*

sauce n : sauciness (see *saucy*), also booze, as in "I better lay off the sauce."

saucepan /sorspən/ n : /sahspan/.

saucepan lids crsl n : kids, *godfors,* (also teapot (child), dustbin, tin, and (Aus) billy lids), "where are the saucepans, then?"

saucy adj : impudent, fresh, syn. *cheeky,* ballsy, smartass, "saucy bugger."

sausages, pork n : *sausage links, links.*

Savile Row n adj : most prestigious street in London for tailors, drawing the rich and famous for *bespoke* suits.

savouries n : savory appetizers or *dessert.*

sawn-off sp adj : *sawed-off.*

sbd abbr n : silent but deadly, a silent fart, also "that one had slippers on."

scallion cf n : kind of onion or shallot with cloves like garlic but milder or onion flavor.

scarper v : to scram, run away, syn. *hightail out.*

scatty col adj : scatterbrained, *crazy.*

scent n : *perfume.*

sceptic, sceptical sp n adj : *skeptic, skeptical.*

Sceptred Isle (poetic) n : the island of *Great Britain*, see *Emerald Isle*.

schedule /shedyool/ n v : /skejool/ (although the British pr. is adopting the American pr.) *timetable*.

scheduled /shedyoold/ n : building or monument officially designated as historic, hence protected or preserved, but if inhabited then known as *listed*.

scheme n : *program,* "a training scheme."

schmutter [Yiddish] csl n : clothing, often dressy or high quality.

school cf n : refers only to *grade school,* never *college*.

scoff v : *gobble down,* syn. *scarf.*

scone /skon/ /skohn/ pr n : /skohn/.

scorch inf v : to move very quickly, "scorch over to Jill's place," syn. *lay down rubber.*

score sl n : *£20.*

Scot n : Scottish person, *Jock, Lallan.*

scotch crsl [scotch egg] n : leg.

scotch n : whisky.

scotch woodcock n : anchovies on toast.

scot-free adj : unharmed, unpunished, "He got off scot-free."

Scotland Yard [name of London street] n : *the Yard,* London Metropolitan police detective headquarters, and also refers to the detectives (*CID*), who also act as consultants to other regional police departments, "Scotland Yard is on the scene."

Scouse, Scouser n : *Liverpudlian,* (Common repartee—"bloody Londoner! Scouse *git!*"). [In Ireland skause is beef stew with new potatoes—Liverpool has a large Irish population. In Maine scouse is like *clam chowder* without the clams.]

screaming abdabs expr n : screaming meemies, literally a description of a lunatic having a screaming fit, and often of psychologically overwhelmed soldiers coming back from overly intense situations, but used as extreme exasperation, "she gives me the screaming abdabs!"

screw sl n : salary, wages.

scrote n : all-around useless, annoying (young) male.

scrubber n : whore, syn. *ho, scrubber, slag, tart, kerb crawler, slapper,* slut.

scrump cf v : steal fruit from orchards, "let's go scrumping," "I think I saw the scrumper in the hedge."

scrumple v : crush, crumple.

scrumpy n : rough *cider,* farmhouse *cider*/cyder, clear or cloudy, still or slightly lively, native to Devon and Cornwall. [Legends abound about the fermentation process (. . . toss in a rusty old iron bedstead to precipitate the tannins, then a dead cow to draw out the maggots . . .) but while it is true that an accumulation of carbon dioxide could cause a mouse scurrying across the surface of the vat to expire and fall in, brewers of old did actually hang in a piece of meat during a long cold spell to keep the yeast viable.]

scuffers n : police.

seaside n : the *beach,* "let's go to the seaside!"

seaside rock n : see *rock*.

season ticket n : commuter ticket, bus or train pass lasting a certain period.

sea wall n : mud embankment or *levee* circumscribing the entire coast of the *British Isles,* where necessary to prevent encroachment of the sea, and generally with a *footpath* along its top.

secateurs n : hand *pruning shears.*

secondary modern hist n : until recently, *secondary school* focusing on practical skills rather than academic studies, see *eleven plus.*

secondary school n : usu. ages 11–18, equivalent to *middle + high school,* offering secondary education following primary education, see *grammar school, secondary modern, primary school.*

seconded v : temporarily sent (on a job,

tour of duty).

seed-cake n : caraway seed-cake, a bit like a bundt cake or *pound cake,* but with whole caraway seeds.

see-saw n : *teeter-totter.*

see you, Jimmy! (Glasgow) expr intj : "I'll fuckin' killya!"

self-service (*petrol* station) n : *self-serve.*

sell-by date n : *expiration date,* "is it past the sell-by date."

sellotape [Sellotape®] n : *Scotch tape,* sticky tape (Aus).

semi- /semee/ prefix : /semie/.

semi cf n : *semi-detached* house, "they lived in a semi."

semi-detached n : tract houses built in pairs side-to-side, but often seen as a symbol of lower class struggle to reach an unenviable middle class, see *duplex.*

send-up cf v n : ridicule by mimicry, also a parody or satire.

senior lecturer n : *assistant professor.*

sent to Coventry v : ostracized, shunned.

seppo [Aus] rsl n : American, syn. *Yank.*

septic tank (hence *seppo*) [Aus] rsl n : American, syn. *Yank.*

service flats n : *apartment hotel.*

serviette n : table *napkin.*

settee n : *couch, love seat.*

sex cf v : syn. *stuff, poke, leg over, shag, frig, have it off, have it away, get your end away, have it up, roger, knob, rumpy pumpy, bunk up.*

shag cf v : *screw,* fuck, "shag off."

shagged, shagged out inf adj : tired out, exhausted, *knackered.*

shampers (play on *champers*) joc n : shampoo.

shandy n : half *beer,* half *lemonade*–sounds *gross* but surprisingly refreshing on a hot summer's day (if any). See also *ginger beer shandy.*

sharking v : going after a specific woman (see *pull*).

shepherd's pie n : baked dish of *minced meat* topped with mashed potato. See *cottage pie.*

sherbet cf n : flavored fizzy candy powder.

shew /shoh/ arch sp v : show.

shicer sl n : swindler or failure.

shilling n : see *1/-.*

shinty (Scotland) n : *shinny,* simple form of hockey.

shirty adj : *huffy,* cf. *stroppy.*

shite n : shit (cf *shoot*).

shooting-break (or **-brake**) n : *station wagon, estate car.*

shop cf n : *store.*

shop sl v : to finger (a criminal, etc).

shop assistant n : *sales clerk.*

shopping precinct n : pedestrian-only shopping area or open-air mall in the center of town.

shopping trolley n : *shopping cart, shopping caddy.*

shop walker n : *floorwalker.*

short list n : list of candidates from which final choice is made.

short-list vt : to put on a *short list.*

shout n : info, as in "give joe a shout," syn *heads up.*

shout expr n : as in 'I think it's your shout' meaning your turn to buy the next round (of drinks), "my shout!"

Shreddies (breakfast cereal) n : similar to *Chex* and Kellogg's Crispix.

shreddies sl n : *manky* or revolting men's (boy's) *pants.*

shtum, schtoom /shtoom/ [Yiddish, common in E London] **shtumf!** /shtoomf/ imp intj : shush! be quiet!

shufti /shuftee/ [Hindustani] v : to look around, to *scope* out, "let's have a shufti," also, just look or look at.

shunt (railway) n v : *switch.*

sick n v : *puke.*

sick squid sl n : £6.

side (side spin) (billiards) n : *English.*

sideboard (furniture) usage n : *buffet.*

sideboards (hair) n : *sideburns.*

sidelights n : *parking lights.*

sideways expr adj : 'make your shit hang sideways' = annoy, "it didn't make my shit hang sideways," or in surprise as in "*shag* me five times sideways."

silencer (car) n : *muffler.*

siling dial [Yorkshire] v : raining very hard, (cf. *kissing*).

silly buggers expr n : tomfoolery, "he's just playing silly buggers."

silly season (press) n : ~August, when the papers pad with frivolous and exaggerated stories (*Parliament* is in recess).

silver top n : bottle of unpasteurized milk with a silver top (see *milk top*) indicating *regular* milk about equivalent to Vitamin D milk in fat content, see *gold top.*

Sindy n : *Barbie* clone.

single n : *single ticket*, "two singles to town, please," (or Gerald Durrell's book *Two Singles to Adventure*, Adventure was actually their destination's town's name).

singlet n : *undershirt.*

single ticket n : *one-way ticket*, see *return ticket.*

sink n : kitchen sink.

sister n : hospital nurse, see *matron.*

sitting room usage n : *living room.*

The Six Counties n : of Northern Ireland.

sixes and sevens expr adj : confused, mixed up, "they are at sixes and sevens."

sixpence n : see *6d*, syn, *tanner.*

sixth form n : final two years of *secondary school*, equivalent to *grade* 11 (lower sixth) and 12 (upper sixth), during which *A levels* (and now *AS levels*) are taken.

sixth form college n : a college just for *sixth form.*

skelp dial v : slap, "if I stepped out of line, she would give me a good skelping."

skew-whiff col adj : askew, also *sqiffy.*

skimmed milk n : *skim milk.*

skin and blister crsl n : sister, see *trouble and strife.*

skins n : tobacco rolling papers, but the term often used by rollers of *joint*s, "make that a 5-skin," "is it ok if I skin up here?"

skint [skinned, pp of skin] sl adj : flat broke.

skin up expr v : roll a cigarette, usu. a *joint*, see *skins.*

skip n : *dumpster.*

skipping rope n : *jump rope.*

skirting board n : *baseboard.*

skive, **skiver** v n : shirk, shirker, loafer.

skivvy derog col n : female domestic servant.

sky n : usu. means satellite TV [provided by the operator Sky or BSkyB] but also refers to any related service thus facilitated, "have you got Sky?"

sky rocket crsl n : pocket.

slag n : whore, *scrubber*, ho, also general deprecatory term, *git*, "*oi* you slag, did you spill my *pint*."

slag sl v : criticize, slander.

slag off expr v : to *dis*, insult, disparage, slander, denigrate, criticize, "she slagged him off something rotten."

slap and tickle col n : fun in first and *second base*.

slapper sl n : whore, *scrubber*, ho, "what a slapper."

slash v : urinate, syn. pee, take a leak, strain the greens.

slate cf vt : scold, criticize.

sledge sp n : *sled.*

sleeper n : railroad *tie.*

sleeping policeman n : *speed bump, hump, speed retarder.*

slimming usage v : *dieting*, "I can't eat that! I'm slimming."

slip-road n : *on-ramp* (on-slip), *off-ramp* (off-slip).

Sloane abbr n : *Sloane Ranger.*

Sloane Ranger n : *pseuds*, well-heeled yuppie scum, upper-class preppies, the *royal*s, their groupies, and other *ankle biters* that frequent the *West End* clubs in and around Sloane Square, and recognized for their own *Sloane Rangese* not so much for its vocabulary as for its delivery. "What's the difference between a Sloane Ranger and a bowling ball? You can only get three fingers into a bowling ball."

Sloane Rangese n : *Sloane Ranger* lingo (lots of horse and dog allusions), such as *ankle-biters*, *bolter*, *motg*, *sofas*, *sohf*, *sr*, *wrinklies*, *wrm*.

slobber v : *drool*.

slodge n : any unidentifiable substance (food, mud) with the consistency of *porridge*.

slog usage n v : long and tedious hard work, work *real* hard, syn. *graft*, "it was a hard slog."

sloppy joe cf n : big baggy *jumper*.

sloshed sl adj : *drunk* (hence *slosh-up*).

slosh-up sl n : *booze-up*.

sloth /slohth / n : /slahth/.

slowcoach n : *slowpoke*.

small hours expr n : the *wee hours*.

smalls (washing) col n : ladies' underwear, though it generally refers to small items of laundry, "Winona came up with a raft of excuses for *half-inch*ing the smalls."

smart usage n : neat and tidy.

smartarse sp n : *smartass*, smarty-pants.

Smarties® (candy) n : 'like *M&M's,* only better.'

smashing intj adj : great, *brilliant*, *awesome*.

smoke, the smoke, big smoke sl n : London, esp. apt prior to 1963 before coal fires were banned and the world famous smog was sometimes as thick as pea soup.

smoo(d)ge (Aus NZ) v : behave in fawning or ingratiating manner.

snags (Aus) inf n : sausages, syn. *links, bangers*.

snakes and ladders (board game) n : *chutes and ladders*.

snap n intj : announced when two like

things occur or said simultaneously—from the so-named card game around announcing snap! when two same-valued cards are played at the same time, see *jinx*.

sneak (school) sl n v : tell-tale, syn. *grass, fink*.

snip n : a bargain, a *score*.

snitch sl n : nose.

snog v n : *neck, mack,* smooch, "they're snogging in the cupboard," "they went for a snog."

snook n : see *cock a snook*.

snooker n : popular game in UK, similar to *pool*.

snooker [from a strategy in *snooker*] v : caught in a bind, "he's snookered."

snout sl n : cigarette.

snuff it v : to die.

sock expr v : see *put a sock in it* and *pull your socks up*.

socket n : *outlet, power point, point*.

sock suspenders n : *suspenders,* garters.

sod [sodomist] n : clod, irritating fool, *oaf*.

sod! intj : "sod!" "sod it!" "*sod off*!"

sod all expr n : nothing, "I haven't done sod all all day," syn. fuck all, *bugger all, sweet FA*.

sod off imp v : scram, *bugger off*.

sofa usage n : *couch*.

sofas abbr n : suitable occupation for a *Sloane*, see *Sloane Rangese*.

soft as shit expr adj : *wet*, pathetic, useless.

soft goods (trade) n : textiles and fabrics.

soft shoulder n : unpaved shoulder of a road such as a grass *verge*, see *hard shoulder*.

sohf abbr n : sense of humor failure, humor impaired, see *Sloane Rangese*.

soigné /swan(g)ay/ [French] adj : chic.

solarium cf n : tanning room.

solder /soldə/ n v : /sahdə/.

soldiers col n : toast cut into convenient strips, esp. for children, for instance for dunking into soft boiled eggs.

solicitor usage n : *lawyer, attorney.*

sonsie, sonsy [Scot] adj : becoming, pleasing, full of life.

soppy adj : *sappy,* effete, wimpy.

sort code (bank) n : a 6-digit bank *routing number.*

sorted, sorted out usage v : to take care of, "he'll sort it out," "the plumber got it all sorted."

sout [Northern dialect] v : *sat,* sitting, "she's sout *ont* chair."

South n : London and the *Home Counties.*

sov col abbr n : *sovereign.*

sovereign n : gold *£1* coin, now used to refer, with a hint of irony, to the new brass pound coin about the size of a squat fat quarter. There are five kinds differing by the inscription on the edge and the design, representing the four countries comprising the UK and the UK as a whole; pound *note*s were done away with in 1986.

sozzled sl adj : *drunk.*

Spanish archer csl n : the elbow (see also *golden elbow*), rejection, *sack,* "so I gave him the Spanish archer then."

spanner n : *wrench,* 'a spanner in the works,' (or John Lennon's book *A Spaniard in the Works*).

spare col adj : to become very distraught, "don't go spare," "he went spare," syn. *lose it.*

spares usage n : *spare parts.*

sparky col n : electrician, esp. on a *construction site.* See also *chippie.*

spaz offen sl n : spastic, person acting in a spastic manner, uncoordinated person, syn *flid*, *spastic*, *clot.*

speciality sp n : *specialty.*

speed retarder n : the official name for a *speed bump.*

spelt sp v : *spelled.*

spend a penny n : go to the *bathroom,* "I've got to spend a penny!" From the days when *public conveniences* required a

penny to be put in the slot to enter.

spiffing (arch) adj : *excellent.*

spike sl n : *doss house.*

spinney n : copse.

spirits n : *liquor.*

spiv col n : swanky but dubious freelance salesperson, syn. *huckster.*

splendid usage adj : *way cool.*

splinter usage n : *sliver* (of wood etc., in the skin).

the splits n : *the split.*

splodge n v : splotch (connotation is with porridge or paint rather than ink or milk).

spod n : *nerd* (thick glasses, pocket protector, socially deficient kind).

spoke with the lord expr v : to swear, "I spoke with the lord."

spond [*spondulicks*] sl n : cash, *money.*

spondulicks [probably from *Spondylus* shells (spiny oyster) which were one of the commodities used as *money* by the Mayans] sl n : cash, *money* (in a previous era used by upper classes, and hence an excellent word for use by lower classes when putting on mock airs and graces or making fun).

sponge bag n : toiletry bag (see *dop kit*).

sport n : *sports,* 'the sport pages.'

spot col n : small amount, "would you like a spot of tea?" but often as ironic understatement, "spot of *bovver,*" syn. *bit.*

spot of bother n : ruction, see *bother.*

spot on adj : *on the nail.*

spots n : *zits,* pimples.

spotted dick (food) n : steamed suet *pudding* with raisins, syn. currant *pudding, plum duff.*

spring onion n : *green onion, scallions.*

sprog (hence sproggie, sprogette, etc.) Scot sl n : baby, small child, sprogs = kids, sprogdrop = *pregnant.*

sprouts cf usage n : brussels sprouts (though often found as brussel sprouts).

sprucer csl n : teller of tall tales.

spuds n : potatoes.

spunk cf n : semen, syn. *spooge,* (Scot) joombye /joombee/.

squash n : concentrated sweetened fruit juice, diluted with water to drink, "do you want lemon squash or orange squash?"

squash usage cf n : *marrow,* zucchini.

squashed fly col adj : see *Garibaldi biscuits*.

squat n : a settled *flat,* see *squatter*. Famous 1970s London squats include Cornwall Terrace, Regent's Park (since it was owned by the *Queen*), Elgin Avenue, and Hornsey Rise, Islington.

squatter n : person residing in an otherwise abandoned or vacant building, see *squat*. At one time a person establishing residency of a property by staying a night (as evinced by their bedding) could only be legally removed by the city council by relocation, not eviction. This 'loophole' was for a time widely exploited.

squib n : *firecracker,* but not quite as sharp as a *banger* (see *damp squib*).

squidgy adj : squashy (like foam-rubber), squeezy, "this one's all squidgy," "squidge in here."

squiffy sl adj : a bit *drunk*.

squint usage col v : peep, "take a squint at this."

the squirts n : *diarrhea,* syn. the *trots*.

the squits n : *diarrhea,* syn. the *trots*.

squiz [Aus/NZ] n v : glance, *check out*.

sr abbr n : sanctioned ritual.

SRN (State Registered Nurse) abbr n : *RN* (Registered Nurse).

staff (academic) n : *faculty*.

stalls (theatre) n : *orchestra seats*.

stand (public office) v : *run*.

standard lamp n : *floor lamp*.

starkers [stark naked] adj : utterly naked, "he was absolutely starkers."

starters n : appetizers.

state school n : *public school*.

sterling, pound sterling n : British currency, syn. *pound*, see *£*.

stewed apple n : *applesauce*.

stick sl n : abuse, criticism, "he gave me a lot of stick."

stick v : abide, "I can't stick him."

sticking-plaster n : adhesive bandage, syn. *Elastoplast, Band-Aid*.

sticks n : *boondocks*.

sticky plaster n : *sticking-plaster*.

stile n : stepping arrangement in fence allowing persons but not animals to cross, common in rural areas where a public *footpath* crosses farmland, "run a mile, jump a stile, eat a country pancake."

stingers col n : *stinging nettles*.

stinging nettles [*Urtica dioica*] n : though occurring in the US, occurs prolifically in areas of the UK. The sharp biting sting caused by injection of formic acid goes away after a day, unlike the oils in *poison oak,* sumac and ivy found in the US.

stitch-up n : situation where one is deceived, frame-up, "the revolution in Kyrgyzstan may have been an insiders' stitch-up."

stocious sl adj : *drunk*.

stockings n : nylons.

stodge n : thick, heavy food.

stone usage n : *rock*.

stone n : 14 lbs, (6.35 kg) "I weigh eleven stone four," "he's an eight-stone weakling."

stone n : *pit.* (large hard seed of plum, peach, apricot, cherry, date, avocado, etc. see also *pip*.)

stone the crows intj : expression of surprise.

stonkered [NZ and Aus] adj : utterly exhausted, *knackered*.

stonking adj : spectacular, "a stonking blend of funk, rock and jazz," "The new apartments would fetch a stonking price."

stony [contr of stony broke] sl adj : broke, syn. *skint*.

stood regional pp v : standing, "I've been stood here all day."

in stook [Yiddish] csl adj : in financial difficulties.

stopping n : filling for teeth.

storage heater n : electrical heater that accumulates heat during off-peak hours for later release.

store cf n : department store.

storey (floor of building) sp n : *story*.

storm in a teacup expr n : tempest in a teapot.

stout n : dark, sweet beer.

straight n : cigarette made of tobacco not cut with *dope*.

straight fight (politics) n : direct contest between candidates.

straight up csl excl intj : honest! (used as a declaration or a question).

strap line (marketing) n : *tag line*.

stream n : *creek*.

stress usage intj n : grief, acknowledgement, response, or statement about a situation, "stress," "it's stress," syn. *bummer*.

strike a light! intj : surprise, disgust.

strimmer (Strimmer™) n : *weed whacker*.

strine [Aus] contr adj : Australian, "in strine, we say . . ."

string and sellotape expr n : standard materials for a good *kluge,* equivalent to '*chewing gum and baling wire,*' duct tape, or 'paper clips and *pull ties.*'

stroll on expr v : expression of disbelief, syn. 'get out of here.'

stroppy col adj : belligerent, bad tempered, awkward to deal with, syn *ornery, bolshie*, *shirty*, *pissy*.

strump [backform strumpet] v : *pull*, stalk, "she's been strumping around," "is strumping her something rotten."

strumpet [strumpet = prostitute] sl n : *ho,* but these days, more of a saucy minx.

stuff v : *screw,* syn. fuck, "*get stuffed*," "stuff the *Queen*."

stumer [Yiddish] csl n : a dud (of checks, coins, people, situations).

stump v : baffle.

sub-editor n : *copy-reader.*

subway cf n : *pedestrian underpass.*

sultana n : large yellow kind of raisin.

summer time n : syn. *daylight saving time,* **British Summer Time**, the actual date varying from year to year, though presently standardized with the EU to be the last Sunday in March, see table of UK Holidays, *winter time*.

summons (law) n : *citation.*

sump (car) n : oil pan, crankcase.

sun cream col n : sun tan lotion.

supermarket trolley n : *shopping cart.*

supply teacher n : *substitute teacher.*

surgery n : dentist's or *doctor's office.*

surgical spirit n : ethanol, syn. *denatured alcohol, rubbing alcohol.*

surname n : *last name,* see **given name**.

suspender belt n : *garter belt* or *garters* for holding up *stockings*.

suspenders n : *garters.*

suss, suss out sl v : *check out,* figure out, *scope* out, "suss that one out."

swankpot col n : a person of swank.

swarf, swarfega (**Swarfega**®) n : mechanics' grease-cutting hand cleaning gel.

swat alt sp v : see *swot*.

swede n : *turnip, rutabaga.*

the Sweeney crsl [*Sweeney Todd*] n : The *Flying Squad*.

Sweeney Todd n : late 18th century Dickensian London barber who, by means of a trapdoor chair, dumped clients into a basement–which adjoined the catacombs of a church–slit their throats with a *cutthroat* (where necessary), robbed them, and dumped their remains into previously used crypts and vaults. Later, the victims flesh found its way into the meat pies of his lover/accomplice's renowned pie shop. They were finally nailed, and in one of the first uses of forensics (because the star witness poisoned herself in her cell) he was successfully tried and executed in 1802.

sweet n : *dessert.*

sweet, sweetie, sweets n : *candy,* "*mummy*, can I have a sweetie?"

sweet FA [sweet *Fanny Adams*, euph for sweet fuck all] n : nothing, syn. *Jack Shit, zilch.*

sweetshop n : *candy store,* syn. *tuck shop.*

swimming costume n : bathing suit, *bathing costume, swimsuit.*

swimming trunks n : swim shorts.

swingeing /swinzhing/ (journalism) adj : severe, sweeping, drastic, "*MP* warns of swingeing *council tax* rises."

swipe v : pilfer.

swish adj : *posh*, fancy, *smart*, fashionable, "it's a bit swish, isn't it."

Swiss roll n : *jelly roll.*

switchback cf n : road or rail that undulates sharply up and down, also roller coaster.

swizz, swiz col n : rip off.

swop alt sp v : swap, *trade.*

swot (also swat) v : to cram (for *exams*).

swot n : an assiduous student, syn. *nerd.*

— t —

ta /tah/ expr intj : thank you.

table cf v : bring forward an issue by putting it on the agenda.

tackies, takkies [South African] n : *sneakers, tennies, trainers.*

Taffy offen col n : person from Wales.

tailback n : traffic jam or congestion, esp. tailing back a long distance.

take away (food) v : *to go, takeout.*

takeaway n : *takeout,* also restaurant specializing in take out food, "Chinese takeaway."

take the mickey expr vt : make fun off, mock, syn. *piss take*, take the mick.

take the piss expr vt : make fun off, deride, syn. *piss take, take the mickey.*

tally-ho expr excl intj : *bye* (as well as the cry).

tam rag sl n : *jam rag.*

tanner sl n : sixpenny *bit, sixpence,* "spare us a tanner, *mate.*"

tap n : *faucet.*

tarmac (Tarmac®) n : *blacktop,* "they scraped him off the tarmac like a lump of strawberry *jam.*"

tart n : slut, *scrubber.*

tat n : *junk*, kitsch.

ta-ta /ta tah/ expr intj : goodbye, syn. *bye, later,* see *TTFN, t'ra* (Midlands pronunciation).

taters /ta?ers/ crsl [taters (potatoes) in the mold] adj : (very) cold, "brrrr!, taters, ayn'it?" "taters, it's cold."

tato /taytoh/ sl n : potatoes.

tatties [Northern] sl n : potatoes, see *neep.*

tatty adj : tawdry, shabby.

tea [introduced to Europe in the 16 C and England in September 1658. Annual production 30,000 lbs (1700), 2,047,000 tonnes (1988)] n : as well as the veritable British institution (served strong hot and milky, see *British Rail tea*), it stands in for a meeting, "let's have tea," the late afternoon meal, "what's for tea, mum?" or a euphemism for anything else such as having a cigarette or a *beer* (see *teatime*). In the working classes, or in the North, it can also means the last meal of the day, usu. at 6pm, and in contrast for the 'upper classes,' or generally in the South, it would be tea and cake (or anything tasty) around 4–5pm, followed by supper around 7 or 8pm (dinner being a more formal meal, see also *high tea*). As for the *cuppa* itself, although most people just drink it, as Americans drink *coffee,* for some the details of the high ceremony are crucial to a good cup, such as warming the pot first, the *mif/tif* issue, the brand, bags or loose (tea bags or loose leaf), the china, the accoutrements, the setting, and endless others. If this seems excessive just think where the 'iced skinny unleaded triple-shot venti no-whip mocha, leave room for cream' will be in a hundred years' time.

tea break n : a sacrosanct mid-morning or mid-afternoon ten-minute period when the universe creaks to a halt, all wars temporarily suspend, all exasperatingly crucial activities are curtailed, and the British workman sits down for an uninterruptible *cuppa*.

teacake n : light flat currant bun, popular toasted with *tea*, but also used to refer to any small sweet cake had with *tea*, such as a *fairy cake* or cupcake.

tea leaf crsl n : thief.

tearaway n : impetuous or reckless young person, kinda like James Dean, though it usu. has negative connotations, syn. *yobbo*.

tearoom (also **tea shop**) n : small cafe, usu. in villages, serving tea and *teacakes*, *cream tea*, and small meals.

teat (baby's bottle) n : *nipple*.

teatime n : traditionally, this meant a specific time in the afternoon such as 4 p.m. or 5 p.m. usu. associated with *tea*, the last meal of the day. As such it can be used for instance to indicate the end of the work day, "I say it's teatime" (i.e. let's finish up and go home, or go out and get dinner), but it's also generally used for any break time, whether or not the break is actually for tea.

tea towel n : *dish towel*.

tele alt sp n : *telly*.

telephone box n : *phone booth*.

telly n : *TV*, syn. the *tube*, the *box*, boob toob, **goggle-box**.

ten bob n : ten *shilling*s or half a *pound*, but usu. referring to the ten *shilling note* (until they went out of circulation in 1971).

tenement n : *block of flats*.

tenner /tenə/ sl n : ten *pound note*, *£10*.

Terylene n : synthetic polyester used as fiber and also the fabric made from it, syn. *Crimplene*, *Dacron*.

text n : see *txt*.

theatre cf sp n : *theater,* musical or live performance, rather than *cinema*.

theatre n : operating theatre, operating room, "the doctor is in theatre at the moment."

thingummy n : *doodad, wotsit*.

thick adj : (of a person) slow, stupid, "he's a bit thick," 'thick in the head,' 'thick as two short planks,' 'thick as *mince'* (Sc), 'thick as a *brick.'* Expr. 'a bit thick' describes something unreasonable, "that's a bit thick, isn't it?"

thicko n : *idiot, thick* person.

think inf usage n : "I had a good think, and have a solution."

Throne Speech, Speech from the Throne (Canada) n : the *Queen's Speech*, done at both the federal and provincial levels of government, and delivered by the governor-general or lieutenant-governor on behalf of the *Queen* (unless she happens to be visiting).

thrush n : refers to the song thrush *Turdus philomelos* since it is common, less common ones being referred to specifically (e.g. the mistle thrush *Turdus viscivorus*). "Is that a thrush or a female *blackbird*?"

tichy col adj : tiny, hence tich, a small person or child, "hey, tich!"

tick n : moment, 'back in a tick,' 'in two ticks,' 'wait a tick.'

tick v, n : *check,* check mark.

tickety-boo col adj : all right, in order, syn, hunky-dory, *copacetic.*

tick off cf v : to scold, "she ticked me off right over the fence," "that really ticks me off."

tiddler col n : small fish (minnow, stickle-back), also small thing or person, "he's just a tiddler."

tiddly col adj : a little *drunk.*

tiddly col adj : small, tiny.

tiddly [winks] crsl n : drink, "I need a *ping pong* tiddly."

tiddlywinks sp n : *tiddledywinks.*

tif acr n : tea in first, "you're a *tif*!" see *mif.*

tiffin n : light lunch.

tights n : *pantyhose.*

timber usage n : *lumber.*

timber yard n : *lumberyard.*

tin n : *can.*

tinker n : gypsy.

tinkle n : *call* (on the telephone), syn. *bell,* "give me a tinkle."

tip n v : *dump,* "council tip," 'no tipping' (sign on side of road), "this place is a tip."

tipper n : *dump truck.*

Tipp-Ex® n : whiteout, correction fluid, syn. *Liquid Paper.*

tip your lid expr v : kowtow.

tired out vi : syn. *fagged out, buggered, buggered* out, *knackered, beat, flaked out, shagged* out, little death (post coital), *jiggered.*

tit sl n : *dork,* idiot.

titbit sp n : *tidbit.*

titfer crsl [tit for tat /ti?fə ta?/] n : hat.

titheads (from their hats) sl n : police.

to, to the usage prep : "I am going into hospital" = admitted as a patient, "I am going to the hospital" = visiting (a friend or as an employee) the hospital, also "I am in hospital" = "I am in the hospital." The same constructions work with some other institutions. See also *thru.*

toad in the hole n : sausage cooked in batter (bit like a *corn dog*).

toady usage n : *apple polisher, brown nose,* suckhole (Aus).

toast and dripping dated n : popular snack, see *dripping.*

toasty, toastie cf n : toasted sandwich.

toby, toby jug n : large mug in the form of a squat 18th C gentleman wearing a tricorne.

tod (on your) rsl expr adj : (on your) own, "Clever boy. He did it all on his tod."

todger sl n : *penis.*

toff sl n : conspicuously upper class or rich, syn *nob.*

toffed (up) adj : spruced (up).

toffee apple n : *caramel apple.*

toffee-nosed sl adj : uppity, snobbish.

togs inf n : clothes.

to hand usage adj : *at hand,* "do you have a calculator to hand."

toilet cf n : *bathroom,* syn. {+} powder room, *cloakroom,* {0} *ladies, gentle-mens, toilet, WC, lavatory,* lavabo, *por-taloo, convenience, public convenience,* water closet, *penny house,* {-} cloaks, *gents, lav,* privy, *dunny,* latrine, {- -} *loo, netty,* cludgie, thunderbox, {- - -} *wazzer,* cottage (public), *carsey, bog.*

Tom crsl [Tom foolery] n : jewelry.

tomato /təmahtoh/ n : /təmaydoh/.

tombola n : a ticket lottery typically drawn from a large rotating drum or barrel at the village *fête.*

tommy crsl n : window.

ton col n : 100 mph, esp. on a motorcycle.

tonning it col v : going about as fast as you can (see *ton*), syn. *pedal to the metal,* floor it.

toodle pip expr intj : bye-bye, *cheerio.*

topper n : top hat.

tootle v : drive (usu.) at a leisurely pace, "I'm going to tootle over to grandpa's."

topping adj : excellent.

torch (electric) n : *flashlight.*

Tory (politics) n : Conservative (see *minority government*).

tosh (term of address) n : *mate.*

tosh col n : nonsense, *codswallop*, "am I talking complete tosh?"

tosheroon sl n : *half-crown.*

toss sl v : *wank*, see also *not give a toss.*

tosser sl n : syn. *jerk, jerk-off, wanker.*

tossy adj (of *tosser*) sl : dreadful, syn. *hosed, heinous.*

totting v : *dumpster diving*, (NZ *poozling*).

totty n : *chicks, babe*age, "that club is wall-to-wall totty."

toughened glass n : tempered glass, more resilient than annealed glass, and breaks into small pieces rather than shards.

towards usage prep : *toward* (see *–ward*).

town usage n : *city.*

townie n : lower or underclass inner-city youth regularly seen hanging out in town centre, see *chav.*

t'ra /tərah/ /te rah/ /trah/ [Midlands] expr intj : *ta-ta, cheerio.*

traf bsl n v : fart, "he traffed."

traffic warden n : syn. *meter maid.*

trainers n : training shoes (for running, aerobics, etc.), syn. *tennies*, tennis shoes, *sneakers.*

train-spotter n : hobbyist, often schoolboy, a bit like a bird-watcher, but who collects train numbers, occasionally spotted huddled alone at the far end of the platform, notebook in hand. Also inf. *nerd, geek*, see *anorak.*

tram, (**tramcar**) n : *streetcar, trolley, trolley car.*

tramp n : *bum, transient, hobo.*

transport café n : roadside café mostly for servicing commercial drivers, similar in function to the *diner* at a *truck stop.*

trapezium n : *trapezoid.*

trapezoid n : *trapezium.*

trash mag n : comic book or any worthless magazine, also porno-*mag*s.

trash rag n : comic book or any worthless magazine, syn. *trash mag.*

treacle n : *molasses.*

treacle tart n : shallow *golden syrup*-flavored pie.

treacle well (also **treacle mine**) n : a better hoax (kind of like a *snipe hunt*), usu. with clear directions on unassuming roadside signs, known to lure even the cluefully abled. According to legend, treacle wells are in half the English counties, with some having up to a dozen or more. See also *Doris trap.*

tread usage v : stand, "someone trod on my chair."

treasure hunt (children's party game) n : *scavanger hunt.*

trendy adj : very fashionable, chic.

trendy n : person who thinks they're chic, syn. *pseud.*

trifle n : *dessert* made from sponge cake with *custard, jelly*, fruit, whipped cream, and rum, brandy, or sherry.

trilby hat n : *fedora.*

trillion cf n : was 10^{18}, now 10^{12}, see *billion.*

tripe [stomach, esp. of ox, prepared as food, cf *chitlins*] n : syn. *codswallop.*

trolley n : *cart, shopping cart, wagon* for serving food and drinks, also *gurney.* See also *off their trolley.*

trolley bus n : (bus version of) streetcar.

trollies (N) sl n : *pants* and *knickers.*

the trots n : *diarrhea*, syn. the *squits*, the *squirts*, see also *bog trotter.*

trouble and strife joc crsl n : wife, *plates and dishes*, see *skin and blister, godfors.*

trousers n : *pants.*

truant v : *hooky.*

truck (rail) n : flatcar, see *bogie.*

trug n : shallow oblong gardening basket.

truncheon n : *nightstick, billy club.*

trundle usage col v : moving like a very

small child, "I just saw that old *geezer* trundling down the street."

trunk call n : *long distance.*

trunk road n : *arterial road*, main road, *expressway,* but not a *motorway.*

ttfn abbr expr intj : *ta-ta* for now, though quite well known now in the States via Usenet and other online chat fora. (Popularized by David Hamilton, 1970s Radio One DJ.)

tube n : *subway, underground*, hence tube ride, tube train, tube ticket, tube station, etc., "get the tube to South Ken."

tuck n : food.

tuck shop n : *candy store,* usu for kids.

tumble v : realize, *twig,* 'he got tumbled' = he was found out.

tup n : ram, hence v. tupping, when rutting with ewe.

tuppence n : phonetic spelling of *twopence.*

tuppenny adj : phonetic spelling of *twopenny.*

turdis sl n : portapotty, esp. ultra-modern, space-age variety, "the turdis is clean."

turk usage cf n : unpredictably willful person, child, "you little turk!"

turmeric /termэric/ pr n : /tэmэric/ /toomэric/ /tyoomэric/.

turn n : spell, a sudden unwell episode, "Walter's having one of his turns."

turn up v : turn down, "he made me an offer, but I turned him up."

turn-ups (*trousers*) n : cuffs, and also the kind of *pants* that have cuffs, "he was wearing turn-ups."

turps col abbr n : turpentine.

tut /t!/ /tut/ intj : expressing irritation. Although /tut/ is heard both in the US and the UK, /t!/ is heard frequently in the UK. (See Pronunciation Guide for pronunciation of /t!/) (*tut* and *tsk* are probably attempts at spelling /t!/ which some readers then pronounce as written. For

instance, I once heard two boys fighting, and one pronounced the 'g' as he said 'aaaargh!' which he'd probably read in war *comic*s.)

tut-tut /t! t!/ /tut tut/ intj : expressing annoyance or disparagement at something or someone else. The scope for the different pronunciations are as for *tut.*

twat, twot sl n : contemptuous person, also female genitals.

twee adj : trite, affectedly dainty or quaint.

twelve noon in China expr intj : your flies are undone, see China in the table of Gestures.

twerp usage n : stupid and annoying person.

twicer [two tales] n : deceitful person.

Twickers inf n : Twickenham, town south of London (home of the English Rugby Union).

twig v : realize, the moment of getting a *clue,* syn. *click*, the *penny drops, tumble, twig, suss,* catch-on, *cotton,* cotton-on.

twister cf col n : deceitful person.

twit n : *idiot*, stupid person.

twitcher col n : bird-watcher avid in pursuit of sighting rare birds, hence v. twitch.

twopence /tuhpэnts/ n : *2d,* two pennies, half *groat*, trifling amount, "I don't care twopence!"

twopence halfpenny /tuhpnee(h)aypnee, tuhpэnts(h)aypnee/ csl n : a trifling or worthless amount.

twopenny /tuhpenee, tuhpnee/ adj : two *penn'orth*, "it's an old twopenny bit," "I'll give you a twopenny stamp."

txt n : text messaging, *SMS.*

tyre sp n : *tire.*

— u —

u [1954] adj : of language, dress, behavior, upper class, see *non-u.*

u-blocker sl n : huge turd, anything grotesque, syn. *bog*-blocker, grogan.

UK abbr n : *United Kingdom*. UK is used as a general British moniker (such as top level internet domain name), but see *GB*.

underground [London Underground 1890] n : *subway, tube*, hence underground train, underground journey, underground ticket, underground station, etc.

underpants n : *pants*, underwear.

uni abbr n : (university) *college*.

Union Jack n : British flag (combines the crosses of St George, St Andrew, and St Patrick), also known as Union flag, cf *Old Glory*.

United Kingdom n : United Kingdom of *Great Britain* and Northern Ireland (UK = *GB* + Ireland since 1801 (Act of Union with Ireland), but *GB* + Northern Ireland since 1927–the 1921 Anglo-Irish Treaty resulted in the creation of the Irish Free State (renamed Ireland in 1949) and Northern Ireland).

unit trust n : *mutual fund,* mutual trust.

unpaved road n : *dirt road.*

upmarket adj : *upscale.*

uppers expr n : on one's uppers = destitute.

upstairs cf n : (usu.) second floor (see *ground floor*).

up the bum sl expr n : sodomy, syn. *rear-ender,jacksie* rabbit, "he likes it up the *bum*" = "he's gay."

up the spout sl expr adj : *pregnant*, syn. up the duff, up the poke, up the pole.

up the spout sl expr adj : useless, hopeless, syn *down the tubes.*

urinal n : syn. the *head, pisser.*

US /yoo es/ sl abbr adj : useless, unserviceable, broken, "the radio is completely US."

— V —

V, V-sign n : the 'fuck off' gesture made by extending the first and middle fingers at the same time as arcing the hand upwards (see *–ward*), palm facing in, and ending with a slight flip, "he *flash*ed the Vs at us," syn. the *bird.*

vacant site n : vacant *lot.*

vagina cf n : syn. *fanny, minge*, bliff, quim (see *quimle*), mapatasi /mapətazee/, mott, *front bottom*, widgey (Ir).

valve (radio) n : *tube,* vacuum tube.

van Gogh /van gof/ n : /van goh/ (Dutch people say /fan khohkh/).

vapour, vaporise sp n v : *vapor, vaporize.*

varnish remover n : *nail polish remover.*

VAT /vee ay tee/ [value added tax] abbr n : similar to *sales tax,* but included in marked prices.

Vatican roulette n : rhythm method, syn. Roman roulette. See also *getting off at....*

Vegemite (Aus) n : *Marmite*, although "Vegemite is *bloody* disgusting, whereas *Marmite* is the food of the gods."

Vera Lynn crsl n : gin.

verge n : *curb,* roadside, *soft shoulder*, 'grass verge' is usu. implied.

verger n : church official with caretaking and attendant duties.

verruca n : plantar wart.

vest cf n : *undershirt.*

vet v : to screen, examine (people and things), "all potential clients are carefully vetted."

veteran cf n : a person with much experience in action, esp. soldier or serviceperson.

video (the machine) usage n : *VCR.*

video nasty col n : esp. violent or horrific video.

virgin polo col n : refers to the Trebor mint, *Polo mint*'s main competition, since it has no hole in the middle.

vitamin /vitəmin/ n : /viedəmin/.

— **W** —

wagger pagger bagger n : *waste paper basket* (an exquisite example, along with *pragger-wagger*, of obsequiously decadent jargonising (see *–er*) whose vein is continued by *Sloane Rangese*).

waggon sp n : *wagon,* generic term for commercial truck, *lorry.*

waistcoat /waystkoht/ /weskət/ n : *vest.*

wallet usage n : *billfold, men's wallet.*

wallop sl n : particularly strong *beer,* or any powerful booze.

Wally n : conspicuous fool, *idiot.* See also *'Where's Wally.'*

wango dingo inf adj : *crazy,* syn. nuts, round the bend, *round the twist,* "You must be completely wango dingo."

wank sl v : masturbate, syn *toss, frig,* thrap (N), box the Jesuit, feed the ducks, stab the cat, Midland Bank, J Arthur (Rank), Jodrell (Bank), Barclay's (Bank), Sherman (tank).

wanker sl n : (masturbator) *jerk, jerk off, tosser,* syn merchant banker, Kuwaiti tanker.

wardrobe n : *armoire, closet.*

washing usage n : *laundry,* "I do the washing every other week."

washing-up n : the *dishes,* "do the washing-up."

wash up cf v : do the *dishes,* "who's going to wash up?"

wasp n : *yellow jacket.* (In the UK, there are bees and wasps. Hornets are known, but most others are not well known or often encountered. cf. *yellow jacket.*)

waste paper basket, waste paper bin n : *trash can.*

water diviner n : dowser.

Watford n : see *north of Watford.*

way out (sign) imp n : *exit.*

waz, wazz v : to pee (also masturbate), hence n. wazzer = *loo,* "go for a whizz in the wazzer."

wazzock col sl n : fool, *idiot, pillock.*

WC [water closet] n : *bathroom.*

weather n : the national pet peeve, and number one topic of conversation, "Britain has no climate, only weather."

wee [Scot] n : small.

wee v n : pee, "mummy, I got to go wee!" (small boy, legs tightly crossed, bright red face).

weed n : *nerd,* "last one in's a *wet* and a weed."

week usage expr n : 'Monday week' = next Monday plus a week, 'last Tuesday week' = the Tuesday prior to last Tuesday, "*Auntie* should be coming Friday week."

Wee's lettuce n : *iceberg lettuce.*

wee wee v n : pee, also *penis* (small child's word).

well good expr adj : *cool,* very good.

wellied adj : *drunk.*

wellies col n : *wellington boots.*

wellington boots n : *rubber boots,* rubber rain boots, *gumboots.*

welly [wellington boot] expr n : elbow grease, 'give it a bit of welly' = put your foot down, kick it, etc.

Welsh dresser n : *hutch.*

Welsh rabbit (rarebit) /rabit/ /rairbit/ n : *cheese on toast* with *Worcester sauce.*

Wendy house n : child's play-house.

West Country n : the south-western counties of England.

West End n : entertainment and shopping (*ponce*y) area of London west of the *City.*

Westminster n : *Palace of Westminster,* where *Parliament* sits, see *Whitehall.*

wet adj : ineffectual.

wet n : feckless or inept individual.

what's up? cf expr intj : what's wrong?

Where's Wally n : *Where's Waldo.* ['Where's

Wally' began as a twilight cry at various festivals (Isle of Wight, Glastonbury, Weeley) in the late 1960s/early 1970s, and via a group of hippies living at Stonehenge (all named Wally), and various conspiracy theories, **Wally** got its present meaning, and the cry begat the popular series of cartoon books and the 1980s TV animation.]

while (N) prep conj : until, "wait while Monday." Because of this confusion (consider 'do not cross track while lights are flashing'), apparently official documents, signs, and instructions (in the N), are supposed to always use *whilst*, but most style guides (produced in the S) encourage using while as it is clear and straightforward.

whilst adv conj : while, but see *while*. (Common in both written and spoken usage.)

whinge /winzh!/v n : whine, pule, *bitch*, esp. incessant, "whinging *poms*" [Aus].

whip v : steal.

whip-round n : pass the hat around (to collect *money*), "let's have a quick whip-round for the old *codger*."

whisky, pl **whiskies** n : Scottish kinds, cf. *whiskey,* see Spelling Table.

whistle crsl [whistle and flute] n : suit.

Whitehall n : where the Civil Service sits, see *Westminster*.

white mice sl n : tampons, for instance, a person unclogging a sewer will complain of too many white mice with the *brown trout*, see also *chuftie*.

white spirit n : *turps* substitute (also called sub *turps*).

white horse n : horse carved into the side of a chalk hill, typically visible from a great distance. There are over 20 in Britain (and a lion 1931), some cut for the millenium, most some hundreds of years old (Cherhill White Horse 1780), and the oldest being the Bronze Age Uffington White Horse around 1200BC, see the **Long Man of Wilmington**.

whitlow n : infection near toe or finger nail.

Whitsun holiday n : fixed in the 1970s to be Spring **Bank Holiday**, the last Monday in May (though it was moved up a week in 2002 for the **Queen**'s Golden Jubilee), see table of British Holidays.

wide sl adj : shrewd.

willy (used mostly by children) n : *penis*.

Willy Wagga Dagger joc n : William Shakespeare, syn. Bill the Quill.

Wimpy's n : English *café*, like Denny's, syn. *diner, greasy spoon,* [not to be confused with Wimpey's construction equipment manufacturer: We Import (Imploy) More *Paddy*'s Each Year].

windcheater n : *windbreaker.*

Windolene n : *Windex.*

windscreen n : *windshield.*

wing n : *fender.*

winkle out v : to extract or displace.

winkle pickers sl n : pointed shoes or boots, once fashionable.

winkles n : a very small edible gastropod mollusk available, like *cockles* and mussels, as a snack, esp. in *seaside* areas.

winter time n : end of *summer time*, currently coinciding with the end of *daylight saving time,* see table of UK Holidays.

wireless dated usage n : radio.

witness-box n : witness stand.

witter dial inf v : prattle, *natter, rabbit*, "What are you wittering on about?"

wobbler, wobbly n : tantrum, 'throw a wobbly' = throw a fit or tantrum, *lose it,* "Don't go wobbly, George"—Margaret Thatcher to George Bush during the 1990–1991 Gulf War.

wodge n : chunk, lump, or amount, "several pre-paid delivery sacks in which to return wodges of papers," "I just whipped up a wodge of XML."

wofter, wofta col n : *bum,* "your dad looks like a *crusty* old wofter."

wog derog n : black and sometimes Asian or Arab person (or any foreigner, even the French, 'the wogs start at Calais'), syn. nigger, *coon*, nig-nog, fuzzy-wuzzy.

wonky adj : unstable, unreliable.

wood louse n : *sow bug, pill bug, roly-poly, potato bug.*

Worcester sauce /wustə/ n : a savory sauce.

Worcs /works/ abbr n : Worcestershire /wustəshə/.

wot joc sp intj pron : popular spelling of what, see *wotsit*, *wotcha*, 'wot, no god?'

wotcha low expr intj : hello, syn. *hi, howdy,* "wotcha, *mush!*"

wotsit [what is it] n : thingamajig, *doodad.*

wrinklies n : parents or persons over 40, see *Sloane Rangese*.

wrm abbr n : what really matters, see *Sloane Rangese*.

— x —

x-directory adj : see *ex-directory*.

xxxx /foreks/ joc sl expr intj : euph. for fuck [because it is sometimes actually written that way—'what the xxxx!'] (also type of Aus. lager).

— y —

yaffle dial n : green woodpecker.

Yank sl n : American, syn. Sherman (tank), *seppo*.

yarbles sl n : *balls*.

the Yard col n : *Scotland Yard*, "Yard denies army unit arson claim."

yard of ale n : bulbous glass with long thin neck that holds a yard (about 2½ *pint*s) of *beer*. Usu. a challenge to drink in one go, or in competition with another.

yertis [here it is] n : the *loo*. Also 'yeah it is' as in 'yertis notisnt yertis notisnt . . .' (cf. *too*).

yeti [Sherpa, Tibetan *meetoh kangmi*–little man-like animal] n : Himalayan version of *bigfoot*, **Abominable Snowman**.

Y-fronts® n : men's *pants*, syn. *tightie-whities*, **nut chokers**.

yobbo, yob [bsl *boyo* [Ir] boy] n : hooligan.

yocker v : spit.

yokel n : country bumpkin, clodhopper, syn. *hick*.

yonks n : long long time, syn. *donkey's years*.

Yorkshire pudding n : baked batter, usu. accompanying roast beef.

— z —

z /zed/ n : /zee/, *A to Z* /ay too zed/, *z-bend* /zed bend/.

zapping (TV) n : *channel surfing*, **channel-hopping**, "he likes to zap."

z-bend /zed bend/ n : *s-curve,* sharp bends in road, syn. *zig-zag bend*.

z-car /zed cah/ n : police car, *panda car*.

zebra crossing /zebrə/ n : *crosswalk* but so indicated by broad black (the asphalt) and white stripes, what the Beatles were crossing on the Abbey Road album cover, syn. *pelican crossing*, *ped xing*.

zig-zag bend n : s-shaped bend in road, syn. *z-bend*, *s-curve*. See also **hairpin bend**.

zizz n : nap, *z's*.

The American language differs from the English in that it seeks the top of expression while English seeks its lowly valleys.
— SALVADOR DE MADARIAGA, *Americans Are Boys*

— # —

! punc : *exclamation point.*

' ` ´ ' punc : single quotes.

" " " cf punc : quotes, double quotes, *quotation marks*, ditto marks.

( ) cf punc : *parentheses*, parens.

[ ] punc : *brackets* or *square brackets.*

{ } punc : *braces, curly braces, wavy* brackets.

< > punc : *braces*, angle brackets.

« » punc : French brackets.

. cf punc : *period.*

/ cf punc : slash, (virgule), forward slash.

cf symb : pound, pound sign, "press the pound key," symbol for pound, "a 5# bag of seed," symbol for number, "apt. #3."

₤ symb : & [and] is sometimes written like a vertically stroked reverse 3.

% symb : sometimes used as a 'please turn over' symbol on the bottom of a letter.

-a cf alt suff : quite a common way, in informal writing, of spelling a phrase closer to how it is actually pronounced (eye dialect), so the -a isn't exactly a suffix but the result of a contraction, collapsing two words where the second one is usu. *of* or *to*. Examples: coupla (couple of) "Coupla other things though . . .," gonna (going to), *gotcha* (got you), gotta (got to), hafta (have to) "do I hafta," kinda (kind of) "kinda felt like I was dreaming," lotsa (lots of), oughta (ought to = should), outa (out of), *seeya* (see you), sorta (sort of), wanna (want to, see *wannabe*), whaddya (what do you), ya (you). See also *hecka, hella*. There are many similar contrac-

tions using vowels apart from a: dunno (don't know), gimme (give [it to] me).

-cian suff : beautician (hairdresser), *mortician.*

-ee suff : a popular way of adding humour, irony, etc. to situation by creating the recipient of some action: muggee (the victim of a mugger), spankee (we assume overtones of sexual deviancy), although many such words are entering regular usage: abductee, advisee, appointee, honoree, retiree.

-ery suff : *beanery*, bootery, *eatery*, winery.

-fest suff : festivalise, see *gabfest*. "Whaddya say—let's skip 7th and 8th [period], go to the mall, and have a calorie-fest."— from the movie *Clueless.*

-head suff : an enthusiast, for instance, Deadhead (Grateful dead fan), *ditto head, gearhead, hose head, jarhead, propeller head*, wirehead (hardware *hack*).

-ize suff : many nouns and adjectives in the US are verbed by appending -ize (final, finalize), but in the UK it is generally -ise though the -ize form is allowed. See the –ize/-ise section in the table of Spelling Differences for a list, which shows no hard and fast rules, and some exceptions (criticise, merchandize, realise, surprize).

-ly suff : in the US this is dropped from many adverbs in informal speech, and also sometimes in writing, "he walked crooked," "he's *real* nice." It is sometimes made up for by using 'all,' "he looked at me all winsome," or appending 'like,' "he went off speedy like."

-or suff : in the US the 'u' is dropped from the spelling of numerous words which in the UK (often) end in -our (a remnant of the French spelling) (*colour*, favourite, flavour, honour, labour, neighbour), see table of Spelling Differences.

-spot n suff : denomination, 5-spot = $5, "can you *spot* me a ten-spot."

-ster suff : highlight an association or affinity for, such as: gamester, hipster, *huckster*, mobster, oldster, teamster, but like the *-ee* suffix, used freely for effect, for instance to draw attention to someone (Pat → Patster–the person being Pat), or something "it's so cold I've turned into a numbster."

-ter suff : many words in the UK ending in -tre (a remnant of the French spelling) (such as *metre*, *theatre*, *centre*) will end in -ter.

-ville suff : substantiates or emphasises the subject, for example, nowheresville (a place of no significance like *jerkwater*), *splitsville*, see *cube*, *city*.

$ symb : symbol for *dollar* [originating from P^s, an abbreviation for Pesos and Pesetas, which as written in the late 18 C slowly became transmogrified into the $, and not from things such as *US → ₴ → $ ↔ $*.

$1 symb : one *dollar*. The dollar *bill* has George Washington (1st president) on face, Great Seal of US on back. There is also a dollar coin (see *silver dollar*) that can occasionally be found in ones change. See also *gold dollar*, *Susan B. Anthony dollar* and *Sacagawea dollar*.

$2 symb : the two dollar *bill* is often associated with bad luck. Face: Thomas Jefferson (3rd president), back: signers of Declaration of Independence or Monticello (Jefferson's self-designed home in Virginia), ($2 gold coin minted 1792).

$2.50 symb : gold *quarter eagle* coins were minted 1792–1929.

$3 symb : gold coins minted 1854–1889, also joke *bills* such as Nixon/Watergate, Clinton/White House, see *three dollar bill*.

$4 symb : gold coins minted 1879–1880.

$5 symb : face: Abraham Lincoln (16th president), back: Lincoln Memorial, ($5 gold coin, *half eagle*, minted in 1795–1929).

$10 symb : face: Alexander Hamilton, back: US Treasury. ($10 gold coin called *eagle* minted 1795–1933).

$20 symb : Andrew Jackson (7th president), the *White House*, ($20 gold coin called *double eagle* minted 1850–1932).

$50 symb : Ulysses Simpson Grant (18th president), US *Capitol*.

$100 symb : Benjamin Franklin, Independence Hall, syn. *c-note*, *benjamin*.

$500 symb : William McKinley (25th president), ornate design, not issued after 1969.

$1,000 symb : Grover Cleveland (22nd and 24th president), ornate design, not issued after 1969.

$5,000 symb : James Madison (4th president), ornate design, not issued after 1969, still legal tender.

$10,000 symb : Salmon P. Chase, ornate design, not issued after 1969, last printed 1949, still legal tender.

$100,000 symb : Woodrow Wilson (28th president), ornate design, federal transactions only.

$1,000,000 symb : Ashton, ornate design, federal transactions only. [I read this somewhere but no such note exists as far as *BEP* is concerned. Perhaps it was designed but never implemented.]

0 (telephone) num : operator number, like *100*.

0-dark 30 expr n : see *oh-dark thirty*.

½¢ symb : half cent, copper coins minted 1793–1857.

1¢ symb : *cent*, syn. *penny* (copper-clad zinc since 1982 (hence clunk when dropped), bronze 1864–1982; large coin 1793–1857).

2¢ symb : copper coins minted 1864–1873.

2–55 n : complimentary air conditioning on cheap cars (two windows rolled down, go 55 mph). Many variants: 'four by sixty air conditioning' (four windows rolled down, go 60 mph), and 10–40 (roll windows down 10%, drive at 40 mph).

2-way stop n : street *intersection* controlled by two *stop signs*.

3¢ symb : coins (silver 1851–1873, cupro-nickel 1865–1889).

4.0 num : see *four point*.

4 by 60 n : *AC*, see *2–55*.

4th July n : *Fourth of July*, syn. *fireworks day*, "When I approached the x-ray, the man said, 'say ma'am, them there bangles need to be removed otherwise we'll light up like the 4th of July.'"

4-way stop n : street *intersection* controlled by four *stop signs*.

5¢ symb : *nickel* (cupro-nickel, since 1966), half *dimes* (silver 1794–1873).

7-Eleven /(seven eleven)/ n : a chain of 24-hour *convenience stores* (that were originally open from 7 a.m. till 11 p.m.). Like Circle-K, the term is informally used generically for any 24-hour *convenience store*.

9/11 /(nine eleven)/ n : the 11th September 2001 terrorist event.

10–4 (trucker jargon) n : ok [message understood], syn. Roger. (CB '10-code,' established by the FCC, is a protocol of 60 messages in the range 10–1 to 10–99, and 10–200. E.g. 10–4 ok message received, 10–9 repeat message, 10–20 where are you "what's your 20?," 10–36 correct time is, 10–70 fire at, 10–200 police needed at.)

10¢ symb : *dime* (cupro-nickel since 1965,

silver 1796–1964), exactly 1mm thick.

20¢ symb : silver coins minted 1875–1878.

24/7 /(twenty four seven)/ num adv : twenty four hours a day, seven days a week, meaning all the time or anything ceaseless. 24/7/365—all days of the year.

25¢ symb : *quarter* (cupro-nickel since 1965, silver 1796–1964).

30 expr n : see *oh-dark thirty, beer thirty*.

40 num n : see *back 40, forty ouncer*.

50 n : see *five-o*.

50¢ symb : *half dollar* (cupro-nickel since 1970, silver 1794–1964, 20% silver 1965–1970).

55 n : 55 mph was the national speed limit 1974–1995, calculated to reduce *gas* consumption and accidents, and is still heard in many expressions, '55, staying alive,' see *2–55*.

80 num n : see *back 40*.

86 adj v : eighty-six, (usu. restaurant, bar use) unwelcome, throw out, don't serve, 'out of order. If we catch you pissing in the sink you're 86'–sign on urinal in *bar* toilet. Also "we're out of it."

101 /(one oh one)/ num : introductory class at university (e.g. psychology 101) and hence used to imply any introductory procedure (driving 101, partying 101).

411 (telephone) num : *directory enquiries*, local *information*, and used as slang meaning information. In some areas 411 changed to 1–411 when it stopped being a free service. In other areas it's not used, see *555–1212*.

420 /(four twenty)/ num : number associated with *stoners* and smoking out, and interjected frequently, "take *highway* 420 and you're there, *dude*!" the time (4:20) the clocks show in numerous movies, [falsely but popularly believed to be the police code for a drug bust].

555- (telephone) num : the unused first three digits of telephone numbers except for a few telephone service numbers (see *555–1212*), and hence used a lot in movies knowing that no such number exists.

555–1212 (telephone) num : *directory inquiries, long distance information, directory assistance.* The number is preceded by the area code for enquiries in that particular area.

911 /(nine one one)/ (telephone) num n : police, fire, and ambulance number, like *999* or *112*. See also *9/11*.

1040 /(ten forty)/ num n : the basic and only too well known *IRS* form for filing taxes. See also *z*, and *2–55*.

1600 Pennsylvania Avenue n : address of the *White House* in Washington, *DC*.

— a —

A1 sauce n : A1 steak sauce is a brown spicy sauce like *HP Sauce*.

A's [Oakland **A**thletics baseball team] n : "how 'bout them A's" is a classic 'let's change the subject' line.

AAA abbr n : Automobile Association of America, syn. *RAC*. "Triple A."

AC, a/c abbr n : air conditioner, "turn down the AC."

accommodations n : *accommodation*, lodgings.

across from usage adj : *opposite*.

acrost /akros/ var /akrost/ adv : across is pronounced by some /acrost/ but usu. it is not noticed as such by the speaker. Hence, it is occasionally written (incorrectly) as shown or in some form, " . . . if you come accrossed any . . .," " . . . with over 65 offices acrost the state to serve you." (Acrost is also found in some traditional UK dialects, including Cockney.)

ad [abbr advertisement] n : *advert*.

adios intj : *bye*.

adjuster, adjustor (insurance) n : insurance *assessor*.

administration n : government, in the sense of the present party in power: "the Clinton administration."

adobe [Sp] n : kind of clay, or earth and straw mix, sun-dried, used as a building material, and the style of houses built with this, common in the Southwest, "it's an adobe further south."

advice columnist n : *agony aunt*.

adz sp n : *adze*.

AFB abbr n : Air Force Base.

afterward adv : *afterwards*, see *-ward*.

aggies n : agricultural students, quite multifarious in Texas and the Midwest.

a horse a piece expr (WI MI MN) n : six of one, half a dozen of the other.

airplane sp n : *aeroplane*.

aisle n : *gangway*.

Aksarben, Ak-Sar-Ben n : popular commercial, institution, business, club name in Nebraska, coined at a time–1895–when everything seemed to be going backwards.

a la mode adj : topped with a dollop of ice cream, 'apple pie a la mode.'

alcohol usage n : as in *liquor*, generic term for any kind of alcoholic drink, "she was caught with some alcohol."

alfalfa n : *lucerne*.

alien usage n : non-*US* citizen, cf. *gaijin*, *gringo*.

alien pods n : source of *pod people*.

all expr adv : a verbal gesture for quoting things said and/or states of being, "He's all *bent out of shape*," "and so I was all 'what's up with you,'" "I was all '<facial expression>whatever,' then I'm all '<shrug>,'" "he thinks he's all *bad*, but he's just a gangster *wannabe*."

all day (SW) usage expr adv : total, "how much money you got?" "I got ten *bucks* all day" = 'ten *bucks* total.'

all-nighter expr n : spending all night to complete something, such as studying, "he *pull*ed an all-nighter again."

all over expr v : 'I'm all over it' = I'm on the task, I'm taking care of it.

allowance, weekly allowance n : (children's) *pocket money*.

all-way stop n : intersection controlled by as many *stop signs* as intersecting streets, the immoral equivalent of a *roundabout*.

the almighty dollar expr n : deification of American money or money in general, which seems to be true of Americans more so than other nations. Winston Churchill called Americans a nation of shopkeepers.

alot usage sp adv : a lot, "using alot less energy."

already [Yiddish] usage adv : used as an intensifier, "let's go already!" See also anymore, yet.

alternate usage adj : *alternative*, "she is expected to find an alternate speaker."

aluminum sp n : *aluminium*.

a.m. /ay em/ usage n : morning, "I'm hoping to head over in the a.m. when it starts."

America col n : United States of America.

American cheese n : a cheese by-product [process cheese food] made from useless by-products of actual cheese production, and found as the cheese in cheeseburgers, *tuna melts*, etc.

American Dream expr n : post war political propaganda where every American could expect to have a nice car, house, and family (2.4 kids and a dog) in beautiful surroundings, and a good job.

American robin n : common backyard bird and harbinger of Spring–a large (10"), red-breasted thrush *Turdus migratorius* closely related, and similar in size, to the European *blackbird*.

amped adj : way excited, pumped up, "amped out of our minds on hormones and shame."

amusement park n : *funfair*. See also *carnival*.

analyze sp v : *analyse*.

anesthesiologist n : *anaesthetist*.

anesthetist cf n : nurse (as opposed to doctor) who gives anesthetic.

angel food cake n : a fancy kind of sponge cake.

antebellum adj : pre–Civil War (1861–1865).

antenna n : *aerial* (on cars, televisions, etc.).

antsy adj : jittery, restless.

anymore [Ir] (esp MW) usage adv : nowadays, as in "we bike to the movies anymore," see also *already, yet*.

anywho, anyhoo (NW) adv : anyhow, *anyroad*.

apartment n : *flat*.

apartment building n : *block of flats*.

apartment hotel n : *service flats*.

apple butter n : *applesauce* cooked down to the consistency of butter and bought in a jar like *jam*.

apple cider n : apple juice.

applejack n : liquor from fermented *cider*.

apple pie expr n : that which represents something sacredly American, "As American as apple pie."

apple polisher n : *toady*.

applesauce n : *stewed apple*, but usu. as bought in a jar like sauce.

appointment book n : *diary*.

area code (telephone) n : *dialing code*, always 3 digits. Some *Midwest* states still have one area code that covers the whole state, but most states have more than one area code covering different areas of the state, some up to 30. See area code tables.

Arkansas /ahkənsah/ n : but the Arkansas River can be /ahkənsah/ or /ahkansəs/.

armoire [Louisiana French] n : *wardrobe*.

armpit n : contemptible place, "Houston is the armpit of Texas."

arroyo [Sp] n : dry river bed, *gully*.

arugula (green leafy vegetable) n : *rocket*.

ascot n : *cravat*.

Asian cf n adj : coming from China, Thailand, etc. Also, coming from any part of the continent of Asia. See *Oriental*.

ass sl n : *arse*. Ass is homophonous with ass, the animal, with resultant puns ("I'm going to ride your ass," etc.). A magazine *ad* shows a rump view of an ass with the caption, "An engineer can save you more than just money." See expr. *haul ass, get your ass in gear*.

ass backward expr adv : *backwards*, all mixed up.

asshole sl n : *arsehole*.

assignment (school) n : homework.

assistant professor n : *lecturer*.

associate professor n : *reader, senior lecturer*.

at hand usage adj : *to hand*, "I have a pencil at hand."

ATM abbr n : automatic *teller* machine, *cashpoint, hole in the wall*.

attorney /aternee/ n : *lawyer, solicitor*.

audit v : monitor a class (maybe taking the test) but without amassing *credits*.

auto, automobile usage col n : usu. a car, but can mean any kind of vehicle.

aw intj : a verbal groan like oh or hey, "aw shucks!"

awesome /ahsəm/ adj : syn. *brill*, "awesome, *dude*."

awesome! /usəm/ intj : delight, admiration, "awesome, possum."

ax sp n : *axe*.

ax (BEV or Ebonics) v : ask (axe is also ask in a traditional North Cumbrian dialect).

— b —

babe /bayb/ n : attractive young woman, syn. *bird, chick, hottie*. Also applied by women to *hot guys*.

baby buggy n : *pram*.

baby carriage n : *pram*.

Baby Ruth n : (chocolate bar) similar to Lion bar.

bach /bach/ (bachelor) v : usu. to bach it, to go it alone, to become or remain single, "he's baching it" meaning, for instance, he's getting an apartment by himself.

back 40, back 80 n : many rural areas, esp. in the *Midwest*, are laid out in one mile *sections*, and these 640 acre units are halved, halved, halved (80 acres), and halved again into convenient 40 acre fields, which become discernible units, as in "go to the back 40," "those 40s on the other side of the river." See also *north 40s*.

back east n : the *East Coast*, and how many Americans not from there refer to it, "He's from back east," "he's a backeaster." See also *out west, the South*.

backpack n : light *rucksack*.

backpacking vt : hiking, sometimes camping.

back up (car) n : *reverse*.

backup lights n : *reversing lights*.

backwoods n adj : remote, culturally backward area, syn. *boondocks*.

bad adj : really good.

badass n : *hard case*.

bad deal n : cheated, syn. *bum steer*.

bad hair day expr n : (having a) socially bad day.

bad-mouth v : talk badly of, swear at, syn. *gobshite, dish the dirt*.

bad news sl n : calamitous, when referring to unsavoury things, people, or places, "that place is bad news."

bag n v : *sack*. The normal bag, provided by the supermarket for your groceries, is a brown paper bag, 7 x 12 x 14" high or 17" high ($^2/_3$ or $^5/_6$ cu. feet). Due to environmentalism, plastic *carrier bag*s became available as an option, see *paper* *or plastic.* Smaller brown bags are used for small or fewer groceries, see *brown bag lunch, sack lunch.*

baggage room n : *left luggage* office in bus terminal or *railway station*, any room used for storage.

bag it expr v : forget the whole thing.

bag lady n : female *tramp* typically carrying all her worldly possessions around in *carrier bags* (or *shopping trolley*, etc.).

bags n : suitcases.

bail (bail out) col v : *quit, scarper*, "she bailed on me."

balcony n : *circle* in *theater* or *cinema*.

ballistic adj : 20 C version of berserk, "Don't tell her what happened, she'll go ballistic," see *flip.*

ballgame, ball game n : baseball game.

ballpark n : baseball *field*. See *in the ballpark.*

ballplayer n : baseball player.

baloney n : *rubbish*, nonsense, also *bologna.*

bam regional col n : *cottonwood.*

band n : ring, see *wedding band.*

band-aid (Band-Aid®) n : *plaster, Elastoplast.*

bangs (hair) n : *fringe.*

bar n : *pub*, typically open from noon until 2am, sometimes open for breakfast. The American bar tends to be more of a pick-up joint or meat market rather than social, which role is moving to the *coffee shop*, see *pub.*

Barbie (Barbie®) n : *Barbie doll*'s name.

barbie (frat) n : BBQ.

Barbie doll n : like *Sindy*, an anatomically incorrect plastic doll with neo-archetypal beauty (unusually long blonde hair, *mongo breasts,* and long legs all the way up to her armpits). A 5'-6" doll would be 35–17–31, but for the average American woman to achieve Barbie-esque proportions she would need to loose 6 inches off

her waist, add 5 inches to her chest, and grow 2 feet taller, embodying perfection at 7'-2" and 39–23–33.

barf n v : cf. *puke*, "makes you wanna barf," syn. *barf, upchuck, toss cookies, honk, ralph,* hurl, *yak, get sick, spit-up, blow chunks, chunks.*

bargeman n : *bargee.*

barrette n : *hair slide.*

barrio [Sp] n : Latin neighbourhood or community, also a Latin ghetto.

BART acr n : Bay Area Rapid Transit, the (partly) underground trains of the Bay Area. (They finally go to SF airport— yay!)

base n : first base–(French) kissing, (but also a breakthrough in that significant contact has been made and there is now promise, of . . .); second base–groping, copping a feel; third base–finger-fucking, mutual masturbation; home run–'going all the way,' *sex*—alt.sex FAQ 1992.

baseboard n : *skirting board.*

basil /bayz-l/ n : /baz-l/ (both *herb* and person's name).

bass ackward /bas/ n : *ass backward*, Spoonerised for emphasis.

bath abbr n : *Realtor* term for bathroom where ½ bath is sink plus toilet, ¾ bath is sink plus toilet plus shower stall, and full bath is sink plus toilet plus bathtub, which acts as the base of the shower.

bathe /baydh/ usage v : wash, or have a bath.

bath robe n : *dressing gown*, usu. made of towel material, typically white.

bathroom n : *toilet*, "I laughed so hard I almost went to the bathroom in my *pants!*" see *bath.* Syn. {+} *comfort station*, {0} *restroom, bathroom, ladies' room*, little girl's room, little boy's room, *portapotty, portapot* {-} sandbox {- -} *head*, biffy (outside), *john, crapper, pisser.*

bathroom tissue euph n : toilet paper.

bathroom sink n : *basin*.

bathtub n : *bath*.

bawl out v : a loud telling off, syn. *rocket*, *chew out*.

Bay Area n : The area around the San Francisco Bay which includes everything from Marin County, San Francisco and Oakland, all the way down to San Jose and the rest of *Silicon Valley*.

Bay Stater n : person from Massachusetts (official since 18th December 1990).

bayou /bieyoo/ [Louisiana French from Choctaw] n : the typically slow-moving streams and tributaries in the often swampy areas of the *South*.

bazoom n : *breasts*, syn. tits, boobs.

BB gun /bee bee/ [from standard shot size, BB=0.175"] n : *air gun*.

beach usage n : sea, *seaside*, "let's go to the beach."

bean sl v : to hit on the head.

beanery n : restaurant, cheap restaurant, *coffee shop*.

beanie n : small round tight-fitting skullcap, see *propeller beanie*.

beano (Beano®) n : natural enzyme supplement to help with gas, or 'drops you can put on your *frijoles* refritos so you don't have to throw sharp looks at Harwood while you're dining with Moira.'

beans cf n : 'anything at all' in expr. such as "he don't know beans."

bean sprouts n : *mung bean* sprouts (as opposed to *sprouts*).

Beantown n : Boston.

bearded clam sl n : *vagina*.

beat it imp v : scram, *buzz off*, *piss off*, *bugger off*.

beat on usage v : to repeatedly hit, "he was beating on him," "let's beat on the keys awhile" = to hack (computerwise).

beat the pants off somebody expr v : defeat, *beat somebody hollow*.

beat up on v : to *bash up*, beat up, *beat on*.

beat yourself up expr v : self-reproachful, overly self-critical or blameful, "don't beat yourself up."

beaucoup (properly /boh koo/ but usu heard /boo koo/, hence the phonetic spellings such as buku or bookoo) sl adj : a lot, *loads*, "beau coup /boo koo/ *bucks*."

bedroll n : rolled up bedding (or sleeping bag) as used by hikers, *tramp*s, etc.

bedspread n : *counterpane*.

beebee n : see *BB gun*.

beefcake n : dude with muscular physique, see *cheesecake*.

beef jerky n : dried beef strips, eaten as a snack.

beemer col n : referring to the BMW car as a yuppie status symbol, with smugness if owner and disdain otherwise.

beer cf n : standard American beer is colorless, odorless, flavorless, sugarless, untainted by calories, alcohol, and caffeine, and contains no IOC banned substances, but is obscenely effervescent and so cold that each sip is a guaranteed *brain freeze*. Happily, microbreweries have been springing up everywhere producing outstandingly fine, normal beers.

beer thirty n : already past due time for a beer.

beet n : *beetroot*.

behoove vt : *behove*.

bellboy, bellhop n : hotel page.

bell pepper n : *capsicum*, green (red or yellow) pepper.

belly washings regional n : drink.

beltway n : *ring road* around city, esp. the one around *DC* where it also refers to the peculiar social and political scene within, 'Inside the Beltway.'

bender n : drinking binge.

Benedict Arnold n adj : traitor, syn. quisling, " . . . every Benedict Arnold company that exports jobs overseas. . . ."

[Successful American general who in 1779 sold out, defected, and subsequently fought for the British.]

benjamin, benji n : *$100 bill, c-note*, "where d'you get all those benjamins?"

bent out of shape expr adj : worked up, syn. 'throwing a *wobbler.*'

BEP abbr n : Bureau of Engraving and Printing, in Washington, *DC*, the place where paper money is printed. *Bills* are sent to one of the twelve Federal Reserve banks from where they are distributed, and this location is printed on the face of the *$1 bill* to the left of the portrait in a seal containing a letter, A–L. (Coins are mostly minted in Philadelphia, PA and Denver, CO (and some in San Francisco, CA). Some coins indicate their place of mint with a letter P or D (or S), near the date for recent years. See *Mint*.)

berry usage n : grain, "*wheat berry.*"

beta /bayda/ cf n : /beeta/ β. Similarly, zeta /zayda/ and the prefix meta- /meda/.

bfd /bee ef dee/ abbr expr n : big fucking deal, often used as a response.

bfe abbr expr n : Bumfuck Egypt, "I'm in bfe, trying to email . . .."

bh jargon abbr n : (one) *butt* hair, usu. found (as revenge) in patrons food (by *dis*sed kitchen staff).

Bible Belt n : areas in southern US (North Carolina, South Carolina, Georgia, Tennessee, Arkansas, Missouri, Oklahoma, Kansas). See also *Borscht Belt*, *Corn Belt*, *Cotton Belt*, *Rust Belt*, and *Sun Belt*.

the Big Apple n : New York.

the Big D n : Dallas.

Big Dig n : a rather stunning feature of downtown Boston for the last two decades, the Big Dig successfully put the bulk of traffic underground whilst not disturbing the existing rusting elevated six-lane highway it finally replaced ['the largest, most expensive, complex and technologically challenging highway project in American history']. (See also *subway*.)

Big Dipper cf n : *the Plough*, part of the Great Bear.

the Big Easy n : New Orleans.

bigfoot n : *sasquatch*, similar reputation as Loch Ness monster, syn. *Abominable Snowman, yeti*.

big hair adj : someone's hair unusually puffed up due to atmospheric conditions (static, wind), overzealous use of some specialty hair care product, or naturally.

the Big Tomato n : Sacramento, capital of California (play on the *Big Apple*).

bill n : *note*, as in dollar bill, all denominations of which since 1929 have been 2.61 x 6.14." Also a notice, see *post*.

bill usage n : peak or visor of cap.

billboard n : *hoarding*.

billfold n : *wallet*.

billion cf n : 10^9.

billy club n : *truncheon*.

binky (Binky®) n : *pacifier*, and occasionally children's pronunciation for *blanky*.

bippi col sl adj : stupid, 'bippi tart' = stupid girl.

bird n : the *finger*, "give him the bird."

bird dog n : *gun dog*.

biscuit cf n : light puffy unsweetened scone-like bun, often served with gravy, regionally popular, 'biscuits and gravy.'

bit n : $12\frac{1}{2}$¢, see *two bits*.

bitch v : complain, whine, *whinge*.

bitchin' col adj : syn. *sweet, neat, cool, fresh, rad, brill, safe*.

bite it v : *wipe out*.

bites v : *sucks*, "that bites."

bite the big one v : die, syn. *snuff it, croak*.

black bean n : a black kind of kidney bean, found in Mexican, South American and Cuban-style dishes, see *pinto bean*.

blackbird n cf : collective term for various kinds of black birds.

blackjack (bludgeon) n : life preserver.

blackjack n : *pontoon*, *twenty-one*.

blacktop n : *tarmac*, road surface (and the bituminous material used to make it).

blah adj : drab, boring, underwhelming, "it's so blah," 'the blahs' = ennui, "I have the blahs."

blanky n : small child's favourite blanket, security blanket, syn. winkie, see *binky*.

bleachers n : simple exposed seating at sports stadium.

blech, bletch, bleh [Yiddish] intj : yuck! term of disgust, "why do they call him Tony Bleh?"

blender n : *liquidiser*.

blinders n : *blinkers*.

blindside v : surprise, catch unawares, or attack from out of view.

blitzed adj : *drunk*.

blooper n : *bloomer*, mistake or error, often humorous or embarrassing, "have you seen the *Star Trek* bloopers."

blow sl v : spend, get rid off.

blow sl v : *sucks*, "that blows."

blow chunks sl v : puke.

blown away v : surprise or favourably impressed, "she blew me away," also to surpass, "our runners blew them away," also to kill, cf. 'I'll be blowed.'

blow off vt : summarily dismiss, ignore, or stand someone up, "she blew me off."

blow off steam expr v : *let off steam*.

BLT n : the ever popular bacon, lettuce, and tomato *sandwich*.

Blue Angels n : US Navy and Marines exhibition flying team, syn. **Red Arrows**, *Thunderbirds*.

bluff n : bank, slope, promontory, 'Council Bluffs, Iowa.'

blunt n : joint made with cigar wrapper, see *Phillies Blunts*.

blvd abbr n : preferred abbr. for boulevard, as part of an address or road sign, see *street*, *cul-de-sac*, *close*, *drive*, *mews*.

boardwalk n : *promenade*, also any kind of plank walk way (the wooden *sidewalks* in cowboy movies) as well as planking across sand, marsh, etc.

Bobbittize v : peotomise, "but dozens of matadors were injured, including one gored in the head and one Bobbittized."

bobby pin n : *hair grip*, *kirby grip*.

bobby sox n : girls' ankle socks.

bodacious adj : outrageous.

Bogart v : to hog instead of share, usu. of a *joint*.

bogey man, boogy man n : sinister mythological stranger, esp. lurking on the horizons of children's imaginations at the suggestion of parents or older siblings.

bogue /bohg/ [from bogus] v : fail, not show, "he bogued."

bogue out v : *bogue*.

bogus adj : tasteless, unacceptable, perhaps offensive.

bolo, bolo tie [bolo rope with weights used like a lasso] [SW] n : a 'tie' made from a cord, often leather, fastened at the neck by a usu. decorative sliding clasp (often featuring turquoise which is found in the *Southwest*), state tie of AZ.

bologna /balohnee/ **baloney** n : kind of cold sliced sausage.

bomb cf v : flop, dismal failure, syn. a *Brodie*, "I totally bombed my test."

the bomb /da bom/ intj n : the best.

bonch sl n : *choad*.

boner /bohner/ n : erection, hard-on.

bonk v : to *screw*, also to '*hit the wall*' whilst bicycling.

boobies n : boobs.

boo-boo n : child's scratch or bruise.

boob toob, boob tube cf col n : TV.

booby hatch n : loony bin.

booger n : snot, *bogey*.

book v : to move or go really fast, "that old Mustang books," "let's book it" = 'let's get *outahere*.'

---

bookoo sl adj : see *beaucoup*.

boondocks [Tagalog *bundok* mountain] n : extremely remote location, syn. *sticks*, *tulies*, *backwoods*, Timbuktu, (German Hintertupfingen).

boondoggle n : wasteful expenditure, useless activity (originally with implication that someone dubiously benefits).

boonies contr n : *boondocks*.

bootblack n : shoeblack, one who shines shoes.

booth n : *call-box*, *kiosk*, *phone booth*, "I'm in a telephone booth at the corner of walk and don't walk."

booty /boodee/ sl n : *butt*, also *babe*.

border n : (national) *frontier*.

borscht or **borsch** sp n : *bortsch* (also *borsch*).

Borscht Belt n : in upstate New York, the Catskills generally, or specifically the summer resorts in Sullivan and Ulster counties. See also *Bible Belt*, *Corn Belt*, and *Rust Belt*.

boss adj intj : the best, *excellent*, *cool*; 'The Boss' = Bruce Springsteen.

boughten regional (NE) v : bought, "I've boughten my ticket."

boutonnière /bootəneer/ n : *buttonhole* (as in the small flower spray worn in the lapel), corsage.

boxers, boxer shorts n : underwear in the style of shorts, ant. *tightie-whities*.

boxers in a bunch expr adj : syn. *knickers in a twist*, *panties in a ruffle*, panties all bunched up, panties in a knot.

bozo n : fool, *clot*.

braces cf n : orthodontal device worn on teeth.

braces, curly braces usage punc n : *brace brackets*, curly brackets, *{ }*.

brackets, square brackets usage punc n : square brackets, *[ ]*.

braid v : *plait*.

braids n : *pigtails*, *plaits*.

brain freeze col n : the painful sensation after drinking an overly cold drink, such as a *slushy*, esp. too fast.

brainstorm n : *brain wave*, as in sudden bright idea.

bravo n : in a triathlon, wearing (skimpy) bathing suit for the whole race–bike and run as well as swim, "more go bravo these days, to save time," cf. *go commando*.

break n : see *give me a break*.

break down v : dismantle, clean up and put away, "break down the *creamers*."

break out v : unpack, "let's break out the beers," see *bust out*.

breasts cf n : syn. titties, ta-tas /tah tahs/, *bazoom*, tits, *jugs*, boobs, hogans.

briefs n : underwear in the style of *Y-fronts*, *tightie-whities*.

bro [black brother] inf abbr n : friend, syn. *mate*, "what's happenin,' bro?"

broad n : woman syn. *bird*, *skirt*, *babe*.

Brodie expr v : usu. to do a Brodie, abject extravagant or spectacular failure, fiasco, flop, also suicide attempt [in 1886 Steve Brodie claimed to have jumped off the Brooklyn Bridge, but failed to have it witnessed].

broil usage v : *grill*.

Bronx cheer sl n : *razz*, about the same as (blowing) a *raspberry*.

brown bag n : informal lunchtime meeting where everyone brings their *packed lunch*.

brown bag lunch n : *packed lunch*.

brown nose vt : brown noser = *toady*.

brownie [*west coast*] n : *snuggie*.

brownie n : small rich chocolate cake.

brownie points expr n : good karma or notional points acquired by which you're marked up a notch, or taken up a peg or two. Although, to some, these points are only scored by obsequiousness, see *brown nose*.

brownstone [from the facing of flaky

brownish-red sandstone originally used] n : elegant high-stooped Italianate style of house, found esp. in *NYC* (e.g. the Manhattan house in the movie *Panic Room*).

brunch [collision of breakfast & lunch] n : late breakfast, usu. had at mid-morning, popular on Sundays and public *holidays*.

brung inf v : brought, "he brung his leg down."

BS /bee es/ abbr euph n v : *bullshit*, "she bs's all the time," "he's *all* bs," "they're bs-ing out back."

BS abbr n : *BSc*.

Bubba [brother] (S) n : nickname, 1. male from *Southern US*, 2. *good ol' boy*, 3. *cracker, redneck, trailer park* resident—from the movie *Bubba Ho-Tep*. 'And then there is the all-important Bubba vote. Some rural men in *pickup* trucks have been swayed by Jindal's religious fervor, and their bumper stickers read "Bubbas for Bobby." [Louisiana].' (Also Yiddish for grandmother.)

bubbler regional n : drinking fountain.

buck n : *dollar*, like *quid* for *pound*.

buckaroo [Sp *vaquero*] n : cowboy.

buckeye n : horse chestnut tree, also *conker*, also person from Ohio (the buckeye state).

buck for v : *root for*.

buckle n : an old fashioned, deep dish fruit desert with a crisp crust.

bud n : marijuana buds, the right buds being particularly powerful, and buds being the readily available form in the US rather than the UK hash or oil.

buddy n : friend, syn. *mate*.

buff adj : burly, well built, but usu. as a result of *working out*, "she's gotten really buff."

buffet (furniture) usage n : *sideboard*.

bug n : any small insect.

bug v : annoy, irritate.

buggy cf n : four-wheeled buggy, also *pram*, also (in the south) shopping *trolley*.

bug out col v : *scarper*, also when some-

body's eyes bug out they get huge.

buku /bookoo/ sl adj : see *beaucoup*.

bull adj : euph for bullshit, "what a load of bull."

bulletin board n : *noticeboard*, syn. *pin board*.

bull honky joc euph n : bullshit.

bullhorn n : *loudhailer*.

bull session expr n : discussion, often around some important topic, of the kind amongst a few friends after a few, syn. bullfest, see *gabfest*.

bullshit sl intj : complete and utter nonsense, syn. crap, *cobblers*, *rubbish*, *codswallop*. See *call bullshit*.

bulrush, also **bullrush** cf n : sedges *Scirpus* esp. Common Bulrush or Club-rush *Scirpus lacustris*.

bum adj : unpleasant, syn. *bogus*, 'bum deal,' '*bum steer*.'

bum cf n : *tramp*, transient.

bumbershoot n : umbrella, and the name of a late Summer music festival in Seattle, WA.

Bumfuck Egypt, Bumfuck Ohio expr n : remote or insignificant place. Some random, usu. *Midwest* state occasionally replaces Egypt since the Midwest is considered remote by most *east* or *west* coast folks, though sometimes they're pointing out the remoteness of that state, "she's driving all the way to Bumfuck Iowa!" although, 'Bumfuck, Idaho,' "West Bumblefuck, Long Island."

bummer cf intj, n : depressing person or situation, syn. *stress*. Also intj. as a consolation.

bummin' adj : miserable, "I'm bummin'," "she's bummin' hard," also intj. as a consolation.

bum out v : to depress, "I was totally bummed out."

bum steer n : *bad deal*, cheated, red herring.

bunch inf n : load, group, many, "a bunch

of people made themselves a bunch of money," syn. pile.

bunk n : nonsense, "that's bunk."

bunny hop n : (usu. of a bicycle) both wheels off the ground and landing at the same time, for instance jumping a *curb*.

bunt v : stop the baseball without swinging the bat.

buoy /booee/ n : /boy/.

bureau n : chest of drawers.

The 'Burgh col n : Pittsburgh.

burglarize v : *burgle*.

burlap n : *hessian*, sack-cloth.

Burning Man n : annual festival (see table 1, American Holidays) deep in the Nevada desert, that fulfills a primal yearning to gather; a rite involving towers of bone, smut shacks, fire cannons, robots, dragons, glitter & neon, princess warriors and exploding men.

burrito [Mexican] n : beans and *salsa* rolled in a *tortilla*.

burro [Sp] n : (small) donkey.

bus v : clean off, "bus your own tables."

busboy n : waiter's assistant who cleans and resets the tables.

bush whiskey col n : *moonshine*.

Business Reply Mail (on envelopes, see also *Official Business*) n : *Freepost*. Instead of the huge hollow "1" next to two fat vertical bars with enough space in between for a stamp it has "No Postage Necessary If Mailed In the United States" in a box above 7 thick horizontal lines.

bust n : (police) raid. Beer bust = hearty drinking session.

bust v : to hit, "he got busted in the face." Also, to work hard, as in 'bust my *butt*.'

busted v : caught red-handed, arrested.

bust out v : emphatic version of *break out*. "bust out those beers before I die of thirst!"

busy signal (phone) n : *engaged tone*.

butt [buttocks] cf n : *bottom*, syn. *ass, fanny*,

duff, keister, patootie, tush, "kiss my butt," cf. *bum*. See expr. *move your butt*.

butt crack n : *builder's cleavage*, between the buttocks where your underwear gets caught, "his *pants* were pulled up so his butt crack wasn't hanging out."

butte /byoot/ n : topped, steep-sided, isolated hill.

butt floss n : thong.

butthead n : obstinate *twit, idiot*.

butthole sl n : anus, "butthole surfers."

buttload n : a lot, more than expected, "buttload of frogs," syn. shitload.

buttmunch sl n : fool, sycopohant.

butt-ugly adj : on a scale of 1 to 10 a butt-ugly photographic subject would cause the camera lens to fracture.

buzzard cf n : turkey buzzard, turkey vulture.

buzz saw n : circular saw.

bye cf intj : syn. *hasta, hasta la vista, later, seeya, outahere, adios*.

— C —

cab n : taxi.

cabana n : *beach hut*.

cabinet n : cabinet members are chosen by the *President* and have nothing to do with *Congress*.

caboose n : *guard's van*.

Caddy inf n : *Cadillac*, "I only take the Caddy out for short trips."

Cadillac n : top of the line American cars and, like Rolls-Royce, frequently used as a superlative, "Hewlett-Packard was the Cadillac of calculators."

cajones /ka hohnays/ [Sp box, drawers] n : see cojones.

Cajun [contr of Acadians, the French driven out of Nova Scotia, Prince Edward Island, and parts of New Brunswick and Maine in the 1750s, moving to the *bayous* of

Southern Louisiana] n adj : the Cajun people, their festive culture, music, and their noteworthy cooking.

calendar book n : *diary*, syn. *journal* (more often "let me put that in my book" where 'calendar' is a qualifier).

call (telephone) n v : *ring up*, *ring*.

call v : *knock up* (from sleep).

call bullshit expr v : call someone's bluff or question their veracity, "I call bullshit!"

call collect v : *reverse charges*.

caller ID [caller identification] n : *calling line identification*.

camel toes sl n : jeans so tight you can read her lips.

Camp David n : *US* presidential retreat (cf. *Chequers*).

camper n : *vehicle* set up for camping, usu. a *pickup* with a *camper shell*.

camper shell n : hard canopy that fits on a *pickup* or an open *truck*, usu. with small windows, vent, and door.

can sl n : jail, syn. the *nick*.

can sl n : *loo*, syn. *john*, "I'm gonna hit the can" = take a leak.

can usage n : *tin*, tin can.

can sl vt : *sack*, *fire*, "I was canned in April."

can it vt : dispose, abandon, syn. junk it, *bin it*.

candy n : *sweets*, a *sweet*.

candy bar n : *bar of chocolate*, or similar.

candy store n : *sweetshop*, confectioner.

cannonball run n : an illegal high speed east coast to west coast car rally that starts in an unspecified place (New York) and time (Spring or Fall) and ends about a day and a half later somewhere (Long Beach). (It actually ran five times in the 1970s.)

canola n : *rapeseed oil*.

canuck, canuk [former logging term] intermittently offen n : Canadian person, (name of Vancouver's National Hockey League team).

Cape Cod turkey n : lamb, calf or hog's tes-

ticles, syn. codfish, *mountain oysters*.

capeesh [It *capisce*] intj : do you understand? (Accompanied by a satisfying sharp little slap, in the movies.)

Capitol n : building where the *Congress* meets, like the *Houses of Parliament*. Each state *legislature* similarly has a state capitol building.

car (train) n : *coach*.

caramel apple /kahr(ə)məl/ n : /karəməl/ *toffee apple*.

caravan cf n : *convoy*.

card v : to check *ID* for age, "they're carding everyone tonight."

carded v : to have been asked for *ID*, such as when buying *alcohol* in a *bar* or at the *store*.

carnival usage n : (travelling) *funfair* or circus.

carousel n : merry-go-round, *roundabout*.

cart n : *trolley*, *supermarket trolley*.

carve (snow boarding, skate boarding) v : *shred*.

car wreck n : *car crash*, *wreck*.

casket usage n : coffin.

Castro District n : the San Francisco neighbourhood that's the center of the *gay* universe, attracting *gays* from around the globe.

catalyze sp v : *catalyse*.

catbird seat expr adj : see *in the catbird seat*.

catch v : "catch a *movie*" = 'go and see a *film*,' "catch some *rays*" = 'get a sun tan.' See also *grab*.

catercorner adj : *catty corner*.

cathouse n : brothel.

catsup n : tomato *ketchup*.

cattail n : *bulrush* (reedmace *Typha latifolia* or genus Typhaceae generally).

cattle guard n : *cattle grid*, syn. *Texas gate*, vehicle pass.

catty corner adj : diagonally opposite, usu. in reference to buildings on a crossroads, syn. *catercorner*, *kitty corner*.

catty wumpus adj : turned about, disoriented, syn. *knickers in a twist*. Also, sometimes used instead of *catty corner*.

caulks /korks/ n : logger's spikes (spiked boots for climbing).

caveat n v : warning, 'watch out!' "there's a caveat though," "we should caveat that with . . .," caveat emptor = let the buyer beware.

cell, cellphone n : *mobile*.

cent n : *1¢* coin about the size of a *new penny*, syn. *penny*. Until relatively recently you might have occasionally found an Indian Head penny (1859–1909) in your change, and you can still find a wheatsheaf penny (1909–1959).

center sp n : *centre*.

CEO abbr n : *MD*, Chief Executive Officer.

cha-ching! intj : costly.

champ n : like the Loch Ness monster, a creature in Lake Champlain that's actually on the Vermont endangered species list, cf. *jackalope*.

change purse usage n : *purse*.

channel surfing (TV) v : flipping around the *telly* channels, *channel-hopping*, *zapping*.

Chapstick® n : *lip salve*.

charge card cf n : credit card.

charged (goods bought) v : *put down*, *entered*.

chaw regional var n : *chew*.

cheapskate col n : stingy person.

cheat v : syn. *bugger*ed, *gyp*, *bum steer*, bunk, *shaft*, *hose bag*, *screw*, *ream*, *scam*.

check (banking) sp n : *cheque*.

check (restaurant) n : *bill*.

check (on a list) n v : *tick*, tick mark.

check v : to leave, as in the *checkroom*, "let me check my coat," "check your cynicism at the door."

check vi : an OK or response, as in verbally ticking things off a list.

checkers (the board game) n : *draughts*.

check in v : *book in*, "I booked a room last week but when I went to check in I was bumped."

checking account (banking) n : *current account*.

check out v : take a look at, or have a try, "check it out!" See also *scope*, *dogging*, *butcher's*.

checkroom n : *cloakroom*, also *left luggage*.

Cheerios n (General Mills Cheerios® breakfast cereal) n : little round loops of puffed oats (see *feel your cheerios*), the most popular brand, and woven into American culture (every child has made a cheerios necklace).

cheese (back-formation of cheesy) n : tackiness, shabbiness, "I've maximized my cheese filter."

cheesecake n : shapely woman, see *beefcake*.

cheese cloth n : *muslin*.

cheese head n : person from Wisconsin.

cherimoya n : *custard apple*, sweetsop, *sugar apple*, *Annona* sp.

cherry (usu. of a car) adj v : to fix up to an enviably pristine condition, often beyond its original new condition, "it's cherry," "I was going to cherry it up, but I sold it."

chew n : chewing tobacco, also a wad of it, "get me some chew."

chewing gum and baling wire expr n : materials at hand for fixing anything, equivalent to '*string and sellotape*,' 'paper clips and pull ties,' see also *duct tape*.

chew out vt : reprimand, syn. *bawl out*.

Chex® (breakfast cereal) n : similar to *Shreddies* (as are Kellogg's Crispix®).

chick n : girl, syn. *bird*, *babe*.

chicory (salad) n : *endive*.

childcare provider n : babysitter.

chill imp v : calm down, relax.

chillin' v : *hang out*, "just some ducks and geese chillin' in the lake."

chill out imp v : *chill*, calm down, relax, take a chill pill.

chinch n : bed bug.

chinook [Salish] n : either a warm wet wind that blows south from the *Pacific Northwest*, or a warm dry wind blowing east off the Rockies. [I'm eating some chinook salmon right now!]

chipmunk n : small light and dark striped squirrel, cute and cheeky, seen at campgrounds darting in and out to get scraps.

chipped beef n : thin sliced smoked dried beef.

chipper adj : cheery and lively.

chips (food) cf n : *crisps*, but also includes corn chips.

chitlins, chitterlings (Southern) n : pig intestines prepared as food, syn. middlins. See also *pork rinds*.

choad sl n : penis. Also the perineum, syn. *barse*, *bonch*, taint (usu. female), notcha.

chocolate chip cookie n : the most popular kind of *cookie*.

chop suey [Chinese *jaahp seui* mixed bits] n : developed in the *US* in an attempt to recreate authentic Chinese food without proper cooking utensils, ingredients or seasonings. (See *chow mein*.)

chowder [Fr] n : thick fish and potato soup, *clam chowder*, NY clam chowder is red by addition of tomatoes.

chow down v : eat voraciously, syn. *scoff*.

chow mein [Chinese *cháau-mihn* fried flour (noodles)] n : an American dish first prepared by Chinese *railroad* workers in San Francisco. (See *chop suey*.)

CHP /chip/ abbr n : California Highway Patrol (pronunciation from popular 1970s TV show *ChiPs*).

Christian crank col n : coffee.

chuck, (chuck up) v : to vomit, *blow chunks*, *upchuck*.

chum n v : baiting fish by throwing chum (made from fish, corn, etc.) in the water. Also a brand of pet food, like *PAL*.

chunks sl n : vomit.

chute (yachting) n : spinnaker.

chutes and ladders (game) n : *snakes and ladders*.

chutzpa(h) [Yiddish] n : nerve, cheek.

CIA n : Central Intelligence Agency, more or less equivalent to *MI6*.

cilantro n : *coriander*, but usu. referring to the leaves for cooking or flavouring.

cider cf n : apple juice, *apple cider*.

cinch inf n v : certainty, ensure.

Cinco de Mayo [Mexican 5th May] n : holiday informally celebrated in many parts of the *US*, esp. on the *west coast*. Originally instigated by the Chicano populations in *southwestern* states, this holiday is actually unknown in Mexico apart from tourist and border towns, although it is the Anniversary of the Battle of Puebla (Victory of General Zaragoza Day), one of the dozen Mexican national holidays.

circular file col n : *waste paper bin*, syn. file 13, "that goes in the circular file."

citation (law) n : *summons*.

city cf usage n : *town*, 'city *dump*,' 'city *shops*,' 'city *slicker*.' Also intensifier, "drag city," "surf city," see *–ville*.

City of Brotherly Love n : *Philly*.

clam sl n : *vagina*, "I got a clam shot."

clam chowder n : clam and potato *chowder*.

clerk /klerk/ n : /klahk/, see *sales clerk*.

client euph n : inmate.

Cliff Notes® n : commercial cheat sheets (usu. about 10 years out of date).

clingons [from Klingons—Star Trek] n : *dingleberries*.

clinker cf n : an utter failure.

clip joint sl n : night club specializing in overcharging.

clique /klik/ n : /kleek/.

closet n : *cupboard*, clothes *cupboard*,

also **wardrobe**, also small storage room like a **box room**, 'a skeleton in the closet.'

clothespin n : **peg**, **clothes-peg**.

clout n : influence, weight.

Clue (game) n : **Cluedo**.

clue expr v : get a clue = **realise**, **twig**.

c-note n : *$100 bill*, or about that value, "had to shell out a c-note."

coach (flying) n : **economy**, **economy class**.

coach (train) n : **economy**, **economy class**.

coaster n : **beer mat** or any similar small round tray, mat or pad for hot or cold drinks.

cobbler n : fruit pie with thick rich crust, usu. served hot with ice cream, reminiscent of a **crumble**, "blueberry cobbler."

cockamamie adj : ridiculous, crazy, absurd.

coed /koh ed/ n : female undergraduate.

coffee [introduced to Europe in the 17 C First English coffee-house in Oxford in 1650. Annual production (1988) 3,553,000 tonnes] n : the common drink in the *US*, like **tea** in the *UK*, syn. *Christian crank*, *joe*. (See *with or without*, *wake up and smell the coffee*.)

coffee shop n : **café**, but a veritable institution ubiquitous across the nation. There are many chains, like Denny's (similar to **Wimpy's**), almost hard not to be found in even the smallest of towns, and a hotel will normally have a coffee shop, and sometimes a full restaurant. Coffee refills are always free.

coffee spitter col n : usu. in reference to a shocking newspaper headline, syn. **marmalade-dropper**, muffin-choker.

coin purse n : **purse**.

cojones /kəhohnays/ [Sp shit!] n : testicles, **balls**, courage, chutzpah, **bottle**.

coke n : general term for any **fizzy drink**, esp. in the *South*, or otherwise cola, "What kinda coke you wan? We got Pepsi, orange, *root beer* and *DP*." "Where I come from we call whatever comes in a bottle *coke*." See also *pop*, *soda*, and *tonic*.

cold call n v : the unsolicited activity of a telemarketer or sales*critter* (phone spam).

collar button n : **collar stud**.

collar stay n : **collar stiffener**.

collect call n : **reverse charges call**.

color sp n : **colour**, probably the most well known word that people from both countries are aware of that is spelt differently, see *-or*.

combo [combination] n : can refer to a musical band, food, "gimme the strawberry-chocolate combo," "I'll take the combo platter," color scheme, or virtually anything where appropriate, "one of the two, or a combo of both," "The sky is blue, the snow white, and to complete the all American color combo, my face is now red."

come-on n v : **lure**.

come on down expr v : Join in (the fun), join us, (usu. after passing some kind of test of worthiness) "Hey! That's good enough for me. Come on *down*."—Anne Lamott, *bird by bird*.

come on to expr v : make a pass.

comforter n : **quilt**, **duvet**, **eiderdown**.

comfort station n : **public convenience**, esp. in hotels, *bars*, restaurants.

comic cf n : the comics refer specifically to the **comic** section of the paper, particularly the Sunday *funnies*.

commercial n : **advert**.

common stock n : **ordinary shares**.

commonwealth cf n : for no particular reason, rather than 'State of . . . ,' they are officially named Commonwealth of Kentucky, Massachusetts, Pennsylvania, and Virginia (and Puerto Rico).

community college n : two-year, post high school college, conferring an Associate Degree, and which can also serve as the preliminary two years of a full degree program elsewhere.

commute n : the journey a commuter makes, "my commute *sucks*."

the Company col n : *CIA*.

compensation n : salary, wages.

complected adj : complexioned, "Is she dark complected?"

complection sp n : not yet an official spelling of complexion.

complimentary adj : without charge, gratis.

comptroller n : financial controller in a company.

concert master n : *leader*.

condominium n : *owner-occupied flat*.

conductor (railway) n : *guard*.

cone n : see *ice cream cone*.

confectioners' sugar n : *icing sugar*.

confuddle [contr] v : confuse + befuddle.

confused usage cf v : mixed up, mistaken.

Congress n : like *Parliament*. Comprises the *House of Representatives* and the *Senate*. "If the opposite of pro is con, then the opposite of progress is congress." See *Capitol, Constitution, elections, president*.

congresscritter inf n : *congressman*.

congressman, congresswoman, congressperson n : like *MP*. Used only to refer to *representatives*, not *senators*. As a title, is used before the name, 'Congressman Joe Smith,' and as an address, "Congressman Smith, do you support the bill?"

connect (telephone) v : *put through*.

connectivity n : state of being connected (rooms in a building, computers with other computers or network), "this design enhances connectivity."

Constitution cf n : written document popularly believed to specify how the American government is organised and to guarantee various rights to the people. In fact the Constitution is silent on such matters as political parties and their *primary*

elections, and while the form of its *Electoral College* procedure is followed today, the way it actually works is nothing like what was intended. As to civil rights, these have been modified almost beyond recognition by judicial interpretation. (E.g. the constitution says "Congress shall make no law respecting an establishment of religion, or prohibiting the free exercise thereof." This is interpreted to mean, among other things, that organised religion **must not** be exercised in tax-funded schools. Although that's a damn good idea, it sure isn't obvious that it follows from the quoted sentence.) Constitutional amendments require the consent of three quarters of the state *legislatures*. Judicial interpretations require the consent of five people (i.e. a majority of the nine *Supreme Court* justices).

construction n : *roadworks*, 'construction ahead,' 'fines double in construction zone,' also any general building or repair, "the *shop* is still under construction."

construction site n : *building site*.

construction worker n : *builder*.

continental United States n : (used primarily for *shipping* purposes) the 49 states on the North American continent, which excludes Hawaii (who call it the mainland), see *lower 48*.

controlled intersection (mostly police usage) n : a road *junction* 'controlled' by traffic lights, a traffic cop, or any other means. See also *stop sign*.

convenience store n : syn. the *corner shop*, the *handy shop*.

converse, converse high-tops [Converse®] n : popular brand and style of tennis shoes with high ankles.

convertible n : open top car.

cookie [Dutch small cake] cf n : sweet *biscuit* but chewier and softer (and larger). The most popular is the chocolate-chip cookie, but cookies also include the *Oreo*, *fig Newton*, macaroon, and gingerbread man. See *cracker*.

cook-out n : festive meal outside, chili cook-out.

cool adj intj : of that which increases sereneness or wa, syn. *brill*, *sweet*, *bitchin'*, *neat*, *fresh*, *rad*, bad, *awesome*, *excellent*!

cool sl v : to die, syn. *snuff it*, "the old guy cooled on me."

cooler col n : fridge.

cooler n : large plastic container serving as an insulated picnic basket.

cool your jets expr v : *chill out*, relax.

coon n : *raccoon*.

coon ass sl n : French-speaking Anglo-American, e.g. *Cajun*.

coon's age inf n : very long time, syn. *donkey's years*, dog's age, *yonks*.

cooter [Southern] n : turtle, generally, but in the Southeast refers specifically to *Chrysemys (Pseudemys)* spp.

cooter [Southern] sl n : *yokel*, as in *redneck*, hick, *hillbilly*.

cooties n : body lice, also used for all kinds of contagious, microscopic, creepy-crawly nasties, syn. the *dreaded lergy*. "Whaddya mean cooties! No cooties on me!"

copacetic, copesetic, copasetic adj : running smoothly, hunky-dory.

cop out v : give up, syn. *bogue*.

copy-reader n : *sub-editor*.

cord n : 4x4x8 foot measure of chopped firewood, etc (in MD, packed tight enough that a *chipmunk* can't run through it).

corkboard n : *bulletin board*.

corn cf n : *maize*.

Corn Belt n : agricultural area in northern states (Illinois, Indiana, Iowa, Nebraska, Kansas). See also *Borscht Belt*, *Bible Belt*, and *Rust Belt*.

corn bread n : dry, semi-sweet cake made from coarse *maize* flour, popular everywhere, though originally from the *South*, syn. *corn pone*, pone bread.

corn dog n : frankfurter fried in *cornmeal* batter, on a stick, similar to *toad in the hole*, staple of county and state fairs across the country, usu. cheapest food there.

corned beef n : *salt beef*.

cornhusker n : person from Nebraska.

corn liquor n : *spirits* made from *maize*.

cornmeal n : coarse *maize* flour.

cornpone [Southern *corn bread*] adj : *down-home*, countrified.

cornstarch n : *cornflour*, fine-ground *maize* flour.

corporation n : *limited company*.

costume party n : *fancy dress party*.

cot cf n : camp bed.

cotton, cotton balls n : *cotton wool*.

Cotton Belt n : cotton-growing region of the South. See also *Borscht Belt*, *Bible Belt*, and *Rust Belt*.

cotton candy n : *candy floss*.

cotton to v : take a liking to, hit it off.

cottonwood n : poplar trees native to N. America, see *bam*.

couch usage n : *sofa*, "couch fishing."

courtesy /kertəsee/ n : /kertəsee/ or /kortə-see/.

coveralls n : *boiler suit*, *overalls*, mechanics *overalls*, see *overalls*.

cow expr v : see *have a cow*.

cowbird n : the Brown-headed Cowbird is parasitic, like the *cuckoo*.

cowboy inf n : a person perceived as tackling his tasks from the seat of his *pants*, but ranges from subtly derogatory to reverential, "The only thing this place has going for it is the salary a *deadbeat* computer cowboy can command," "I like my eggs dirty on both sides"—an old cowboy.

cowpea (also blackeye pea) n : *blackeye bean*.

cowpoke n : cowboy.

cow tipping v : a *high school* or *college* prank of sneaking up to a standing sleeping cow and pushing her over (really funny, can injure cow, felony in most states).

CPA abbr n : Certified Public Accountant, equivalent to a *chartered accountant*.

crab grass n : *couch grass*.

crack n : *vagina*, also *butt crack*.

cracker n : *cream cracker*, includes the *saltine*, ritz, and wheat thin. See *cookie*.

Cracker n : person from Florida or Georgia.

cracker sl n : lower-class *white trash*.

crank n : kind of speed (methamphetamine), *downer*.

cranky cf adj : bad tempered.

crapper n : *toilet*, syn. *bog*.

crawdad, crawfish n : *crayfish*. Crawdad and crawfish are used in the west, but crayfish is generally used in the east.

crazy cf adj : syn. insane, *unglued*, kooky, *flakey, unhinged*, wacky, out of one's tree.

cream n : *half and half*.

cream v : annihilate.

creamer n : small milk jug.

creamer n : white non-dairy cream substitute powder for adding to *coffee*, *tea*, etc.

credit n : the value of a *school* class, "I need three more credits to *graduate*."

creek /kreek/ or /krik/ cf n : *stream*, brook. The different pronunciations are regional, though some consider the latter white trash, "a creek is a crik if it has a rusting truck in it."

crêpe cf n : *pancake*.

crib n : baby's *cot*.

crib inf n : house, flat, place.

critter n : creature, "cute little critter," "after the fire, there was a *bunch* of crispy critters," and occasionally pejoratively of people to highlight their rodent or insect-like nature, salescritter (see *cold call*), congresscritter.

croak v : die syn. *snuff it*, bite it.

crock cf n : rubbish, crap, "what a load of crock," "what a crock," also hypochondriac.

crossing guard n : *lollipop man*.

crosswalk n : *pedestrian crossing*, syn. *zebra crossing, pelican crossing*.

crost v : cross, see *acrost*.

crotch n : *crutch*.

cruet usage n : vinegar and oil bottle.

cruise v : to flow easily in a situation, "cruising down the *freeway*," also to leave or take off, "I'm cruisin'" syn. *jam*, also to *pull*, "cruisin' for *babes*."

crumple n : *buckle*.

crunchie col n : *east coast* term for a *granola*.

crunk adj : *amped*.

crust v : uncomfortably psychologically miserable, "he's crusting hard," or physically as in smelly, dishevelled (see *cruster*).

cruster n : usu. a *transient*, or anyone visibly down on their luck, and occasionally literally as when a transient or drunk wakes and his hair is held in place by the dried *gook* he fell asleep in. (PC term: person of *crust*.)

cube n : office cubicle, hence cube farm—large open-plan office full of cubes, cube fever, cube rat (peon, corporate minion), cubeville, "sentenced to cubeville," see *prairie dog*, "the cube where we did the most *heinous* debugging was called the penalty box."

cuffs n : *turn-ups* on *trousers*, as well as on shirts.

cup n : 8 *fluid ounces*, or 2 cups to a *pint*, see table of measures.

cup n : *box* (genital protector in sports).

curb sp n : *kerb*.

cursive n adj : *joined up writing*.

cuss v : curse or swear, "cussed a blue streak," "Yeah, I cuss when I get *real mad*, but I run it out the back door. I don't take it out on the wife and kids."

cussword n : swear-word.

custard cf n : specifically, egg custard, but generally, a base for making desserts like a thick custard that sets firm.

custom-made adj : *bespoke*.

cut v : give, issue, make available, "cut a *check*" (to write a *check*), "cut that *crazy dude* a wide circle" (avoid the *dude*), "cut Spock some *slack!*" (give Spock a chance).

cute adj : attractive, "she's cute," also a choice situation, as in "that was cute."

cut loose expr v : depending on the context, it ranges from letting your hair down to getting the *sack* to going completely berserk. "Attila tended to eat and drink lightly during banquets, but on his wedding night he really cut loose."

cutting the cheese (Indiana) expr v : farting.

– d –

DA abbr n : *district attorney*.

Dacron n : synthetic polyester used as fiber, syn. *Terylene*, *Crimplene*, (Trevira in Germany).

daddy-long-legs n : harvestman.

dahlia /dahleeə/ /daleeə/ n : /dayleeə/ [Named after Swedish botanist A. Dahl, d. 1789, pronounced /dahl/, hence American pronunciation is closest.]

Daisy Dukes [Daisy in the Dukes of Hazard] n : cut-off jeans further cut off and/or rolled up to expose as much cheek as possible.

dame dated n : woman.

darn cf intj : exclamation of surprise, annoyance, syn. {++} *awesome*, *way cool*, *totally rad*, *right on*! {+} *wow*, gee,

cool, *rad*, *radical*, whoa!, {0} *shucks*, Jiminy Cricket! {-} *sheesh*, jeeze, jeepers creepers, jeepers, criminy, dang (it), *darn* (it), heck, gosh darn (it), *gol dang* (it), *blech*, yuk, foo, *phooey*, pshaw {- -} damn, *shoot* {- - -} (the usual stuff).

darned adj : syn. *flipping*.

darn it intj : syn. *sod* it, *flip* it.

data /daydə/ n : /dahtə/.

date n v : anything from spending time with a *buddy* to a lovers' tryst, often somewhere in between and sometimes with the hope of becoming the latter, "We're on a date." Also, the person with whom you are 'on a date,' "who is your date tonight?" "95% of people are undateable" (Jerry Seinfeld).

date book n : *diary*.

davenport n : ample couch, sometimes a sofa bed.

daylight saving time n : syn. *British Summer Time*. There are four time zones in the US—eastern, central, mountain, and Pacific, which are abbreviated to EST, CST, MST, PST, and EDT, CDT, MDT, PDT (standard time and daylight time). There's also Atlantic, Alaska and Hawaii time zones. See table of US Holidays.

Daytimer® n : *Filofax®*.

DC abbr n : Washington, DC (District of Columbia). [Over on the other side of the country, in the 19th century, a new territory (later a state) was created and needed a name. Columbia was considered, but was felt it would be confused with the District of Columbia. So they named it after Washington instead. *Doh!*]

deadbeat cf n : loafer, welcher.

dead end (street sign) n : *cul-de-sac*.

dead ringer n : identical, lookalike.

dead week (college) n : week before finals each term, when students *pull all-nighters* to catch up a term's worth of studying (and hence look dead).

dealie, dealy, dealy-bop, deal col n : an item or thing, usu. when the name doesn't come to mind, "where's the dealie," "bring me that deal over there," see *doodad*.

death tax n : *death duty*, *estate tax*, inheritance tax (current term), termination tax.

deb [debutante] n : bimbo.

debark n : *disembark*.

debit card n : *payment card*.

decal n : plastic transfers for cars.

deck n : *pack* (of cards).

deep-six [the regulation minimum six fathom depth of nautical burials as sounded off on a standard sounding line to the sixth deep or mark] n v : to bury or kill, and hence to discard, throw away, also to beat an opponent decisively.

Deep South n : AL, GA, LA, MS, SC, and maybe parts of FL, TX. See also the *Southern States*.

defense sp n : *defence*.

deli [contr delicatessen] n : *sandwich* shop that also slices meats and cheeses, (The Digital Deli in *Silly Valley* sold a smorgasbord of ready to go electronic and computer parts).

den n : a separate room for hobbies, study, etc.

denatured alcohol n : syn. *methylated spirits*, see *rubbing alcohol*.

deplane v : *disembark* (from a plane).

depot /deepoh/ (/depoh/) cf n : bus or *railway* station.

derby /derbee/ cf n : *bowler hat*, hard hat.

desperado [Sp] n : criminal.

dessert n : *pudding*, *afters*, *sweet*.

detail v : to clean, vacuum, wash and polish a car, "our autos are detailed every three shifts," "we also do auto-detailing."

detour n : *diversion* (road sign/instruction).

diaper n : *nappy*.

diarrhea sp n : *diarrhoea*, syn. *Montezuma's revenge*, *touristas*, sour-apple quickstep.

diary cf n : personal *journal* or note book.

diatomaceous earth n : *kieselguhr*.

dibble n : dibbing-stick, *dibber*.

dibs n intj : a claim, *bag*, "I have dibs on that."

diddle cf v : waste time, syn. *faff*.

diddly, diddly-squat n : worthless, miniscule, insignificant, "he don't know diddly," syn, *Jack*, *sweet FA*.

diesel (fuel) n : *derv*.

dieting usage v : *slimming*.

dig inf v : understand, appreciate, admire.

dime n : *10¢* coin, a little smaller than a *sixpence* or about the size of a *½p*.

dime sl n : $10 worth of *dope*, usu. marijuana.

diner n : restaurant, but usu. at the *transport café*, *greasy spoon*, cheap café, *coffee shop* end of the scale. [Originally, from the dining car of a train, some of which were converted to buildings, and other restaurants which were styled after them, the intention being to recreate a '50s ambiance.]

ding-a-ling col n : idiot.

dingbat n : stupid person.

dinky cf adj : inconsequential, also shabby.

dip n : such as *guacamole* or bean dip (mashed beans with seasonings) or sour cream dip (sour cream with seasonings) eaten by dipping in sliced vegetables, or *chips*.

dip [dipshit] n : *tosser*, *dork*, see *dipped*.

dipped expr adj : surprise, usu. 'I'll be dipped' (in full, 'I'll be dipped in (dog)shit'), syn, 'I'll be damned,' 'well, I'll be,' 'I'll be *blowed.*'

directory assistance (telephone) n : *directory inquiries*, *information*, 411, 555–1212. This is now the official term since some folks would call information thinking it was a general *information* service, "this is directory assistance. Try the zoo. Please hold for that number."

dirt road n : *unpaved road*.

dis (disrespect) v : put down, disregard, "don't be dissin' me."

discombobulate vt : upset, confuse.

dishes (usu **the dishes**) v : *washing up*, "do the dishes."

dish towel n : *tea towel*.

disk (computer) n : *disc*.

the District n : Washington, DC.

district attorney n : *public prosecutor*.

ditto head n : Rush Limbaugh fan, whether or not they agree with what he says.

ditz n : ditsy person, dithering woman, syn. dumb blonde.

divided highway n : *dual carriageway*.

Dixie n adj : the *Southern States*, also *Southern* culture, esp. music.

DMV abbr n : Department of Motor Vehicles, the place where you obtain a *driver's license* and take the test. BMV (bureau) in some states, syn. *DVLA*.

docile /dosl/ n : /dohsiel/.

doctor's office n : *surgery*.

dog v n : *dis*, "he dogged you," unsatisfactory, substandard, "*aw*, man, it's a dog."

dogging col v : giving someone a dirty look.

doghouse n : kennel. See *in the doghouse*.

doh! /doh/ /doh?/ intj : expression of incomprehension (at something said or done), usu. self-referential [Homer Simpson's exclamation of exasperation and frustration], see *duh!*

doing donuts v : driving in circles (leaving *donut*s in the snow, mud, grass, gravel).

dollar [the word comes from Joachimsthaler, shortened to thaler (now Taler), a 3 mark coin minted since 1519 in St Joachim's Valley in Bohemia] n : the primary unit of US currency. See *$* and *$1*. "the [Spanish] dollar is a known coin and most familiar of all to the mind of the people"—Thomas Jefferson.

done sl usage v : has already, "he done *book*ed."

done deal expr n : completion (of some deal), often used in the future sense, "it's a done deal" = it's as good as done.

don't sweat it expr v : don't go to great lengths, don't worry about it.

donut sp n : doughnut. (See *doing donuts*).

doodad col n : an item, a thing, syn. thingummy, gimcrack, doojie, *doohickey*, *dealy*bob, puppy ("gotta nail that puppy down before it'll fly"), *gizmo*, gazinta (e.g. an electrical *socket*), thingy, *dealie*, *jobby*, whatsit, such and such, whosit, what's his face, so and so, whachamacallit. See *widget*.

doofus inf n : *oaf*.

doohickey col n : gadget.

doorman n : *porter*.

dope cf n : general term for drugs.

dope col adj : *cool*, really good, "this jacket is dope," "it's the dope" (the best), "diggety dope."

dop kit n : men's toiletry bag (see *sponge bag*).

dork n : stupid and graceless person, syn. *gormless*, *nerd*, *jerk*, also *penis*, (also v. *sex*).

dose col n v : (one hit of) LSD, "*kind buds*, doses, *shrooms* and ecstasy," "are you going to dose?"

DOT n abbr : Department of Transportation, *DfT*, ODOT /oh dot/ = Oregon or Ohio DOT.

double eagle n : *$20* gold coin minted 1850–1932.

double whammy n : hex, curse, evil eye, and hence resultant debilitating episode such as 'caught between a rock and a hard place.'

downer n : the depressant drug, but also any depressive person or situation, syn. *bummer*.

down-home adj : simple and unpretentious, but often referring to *Southern* small-town quality, or rusticity, "us down-home boys gotta stick together," "he's a down-home kinda guy."

down the tubes expr adj : *down the pan*.

downtown n adj adv : *city centre* or business centre.

doy, doi /doy/ intj : var. of *doh*! and *duh*!

DP abbr n : Dr Pepper, a popular brand of *fizzy drink*, originally carbonated prune juice, see also *root beer* and *coke*.

draft n : *conscription*.

draft sp n : *draught*.

drag sl n : influence, persuasiveness.

drag sl n : *street*.

drapes n : *curtains*.

drinks party n : cocktail party.

driver's license n : *driving-licence*. The American driver's license, available to anyone over 16 (most states, varies) upon completion of a written and a driving test (easy compared to the British driving test), is issued by each state, and is renewed every four years. It seconds as the primary American *picture ID*, and as such has anti-tampering devices such as holographs. Indeed, the *DMV* issue them as ID cards for underage kids and those who don't drive.

driver's permit n : the permit required for the *learner drive*r before passing the test. It is available to anyone over 15 (though to drive they must be accompanied by someone with a valid *driver's license*). "I'm going to the *DMV* to get my permit."

drool v : syn. *slobber*, *dribble*.

drop n : see *mail drop*.

drop v : to withdraw from, "today is the last day to drop this class without being penalized," "I dropped chemistry," 'To have the charges removed, you must officially drop during the refund drop period.'

druggist n : *chemist*.

drugstore n : *pharmacy*, *chemist's*.

drunk cf adj : syn. *blitzed*, tanked, *three*

sheets to the wind, canned, faced, full, *plowed*, slug-nutty, squizzed, squashed, jagged, smashed, tie one on, corn'd-up, crocked.

dry goods store n : *draper*.

dryly sp adj : *drily*.

duck tape, duct tape n : *gaffer tape*, "It ain't broke, it just lacks duct tape."—The Duct Tape Guys, 'it has no downside' (see *chewing gum and baling wire*).

dude (term of address) n : cf. *mate*, syn. {+} *buddy*, *dude*! {0} *guy*, *sir*, *dude*, {-} *pal*.

dude n : fellow, cf. *bloke*, syn. {+} *buddy*, *hunk*, *hombre*, stud, {0} *dude*, {-} *pud*, *dummy*, *wienie*, *dingbat*, *dweeb*, *nerd*, *wonk*, *ding-a-ling*, *klutz*, {- -} *fink*, *stoopid*, *ditz*, *dork*, *bozo*, *dumb-ass*, *flake*, {- - -} *tard*.

dude! intj : admiration.

duff (anat) n : *bottom*.

duffer n : person selling cheap and flashy trinkets.

dufus sp var inf n : *doofus*.

duh! (intoned differently (with up to three syllables) to generate different meanings) /də/ /duh/ /der/ /du/ intj : silly! what a twit!, ignorant fool! syn, *doh*! *doy*! doi! (usu. referring directly to another person (because of something they've just said or done), but can be self-referential, see *doh*!).

dumb adj : stupid, "you're dumb!" "how can you be so dumb!?" "dumb ass!"

dump n v : *tip*, *rubbish tip*, 'City Dump,' "no dumping."

dump v : jilt, "I've been dumped! (boo hoo hoo . . .)."

dump v : to have a crap, "I've gotta take a dump."

dump on expr v : the full range from crying on someone's shoulder to verbal abuse.

dumpster n : *skip*.

dumpster diving v : *totting*.

dump truck n : *tipper*.

Dun & Bradstreet n : The business financial reference.

dunk v : *duck* (someone under the water as a joke).

duplex n : house sold or rented as two separate units or *flat*s (front and back or upper and lower floors), see *semi-detached*.

dust sl v : surpass (in games), syn. kill, cream.

dust devil n : whirlwind of dust anything from a few feet to hundreds of feet high.

duty /doodee/ n : /dyootee/ or /jootee/.

dweeb sl n : ineffectual and perhaps vulnerable person, syn. *nerd*, *twit*.

— e —

eagle n : $10 (from the $10 gold coin of the same name, minted 1795–1933. There was also a *half eagle*, *$5*, a *quarter eagle*, *$2.50*, and a *double eagle*, *$20*.)

East Coast n : esp. the urban corridor *thru* Boston MA, RI, CT, NY, NJ, DE, MD, DC, see *Northeast Corridor*, *back east*, *out west*, *The South*, *Midwest*.

Easter Bunny n : a rabbit (symbol of fertility) that leaves Easter eggs (and other presents) hidden here and there around the *garden* for kids at Easter.

Eastern Seaboard n : East Coast.

eatery n : place to eat (restaurant, snack bar, etc.), syn. *noshery*.

eats col n : food, syn. *grub*.

edgewise adv : *edgeways*.

editorial (newspaper) n : *leader*, *leading article*.

eggnog n : *egg flip*.

eggplant n : *aubergine*.

eh? [Canadian] intj : often added to statements in typical Canadian and popularised in the US by Bob and Doug McKenzie in their movies, see also *hoser*.

eighteen-wheeler n : very large *lorry*, syn. *juggernaut*, *semi*.

eighty six adj v : *86*.

el [elevated] n : the *L* (in Chicago, see *subway*), "catch the el."

Election Day n : elections for all manner of offices (and *propositions* too, in states where they use them) occur simultaneously on the Tuesday after November 1. See also *Congress*, *Electoral College*, *lame duck*, *off-off-year election*, *off-year election*, *president*, *primary*.

elections cf n : elections are held every 2 years for all *House* seats and a third of the *Senate* seats each time, so *senators* have a 6-year term.

the Electoral College n : nominally independent body of 'electors' that actually elects the *president* and *vice president*. If 50.1% of voters in California vote for the Democratic candidate for president, say, then what actually happens is that all 54 of the electors nominated for California by the Democratic Party are elected to the Electoral College. The 54 electors meet just once, remaining in California (the entire Electoral College never meets as a body), for the purpose of casting 54 votes for the Democratic candidate for *president* and also (nominally separately) 54 votes for the Democratic candidate for *vice president*. The 538 votes from the Electoral College must produce an actual majority for the winning candidates (which happens practically always—see *third party*), or else they are ignored and a special voting procedure in *Congress* determines the winners.

electric cord n : *flex*.

electric heater n : *electric fire*.

electrical outlet n : *power point*, *socket*.

elementary school cf n : *primary school*, grades *K-5*, (could be *K*-4, *K*-8, 1–4, or 1–8).

elevator n : lift.

elk cf n : red deer *Cervus elaphus*, makes stunning bugle sound, (also *wapiti C canadensis*), also *moose*.

emcee n v : *MC, compère*.

Emerald City n : Seattle (rumoured Rain Festival, October *thru* May, is to dissuade tourists, see *PNW*).

enchilada n : baked *tortilla* stuffed with beans, rice, meat and spicy seasonings, a staple of Mexican fast food joints. See *whole enchilada*.

endive n : *chicory*.

energy bar n : *granola bar*, originally designed as easy food for extreme athletes, but now a popular 'power' food (popular brands being Cliff bar and Power bar).

engagement calendar n : *diary*.

English (billiards) n : *side*.

English muffin n : *American muffin*, *muffin*, available toasted at *coffee shops*.

entrée cf n : main course.

epic (skater) adj : of a really good day.

eraser n : *rubber*.

escrow n v : most major transactions (such as buying a house) are facilitated by escrow whereby a third party holds all contract, monies, etc, until all conditions are satisfied, "I'm still in escrow but looking forward to getting in there."

Esq [Esquire] cf abbr n : letters after a name to indicate a lawyer.

estate tax n : *death duty*, *death tax*.

E ticket col n : a good time. From the tickets at Disneyland (till 1982) which were bought in books; A tickets were for the *wimpy* rides and E tickets were for the *funnest* rides.

Euell Gibbons n : health buff famous for surviving in the wilds on nuts, berries, (and purportedly rocks); did *commercials* for health foods; died of a heart attack at 64. "No matter what Euell Gibbons says,

there's some parts of a tree you can't eat"—mountain biker after crashing into a tree.

evidently usage cf adv : apparently.

excellent intj : *spiffing*, *awesome!*, *radical, dude!*

exclamation point punc n : *exclamation mark*, *!*

exit (sign) n : *way out*.

exit n : *freeway junction*, typically numbered, "I'm getting off at exit 980."

expensive usage n : *dear*.

expiration date n : *expiry date*, *sell-by date*. US groceries usu. have a date printed on the packaging, sometimes adjacent to a 'sell by' and occasionally 'best before,' or sometimes just labelled 'expiration date.'

explorer n : dental probe.

expressway n : urban *highway*, usu. *freeway*.

eye candy n : something easy or enticing to look at, like soft porn or cool computer graphics.

— f —

fabric usage n : *material*.

face cloth n : *flannel*, *wash cloth*, *face flannel*.

face plant expr v : to land on your face, usu. unintentionally during some activity such as skating, cycling, etc.

faculty n : *staff* (academic).

fag, faggot cf offen sl n : *gay* person.

fall n : *autumn*, "Fall is my favorite season in Los Angeles–watching the birds change color and fall from the trees"— David Letterman.

fall guy n : scapegoat, syn. *patsy*.

fanny cf n : *bottom*, see *fanny pack*.

fanny pack n : small bag worn around waist, syn. *bum bag*, plastic sporran.

farmer john adj : *dungaree*-style–one

piece trousers with bib and straps, usu. applied to *overalls*, but also wet suits, etc (as opposed to jumpsuit-style like *boiler suit*, *coveralls* and *overalls*).

fatty n : *joint*, originally so named (1980s) due to its girth, but more often now in reference to its quality, "a nice fatty."

faucet n : *tap*.

fava bean n : *broad bean* Vicia faba.

FBI abbr n : Federal Bureau of Investigation, more or less equivalent to *MI5*.

FCC abbr n : Federal Communications Commission.

FDA abbr n : Food & Drug Administration, the body that oversees food and (medicinal) drug manufacturing by, for instance, monitoring food additives, requiring all food products to list their contents, and making sure drugs are tested for safety, 'FDA Approved.'

fear and loathing [*Fear and Loathing in Las Vegas* Hunter S. Thompson] n : apprehension prior to inevitable wretchedness, "when's the next fear and loathing ride?" "the most lyrical sort of fear and loathing."

fedora n : *trilby hat*.

feel one's cheerios v : *amped*, feel one's oats (see *Cheerios*).

fender n : *wing*, *mudguard*.

fender bender n : minor car accident, *prang*.

Ferris wheel n : *big wheel*.

fiber sp n : *fibre*.

field n : *pitch*, "*football* field."

fifth (of a *US* gallon) n : bottle of scotch, vodka, rum, etc, about ⅓ *pints* or ¾ litre (see *fluid ounce*), "the cop made him empty his fifth into the gutter."

fifth expr v : see *taking the fifth*.

fig newton n : *fig roll*.

figure v : consider.

fillet /filay/ n : /filit/.

fin n : *$5 bill*.

finger, the finger n : the 'fuck off' gesture made by thrusting out the upturned fist with the middle finger pointing up, syn. the *bird*, the *V*s, "he gets the finger."

fink n v : *creep*, also *sneak*.

fire usage v : to *sack*, *can*.

firecracker n : a firework, esp. the Chinese kinds like strings of small *bangers*.

fire department n : fire service, *fire brigade*.

firefighter n : fireman.

fire truck n : *fire engine*.

first base n : see *base*.

first-degree adj : most serious of crimes, 'first-degree murder.'

first floor cf n : *ground floor*, (US: 1st or ground, 2nd, 3rd, 4th . . . , UK: ground, 1st, 2nd, 3rd . . .).

first name n : *Christian name*, *forename*, see *last name*.

fish sticks n : *fish fingers*.

five expr v : 'take five' = five minute break, 'back in five' = back in five minutes, although cf. *seven*.

five finger discount expr n : in reference to stolen goods, syn. *off the back of a lorry*, "I got these on a five finger discount."

five-o n sl n : police, "look out, five oh!"

five second rule n intj : invocation conferring immunity from germs when eating dropped food item if picked up within specified time period, occasionally heard as ten second rule (drunk version) or other amount. [Coined by Ghengis Khan but with a half-day grace period (reflecting a slower pace of life).]

fix col v : neuter.

fix v : to prepare, "shall I fix rice or potatoes for dinner?" "She's fixing her hair."

flack n : publicist, one who engages in flackery (all slogans and buzzwords).

flake n : *pseud*, *hoser*, unreliable person.

flaky adj : *dodgy*, also (of a person) eccentric,

crazy, peculiar, unstable, unreliable.

flaming adj : impassioned. Flaming *gay* = very overtly *gay*.

flapjack cf n : pancake.

flashlight n : (electric) *torch*.

flatbed n : kind of *truck* with carrying part a flat surface with no sides or enclosure. Also, just the carrying part, that can be hitched up to a *truck* or car.

flat tire (regional) v : treading on someone's heel while they're walking.

flatware n : cutlery, knives forks and spoons.

flip, flip out v : loose control, usu. by throwing a spectacular tantrum, "she just flipped when I told her," also when a person actually suddenly becomes insane, or when an unstable person has an episode, syn. *tweak, lose it, wig out*, go *ballistic*, go *postal*, **throw a wobbly**.

flip off vt : to give the finger, syn. *flash the Vs*.

flip the bird vt : syn. *flash the Vs*, "he flipped me the *bird*."

floor lamp n : *standard lamp*.

floorwalker n : *shop walker*.

flophouse n : *doss house*.

flub v : to fluff, *botch*, bungle.

fluid ounce cf n : 29.6 ml (larger than a *UK* fluid ounce by 1.2 ml), 16 to a *pint*, see table of measures.

flunk v : fail, "I think I flunked that test," "the prof's gonna flunk me."

flutist /flootist/ sp n : /flortist/ *flautist*.

fly adj : intensely *hot*, "she is so fucking fly!"

Flying Elvi n : Elvis-impersonating skydiving team (featured in the movie *Honeymoon in Vegas*).

folks col n : parents, family, "wait till the folks back home here about this."

foo inf intj : versatile word used as everything from metasyntactic variable in computer programming to euph. intj. for fuck (see *phooey*, and the probably related

fubar, and *snafu*).

foot n : the ordinary American foot has been the same (international foot) as the British (used to use) since 1959, an inch of which is exactly 2.54 cm. The *US* survey foot is still used in surveying, and is the one where exactly 39.37 inches are a *metre*. Although the difference is only two parts per million, if you were racing from NYC to LA and based your calculations on the wrong foot, you'd have to get out and push the last 29 feet.

football cf n : American football.

forsythia /forsitheeə/ n : /forsietheeə/.

forty, forty ouncer sl n : a 40 *ounce* screwtop bottle of *beer* (over two *pint*s), handily available at *convenience store*s and popular with underage kids and winos, "a forty in his hand."

four point average n : *4.0 GPA* (the highest theoretically achievable, although with extra credit, some kids have managed 4.2), "she had a four point average all through school."

Fourth of July n : *Independence Day* celebrated nationally as a public *holiday* and with fireworks shows, "what are you doing for the fourth?" see table of American Holidays.

four way stop n : see *4-way stop*.

frat n : fraternity, "frat boy" (member of a fraternity), "that's a frat *bar*."

frat brat sl n : obnoxious *Greek*.

fred (bicycling) sl n : conspicuously overdressed neon pseudo-bicyclist.

freebie n : free item.

freeway n : *motorway*, the *interstate* freeway system started in 1956, see *US highway*.

freight car (railway) n : *goods truck*, *goods van*.

freight hopping v : travelling (*hoboing*) by means of *railroad freight cars*.

French fries n : *fries*.

fresh col adj : syn. *sweet, bitchin', neat, cool, safe, rad, brill.*

freshman n : *fresher*, 1st year (applies to both *high school* and *college*, and to both sexes), see *sophomore, junior, senior.*

freshman 15 expr n : the supposed 15 lbs college *freshmen* put on due to late nights (studying) and dubious eating habits on their first stint away from home.

fries n : *chips*, but thinner and less greasy.

frijoles [Sp] n : beans, usu. seen on a menu where it typically refers to cooked or refried beans.

from hell col expr adj : worst, "this *beer*'s from hell," "I'm now on the mailing list from hell"—Matt Groenig, *Life in Hell.*

from the wrong side of the tracks expr adj : from the *scuzzy* part of town, usu. in reference to an undesirable person, ant. 'from the right side of the tracks.'

front desk (hotel) n : *reception.*

frosh n : freshman.

frosting n : *icing.*

fruit n : *queer*, "do you have any fruit? Just those that walk in."

fruit fly n : *gay*, also fag hag.

fubar [orig military] acr adj : fucked up beyond all recognition.

full professor n : *professor*, "is Professor Jones a full professor?"

fully adv : completely, totally.

fumes expr n : see *running on fumes.*

funch sl n: (pun on *brunch*) contraction of fuck-it lunch, to pop out at lunch time for more than just lunch, cf. *dirty weekend.*

fun house n : *ghost train.*

funnest n : most fun (quite common usage).

funnies col n : the cartoon section of the Sunday paper, "who's stolen the funnies?" "in the Sunday funnies."

futz v : futzing around = *faff*ing around.

— g —

gabfest n : incessant talking session, gossiping, syn. *chinwag*, chinfest, talkfest, bullfest, *bull session, shoot the shit*, see also *rabbit.*

gaijin, gaigin [Japanese *gaíjìn*] /giejeen/ n : foreigner, alien (gaikokujin = foreign people, more polite), syn. *gringo.* (American in Chinese is /may gwo ren/ (beautiful land person), and foreigner in Chinese is /way gukin/ or *wei guo ren* /way gwo ren/ (different land person), in Korean is /way guk salang/, and in Thai is /farang/.)

game usage n : *match.*

gandy dancer n : itinerant labourer, also *railroad* worker.

gangbusters, like gangbusters inf adv : enthusiastically, energetically, quickly, like *billy-oh.*

garage /gərahzh/ n : /gərahj/ /garij/.

garage sale n : *yard sale*, sale of secondhand or used household items from *yard* or driveway (mouth of garage), usu. on weekends, similar in nature to a *car boot sale.*

garbage n : *junk, rubbish.*

garbage bag n : *dustbin bag.*

garbage can n : *dustbin.*

garbage dump n : *rubbish tip.*

garbage man n : *dustbin man.*

garbage truck n : *dustbin lorry.*

garbanzo n : *chickpea.*

garden cf n : flower bed, or vegetable patch.

garter belt n : *suspenders, suspender belt.*

garters n : *suspenders, sock suspenders.*

gas, gasoline n : *petrol, petroleum.*

gas station n : *petrol station, garage.*

gated community n : a street with restricted access via locked gates, often taken as a slight on the rest of the neighborhood rather than protection from it. "makes it possible for us to step outside our internal gated communities."

gator abbr n : alligator.

gay n : cf. *queer*, syn. fairy, *fag*, *troll*, *fruit*, *gay*.

gaydar n : ability to detect *gays*.

G-dog /jee dahg/ (term of address) n : friend, *mate*, "Hey g-dog, good to see ya."

gearhead inf n : *nerd*, person preoccupied with the technology, e.g. in bicycling, a cyclist exclusively interested in his equipment rather than the *countryside* he's cycling through, see *–head*, *fred*.

gearshift n : gear lever, *gear stick*.

GED abbr n : General Education Diploma, a lesser alt. to graduating from *high school*, though the GED is usu. taken by kids who'd dropped out of *high school* but wish to have at least its equivalent for employment purposes, or wish to continue their education at *community colleges* and universities, where it would be required.

geek [person who bites heads off chickens in a carnival side show] n : *nerd*, characterised by obsessive involvement (and usu. considerable expertise) in some field and a deficiency in social skills from which the concentration on the specified field serves as a shield, 'out of step with' normal people.

generator (car) n : *dynamo*.

gerbille sp n : var. of gerbil.

German shepherd (dog) n : *Alsatian*.

gerrymandering v : creatively changing the *electoral* district boundaries for political purposes, "Clinton's proposal to use statistics to extrapolate the census is a clever attempt at gerrymandering."

get off v : have a good time, get high, also to have *sex*.

get real col imp v : be realistic.

get sick v : throw up.

get the short end of the stick expr v : to get the worse part of a deal, or be in the less favourable situation.

get your ass in gear expr v : get going, get moving, *get cracking*.

ghetto bird col n : police helicopter.

gift basket n : open basket of luxury food, like a *hamper*.

gift certificate n : *gift voucher*.

GI Joe (GI = soldier) n : sort of military equivalent of *John Q. Public*, and now the name of a doll.

Gila monster /heelə mahnstə/ [their habitat around Gila river by Gila /heelə/ AZ] n : the orange and black Gila monster *Heloderma suspectum*, the largest US lizard (up to 20"), and its only relative, the Mexican *H. horridum*, the beaded lizard (up to 35"), are the world's only venomous lizards.

gimp n : lame person.

Girl Scout n : *Guide*, *Girl Guide*.

Girl Scout cookies n : national cookie drive by the girls, held every *Autumn*, to help fund the organisation.

gism /jizm/ alt sp n : *jism*.

give me a break expr v : *leave off*. It can be used as 'don't try and pull that on me,' or 'give me a chance.'

given name n : *Christian name*.

giving the bird gesture v : syn. *flip*, *flip off*, *flipping the bird*, see *finger*.

gizmo n : complicated or obscure device, syn. *widget*.

glom v : to stick to like a big lump of snot.

gnar /nah/ abbr adj : *gnarly*.

gnarly /nahlee/ adj : unpleasant, syn. *bogus*, *gross*, but also of something imposing a great challenge, "gnarly waves, *dude!*"

gobbledygook n : *double Dutch*.

gofer [go for] n : *tea boy*, general errand boy, *dogsbody*.

go figure (usu at some slightly perplexing

situation) expr v : how about that, whaddya know.

going down col vi : to happen, usu. of something dramatic, "something's going down. I saw a *bunch* of *fire trucks* and cop cars," "it's going down on 4th street" (of a raging party).

goldbrick n : *skiver*, lazy person.

gol dang it euph intj : quaint regionalism, syn. *darn*.

gold dollar n : golden *dollar* coins (1849–1889).

goob (Southern) n : syn. *loogie*.

goober [Kongo *nguba*] col n : peanut, also *Southerner*.

good usage adv : authentic, also well, "he did good," "looking good."

good-driver discount n : *no claims bonus*.

good enough for government work expr n : barely adequate, said with overtones of that's all the job (or boss) deserves, or (smugly) that's what I can get away with.

goodies n : tasty foods or *sweets*, choice little gifts.

Good Neighbors (TV show) n : The *Good Life*.

good ol' boy sl n : easygoing, bluff, *Southern* guy, high on loyalty (to family, friends, church, business, politics) and influence in the community, low on smarts, tolerance, imagination.

goof v : err.

goofball col n : drugs or medication, esp. pill form, esp. with strong side effects, "he's all *hopped-up* on goof balls," also *goofy* or clowning person.

goof off n v: *skiver*, to *skive*.

goofy adj : silly or ridiculous.

gook derog n : person from Far East or Orient.

gook n : yucky stuff, "the alien retires to feed and create its slimy gook."

goon n : thug.

goose v : to poke the *butt*.

goose bumps n : *goose pimples*.

gopher n : rabbit-sized burrowing rodent found all over US, also some kinds of ground squirrels in the prairies (see G*reat Plains*), also *gofer*.

got usage v : have, 'why does porn got to hurt so bad?' 'you've got mail.'

gotcha n intj : unsuspecting event, such as getting a *splinter*, a *pratfall*, or getting caught on something, see *Doris trap*, also upon catching someone red-handed.

gotten v : got (pp. of get), "my driving's gotten better." (UK remnants: begotten, forgotten, gotten up, ill-gotten gains, misbegotten, and unbegotten.)

governor n : governs the state, as the *president* governs the country. See *congresscritter, legislature*.

GPA abbr n : grade point average, a scale from 0–4, given up to one decimal place, "I have about a 3.5," see *four point average*.

grab n : get, "Grab a sweater. It's cold outside," "let's grab a *sandwich* before we go," or have, "could I grab one?"

grade (road) n v : used like slope as in 'steep grade' or 'grade the road' meaning to level the road, hence grader–the scraping machine used to level or smooth road surfaces under *construction*.

grade (school) n : *class, form* (see *elementary school, middle school, high school, K-12*). To figure the age, think grade + 6, for instance a fourth grader is usu. about 10, see *K-*.

grade crossing (railway) n : *level crossing*.

grades (school) n : *marks*, "she got good grades all through high school," see *GPA*.

grade school n : in particular, *primary school* or *elementary school*, in general, *K thru 12* as opposed to university or college.

graduate n : usu. specified, *high school*

graduate, college graduate (=*postgraduate*) (*BS* or BA).

graduate degree n : *postgraduate degree* (masters or PhD).

graduate school n : department for grad students (studying for masters or PhD).

Graham Crackers® /gram/ n : these are like a semi-sweet *biscuit*, similar in texture to a light *digestive biscuit*, and eaten as is, and also often crushed to make a pie crust.

grand cf sl n : *$1000*.

granola n : like *muesli*, but typically toasted and crunchy.

granola col n : stereotypical environmentally conscious, *granola*-eating (health conscious), hemp clothes/tie-dye wearing, ex-hippie/yuppie, "lota granolas in Oregon." Maybe a *West Coast* term, see *crunchie*, *muesli*, and also *anorak*.

granola bar n : *energy bar*.

grape jelly n : *jam*, very popular with children, often the kind found in *pbj* sandwiches. In the US grape occupies the same culinary niche as *blackcurrant* in Europe (grape jelly, grape juice, *soda* and *candy* flavour).

graveyard shift n : night shift, "I work three graveyards this week."

gray sp adj : *grey*.

Gray Lady n : *New York Times* (because until recent decades no pictures appeared on the front page, and certainly not in *colour*).

GRE abbr n : Graduate Record Exam, a half-day test of verbal, mathematical, and analytical skills, required for entrance into graduate programs at most colleges.

greasy spoon n : low quality *café*.

Great Plains n : prairie lands between the Rockies and the Missouri River from ND to TX.

Greek n : member of university sorority or fraternity, which are named using two or three Greek letters, such as the fraternity Phi Alpha Tau ΦAT or Delta Tau Delta ΔTΔ, or the sorority Kappa Alpha Theta KAΘ or Tri-Delts ΔΔΔ (there are over a thousand combinations in use). Rampant parodies include: eta bita pi HBπ, tappa kegga brew, I felta thigh, and of course ΦYK.

greenback n : a dollar bill, or US paper money in general.

green beans n : *French beans*.

green card n : [Alien Registration Receipt Card, credit card-sized, originally green] allows recipient to live and work in the US, "I'm a resident *alien*."

green onion n : *spring onion*.

green plum n : *greengage*.

green thumb n : *green fingers*.

grifter n : swindler; to shopgrift–to return used item for full refund.

grilled cheese sandwich n : a greasy cheese *sandwich* grilled till the cheese melts.

grinder n : *submarine sandwich*.

gringo [Mexican] /gringoh/ n : foreigner, often used disparagingly, syn. *gaijin*.

grip n : suitcase, or other travelling bag.

grits n : coarse-ground *maize*, and the *porridge*-like dish made from it, see *hominy* grits and *cornstarch*.

grody adj : unpleasant, syn. *gross*, *gnarly*, *grotty*.

grok [*Stranger in a Strange Land*—Robert Heinlein] vi : to intuitively understand completely and naturally, be soaked in meaning, to wrap your mind around.

gross adj : unpleasant.

grossening col v : to make unpleasant.

gross out v : to disgust.

ground (electrical) n : *earth*, 'ground wire,' 'ground fault interruptor.'

ground vt : to punish kids by confining them to the house, "you're grounded for the weekend," "Harry Potter was grounded for life!"

ground cloth n : *groundsheet*.
grounded (electric current) v : *earthed*.
groundhog n : *woodchuck*, a kind of marmot found in *northeast*ern US.
Groundhog Day n : February 2nd. If the groundhog sees his shadow on this morning he is scared back into hibernation, indicating six more weeks of winter, but if it's cloudy, hence no shadow, it indicates an early spring. [This myth perpetrated by Clymer Freas on February 2nd 1886–actually they're out *scop*ing for *chicks*.] Several localities have official groundhogs–the most famous being Punxsutawney Phil–whose 'predictions' are reported in the news media. (There's an ancient superstition in *East Anglia* (probably deriving from a similar Roman moonlight event), that if a *hedgehog* awakes on Candlemas (Sunday closest to February 4th) and sees the sun, it'll be a long cold winter. Since East Anglians were some of the main emigrants to *New England*, the tradition of Groundhog Day may have transferred from that.)
grunge n : style of generation Xers, which tends to look like a young clean *transient* with freshly laundered clothes, but the holes still in the knees of the (sometimes baggy) jeans. Follow the *skater* thread.
guacamole /gwahkəmolee/ n : *dip* made from mashed avocado plus one or more of diced onions, *jalapeños*, garlic, tomatoes, and seasonings.
gubernatorial adj : of a *governor*.
guess expr v : as in 'I guess' = I suppose.
gulch n : *gully*, ravine, esp. with (seasonal) torrent.
Gulf Coast n : the coastal region of the *Gulf States*.
Gulf States n : the states along the Gulf of Mexico TX, LA, MS, AL, FL.
gully n : ditch, but esp. caused by water erosion, syn. *gulch*, wadi.

gully washer [S, cowboy term] n : hard rain, esp. sudden as would cause a flash flood.
gumbo [Afr] n : stew thickened with *okra*, also *okra*. See also *jambalaya*.
gummy/i bears n : like *jelly babies* but in the shape of little teddy bears, also generic round ones called gummy candy roll, and here and there gummi frogs, fish, worms, octopi, salamanders, and dinosaurs.
Gunks n : the Shawangunks cliffs in NY, 90 miles north of Manhattan, which is a popular climbing spot and includes some hard climbs.
gurney n : *trolley*, wheeled stretcher.
the gut n : the main *drag* through town where *high school* boys drive their hot rods on a Saturday night, cruisin' for *babes*.
gut course (university) n : an easy course, *blow-off*, "that's a gut course, it's a *no-brainer*."
guy expr n : *bloke*. By itself, neutral, but in expressions such as 'some guy,' '*neat guy*' positive. Guys can refer to a group of people regardless of gender. Also term of address, "Hi guy."
gyp v : cheat.

– h –

haberdashery cf n : men's clothing.
hacienda [Sp] n : usu. refers to a spacious single-*storey* Spanish style house that would otherwise be the main dwelling of a hacienda or estate (often a plantation).
hack n : hacker, person who works on something with compulsive dedication, such as a hardware hack. Also a prank, particularly the more sophisticated and elegant.
hack v : to explore and create with exhaustive diligence (usu. something related to computers, but could be anything).

hairpin corner, hairpin turn n : *hairpin bend*.

hair spray n : *hair lacquer*.

half and half n : milk and cream, available in cartons just like the normal milk, and the milk of choice for adding to *coffee*.

half dollar n : cupro-nickel coin occasionally found in one's change, the size of a thick *old penny* with Kennedy (35th president) on front (since 1964, see *50¢*) and the Great Seal on back.

half eagle n : *$5* gold coin (1795–1929).

hamburger, hamburger meat n : *minced meat*, and all the connotations, "after the fall my thigh looked like hamburger meat."

hamper cf n : *laundry* basket.

hand truck n : *barrow, sack barrow*.

hang v : hang around, *hang out*, "I'm hanging with him," "They're *wannabees*, 'cos they can't hang with the big dogs."

hang v : to do, "we're lost, better hang a *u-ee*," "hang a left turn," see also *pull*.

hang in there (also *hang tough*) expr v : stick it out, (keep a stiff upper lip).

hang out v : to idle, *visit*, do nothing in particular.

hang out a shingle v : proclaim a new business (as if written on a wooden shingle).

hang ten v : relax, *chill*.

hanky-panky cf n : *jiggery-pokery*.

happy camper expr n : satisfied or engaged person in some situation, "apart from Joe, they're all happy campers."

hard candy n : *boiled sweets*.

hard hat n : provocative hat worn on *building site*s. (Oh! protective hat . . .) Sign at entrance to *building site*s, 'Hard Hat Area.'

hardware store n : *ironmonger*.

Harry Potter and the Sorcerer's Stone n : *Harry Potter and the Philosopher's Stone*.

harsh adj v : *gnarly*, ruin, 'harsh my mellow,' 'harsh my boner' = to irritate, upset, get on my nerves, "*Chill, dude!* You're harshing my buzz."

hash browns n : fried grated potato.

hasta /asta/ expr intj : bye, see you later.

hasta la vista [Spanish bye, until I see you] expr intj : bye, see you later.

haul ass expr v : to go all out.

haulers (trucking) n : *hauliers*.

have a cow expr v : incensed, *unhinged* state caused by undue provocation, "Don't have a cow, man"—Bart Simpson to his exasperated dad.

Hawkeye n : person from Iowa.

haze v : disconcert or bully, esp. of a *freshman*.

hazing n : strongly deprecated *high school* and college fraternity initiation rituals.

head, usu **the head** n : urinal, toilet.

headcheese n : *brawn*, pork luncheon meat (made from head, feet, heart, tongue).

headcheese sl n : *cock cheese, knob cheese*.

head fake [*football*] n : trick, (when a running back looks one way while the real move is the other).

head honcho n : *honcho*.

heads up expr n imp : notice, alert, "thanks for the heads up," syn. *shout*.

hecka [heck of a, see -*a*] col adv : very, really, "he's hecka fine!"

heinous usage adj : of a *gross* situation, dreadful, another word reinvigorated by *Bill & Ted's Excellent Adventure*, along with upstanding, triumphant, *bogus*, *bodacious*, awesome, and of course most *excellent*.

hella [hell of a, see -*a*, considered the slang or vulgar version of hecka] col adv : very, really, syn. *hecka* "he's hella fine!"

herb /erb/ /herb/ n : /herb/, "an herbal beverage" (Americans pr. the h as in heir, honour and honest. See also *homage*), also syn. of pot.

Herb /herb/ n : stereotype–overweight middle aged guy bereft of style (apart from his Gaucho's). See *rube*, *Herbert*.

hero sandwich n : French loaf *sandwich* buttered with *mustard* and *mayo* and generously filled with cold cuts, cheese, lettuce, onion, tomato and *pickles*.

hi intj : hello, hiya.

hick n : *yokel*.

hickey n : *love bite*.

hickory n : native N. American nut bearing tree (along with pecan in the *south*) of the genus *Carya*, related to walnut.

highball (drink) n : spirits and soda.

highball (train) n : full speed ahead signal.

highballing v : moving fast.

high school n : grades 9–12 (ages about 15–18), see also *senior high*.

high school diploma n : *high school* graduating certificate, which can be obtained as soon as enough *credits* are accumulated. *High school* dropouts are those that leave without graduating, see *GED*, *K12*.

high-tail (out) v : *scarper*.

highway n : main road, like an *A-road*, can refer to *freeway*, see *route*.

hike (salary) v : *boost*, *rise*.

hillbilly n : *yokel*, *backwoods* person.

hire cf v n : employ (someone), "where's the new hire."

hired hand n : help, esp. on farm or ranch.

history adj : absent, gone, also as good as dead, *toast*. "I'm history," depending on context, means I'm leaving (see *outahere*) or I'm done for.

hither and yon expr n : *hither and thither*.

hit on v : *chat up*.

hit the wall (running) n : run out of steam during a run, such as at mile 20 in a marathon.

HMO [Health Maintenance Organization] abbr n : kind of health insurance— basically your doctor is your 'primary care provider' and insurance is only pro-vided for services by other specialists if he/she refers you. See *PPO*.

ho [whore] /hoh/ n : slut, "don't be callin' me no ho!"

hoagie, hoagy n : *hero sandwich*.

hobo n : *tramp*.

hoboing v : living the life of a *tramp*, which traditionally may include *freight hopping*.

hockey cf n : ice hockey.

hodad n : hand mattock used for *dibbing* seedling trees.

hodad n : pseudo-surfer.

hodag n : *Bovinus spiritualis* a clawed, grinning ox-like creature with speared tail and squarrose ridgeback, thought to be confined to Wisconsin, though cave sightings of similar but much smaller creatures have been reported in eastern parts of the US, cf. jackalope, squonk.

hodgepodge n : *hotchpotch*.

hoedown n : square-dance, esp. rowdy, and of such parties in general.

hogwash n : *codswallop*, twaddle.

ho-hum adj : dreary.

hokey adj : cheap and nasty.

hold v : exclude, hold the *mayo* = no mayonnaise.

holiday (see table of American Holidays) n : There are 8 national holidays, which are observed by the whole country (New Year's Day, Memorial Day, *Independence Day*, Labor Day, Columbus Day, Veteran's Day, *Thanksgiving*, and Christmas). Federal holidays are holidays observed by federal workers, which include the national holidays, Martin Luther King, Jr.'s birthday and President's Day. A *legal holiday* is one established by law, which may be confined to an area such as a state, or in the case of all the above, nationally.

holler n vi : yell or cry out, "you should have heard him holler!"

Holstein [area in NW Germany] n : the black and white patterned *Friesian* cows.

homage /ahmij/ /hahmij/ n : /homij/ (see also *herb*).

hombre [Sp man] /ahmbray/ n : big guy, *dude*.

home boy n : fellow gang member.

homely cf adj : (of a woman) plain, and euph. for ugly, unattractive.

home slice [black col] n : girlfriend or close female friend.

homie [black col] n : boyfriend or close male friend, "homie G" [G from gangster].

hominy, **hominy grits** n : *grits* (hominy is *corn* treated, usu. by soaking in *lye*, to remove hulls, resulting in a bleached, tasteless, and sterile (good for storage) grits).

honcho [Japanese *han-cho* squad leader] n : boss, syn. *gaffer*.

honk v : throw up.

honky n : white man, white person, syn. *white trash*.

hooch [from the Hoochinoo tribe noted for its homemade liquor] col n : *moonshine*, illicit or low grade *liquor*, syn. *poteen*, white lightning, white mule.

hoochie-coochie adj : alt. sp. of *hootchy-cootchy*.

hoochie mamma n : promiscuous young woman.

hood n : *bonnet*. (see also *under the hood*.)

hooker n : whore, *scrubber*.

hook up v : get laid, "college kids don't *date* anymore. They hook up or *hang out*."

hooky (usu 'to play hooky,' also **hookey**) cf v : *truant*.

Hoosier /hoozhə/ n : person from Indiana. [One derivation is 'who's there?'—James Witcomb Riley, Hoosier poet, and used in the story Little Orphan Annie. Another story–during many a bar room brawl an ear would get bitten off (in Mike Tyson-esque style) and people would ask, "Whose ear?"]

hootch col n : alt. sp. of hooch.

hootchy-cootchy adj : relating to sensual or sexy activities [from name of erotic dance].

hootchy mamma n : alt. sp. of *hoochie mamma*.

hooters n : big tits.

hope chest n : bottom drawer.

hopped-up adj : drugged up, under the influence of narcotics (usu. referring to medication rather than recreational type drugs), also *amped*.

horny adj : *randy*.

horse n : see *a horse a piece*.

horse apples joc n : horse droppings.

horse opera (film) n : western.

horse pucky joc euph n : horseshit (as in nonsense). See *bull honky*.

hose v : to fuck, in all of its senses, but not an offensive word, "I was *hosed*" (cheated), "I wouldn't mind hosing her garden down."

hose bag v : cheat, swindle.

hosed adj : useless, *naff*, bogus, screwed, destroyed, "my hard drive is hosed," also *drunk* or stoned.

hose head n : hollow headed person.

hoser n : syn. clown, *creep*, *bender* "hoser from the *north 40s*, eh?"—Bob and Doug McKenzie (Rick Moranis & Dave Thomas), *Strange Brew*.

hostess (restaurant) n : girl or women who seats you.

hot adj : very sexy.

hot dog bun n : *bridge roll*.

hot tea n : usu. sweetened and taken with a slice of lemon (no milk), syn regular tea (NY).

hottie [noun form of *hot*] n : attractive person, *babe*, "he's a hottie."

the House n : the *House of Representatives*.

housebreak v : *house-train*, potty train.

House majority/minority leader n : see *majority leader*.

House of Representatives n : The House now comprises 435 seats representing the states by population. See *Congress*.

housing project n : low-income housing, *council estate*.

howdy intj : how are you?

howdy doody joc intj : *howdy*, but equivalent to, and probably making fun of 'how do you do.' Howdy Doody was also a popular children's *TV* show, 1949–1960, featuring the namesake marionette, and starting with a chorus of kids yelling "It's Howdy Doody time!"

huck col v : to toss, lob, *bung*, but skiers and snowboarders huck cliffs by skiing off them and doing zero or more tricks, twists, and flips before landing.

huckleberry n : *Gaylussacia* and its edible berries, and also another name for blueberries, (also in Britain another name for whortleberries, see *bilberry*).

huckster n : foister of *junk* with hard sell, syn. *spiv*.

huffing col v : glue sniffing, actually sniffing anything to get high, "have you tried huffing highlighters or markers?"

huffy adj : *shirty*.

huh? intj : syn. 'I beg your pardon?' what?

human resources [PC euph. for manpower] n : personnel.

hump v : *screw*.

hunk n : gorgeous man, syn. stud.

hunker down v : squat down, keep a low profile.

hunyack (cowboy term) sl n : the ring of hair around the *butthole*.

hush puppies n : deep-fried corn balls (cornmeal-egg dough), often also includes onions.

hustler n : person on the make.

hutch n : *Welsh dresser*.

hype n : sales talk.

hyped adj : excited, syn. *amped*.

I abbr n : *interstate*, e.g. I-5 is *interstate* 5, the main freeway up the west coast from Mexico to Canada.

ice box n : fridge.

iceberg lettuce n : *Wee's lettuce*.

ice cream cone n : *cornet*, ice cream.

iced tea n : tea served over ice (no milk); see also *hot tea*, *sweet tea*.

icky adj : distasteful, nasty, (*gross* and sticky).

ID /ie dee/ n v : identification, often being the *driver's license*, which includes a picture and state of residence, though generally anything similar, esp. with a picture (passport, student ID card, birth certificate), "I need to see a piece of ID," "you need two *picture IDs* to get in here," "Can anyone ID the author for me?"

idiot cf n : syn. *bozo, nebbish, stoopid, ding-a-ling, tard, retard, dork, nerd, dingbat, dumb*, see *short bus*.

impatience n : *busy Lizzie, Impatiens*.

in back of prep : behind, "the *dumpster*'s in back of the *store*," 'in back of beyond' = way out in the *tules*.

inc abbr adj : incorporated, syn. *Ltd*.

incorporated n : *limited company*.

Independence Day n : *Fourth of July*.

Indian burn n : *Chinese burn*.

indict /indiet/ (law) v : officially charge with a crime.

inexpensive adj : euph for *cheap*, or costing just the arm and leg below the knee.

information (telephone) n : now officially *directory assistance*, **directory inquiries**, dial 1 <*area code*> *555–1212*, "call information," "I woke up this morning and couldn't find my socks, so I called information. She said they were behind the *couch*. She was right."—Steve Wright.

in heat v : *on heat*.

innie n : indented belly button, see *outie*.

inquire usage sp v : *enquire*.
inseam (clothing) n : *inside leg*. (See *outseam*.)
inside lane cf n : *outside lane*.
installment plan n : *hire purchase*.
intermission n : *interval*.
intern n v : student or *graduate* working to receive training or practical experience (in industry, hospital, *White House*, etc).
intersection (road) n : *junction*, crossroads.
interstate n : national *freeway* system. North/south roads numbered oddly, I-5 (west coast) to I-97 (east coast), east/west numbered evenly, I-4 (south) to I-96 (north), with I-5, 10, 15, 20 . . . being transnational. Three-numbered *freeways* end in a *city* (start with odd number, e.g. I-580 ends in the *Bay Area*) or go through or around a *city* (start with even number, e.g. the San Diego Freeway I-405 goes through and around *LA*).
in the ballpark col expr adj : acceptably close enough, "well, it's not the right answer but it's in the *ballpark*."
in the cards expr n : *on the cards*.
in the catbird seat expr n : exultant, on top of the world.
in the doghouse expr n : in trouble, usu. with wife or girlfriend.
IRA /eirah/ [financial] cf n : individual retirement account, a popular retirement savings plan. (Ira is also a person's name.)
IRS abbr n : Internal Revenue Service, equivalent to the Inland Revenue. See also *1040*.
Ivy League adj n : relating to scholastically and socially prestigious eastern *US* universities. (The eight Ivy League colleges are Brown, Columbia, Cornell, Dartmouth, Harvard, Pennsylvania, Princeton, and Yale, which originally formed a league in the 1940s to play intercollegiate *football*, and also consistently represent top US colleges. Other top state schools include UC Berkeley, UCLA, Virginia, North Carolina, Michigan, and Illinois, and top private schools include MIT, Johns Hopkins, Northwestern, Duke, Rice, Caltech, Carnegie Mellon, and Stanford). See also **redbrick**, *Seven Sisters*, **Oxbridge**.

– J –

jack euph n : *Jack Shit*, "he don't know Jack," "I know Jack about . . . ."
jackalope n : *Lepus Anteoculae* cross between a jackrabbit and (pronghorn) antelope, ranging in size from a bunny to a horse, very shy in its native habitat—western plains and deserts–but well represented on postcards in *tacky* tourist shops (and occasional trophy mounts), cf. *bigfoot*, bunyip, *champ*, *Jersey Devil*, *hodag*, *sasquatch*, *shagamaw*, *snipe hunt*, *squonk*.
jackhammer n : *pneumatic drill*.
jack Mormon n : backsliding Mormon, a sheep who has strayed from the flock, less divinity but still ovinity.
jack off v n : masturbate, syn. *wank*, *toss*, also a *wanker*, syn. *jerk off*, snap the radish.
jack shit expr n : nothing, syn. *sweet FA*, "he don't know Jack Shit."
jack-tar n : sailor.
jail n : *gaol*.
jalapeño /haləpenyoh/ n : a kind of chili pepper, very popular in many Mexican dishes, and ranging from mild to damn hot.
jam v : to take off in a big hurry, "gotta jam," also to flow smoothly in a situation, "she's jammin," syn. *cruise*.
jambalaya [Fr] n : rice dish made with heavily seasoned meat or seafood, and a

notable element of Louisiana cooking and culture.

Jane Doe n : female *John Doe*.

janfu acr n : joint army and navy fuckup, see also *fubar*.

janitor usage n : *caretaker*.

jarhead sl n : marine.

Jayhawker n : person from Kansas.

jazzed adj : excited.

jello (Jell-O®) n : jelly. The common spelling is jello, but formally it's Jell-O.

jello shooters n : *slimers*.

jelly n : *jam*.

jelly roll n : swiss roll.

jerk n : *wanker*, *git*.

jerk off n : *jerk*.

jerk off v : masturbate, *wank*.

jerkwater adj : an insignificant or small town, usu. referred to as in, "they came from some jerkwater town," see *boondocks*.

jerky [Quechua] n : dried strips of meat, eaten as a snack, *beef jerky*.

jerry-rig v : creation of a slapdash construction (as opposed to a temporary construction as in *jury-rig*), although they're probably used synonymously without awareness of the nuance.

Jersey Devil n : a fierce, horned dragon-like creature that's been plaguing the Pine Barrens of New Jersey for several centuries, with sightings augmented by strange (two-legged) tracks in the snow, angry part-human cry, and crack of leathery wings, cf. *jackalope*, *squonk*.

jibbers, **jibonks** [from bonking off *kerb*s, etc.] col n : older *skater*'s term for the new breed of *skaters*.

jicama /hikəmə/ [Sp] n : white sweet salad vegetable (root) crisp like a radish.

jimmies (confection) n : rod-shaped *hundreds and thousands*, either chocolate or multi-coloured, syn. *sprinkles*.

jimmy (short crowbar) n, vt : *jemmy*.

jinx intj : announced when two people say the same thing simultaneously, (in some versions the person to first say jinx declares a forfeit), see *snap*.

jism (jizm, *gism*, and many other homophonous spellings) n : semen, syn. *wad*, *spunk*, *spooge*, *load*.

jobby col n : thing, *wotsit*, "what are those jobbies for?"

jock n : athlete, also proficient specialist, as in computer jock.

joe n : coffee, "let's go *grab* a cuppa joe."

Joe Blow n : *Fred Bloggs*, syn. *John Doe*.

Joe Schmo sl n : nobody, *loser*, *schmo*.

john usu **the john** n : men's toilet, *lavatory*, syn. *loo*, can.

john sl n : *punter* (male client of a prostitute).

John Doe n : name, like *John Smith*, assigned to an unknown person, such as a corpse or amnesiac, syn., *Fred Bloggs*, *Joe Blow*, *John Q. Public*.

John Hancock n : signature, "put your John Hancock here."

John Q. Public n : used often as 'your name here' in *ads* for, say, credit cards: John Q. Public, 123 Main Street, Anytown USA; and hence used as: man in the street, silent majority, unwashed masses, *man on the Clapham bus*, syn. *Joe Blow*, *Fred Bloggs*.

Johnson sl n : *John Thomas*.

joint cf n : joints in the *US* are usu. made with straight marijuana, and usu. rolled with one cigarette paper, although pipes seem the mode of choice, and *bongs* where convenient.

jollies n : kicks, good time, whatever gets you off.

jones sl v : crave, "jonesing after women," "here's the stuff that feeds my jones," "he's got a bad jones" (=serious addiction).

journal usage n : personal notebook, *diary*.

jugs sl n : large tits.

juicy boy n : beyond *hot dude*.

July 4th n : *Independence Day*, see *Fourth of July*.

jumper cf n : *pinafore* or dress worn over blouse.

jumper cables n : *jump leads*.

jump rope n : *skipping rope*.

jump the shark expr v : an event (during some project) after which everything seems to go downhill [Fonzie jumps the shark on water skis on *TV* show *Happy Days* (1974–1984) after which the show was deemed to degenerate].

junior n : 3rd year, or second-to-last year in case of two- or three-year programs, see *freshman*, *sophomore*, *senior*.

junior college n : see *community college*.

junior high n : junior *high school*, grades 7–9 (see *senior high*, *middle school*).

junk man n : *rag and bone man*. Fred Sanford, the most famous US junk man, from the TV show *Sanford and Son*, based on Steptoe and Son.

jury-rig v : to build a makeshift construction, *jerry-rig*.

juvy n : *juvenile hall*.

juvenile hall n : youth detention centre, *Borstal*.

– k –

K- n : designating 'kindergarten *through*,' such as K-5 (kindergarten *thru* 5th grade, representing *elementary school*).

K12, **K-12**, **K thru 12** n : US range of education, grades K (kindergarten starting at about age 5) and 1 to 12 (ending at about age 18), compulsory until about grade 10.

Kamikaze Club n : a club of owners of very high performance cars, such as Lamborghinis, and typically extremely expensive (a tune up could cost $125,000). *CHP* equipped themselves with souped-up Mustangs in order to be able to pursue them.

keener (Can) sl n : very eager, enthusiastic person, sometimes obviously trying to get into someone else's good books, syn. *brown-noser*, suck-up, bootlicker.

keep you posted expr v : keep you informed (of progress).

keister sl n : *butt*.

Ken n : *Barbie*'s boyfriend.

Kentucky Derby n : 'the run for the roses,' **the** annual horse race in Kentucky, first Saturday in May, syn. *Derby*.

kerosene n : *paraffin*.

ketchup n : tomato ketchup.

kewl sp adj : *cool* spelling of *cool*, which also highlights the pronunciation when used as an intj. indicating something particularly *cool*.

Key lime n : a tropical lime grown in the Florida Keys, like the Mexican lime as used in bars (as distinct from the subtropical Bearss or Persian lime, which is larger, juicier, and less tart).

Key lime pie n : like a lime flavoured lemon meringue pie, the filling (*custard*) being green instead of yellow.

kick-ass expr adj : powerful, "that's one kick-ass car," "that's a kick-ass tape," "your kick-assin'est CD."

kick back adj v : relaxed, relax, mellow, "he's a kick-back kind of guy," "I'm just kicking back."

killer adj : syn. *totally awesome*.

Kilroy n : the 'Kilroy was here' slogan adopted the *Mr Chad* graphic.

kind /kien/ [surfing jargon] adj : quintessential, usu. applied to surfing conditions, "kind *buds*," "you'll need kind veggie burritos."

kine /kien/ adj : see *kind*.

king n : 'The King' is Elvis Presley (1935–1977), "Frank is my Elvis"—Matt Groening.

kissling (Pennsylvania) col v : freezing rain (cf. *siling*).

kitty corner adj : *catty corner*, diagonally opposite.

kiwi fruit, kiwi n : *Chinese gooseberry*.

kludge cf sp n : alt. sp. of *kluge*.

kluge (though often *kludge*) /klooj/ n v : /kluhj/ *bodge*, *lash-up*, though normally one that works well; typically applied to hardware and software fixes that, though a bit *Heath-Robinson*, elegantly solve the immediate problem.

klutz [Yiddish] n : clumsy person, syn. *cack-handed* person.

knickers cf n : knickerbockers, *plus-fours*.

knock up cf sl v : to make pregnant.

kook inf n : eccentric.

kumquat n : citrus fruit like an ovoid miniature orange, the inside is tart like a lemon and the rind is sweet.

kvetch [Yiddish] n v : bitch, *whinge*.

– I –

L n : the Chicago 'L' (Chicago Elevated) *subway* (much of it is on trestles in the city), "get on the 'L.'"

LA /el ay/ abbr n : Los Angeles [El Pueblo de Nuestra Senora la Reina de Los Angeles de Porciúncula], "LA sucks. I love it." (LA—six suburbs in search of a city—Clive James.) LA is also the abbr. for Louisiana, and does cause confusion.

ladies' room n : *ladies*.

ladybug n : *ladybird*.

lagniappe /lanyap/ [Quechua] [LA & MS] n : something extra (gift, pleasant surprise).

laid back adj : mellow, *kick-back*, very relaxed.

La Jolla /la hoya/ n : town near San Diego, known for its famous theatre.

la la land n : Los Angeles.

lame sl adj : syn. *bogus*.

lame duck n : a politician who is still in office but whose replacement has been elected already. (Many elective political offices in the US do not actually change hands for many weeks after *Election Day*. The new *president* is not inaugurated until 20th January, for instance, and until the 1930s the date was 4th March.)

landscaping v : general *garden* maintenance, by professional landscapers, as well as the setting up and maintenance of the grounds around large commercial businesses.

last name n : *surname*, see *first name*.

Las Vegas [Sp the meadows] n : [The entertainment and gaming capital of the world] A phenomenon well worth visiting to experience world-class *cheese*. Europeans that dislike America feel the same as Americans that dislike Las Vegas. The city, built around an oasis in the deserts of Nevada, famous for its connection with the mob, gambling, prostitution, and shows, is now also a popular place for conventions. Every new hotel is built to out-rival the last; castles, pyramids, volcanoes, better than the real thing; inside amusement parks, inter-hotel monorails, and a vast acreage of slot machines in each *lobby*. See The *Strip*.

later [contr 'see you later'] intj : bye, syn. *tata*, *outahere*, *adios*, *seeya*.

latex paint n : *emulsion paint*.

laundromat n : *laundrette*, *launderette*.

laundry usage n : *washing*, "I have to do the laundry."

lawyer n : *solicitor*, syn. *attorney*.

LAX /el ay eks/ abbr n : Los Angeles airport (from its airport code).

lay down rubber v : to take off (to go somewhere) extremely rapidly, syn, *scorch*.

lazy boy (La-Z-Boy™) n : easy chair usu. with foot rest that rises from base as back is pushed back, syn. *recliner*, Barkalounger.

lazy Susan n : circular tray on bearings used in dining (popular in Chinese restaurants), sometimes two-tiered, used in kitchen cupboards.

learning curve n : referring to the ease or difficulty of acquiring a new skill, "that [computer] language has a steep learning curve," "her learning curve is fractal."

lease v : *let* or *rent*, usu. contracted for a specified period.

left field expr adj : see *out of left field*.

legal n : paper size (8½ x 14"), see also *letter*.

legal holiday n : *bank holiday*.

legal pad n : pad of ruled *legal* paper, usu. yellow.

legislature n : the federal legislature is administered by *Congress*. Most state legislatures have the same form as the federal government, with a state *House of Representatives* and a state *Senate*, but the term *Congress* is reserved for the federal legislature, and instead of 'state president' it's state *governor*.

leisure /leezhə/ and /lezhə/ n : /lezhə/.

lemon n : *duff* car, but typically refers to the statistical one-in-a-million car that rolls off the production line like all the rest, but for some inexplicable reason just doesn't work.

lemonade cf n : lemon *squash*.

let's don't regional usage v : *don't let's*.

letter n : *school* or *college* initial as a mark of proficiency in athletics, "I lettered in basketball," cf *blue*, *colours*.

letter n : standard paper size (8½ x 11") equivalent to *A4*, see *legal*.

levee n : embankment on river, similar to the *sea wall*.

lever /lever/ and /leever/ n v : /leever/.

leverage (commerce) v : *gearing*.

license plate n : *number plate*.

license plate number n : *registration number*.

licorice sp n : *liquorice*.

lieutenant /lootenənt/ cf n : /leftenənt/ the American pr. preserves the original French.

life preserver cf n : *life-jacket*.

life ring, **life saver** (sp life buoy) n : *lifebuoy*, *lifebelt*.

Lifesavers ® n : sweets equivalent to *Polo*.

life vest n : *life-jacket*.

light bulb cf n : US light bulbs screw in.

lightning bug n : firefly.

lightning rod n : *lightning conductor*.

light switch cf n : in US, down is off, up is on.

lima bean [Quechua] n : *butter bean*.

limey n : person from *GB*, "slimy limey."

line n : *queue*, "get in line," "I saw her in line," "form a line," "stand in line," "standing *on* line" (NY).

lineup n : *identification parade*.

line up imp v : *queue up*.

links n : *sausages*, syn. *bangers*, *snags* (Aus).

lint n : *fluff*, "dryer lint."

Liquid Paper ® n : whiteout, correction fluid, syn. *Tipp-Ex*.

liquor n : *spirits*.

liquor store n : *off licence*, *packy*.

Little Dipper (constellation) n : Little Bear.

liverwurst n : *liver sausage*.

living room usage n : *sitting room*.

load col sl n : *wad*, "she bared her chest at the man bearing good tidings causing him to drop his load."

lobby n : *foyer*.

lollapalooza, lalapalusa, etc. n : very striking or unusual person or thing, and now the name of a Woodstock-style annual music concert (1991–1997).

long distance n : *trunk call*. Local calls are (generally) free, and any calls outside the local are long distance, for which a tariff is charged.

looey, looie, Louie n : syn. *loogie*.

loogie /loogee/ n : phlegm syn. *gilbo*.

looking good adj : spectacular.

loquat n : sweet, greenish-yellow fruit the size of a small plum that tastes a bit pear-like, and contains two very large seeds. The tree is quite popular in landscaping in states with Mediterranean or tropical climates, such as California and Florida.

lose it v : 'lose your *cool*,' lose control or composure, syn. *flip* out, throw a *wobbly*, "he just lost it."

loser n : failure, syn. *hoser*, 'uniquely-fortuned individual on an alternative career path, person with temporarily unmet objectives'—The Official Politically Correct Dictionary.

losingest inf adj : most losing, ant. *winningest*.

lost and found n : *lost property*.

Lost Wages expr n : *Las Vegas*, the canonical legal gambling haven.

lot lizard (truckers) sl n : prostitute working *truck stops* (by canvassing drivers in the *parking lot*).

lot n : site (as in *building site*, *vacant site*), see parking lot, "there are six lots but only three have houses on them."

love seat n : two-person *settee*.

lowboy n : low chest or table, with drawers, about three feet high on short (usu. cabriole style) legs. Also, a kind of *flatbed* trailer hitched up to a *truck*.

Lower 48 (esp Alaska) n : the contiguous 48 states and *DC*, which excludes HI and AK. See *continental United States*.

lox [Yiddish] n : smoked salmon, popular on bagels with cream cheese (and capers), 'lox & bagels.'

Ltd cf n : prestigious line of large Ford cars.

lumber usage n : *timber*.

lumberyard n : *timber yard*.

lummox n : clumsy person.

lush n : alcoholic.

lye n : *caustic soda*.

– m –

M&M's® (sweets) n : *Smarties*, the green M&Ms have an aphrodisiac reputation, the red ones went out of circulation in the 1970s till 1986 due to *FDA* issues, and the blue ones appeared in 1996 by popular vote.

ma'am n : formal term of address, syn. *missus*.

macho /mahchoh/ [Sp machismo] adj : manly, adopting the stance of a *hard case* or *tough guy*.

Macintosh (computer) usage n : *Apple Mac*.

mack v : kiss, *snog*, *neck*, also, to eat voraciously, "I macked on that sandwich."

mad cf adj : angry syn. *pissed*, *cross*.

Madison Avenue n : American advertising industry (formerly centered on Madison Avenue in New York).

mail n v : *post*, "the *check*'s in the mail," "I'll mail it in the morning."

mailbag n : *postbag*.

mailbox n : *pillar box*.

mail drop n : a box, in a hotel *lobby*, etc. for letters.

mailer n : container (tube, box, stout envelope) for *post*ing things "I'll throw it in a mailer in the morning."

mailman n : *postman*, letter carrier (Canada), mail delivery person (PC term).

mail slot n : *letterbox* in door.

Main Street n : *high street*.

maître d n : *head waiter*.

major adj : an intensifier, "That was a major screw up," "He was majorly sick."

major n v : main subject of study, "my major is computer science," "I'm majoring in general studies."

majority cf n : number or part greater than half.

majority leader n : Each party's current contingent in each house of *Congress* chooses one member as a leader, who is known as the *House* or *Senate* "majority leader" in the case of the party with the most seats *in that house* (irrespective of the other house or the presidency) and the *minority leader* in the case of the other party (see *third party*).

make v : seduce.

make reservation v : *book*.

making out v : petting to heavy petting.

mall n : shopping mall, see also *strip mall*.

mamma [Southern] n : *momma*, *mummy*.

mañana [Mexican tomorrow] intj n : do-it-later philosophy.

marathon bar (candy bar) cf n : *curly wurly* (Cadbury) (Mars marathon bar 1973–1981).

margarita n : tequila and lime cocktail.

marines cf n : U.S. Marine Corps.

marquee cf n : canopy, cover projecting out from entrance to hotels, theatres, etc.

mashing v : *snog*ging, *making out*.

Mason-Dixon line [a survey line fixing the boundary between the states of Pennsylvania and Maryland] n : considered a boundary between the North and the *South*.

masonite n : *fibreboard*.

math n : *maths*.

mauve /mahv/ or /mohv/ n : /mohv/ (rhymes with faux, taupe).

maven n : expert.

maverick n : unpredictable person.

mayo abbr n : mayonnaise, a popular *sandwich* condiment along with *mustard*, salt, pepper, *pickles*, oil, vinegar, and ground herbs and spices, see *hold*.

MC [master of ceremonies] abbr n v : emcee, *compère*.

mean cf adj : nasty, unpleasant, "mean people suck."

meat usage n : kernel of a nut.

meat grinder n : *mincer*.

mechanical pencil n : *propelling pencil*.

median, median divider (road) n : centre or *central reservation*.

meet with usage v : meet.

mega col adj : great, big, large, "she's a mega-pain."

melt n : usu. *open* sandwich with melted (*American*) cheese on top.

melvin v : *snuggie*, *wedgie* [E. Coast], *brownie* [W. Coast] .

men's room n : *gentlemen*, *gents*, *mens*.

men's wallet usage n : *wallet*, *billfold*.

meow sp v n : miaow.

mesa [Sp table] n : plateau.

meter maid n : female *traffic warden*, 'meter maids eat their young'—bumper sticker in San Francisco.

metro n : name of *subway* system in some cities (like Paris Metro).

mezzanine (theater) n : *dress circle*.

Mickey Finn n : spiked drink, 'slip a Mickey' = to surreptitiously knock out by spiking someone's drink (chloral hydrate being a favourite).

Mickey Mouse adj : cheap and nasty, syn. *made in Hong Kong*.

Mid-Atlantic, Middle Atlantic n : NY, NJ, PA, DE, MD, see *East Coast*.

middle school n : secondary school, *grades* 6–8 (sometimes 5–8). See *junior high*, *senior high*, *high school*.

midterms n : midterm *exams*.

Midwest n : the *North Central* states (the West isn't where it used to be) including ND, SD, MN, IA, NE, KS, MO, WI, MI, IL, IN, and OH (culturally Midwestern but East *wannabes*), "he's a Midwesterner." See also *Great Plains*, *back east*, *out west*, *mountain states*, *the South*.

mighty usage adv : greatly, very, "that was mighty tasty," "he was mighty *pissed*."

Mile-High City n : Denver, CO.

Milky Way (candy bar) n : *Mars bar*.

minority leader n : see *majority leader*.

Miranda n : a rule (established in 1966)

requiring police to advise subjects prior to arrest of their rights, including the right to remain silent, and anything they do or say could be used against them.

MLK abbr n : Martin Luther King, Jr., his name being used increasingly to name roads, bridges, etc. and often informally referred to as MLK Blvd, etc. See January 15th in the American Holiday table.

mob n : criminal gang, 'the Mob' = organised crime, Mafia, Cosa Nostra.

moby [Moby Dick] adj : really huge.

molasses n : *treacle*.

mold sp n v : *mould*.

mollusk sp n : *mollusc*.

molt sp n v : *moult*.

mom /mahm/, **mommy** sp n : *mum* /mum/, *mummy*.

mom and pop diner n : small family-owned restaurant, "you should check out that great mom and pop hamburger joint over on Fifth."

mom and pop store n : small family-owned *shop*.

momentarily cf adv : in a moment, very soon, "the plane will be landing momentarily."

momma n : *mamma, mummy*.

Monday morning quarterbacking expr v : being unfairly critical in hindsight, syn. glibido, hurler on the ditch (Ir), see all *mouth and trousers*.

mondo [Italian the world] sl adv : completely, absolutely.

mongo [contr] adj : humongous.

mononucleosis n : *glandular fever*.

Montezuma's revenge n : diarrhoea or even dysentery suffered by tourists.

moomoo n : see *muumuu*.

moon pie (food) n : nasty combination of cheap chocolate, marshmallow sauce and something akin to *Graham crackers*.

moonshine n : illicitly homemade *corn* whiskey.

moose n : *Alces alces*, *elk*.

moot cf usage adj : dead, as in "that issue is moot" meaning 'that issue is dead,' probably from the legal meaning–'deprived of practical significance.'

mortician n : undertaker, *funeral director*.

mosquito eater n : crane fly, *daddy-long-legs*.

motel [motor + hotel] n : rooms are accessible from outside (car park), whereas in a hotel the rooms are accessible from the inside.

motor home n : large vehicle built like a motorised *caravan*, for living in *whilst* touring, etc.

motor mouth sl n : unremitting talker, see also *gabfest*.

Motown, Motor city n : Detroit.

mountain oysters n : lamb, calf or hog's testicles, syn. codfish, *Cape Cod turkey*.

mountain states n : MT, ID, WY, NV, UT, CO, AZ, NM, see *West Coast*, *Midwest*, *East Coast*.

move your butt expr v : get a move on, get out of the way, syn. 'mind yer backs.'

movie n : *film*.

the movies n : cinema, *theater*, syn. the flicks, the *pictures*.

moving van n : *removals* van, *pantechnicon*.

MS abbr n : *MSc*.

muddle v : to mix and crush (cocktails, etc).

mud flap girl n : large-breasted naked reclining woman silhouette seen on *truck* mud flaps, syn, truck flap girl.

muff sl n : *vagina*, pubic hair.

muff diving sl v : cunnilingus, syn *gamahuche*.

muffin cf n : like a tea cake or small cake, available in many flavours: bran, blueberry, poppyseed, etc.

muffler (car) n : *silencer*.

mug sl n : thug, *punk*.

mugwump n : boss, syn. big chief.

mullet n : short haircut left long in the back, popular with country-western singers, (1980s) *football* stars, and *trailer trash*, 'business up front, hippie in the rear,' "without a beard and mullet, it just ain't Jesus."

mums n : chrysanthemums.

mung rag n : tea towel to sop up beer slops at a party at a house.

muscle car n : *macho* car, souped-up engine, for instance: 'Vette (Chevrolet Corvette), Chevy Nova, Camaro (Chevrolet), Duster (Plymouth). [Performance sells cars, not fuel economy.]

muss col v n : mess.

mussy col adj : messy (of hair, makeup).

mustard cf n : American mustard is bright yellow and non-spicy hot, for which they resort to Dijon or Grey Poupon.

mutual fund n : *unit trust*.

muumuu /moomoo/ [Hawaiian] n : voluminous, loudly patterned dress, usu. worn by women of size.

— n —

nachos [Mexican Nacho, diminutive of Ignacio] n : *corn chips* with melted cheese on top, and often sliced *jalapeño*.

nail enamel n : *nail varnish*.

nail polish n : *nail varnish*.

nail polish remover n : *varnish remover*.

napkin cf n : *serviette*, esp. paper, available freely at most fast food places.

narc sl n v : narcotics agent, also telltale, esp. on (fellow) drug users, cf. *nark*.

narly adj : see *gnarly*.

natch [contr] adv : naturally.

neat cf adj : excellent, enjoyable, pleasant, syn. *sweet, bitchin', cool, fresh, rad, brill, safe*.

neatnik n : typically anal person who is excessively neat and tidy.

nebbish [Yiddish] n : fool, *loser*.

neck v : *snog*.

nerd n : socially maladroit person, but esp. used to describe the gangly archetypal scientific (esp. computer) nerd with dishevelled hair, horn-rimmed glasses, goofy (buck) teeth, spotty complexion, untucked shirt replete with *nerd pack*, and *trousers* a few inches too short, whose belt is solely for hanging a calculator off. The term has expanded beyond the syn. *geek* to include just about any unidimensional person with a discernible social deficiency. But qualified, it means enthusiast and indicates specialty, 'computer nerd,' 'math nerd.'

nerd pack n : plastic pocket protector (worn in shirt pocket) often stuffed with *biros*.

nervy cf adj : brash, bold.

Nestlés /neslees/ n : /nes-ls/.

newbie n : neophyte, of new people to some activity, and therefore guileless, 'clueless newbie,' originally confined to online activities [originated in newsgroup:talk.bizarre].

New England n : all the northeastern corner states: ME, NH, VT, MA, RI, CT.

newf, newfie, pl **newfies** (Canadian) n : person from Newfoundland. Also the breed of dog.

newsstand n : *bookstall*.

New York minute n : less than a minute.

niche /nich/ n : /neesh/.

nickel n : 5¢, a fat cupro-nickel coin like a large fat *1p*.

night crawler n : large earthworm.

nightgown n : *nightdress*.

nightstick n : *truncheon*.

nipple (baby's bottle) n : *teat*.

nite inf sp n : night.

no-brainer n : no thought required, the obvious choice.

nod n : approval, "he got the nod" (the go ahead).

no dumping (sign) imp v : *no tipping*, (see *dump*).

no-no n : *not done, not cricket*.

noodle col n : head, syn *noddle*.

noogy n : having your scalp rubbed hard with someone's knuckles, "our brothers used to hold us down and give us noogies," "a colleague got him in a headlock and gave him 'noogies.'" See also *snuggie*.

no place n : nowhere in particular.

no problem expr intj : easy, no big deal, not a problem, no worries (Aus).

normalcy usage n : normality.

north 40s n : Canada–the 49th parallel divides the western parts of the US and Canada, most of the eastern part is above the 45th parallel, and most of the population is within 100 miles of the US border. See also *back 40*.

North Central n : West: ND, SD, MN, IA, NE, KS, MO, East: WI, MI, IL, IN, OH, see *West Coast, Midwest, East Coast*.

Northeast Corridor n : route between Boston and *DC* via *NYC*, see *East Coast*.

Northeast n : *New England + Mid-Atlantic*.

no see um [no see them] n : Ceratopogonidae, virtually invisible biting midges.

no sweat adj : easy, no big deal.

not! intj : unexpectedly added to the end of a statement to reverse its meaning (popularised by Wayne and Garth in Wayne's World).

notary public n : *commissioner for oaths*.

nothing but net expr adj : an expression used from basketball, now replacing *swisher*.

notions n : *haberdashery*, etc.

no way intj : expression of disbelief, syn. you're kidding, you've gotta be joking. A smart alec reply is "*way!*"

NSA abbr n : No Such Agency, also known more officially as the super-secret National Security Agency (electronic security, cryptography, etc).

nuke v : to microwave, also to figuratively obliterate (an object, an opponent).

nutria [Sp otter] n : *coypu* (*Myocastor coypus*).

nuts usage sl n : testicles, syn. *goolies, knackers, knacks*.

NYC abbr n : New York City, *the Big Apple*.

— O —

oatmeal n : *porridge*.

ocean usage n : sea, *seaside, beach*.

off-color adj : in bad taste, a bit *rude* (as well as a *bit off*, etc.).

Official Business (on envelopes, see also *postage-paid return*) n : equivalent to *On Her Majesty's Service*.

off of prep : off. The Quingawaga squeaks and moans / While dining off of ankle bones.—Edward Gorey.

off-off-year election n : election in an odd-numbered year, for local offices only.

off-ramp n : *slip-road* (off-slip).

off the wall sl adj : unconventional.

off-year election n : election in a year that is an odd multiple of 2, when there is voting for *Congress* but not for *president*.

oh-dark thirty n : an ungodly time of the morning, when morning show announcers have to be at work, "we got an oh-dark thirty wakeup call on the ranch."

oil pan (car) n : *sump*.

OJ /oh jay/ abbr n : orange juice, "we're out of OJ."

Oklahoma skylight n : opening in building installed by tornado.

okra n : *ladies' fingers*, bhindi, see *gumbo*.

Old Blue Eyes n : Frank Sinatra.

Old Glory n : American flag.

on usage prep : "he beat up on him," "he thrashed on him," "standing on *line*"

(NYC), "we were still on our good behavior."

one-armed bandit n : *fruit machine* operated using a lever on the side.

one-way ticket n : *single ticket*.

on-ramp n : *slip-road* (on-slip).

on the nail expr adj : *spot on*.

on the rag adj : testy, also a woman on her period.

open-face adj : open-faced *sandwich = open sandwich*.

opine v : express an opinion.

orchestra seats n : *stalls* (theatre).

ordinance n : *by-law*.

Oreo cookies n : chocolate *biscuit*s with cream filling.

Oriental cf adj : an object from China, Thailand, etc. (rather than a person (except as a dated term), when it's considered offen. or demeaning), see *Asian*.

ornery adj : irritable, cantankerous, *bolshie*, *stroppy*.

ottoman n : *pouf*, *pouffe*.

out suff : appended to a verb (*chill out*, freak out, munch out, *tweak* out) and, where such expressions are common, can be left off and still be understood, "she freaked," "*chill*, will ya, buddy!" "I'm tweakin'." Also found in expressions such as '*bawl out*' and '*chew out*.'

outahere [out of here, see *-a*] intj vt vi : depending on context it can mean 'let's leave,' let's get out of here,' or the same as [I'm] leaving, syn. *later*, bye, [I'm] gone, [I'm] *history*, "I'm outahere," (many sp. var. "I'm outta here"), or as an vi. scram, *beat it*.

outasight [out of sight] col adj : *way cool*.

outie n : protruding belly button, "do you have an *innie* or an outie?"

outlet n : *socket*, *power point*.

outlet, outlet store n : *store* (sometimes in an outlet mall) selling returned, slightly defective, or less popular merchandise of

a particular manufacturer, usu. at greatly reduced prices.

out of left field expr adj : very unexpected, usu. of an idea or of some action, "this dictionary is out of left field."

outseam n : *outside leg*. (See *inseam*.)

outside lane cf n : *inside lane*, lane furthest from *central reservation*, i.e. the slow (rightmost) lane.

out west n : anything west of the Rockies, "He's from out west." See also the *West Coast*, *back east*, *the South*, *Midwest*.

over adv : over again, "do it over," "I'm going to start over."

overalls cf n : *dungarees*, cf. *boiler suit*.

over easy adj : eggs fried both sides but without cooking the yolks.

overhead n : *overheads* (running costs).

over medium adj : eggs fried both sides and with the yolks slightly cooked.

overpass (road or rail) n : *flyover*.

oy vey, oy vay [Yiddish] intj : expression of distress, alarm, syn. oh no!

oz n : see *fluid ounce*.

— P —

Pacific Crest Trail n : 2400 mile *footpath* forged through the Sierras and Cascades going from Mexico to Canada through California, Oregon and Washington.

Pacific Northwest n : *PNW*, WA and OR, aka Pacific NorthWet (see *Emerald City*).

pacifier n : baby's dummy.

package store [Massachusetts] n : *off-licence*, liquor store.

pack rat n : person who hoards, from the wood rat *Neotoma* spp. who hoards interesting things in their big stick nests, like a magpie.

packy [NE] col n : *offie*, *package store*.

paddle col v : spank.

paddle usage n : bat (ping pong).

page (wedding) n : *pageboy*.

pal n : term of address conveying mild hostility, "hold your water, pal."

palmetto bug n : particularly large, robust, light-insensitive cockroach that can fly, encountered esp. in south Florida.

panhandle v : beg for money, usu. by a *transient* on the street, also the long narrow part of a state (FL ID MD OK TX WV).

panties n : *knickers*, undies, women's underwear.

panties in a ruffle expr n : syn. *knickers in a twist*, *boxers in a bunch*, panties all bunched up, panties in a knot, jock in a bind.

pantry usage n : *larder*.

pants cf n : *trousers*.

pant suit n : woman's trouser suit.

pantyhose n : *tights*.

pantywaist n : sissy, *big girl's blouse*.

papaya n : *pawpaw, papaw*.

paper cutter usage n : *guillotine*.

paper hanger n : *decorator*.

paper or plastic expr adj : common refrain at the supermarket checkout, see *bag*.

papier-mâché /payper mashay/ n : /papiay mashay/.

paraffin n : *paraffin wax*.

Parcheesi (game) n : *ludo*.

parentheses usage punc n : *brackets*, *round brackets ( )*.

parka [Aleut] n : *anorak*.

parking lights n : *sidelights*.

parking lot n : *car park*.

parkway cf n : ostensibly landscaped *highway*.

parterre n : the ground floor behind the orchestra in a theatre.

party n : group, "there's a party of six waiting at the bar," "party of one for dinner."

party favor n : trivial knick-knacks and *sweets* given out at (children's) parties as gifts.

pass v : *overtake*.

passing tone (music) n : *passing note*.

patch n : insignia or design on fabric which is then sewn on clothing, "Americans often sew a Canadian flag patch on their *backpacks* when travelling abroad."

patch kit n : *puncture outfit* for repairing punctures in bicycle (and motorcycle) *tyre*s.

patootie /patoodee/ col n : *butt*, "it's a big pain in the patootie."

patsy n : scapegoat, *fall guy*, *sucker*, "He cannot play the patsy any longer."

patty n : flat cake of chopped food or *mince* (*hamburger* patty), flat *boiled sweet* (peppermint patty).

pavement cf n : road surface, *carriageway*, asphalt, or any paved surface, "traffic offenders are made to see the *Red Pavement* video."

pbj, **pb&j** abbr n : peanut butter and jelly, "do you want *sloppy Joe* or a PB-n-J sandwich?"

PC [Politically Correct] n adj : "that wasn't very PC," "she is so PC." Although a supposedly non-offensive-to-any-group way of referring to said group it ends up being a method of euphemizing by using 'adverbially premodified adjectival lexical units' to make phrases such as 'cluefully challenged,' meaning *retard*, and 'involuntarily leisured,' meaning *fired*. Ant. Historically Correct. [Since I'm only recently a survivor of being a (not yet) terminally inconvenienced, scrotally-advantaged ice person of noncolor, I have nothing more to say about this.]

PD abbr n : Police Department, well known examples: LAPD (Los Angeles), NYPD (New York). [Apparently there is an ominous evolution: Police Force → Police Department → Police Service. See *PC* for implications.]

peavey, **peavy** n : cant dog, logger's long-handled spike with a hooked arm, used for shifting heavy logs.

pecker cf n : penis.

pedal to the metal expr n : floor it, *haul ass*, "I had the pedal to the metal the whole way."

pedestrian underpass n : *subway*.

ped xing (road sign 'pedestrian crossing') n : *zebra crossing*.

peekaboo intj : *peepbo* (game with babies).

pendejo /pendayhoh/ [Mexican] n : *asshole*, *dufus*, slime.

penis cf n : syn. *pecker*, *Johnson*, dick, schlong, meat, bone, whanger, *weenie*, *wiener*, pee pee, peter, percy, *choad*, *dork*, *pud*.

Pennsylvania Avenue n : see *1600 Pennsylvania Avenue*.

penny cf col n : *cent*.

perfume n : scent.

period punc n : *full stop, full point*.

person to person n : *personal call*.

pesky adj : troublesome.

pets [Fr péter] (French Canadian) n : farts, petting=farting.

pharmacist n : *chemist*.

pharmacy n : *chemist's*.

Philadelphia Lawyer n : unscrupulous or extraordinarily clever person or lawyer.

Phillies Blunts n : a brand of cigar, about 5" by ½", popularly used by *stoners* by splitting, replacing the contents with marijuana, and resealing. 'Smokin' the blunt' has become so popular that tee shirts, bumper stickers, lyrics, and even a band can be found with reference to it. The cigar company, although apparently concerned, made $53,000 in 1994 in tee shirt royalties (which they gave to charities).

Philly sl n : Philadelphia.

phone booth n : *call-box, kiosk*.

phonograph n : *gramophone*.

phooey intj : *darn, whatever*.

pick n : pickaxe.

pickle cf n : a large *gherkin*, 'dill pickle.'

pick-up v : *pull, chat up*.

pickup, pickup truck n : light truck (½ or ¾ ton), enclosed cab, open body.

pick-up line n : *chat up line*.

picture ID n : *ID* that includes the owner's photograph, such as a *driver's license*. Some fascist establishments (requiring picture ID for entry) require a valid state *driver's license*, not accepting passport, birth certificate, or another form such as an (international) student card even though it has a sealed in photograph with signature.

piece usage n : some, "he wore a funny piece of jewelry," 'a piece of fruit' = a piece of a fruit, one fruit, or some fruit.

pierogi n : a potato-cheese filled dumpling.

pigpen n : *pigsty*.

pill n : annoying, unpleasant or tiresome person (often child or woman).

pill bug n : *wood louse*.

pin n : *badge*, the kind you pin on, like a *golliwog* badge, or a boy scout badge. Cf patch.

piñata /pinyahdə/ [Mexican] n : children's party game where a two-foot model of a cow, rabbit, guitar, or some such, made out of something akin to *papier mâché*, festooned in colorful ribbons and filled with *candy* and *party favors* is swiped at in turns by a blindfolded child with a big stick or baseball bat, in the hopes of breaking it, when all the children rush in to gather the rain of *sweets* and knickknacks.

pin board n : *noticeboard*.

pine nuts n : up to 1" waxy edible seeds of western N. American pines.

pinkie n : little finger.

pint cf n : the *US* pint (473 ml or 16 US *fluid ounces*) is substandard and always leaves you hankering after that last swig, being about 17% smaller than the UK pint (568 ml or 20 UK *fluid ounce*s), see table of measures.

pinto adj n : (paint in TX) *piebald*.

pinto bean n : a pink and brown speckled kidney bean (brown when cooked) found in *southwest*ern and Mexican-style dishes, and is usu. the refried bean (*frijoles*, in *burritos*, *tacos*, etc), and exchanged with *black beans* for variation.

pirogi n : *pierogi*.

pissed cf adj : *pissed off*, "she was so pissed."

pisser n : urinal.

pit n : *stone*. (large hard seed of plum, peach, apricot, cherry, date, avocado, etc. see also *pip*.)

pitch n : line of sales talk.

pitch v : to toss out, get rid off, "Pitch In" (instructions on the side of public *trash cans*), "anything illogical will be pitched," "Don't pitch that can. You can recycle it."

pitcher n : *jug*.

pitcher (baseball) n : equivalent to cricket *bowler*.

pizzazz n : stylish or glamourous vigour.

plaid /plad/ adj : tartan or any similar rectangular design on material.

plank sl v : sex.

planner, day planner n : *diary*.

play-doh [Play-doh®] n : *Plasticine*.

play possum v : play dead, syn. lie doggo.

Plexiglas n : *perspex*.

plowed sl adj : drunk.

plumber's crack n : *butt crack*, *builder's cleavage*.

plunk down v : *plonk down*.

pms [premenstrual syndrome] n : of an irrationally highly emotional person, "she was very pms-y to me," syn. *pmt*, *period drama*.

PNW abbr n : *Pacific Northwest*. The people are characterised as being pioneers but *buttheads* ('we found paradise, now leave us alone,' 'don't californicate Oregon,' see *Emerald City*), and the region beautifully lush and forested with a high rainfall.

pod n : a *pod people*.

podiatrist n : *chiropodist*.

pod people [from the scifi classic *Invasion of the Body Snatchers*] n : the social archetype epitomizing the *gormless* drones hatched from (alien) pods, but also a person acting surprisingly out of character, usu. better, like a *mean* boss giving you a *raise* or the day off.

pod speak v : mindless drivel.

Podunk n : an actual village in MA (and CT, MI, NY, VT) that has become figurative for some small unimportant backwater *hick* town. Other unusual American town names (many from Native American), some of which are used like Podunk, include Boring, Drain, Bend, and even Wanker's Corner OR, Bat Cave NC, Bugtussle (TX, OK) and Bug Tussle (KY, TN), Cool, Weed CA, Hoboken NJ (AL, CA, GA), Ho-ho-kus NJ, Kalamazoo MI (AR, FL, WV), Kankakee IL, Keokuk (IA, TX), Kokomo (AR, CO, HI, IN, MS, TX), One Blink, Two Blink TX, Oshkosh WI (NE), Peculiar MO, Punxsutawney PA, Skaneateles NY, Truth or Consequences NM, Virgin UT, syn. *Neasden*, *Purley*. Mythical places would include *San Placebo* CA, and *Dacron* Ohio. See *BFE*.

poison oak, poison ivy, poison sumac n : They contain an oil which in many people causes irritation that can last for weeks, and in some sensitive people can be miserable and debilitating. They are common hazards of shrub and woodlands, in a similar way to nettles. The oak and sumac are shrubs, and the ivy is a vine. The oak tends to be found in the West, the ivy in the East.

pole usage n : used generically where rod might be expected, "my other fishing pole is a fly-rod," *"pole bean."*

pole bean n : *runner bean.*

polliwog, pollywog n : tadpole.

pony keg n : smaller or half keg.

pooch n : dog.

pool n : game, like *billiards*, popular in the US and found as standard entertainment in bars. [45,000 pool tables in British *pub*s in 1986 (*The Color of Money*), up from zero in 1961 (*The Hustler*).]

poop n : the facts, syn. the skinny.

pooped adj : exhausted, syn. *shagged* out.

pooper-scooper n : long-handled scoop for taking care of dog poop in the *yard*.

poor boy, po' boy (Southern) n : *submarine sandwich* but sometimes on toasted bread roll.

poor girl (Southern) n : smaller *poor boy*.

poot sl n v : fart.

pop n : general term for any *fizzy drink*, esp. in the *Midwest* and West. See also *coke*, *soda*, and *tonic*.

pop v : syn. screw, "I popped her, once."

pop v : to ingest, often pills.

pop v : to open, esp. with a pop, "pop a cold beer," *"pop the hood."*

pop a wheelie expr v : to suddenly do a wheelie, "he's out in the *parking lot* poppin' wheelies."

popcorn land n : *LA*.

poplar cf n : Tulip tree *Liriodendron tulipifera*, also called tulip poplar, yellow poplar.

popsicle (Popsicle™) n : *ice lolly, lollipop*.

pop tart [kind of commercial fruit pastry designed to go in a toaster] sl n : stupid girl.

pop the hood expr v : to look inside, examine in detail, "power users rarely pop the hood and tinker around with the bits inside."

pone (S) n : *cornpone*.

pork rinds n : strips of pork skin, rendered of the fat, available, like crisps, as a popular snack, syn. cracklings, pork scracklings. See also *chitlins*.

portapotty, portapot (Portapotty) col n : *portaloo*, (one *West Coast* brand is Honey Bucket).

POS /pee oh es/ acr n : piece of shit, "it's a Chevy POS."

possum (opossum) n : America's only marsupial, like a large rat but almost white fur, almost blind, generally disliked, and heard scuffling around outside in the wee hours.

post cf v : to publicly display a sign or message, "the announcement is posted in the library," "the posted speed is 35 mph," 'NO TRESPASSING—POSTED,' 'POST NO BILLS.'

postal expr v : 'go postal' = go berserk. (Apparently, U.S. *mail* workers have a high incidence of *flip*ping out due to stress.)

Postal Service n : equivalent to *The Royal Mail*.

posted expr v : see *keep you posted*, see also *post*.

postgraduate cf adj n : continuing studies after advanced degree (masters or PhD).

potato bug col n : although this is really the Colorado potato beetle, many use it informally (esp. children) for the *wood louse*.

potato chips n : *crisps*.

pot holder n : *oven cloth*.

pot plant cf n : marijuana plant.

potty mouth n adj : foul-mouthed, "you're such a potty mouth," cf *gobshite*.

potty train v : *house-train*.

pound cake n : *Madeira cake*.

PPO [Preferred Provider Organization] abbr n : kind of health insurance–basically you can see whichever doctor you wish, but percentage coverage tends to be less than the equivalent in an *HMO*.

prairie dog n : kind of ground squirrel (that barks) living in colonies in the prairies (see *Great Plains*), see also *gopher*.

prairie dog v : the popping-up in your cubicle to see what's going on, "the nanosecond the network goes down, all the *nerds* start prairie-dogging in their *cubes*."

pratfall n : a fall on the *butt*, also any splendid blunder.

precinct cf n : district.

prefunk col v : 'all about the funk,' preparations (as in getting stoned, etc.) prior to the party proper.

preppy, preppie n adj : by the neat and tidy (*spendy*) clothes, a tell-tale sign of a well-off, sheltered upbringing and conservative attitudes, ant. punk, goth.

presently cf adv : at present, at the present time, at this moment, immediately, "you have to do this presently."

president (business) n : managing director, *MD*, and now often called 'president and *CEO*.'

president (politics) n : elected along with a vice president in years that are multiples of 4, see *Election Day*, *Electoral College*, *primary*. *Elections* for *Congress* are separate (though simultaneous). Presidential election campaigns tend to start gradually about 18 months before the election, and get into full swing over the last few months. If the president dies or resigns, the *VP* becomes president and (since 1965) then names a new *VP*, who must be accepted by *Congress*. See *git*.

primary, primary election n : a form of election, held some months before *Election Day*, where voters affiliated with one party choose between candidates nominated by that party. Often both parties (see *third party*) will hold their primaries on the same day. Practice varies from one state to another and sometimes from one party to another as to what offices primaries are held for and when they happen. To finally choose a candidate for president, each party holds a national convention after the primaries; the delegates from those states that had a primary vote according to its results.

primary school cf n : grades 1–3, sometimes *K*-3, see *elementary school*.

prime the pump expr v : get something going (such as infusing a project with money).

principal n : *head master*/mistress.

private school cf n : *school* primarily supported by non-government agency or tuition fees, see *public school*.

proctor cf n : *invigilator*.

produce /prohdoos/ n : /prodyoos/ fruits and vegetables.

program n : *scheme*, "a training program."

program sp n v : *programme*.

the projects n : *housing project*, "she's from the projects."

prom n : formal *high school* dance that generally marks the graduation therefrom, which actually occurs about a month later, "who was your prom date?" No expenses spared on *tux*es, dresses, limos, hotel suites, *alcohol*, condoms, pictures, etc. For many Americans prom is a rite of passage.

propeller beanie n : *beanie* with a propeller on top.

propeller head n : *nerd*, who may actually be wearing a propeller hat (*beanie*).

proposition n : a mechanism for interest groups to bypass the *legislature* in many states. If they can get a certain number of people to support a law they propose, then the next election will automatically include a binding referendum on it: subject to some limitations, a majority of Yes votes from the public will then make it law.

pruning shears n : *secateurs*.

pry open v : *prise* open.

pshaw /pshah/ intj : expression of contempt or irritation, *pah*!

psych! /siek/ intj : just messing with your mind, just kidding, fooled you! "we just got married ::pause:: psych!"

public restrooms n : *public conveniences*.

public school cf n : state school, non-fee paying, tax supported and controlled by local government, see *private school*.

pud /puhd/ cf n : oaf, a harmless fellow, a little slower than the rest. Also means *penis*, and is sometimes used in this sense (apparently pud is an old word for sausage).

pudding cf n : sweet *slodge*, a thick *custard* in various flavours (butterscotch, chocolate, strawberry, vanilla), served cold, like chocolate mousse, "would you like a chocolate pudding?"

puhleeeze intj : please, spelled (along with many similar variants) to indicate exasperated entreaty.

pull inf v : to do, but usu. with extra effort, "pull an *all-nighter*." See also *hang*.

Pullman, Pullman car (train) cf n : sleeping car.

pull-off (road) n : passing point, *lay-by*.

pull tie (electronics) n : ribbed plastic strip with a self-gripping eye at one end through which the other end is threaded and pulled taught, syn. cable tie, "there's nothing that can't be fixed with paper clips and pull ties."

pumps cf n : *court shoes*, high heeled shoes, "she was wearing those bright red 'fuck-me' pumps."

punk n : thug, hoodlum, also person wet behind the ears.

purse cf n : lady's *handbag*, bag.

purty adj : the pronunciation, and hence spelling, of pretty by some speakers, and affected for effect by others.

pussy n : *vagina*.

putter v : *potter*.

putty cf n : a color–pallid greyish brown to pale brownish grey.

— q —

Q-tips® n : cotton buds, cotton swabs, safety swabs.

quart cf n : an American quart is slightly less than a liter (0.946352946 l), see *pint*, and table 8, Measures.

quarter n : 25¢, twenty-five cents.

quarterback (*football*) n : leader of the team's offense, see *Monday morning quarterback*.

quarter eagle n : gold $2.50 coins (1792–1929).

quasi- prefix : pseudo-.

que pasa /kay pasa/ [Sp] expr intj : *what's up?* what's happening?

quit v : cease, stop, "will you quit that!" "an addict is a person who enjoys quitting."

quite cf usage adv : very, e.g. "I quite like you" = "I like you a lot," 'quite good' = excellent, "quite ill" = seriously ill.

quitter usage n : person who gives up too easily, see *quit*.

Quonset hut n : like a *Nissen hut*.

quotation marks usage n : *inverted commas*, " " ".

— r —

raccoon [shortening of Algonquian *arocoun, raugrougheun*] n : N. American mammal the size of a large cat with bushy ringed tail and masked eyes.

rad intj adj : syn. far out, *awesome, sweet, bitchin', neat, cool, fresh, brill, safe*.

radical intj adj : full form of rad and heard perhaps a little less than *rad*.

rag adj : see on the rag.

railroad n : *railway*.

railroad car n : *railway carriage*.
railroad crossing n : *level crossing*.
railroad tie n : railway *sleeper*.
railroad tracks n : *railway line*.
rain check n : (guarantee of) postponement, deferment (rather than cancellation).
raise (pay) n : *rise*.
ralph (onomatopoeia) sl v : throw up.
rambunctious col adj : *rumbustious*.
range n : electric or gas *cooker*.
rap v : chat, "they've been rapping all day."
rate usage v : be esp. deserving, "you guys must rate!" = you folks must rate highly in the scheme of things.
rays col n : sunshine, sun rays, "*catch* some rays" = 'get a suntan,' "*catch* the last few rays before sunset."
razz n v : sound of, and blowing, a *raspberry*, syn. *Bronx Cheer*, also derision, contempt, "quit razzing me."
real adv : really, "that's real *neat*."
really cf adv : usu. a response indicating agreement.
Realtor (yes, Realtor is capitalised) n : *estate agent*.
ream v : scrape, bore out a hole, and hence, by allusion to *buggery*, be ripped off, "I've been reamed!"
rear deck [Canadian] n : *boot*.
recess (school) n : *break*.
recliner n : reclining chair, see *lazy boy*.
recon n : reconnaissance, 'recon mission,' cf *recce*.
red-eye inf n : overnight flight, "I'll get the red-eye to Boston."
redneck derog n : rural or small town white labouring class *guy*, typified by bigoted, ultraconservative, conventional, and loutish disposition, who drives a truck decked out with empty beer cans and *coon* huntin' trophies, and has loaded *varmint* guns in the gun rack. Common last words, "hey guys, watch this."
reef (on) v : both castigate and thrash.

reform school n : *Borstal*.
regular usage adj : *normal*, *ordinary*.
religious issues cf n : PC vs. Mac (was Unix vs. VMS), Pepsi vs. Coke, *boxers* or *briefs*, cat or dog person, 'just do it' or 'just say no,' tinsel on Christmas tree or not, *may*onnaise vs. *mustard*, spit or swallow, *East Coast* rap (Biggie Smalls) vs. *West Coast* rap (Tupac Shakur), pro-choice vs. pro-life, Democrat vs. Republican.
relocate usage v : move.
Reno n : 'biggest little city in the west' (like a second *Las Vegas*).
rent usage v : *let*, *hire*, *lease*, (the sign 'for rent' = 'To Let').
rent-a-heap, rent-a-wreck, rent-a-dent n : car hire firm specializing in economical but slightly dinged vehicles.
rental n adj : a house that's rented, or a car that's rented, or referring to any rented item, "I live in a rental," "it's a rental bike."
representative n : *congressperson*.
reservation v : see *make reservation*.
rest area, rest stop n : *lay by* on *freeway* usu. with *toilet*s, parking and free coffee.
restraining order n : legal restriction against someone from bothering somebody, e.g. a paparazzi. See *ASBOs*.
restroom n : *toilet*.
résumé n : *curriculum vitae*.
retard /reetard/ [mentally retarded] sl n : stupid person, syn. *spaz*, *flid*, *bozo*, *tard*.
retired v : to be laid off.
retread (tire) n : *remould*.
Reuben [Reuben sandwich] n : an excessive grilled sandwich made with *corned beef*, Swiss cheese, and sauerkraut, on pumpernickel or (Russian) rye bread.
rhinestone n : *diamanté*.
rhubarb cf sl n : heated dispute.
ride (car) n : *lift*.
riff n v : witty comment, esp. in banter.
righteous sl adj : genuine, *cool*.

right on! intj : *way cool*, syn. hear, hear.

ringer n : (usu. dead ringer) look-alike, also a falsely-represented competitor (horse or athlete), e.g., a company softball team playing a non-employee.

ringing off the hook expr adj : describes the phone ringing incessantly, these days mostly due to telephone *solicitors*.

RN (Registered Nurse) abbr n : *SRN* (State Registered Nurse).

roadkill n : the remains of some *critter* after it's been run over, "I can't believe this venison is roadkill."

roadster n : open two-seater.

roast n : *joint*.

robe n : *bath robe*.

robin cf n : *American robin*.

rock usage cf n : *stone*.

rock col n : jewel.

Rocky Mountain oysters n : *mountain oysters*.

rolodex (Rolodex®) n : file of names and addresses on small cards threaded onto a straight or circular rod for convenient access, "let me check my rolodex."

roly-poly inf n : *wood louse*.

romaine lettuce n : *cos lettuce*.

roofies n : similar in effects to valium and famous as the date rape drug of choice (sedative flunitrazepam (rohypnol)).

rookie n : new recruit or team member.

roomer n : lodger.

rooster n : *cock*.

root beer n : popular *fizzy drink*, the root flavour being sarsaparilla, see also coke and *DP*.

round-trip ticket n : *return ticket*.

route /rowt/ and /root/ n v : /root/ route, expr. "go that route"="go down that path," "The Net treats censorship as damage and routes around it"—John Gilmore.

route (road) n : both *US* and state *highways*, route 66 is *US* 66, originally the main road from Chicago to *LA*.

routing number (bank) n : *sort code*, though its 9 digits (8 + 1 check).

rubber cf n : condom, syn. *johnny*, Trojan (brand).

rubber band n : *elastic band*.

rubber boots n : *wellington boots, wellies*.

rubber cement n : *cow gum*.

rubberneck v : gawk, *gander*, esp. drivers sidetracked by freeway accidents, thus causing traffic jams.

rubbers n : *galoshes*.

rubbing alcohol n : usu. isopropanol, sometims ethanol, syn. *surgical spirit*.

rube n : simpler soul, *twit*, "baffle the rubes in Peoria."

Rube Goldberg [cartoonist] adj : syn. *Heath Robinson*.

rude cf usage adj : discourteous, abruptly impolite.

Rudolf the Red-Nosed Reindeer n : 1930s marketing gimmick which has been leading Santa astray ever since.

rug rats joc n : kids, *sprogs*.

run n : *ladder* in stocking.

run v : *stand* for public office, run for = bid.

runaway ramp (road) n : *escape road*.

running on fumes expr n : running on empty, "He had expended so much energy in the first 50 meters that he was racing on fumes the final 50."

rush n v : a week at the beginning of the college year for joining *greeks*, signing pledges, etc, "I'm being rushed by Alpha Psi Omega."

Rust Belt n : declining heavy industry (like the opening sequence of *The Full Monty*) in northern states (New Jersey, Pennsylvania, Ohio, Michigan, Indiana). See also *Borscht Belt*, *Bible Belt*, and *Corn Belt*.

rutabaga n : *swede*.

RV [recreational vehicle] n : *motor home*.

— S —

S&H, S and H abbr n : *shipping* and handling.

S&L abbr n : *savings and loan.*

Sacagawea dollar /se kah gə wee ə/ /shə ka gə way/ /saka joo ee ə/ [Shoshone bird woman, crucial guide on Lewis and Clark's expedition] n : introduced in 2000, same size as a *Susan B. Anthony dollar* but gold coloured.

sack n : bed, "hit the sack," "got her in the sack."

sack regional n : paper *bag*, grocery *bag.*

sack lunch n : *packed lunch*, *brown bag lunch.*

sagging v : providing a *panty* peek by wearing low-riding *pants.*

sales clerk /clerk/ n : *shop assistant.*

sales tax n : tax added to purchases (even food in some states), similar to *VAT*, but not included in the advertised price. It varies from 0% (AK, DE, MT, NH, OR) to 7% (MS, RI, TN) averaging a little over 5%. Additional local taxes, such as city tax, vary from 0%–7%, such that actual tax varies from 0%–11%, averaging over 7%. Purchases shipped from out-of-state are charged the in-state tax. Tax on lodging and meals, where foisted, is separate.

salsa adj : of spunky Hispanic style (salsa music, salsa food).

salsa n : spicy condiment made from chopped tomatillo /tomatiya/, *jalapeño*, and perhaps onion, garlic, *cilantro*, tomato, and oil. Commercial varieties have a thermometer on the label indicating mild, medium and hot, which some perceive as regional (California medium = Oregon hot).

saltine n : salted cracker.

salutatorian n : second-highest ranking graduating *high school* student, who gives the class's salutatory address, if

any, at the graduation ceremonies, see *GPA*, valedictorian.

same ol,' same ol' expr intj : same old thing, same old stuff, often in answer to 'what's happening?' (what are you up to these days?).

sandbag v : coerce.

sandbag v : feign weakness, "he was sandbagging in that race."

sandbox n : *sandpit.*

sandwich cf n : the American sandwich is not usu. buttered, and usu. has at least two ingredients, often more, see *BLT*, *grilled cheese*, *grinder*, *hero*, *hoagie*, *mayo*, *pbj* (most popular amongst kids), *poor boy*, *Rueben*, *submarine*, *Togo's*, *torpedo*, and *tuna melt.*

sanitary napkin n : *sanitary towel.*

San Placebo n : a mythical CA city, see Podunk.

Santa, Santa Claus usage n : *Father Christmas.*

Santa Anas n : usu. hot, dry, often dusty, wind that blows across the desert into Southern California, esp. in the winter, and seems to make everyone grouchy (positive ions).

sappy adj : *soppy.*

Saran Wrap® n : thin plastic sheet for food, *cling film.*

sasquatch [Salish hairy men] n : seven-foot *yeti* indigenous to *PNW* and Canada.

sassy adj : brazen, *saucy*, *cheeky*, also canny and hip, "she's a sassy lassy."

SAT n : (formerly abbr. for Scholastic Aptitude Test) standardised high school maths and English test widely used, along with *GPA*, as college entrance criteria. See *GRE.*

saucepan /sahspan/ n : /sorspən/.

sausage links n : (pork) *sausages*, *bangers.*

savings and loan n : equivalent to a *building society.*

sawbuck sl n : saw horse with X-shaped

ends, also $10 (X=10), ten dollar bill.

sawed-off sp adj : *sawn-off*.

scab n : *blackleg*.

scads adj : large quantities, syn. *lashings*.

scagy [scag = heroin] adj : dishevelled, dubious, *crusty*.

scallions cf n : *spring onions*.

scam n v : to cheat, swindle, play a con, also to scrounge, "I'm going to scam for more information," also to *pull*, "let's go down town and scam on babes."

scanky adj : see *skanky*.

scarf v : to gobble down, syn. *scoff*.

scavanger hunt (children's party game) n : *treasure hunt*.

schedule /skedjool/ n v : /shedyool/ timetable.

schlemiel [Yiddish] n : *chump*.

schlep [Yiddish] v : carry or drag oneself or a load, work or move tediously.

schlock [Yiddish] n : *rubbish*.

schmaltz [Yiddish] n : exessive sentimentality, *sappi*ness.

schmo, schmoe [Yiddish] sl n : *twerp*, dull or stupid person.

schmuck [Yiddish] n : *twit*, dickhead.

school cf n : refers to university or college, as well as *grade school* (*K-12*), generally any learning institution, "I'll be in school three more years."

schwag [faux-Yiddish swag] n : corporate logo-encrusted baubles and trinkets, syn. gewgaw /googah/, tchotchke /chotskə/ /sotskə/.

scone /skohn/ pr n : /skon/ actually, an increasing third of British pronounce it the same as Americans.

scope col v : to *check out*, esp. *babe*s, "prepare to be scoped on" (by a woman heading out for a night on the town).

score inf n : bargain, good deal.

score v : obtain, buy, esp. *dope*.

score! intj : meaning, you've *scored* a bargain.

Scotch® tape n : *Sellotape*.

scratch (pool, billiards, snooker) v : *foul*.

scratch pad n : scribbling pad or block.

screamer n : a mountain climbing fall, "I took a 25' screamer at the *Gunks*," also a sensational headline.

screaming meemies n : screaming *abdabs*.

screw v : sex, syn. fuck, *stuff, poke*.

screw anchor n : *Rawlplug*, plastic plug used for holding screws in masonry.

screw-up n v : *cock-up*.

scrim n : theatre backdrop, opaque when frontlit and transparent when backlit.

scrog v : *sex*.

scrump sl v : *sex*.

scrunchy n : cloth covered elastic band used to tie back hair, usu. in a ponytail.

scuttlebutt n v : rumour, gossip, scoop (journalism sense).

s-curve (s-turn) n : *zig-zag bend*. See also *hairpin turn*.

scuzzball n : *scuzzy* person.

scuzzy adj : vile, *grotty*.

second base n : see *base*.

second floor n : *first floor* (see *first floor*).

second-last usage adj : second to last, second from last, penultimate, last but one.

section n : a US surveying unit of a square with mile long sides, (one square mile, 640 acres), see *township, back 40*.

sedan (car) n : *saloon*.

see a man about a dog expr v : take a leak.

seeya [see you] intj : bye, but also used to emphasise smugness, (along with stress on the first syllable), "seeya, but I wouldn't wanna be ya!"

self-serve (*gas* station) n : *self-service*.

semi /semie/ [semitrailer] cf n : *articulated lorry*, syn. very large *lorry, juggernaut, eighteen-wheeler*.

semi- /semie/ prefix : /semee/.

Senate n : in the Senate each state gets two seats in *Congress*.

Senate majority/minority leader n : see *majority leader*.

senator n : member of the *Senate*, and also term of address, "Senator Wellstone was the coolest."

send up cf v : sentence to imprisonment.

senior n : 4th year of *high school* or college, or last year in case of two- or three-year programs, see *freshman*, *sophomore*, *junior*.

senior citizen n : *OAP*, *old age pensioner*.

senior high n : senior *high school*, grades 10–12 (ages about 16–18).

set off usage v : *let off*, "the kids are setting off *firecrackers*."

seven expr n : 'back in seven' = back in a week, in the right context, cf. *five*.

seven eleven n : see *7-Eleven*.

seven layer death torte n : particularly rich cake containing lethal doses of chocolate.

Seven Sisters n : seven highly regarded women's colleges (two are now *coed*) in the eastern US–Barnard, Bryn Mawr, Mount Holyoke, Radcliffe, Smith, Vassar, and Wellesley–whose name came about when they self-organised in 1927 to promote private, independent women's colleges. See also *redbrick*, *Ivy League*, *Oxbridge*.

sewer pipe, **soil pipe** n : drain (indoors).

sex cf v : syn. *pop*, *screw*, shaft, ride, *bonk*, cram (*Chicago*), *scrog*, *get off*, jazz, *plank*.

shaft v : *cheat*, treat unfairly.

shag cf n v : kind of dance, also a kind of thick carpet.

shagamaw n : mythical Maine creature *Bipedester deleuissimus* with two bear forefeet, and two moose hindfeet, which it varies alternately, making it tricky to track.

shake n : shingle, but split from log rather than cut from it.

shaping up expr v : developing.

sheers n : *net curtains*.

sheesh intj : *harrumph*!

sheet rock n : *plaster board*.

sherbet cf n : flavoured ice, sorbet.

shift (car gears) n : *change*.

shim n : thin strip of metal or wood.

shinny n : *shinty*, children's simple form of hockey game.

shingle n : see *hang out a shingle*, *shit on a shingle*.

ship v : to send by *post*, a parcel service, or private courier, as well as commercial shipping agents and actual ships.

shipping n : postage, the amount for shipping, "how much is the shipping and handling."

shit on a shingle (army) sl n : creamed *chipped beef* on toast.

shoofly pie n : traditional Pennsylvania Dutch *dessert* made with brown sugar, *molasses* and butter.

shoot euph intj : shit.

shoot the shit sl expr v : talk, *natter*, gossip, see *gabfest*.

shop cf n : workshop, garage; city shops = place where city vehicles (police cars, buses, fire engines, etc.) are fixed. But see *coffee shop*.

shopping cart, **caddy** n : *shopping trolley*.

short bus regional n : innuendo of retarded person, because of the mode of transport typically employed for them. "She came on the short bus," "don't catch the short bus" (do something stupid).

shorts (underwear) n : *pants*, *underpants*, "I was so scared I had to change my shorts," see *boxers*.

shot n : (1 fluid oz. of) liquor or any other drink, "let's go and shoot shots," "I need a shot of espresso."

shot n : *jab*.

shotgun intj v : *dibs* on riding shotgun–to ride next to the driver in a car–popular with kids, "I've got shotgun."

show n : *movies* or any public or group entertainment, "go to the show."

show v : show up, "she never showed," "do you think he'll show," and the psychological sense of show up, be present, be there for me.

shred (snow boarding, skate boarding) v : the smooth and easy actions performed by a superior *skater* or snow boarder (shredder), syn. *carve*, "he shreds."

shred inf v : lambaste, excoriate.

shrimp n : *prawn*.

shrooms [contr mushrooms] n : psychoactive mushrooms, and by humorous analogy applied to *regular* mushrooms, "put shrooms on that *za!*"

shtick n : métier.

shuck n v : to husk (esp. *corn*) or shell, to take off (coat, etc.).

shucks intj : *darn*, nuts, '*aw* shucks.'

shyster inf n : dubious, unpleasant businessman, also dishonest and immoral lawyer or politician.

sidebar [from sidebars in magazine articles] col n : an aside.

sideburns (hair) n : *sideboards*.

sidewalk n : *pavement*.

signal (car) v : *indicate*, see *turn signal*.

Silicon Alley col n : Chelsea, a Manhattan neighbourhood in New York, where many internet development companies are located. See *Silicon Valley*.

Silicon Forest col n : the Beaverton area east of Portland OR, which includes such computer companies as Intel, Tektronix, Center Point, and Hewlett-Packard. See *Silicon Valley*.

Silicon Valley n : San Jose and surrounding or nearby cities (Cupertino, Santa Clara, Fremont, and Scotts Valley) in the southern part of the *Bay Area* that has myriad computer (and related) companies, many of whom have (had) their headquarters there (Hewlett-Packard, Apple, Everex,

Taligent, InfoWorld, Sun, Santa Cruz Operation, Atari, DEC, Xerox PARC, SRI, Stanford University, Borland, and Mountain Computer). By association, certain other areas that have many computer companies are nicknamed similarly, such as *Silicon Alley*, and *Silicon Forest*.

Silly Valley col n : *Silicon Valley*.

silver dollar n : dollar coin (they were actually silver 1794–1935). Recent commemorative ones are the cupro-nickel Eisenhower dollars (1971–1978, also 40% silver 1971–1976) and these are huge, like the old *half-crowns*. See also *Sacagawea dollar*, *Susan B. Anthony dollar*.

sir n : a common form of address, esp. of boys to their fathers, store *clerks* to customers, and strangers getting another's attention, "excuse me, sir."

skank sl n : *ho*.

skanky adj : *sketchy*, *crusty*, dubious, dingy, dishevelled, grimy, dirty.

skater n : semi-post-pubescent skate board (and also snowboard) fanatic who, with the rest of the pack, have an uncanny ability to locate *whatever*'s *going down*, in a blur of high-speed, building-scaling, *sidewalk*-traversing baggy *grunge*. (The *pants* are so baggy the *crotch* is almost at ground level.) Of course, there is a lingo (*bail*, catch air, cone, *face plant*, fakie, fatty pow pow, goofy, ollie, *shred*, ...).

skeeters (esp S) col n : mosquitoes.

skeptic, skeptical sp n adj : *sceptic*, *sceptical*.

sketched col adj : *sketchy*, "that's sketched!"

sketchy col adj : of a person of questionable motives, morals, whatever, of a dubious or suspect situation or thing.

skillet n : frying pan.

skim milk n : *skimmed milk*.

skinny n : info, truth, "what's the skinny on actresses?" syn low-down, *poop*.

skinny-dip v : nude bathing.

skirt dated n : woman, syn. *bint*, (popular with Humphrey Bogart).

slack n : tolerance, leniency, 'cut me some slack' = 'give me a *break*,' also *cool*ness.

slate cf vt : schedule, arrange, "the game was slated for tomorrow."

sled sp n : *sledge*.

sleeper n : slow-burning bestseller or success (*movie*, book).

slick n : *glossy magazine*.

slick usage adj : slippery, "it's slicker 'n cow snot," "slick Willy."

slicker n : (oilskin) raincoat, also snappy city *dude* (city slicker), also clever rogue.

slimers n : J*ell-O* made with vodka, popular amongst *high school* kids, syn. *jello shots, jello shooters, jello* poppers, atomic *jello*.

slingshot n : *catapult*.

sliver usage n : *splinter* (of wood, etc. in the skin).

sloppy Joe cf n : hamburger made by scooping or pouring a porridgey sauce of ground beef and tomato paste cooked in a *skillet* onto buns, sometimes served *open-faced*. Manwich® is a ready-made sauce in a can.

sloth /slahth/ n : /slohth/.

slowpoke n : *slowcoach*.

slushy n : drink made of soda or fruit punch blended with crushed ice.

smackers, smackeroos sl n : *dollars*, money.

smarts n : brains.

smartass n : *smartarse*, smart aleck.

smock n : *overall*.

smoking gun expr n : evidence serving as conclusive proof.

smore, s'more n : popular campfire snack of toasted marshmallows sandwiched between *graham* crackers with a square of chocolate, "I'm making smores" [they're so tasty you want s'more].

SMS abbr n : Short Message Service, text messaging, *txt*.

smudge n v : protect (from frost, insects) by means of smouldering mass, also to bless, purify with smoke from smouldering herb bundles (Native American ritual— equivalent to censer or thurible in Judeo-Christian rituals).

snafu [acr, orig military sl] n : situation normal, all fucked (fouled) up.

snap, snap fastener n : *press stud, popper*.

snap bean n : green bean grown for its pods (as opposed to shell bean).

snap pea (also sugar (snap) pea and snow pea) n : sugar pea, *mange-tout*.

snatch n : *vagina*.

sneakers n : *plimsolls, trainers*.

Snickers (candy bar) n : *Marathon bar*.

snipe hunt n : a ruse to entice the naïve into the woods (for whatever reason), holding a sack to catch snipe, which will supposedly be scared out by the perpetrators, "ok guys! Let's show the new people how to hunt snipe," and generally any prank played on *newbies*, see *gotcha*.

snipes n : *fag-end*s, shoot snipes = picking up *dog-end*s.

snit n : a sulk, "she's in a snit."

snow bird n : New Yorker (and *east coast*er and Canadian) who migrates to Florida for the winter, and also those (*west coast*ers) wintering in Mexico, or even the Midwesterners found in Arizona.

snuck v : sneaked.

snuff v : die, kill.

snuggle n : having your *trousers* (shorts) yanked up sharply, usu. from behind, *wedgie*.

soccer /sahker/ n : /sokə/ *football, footer*.

soda n : general term for any *fizzy drink*, esp. on the *West Coast* and the *northeast*. See also *coke, pop,* and *tonic*.

soda cracker n : *cream cracker*.

solarium cf n : conservatory, sunroom.

solder /sahder/ n v : /solde/.

solicitor n : canvasser, "No Soliciting" (sign seen on doors of office buildings).

solitaire (game) n : *patience*.

someplace usage n : somewhere, "you can tell he's from someplace else."

soo-ee, soooey, sewee n : pig call (with a rising pitch).

Sooner n : person from Oklahoma. "[In 1889] the last big tract of Indian land was declared open for settlement, in [what is now] Oklahoma. The claimants and the speculators mounted their horses and lined up like trotters waiting for a starting gun. The itchy ones jumped the gun and were ever after known as Sooners–and Oklahoma was thereafter called the Sooner State."—Alistair Cooke, *America* 1973.

sophomore n : 2nd year, see *freshman, junior, senior*.

sophomoric adj : immature and overconfident.

sosh /sohsh/ [social] col abbr n : pronunciation and sometimes spelling of soc, "I'm a soc /sohsh/ student" (social studies at university), "I never read the newsgroups soc /sohsh/ whatever" (news:soc.*).

South, The South n : the southeastern part of the US, the *Southern States*, see *Southern*.

Southern adj : attitude, mores, accent, and history of the southern folk hailing from the Chesapeake Bay area of VA, NC, SC, GA, Gulf States (AL, MS, LA, eastern part of TX). See also *Southern States* and *Deep South*.

Southern Belle n : beautiful *Southern* woman.

Southern drawl n : the *Southern* accent or way of speech.

Southern States [from the original eleven states of the Confederacy during the American Civil War] n : *Dixie*, the four states of the upper South (AR, NC, TN, VA), plus the seven states of the *Deep South*. Culturally, parts of DE, KY, MD, MO, and WV are considered *Southern*, and parts of TX are not.

southpaw n : left-handed person. [Baseball diamonds are traditionally laid out so batters won't be blinded by the setting sun, which results in the pitchers left hand being south.]

Southwest n : AZ, NM and parts of CA, (NV), and TX, see *West Coast*.

sow bug n : *wood louse*.

spackle n v : like *Polyfilla*, can use toothpaste in a pinch.

spare parts usage n : *spares*.

spatula n : *fish slice*.

specialty sp n : *speciality*.

speed bump n : *speed retarder*.

spelled sp v : *spelt*.

spendy col adj: expensive, *dear*.

spiel n : line of talk.

spiffy adj : *spiffing*, looking good, "that's pretty spiffy."

spin doctor [1984] n : sophist, rhetorician, yarn spinner, usu. *whacked* re-interpreter of events, usu. political and spawned in DC.

spit-up n v : esp. baby spit-up (=baby *sick*), regurgitate or vomit.

the split n : *the splits*.

splitsville n : state of leaving (splitting)– everything from 'popping out for a mo' to breaking up a relationship 'Welcome to Splitsville, Population: 3, You, Ben & Jerry.'

spooge n : cum, semen, *jism*.

spook col n : *CIA* agent, or of any of the other entities (*NSA, FBI,* etc.).

spook v : scare.

spool usage n : *reel*, bobbin, "spool of *thread*."

sports n : *sport*, 'the sports pages.'

spot v : support, yield, lend, advance credit, "can you spot me a ten-spot."

spreckles n : *sprinkles*.

sprinkles (confection) n : *hundreds and thousands*, syn. *jimmies*.

sprouts cf usage n : *alfalfa* sprouts, used like mustard and cress, popular in *sandwiches* particularly on the *West Coast*, "do you have any *sandwiches* without sprouts?"

spunk cf n : liveliness, excitement, courageousness.

squash [shortening of Algonquian *asquatasquash*] n : any cucurbit fruit (gourd family), see *winter squash, summer squash*.

squonk n : *Lacrimacorpus dissolvens* a warty, loose-skinned, *butt-ugly* (and hence wretchedly shy) creature of the northern Pennsylvania hemlock forests, that when sought *plays possum* by dissolving in a surfeit of melancholy.

stall n : individual cubicle in public toilets.

stand up v : not showing up for a *date*, "don't stand him up!" "she stood him up," "I've been stood up."

star n : *pip*, "three-star general."

Stars and Stripes n : *US* flag, see *Old Glory*.

state highway n : numbered *highway* within a state, "Highway 99 will take you into the capital," see *US, interstate*.

State of the Union n : like the *Queen's Speech*. Today this takes the form of an annual speech by the *president* to Congress, delivered with much ceremony and covered as a major news event. "The President shall from time to time give to Congress information of the State of the Union and recommend to their Consideration such measures as he shall judge necessary and expedient."—Article II, Sec. 3, U.S. Constitution.

station wagon n : *estate car, shooting break*.

stick, stick shift (car) n : *manual*, "do you drive a stick?"

sticker n : decorative self-adhesive label, transfer, *decal*.

stogie, stogy /stohgee/ n : cigar or specifically a cheap slender cigar.

stoked sl adj : *chuffed*.

stomp v : stamp, tread heavily.

stoner n : person for whom getting stoned is part of their lifestyle.

stoopid adj : stupid emphasised by sp. and also term of address.

stoplights n : traffic lights, "I got another ticket for running a stoplight," "I live in beautiful, scenic Milpitas, which is Spanish for land of a thousand stoplights."

stop sign n : large red octagonal road sign, emblazoned with a large white 'STOP,' found at most street intersections. Due to the rectangular grid layout of American towns (see *township*), intersections are two streets crossing at right angles, which are then controlled by four stop signs (4-way stop) or a pair (2-way stop) giving precedence to one of the streets. cf. *give way*.

storage cell n : *accumulator* (rechargeable electric cell).

store n : *shop*, 'let's go to the store' means 'let's go down [to] the *shop*s.'

story (floor of building) sp n : *storey*.

stove n : gas stove, *cooker*.

straight, straight-up (drink) adj : *neat*.

straight razor n : *cut-throat razor*.

street usage n : *road*, cf. *cul-de-sac, close, drive, blvd, mews*.

streetcar n : *tram*, trolley, *trolley car*.

street legal adj : certified roadworthy, typically of an unlikely looking car.

string beans n : *French beans*.

The Strip n : the main *drag* through *Las Vegas* chocked with surreal hotels emblazoned with flashing neon.

strip mall n : string of *shop*s, usu. set back a bit off the road for parking, etc.

stroller n : *pushchair*.

strut v : stroll proudly, walk tall, swagger, "she was strutting her stuff." (See *mince*.)

stucco n : plaster for interior or exterior decorating. Like *Artex*.

student driver n : *learner*; student drivers can drive any car, accompanied by qualified driver, with no external indication such as *L plates*, though they need a *driver's permit*.

student driver car n : professional instructor's car, which usu. has a huge sign on top indicating status of occupant and the school's particulars.

studio apartment n : *bedsit*, studio flat.

studly inf adj : manly, *macho*, "he's studly," 'studly Dudley' (impressively tough *dude*).

stump v : politician making the campaign rounds, 'on the stump' = campaigning for an *election*.

stylin adj : working out exceptionally well "he's stylin," "styling place you got here."

sub [contr] n : *submarine sandwich*.

subdivision n : a housing tract, like a *housing estate*, "she lives in that new subdivision north of town," but technically the actual tract of land being subdivided [originally previous farm-sized properties] for new houses, usu. as a town expands.

submarine n : *hero sandwich*.

substitute teacher, substitute, sub n : *supply teacher*.

subway cf n : *tube*, *underground*, *metro*, (San Francisco *BART*, the Chicago '*L*,' the T in Boston (MBTA includes buses and subway), New York subway (that used to have an '*el*'), *DC* Metro (Metrorail)).

suck v (adj **sucky**) : bad, "that sucks," "I had a sucky day."

sucker n : *lollipop*.

sucker n v : dupe, to cheat, fool, "he suckered me into it."

suck face col v : *snogging*, *mashing*.

suds col n : beer.

sudser (TV) n : soap opera.

sugar apple n : *cherimoya*, sweetsop, *custard apple*, Annona sp.

summer squash n : tend to be tender and green, such as vegetable *marrow*.

Sun Belt n : sunny states like CA, AZ, NM, and FL, but also the *Gulf States*. See also *Borscht Belt*, *Bible Belt*, and *Rust Belt*.

sunny side up adj : eggs lightly fried without turning them over.

sunshower n : rainfall whilst sunny.

Superman [the super hero] n : the quintessential *alien*, working hard to fulfill "truth, justice, and the American way," see the *American Dream*.

sure adv : surely, "he sure is fun."

Susan B. Anthony dollar n : smaller sized *silver dollar* (cupro-nickel, 1979–1981), the size of a *2p*. Popular in *Las Vegas* for use in the slot machines, and found only occasionally elsewhere. See also *Sacagawea dollar*.

suspenders n : *braces*.

suzy, suzy B col n : *Susan B. Anthony dollar*.

sweater n : *jumper*.

sweet col adj : syn. *safe*, *bitchin'*, *neat*, *cool*, *fresh*, *rad*, *brill*.

sweetie n : term of endearment, syn. *poppet*, honey.

sweet tea [Southern] n : sweet *iced tea*, the sugar added prior to the tea being poured over ice; typical drink of the *South*, along with (iced) *lemonade*, ant. *unsweet tea*.

swell adj : splendid, excellent.

swimsuit n : *swimming costume*, *swimming trunks*.

swisher n **swishingly** adv : airball, a basketball shot so good it completely avoids the rim and 'swishes' through touching only net, see *nothing but net*.

switch (railroad) n : *points*.

switch (railroad) v : *shunt*.
switchback cf n : rail or road that *zig-zags* sharply, esp. in hilly terrain.
switch blade, swish blade n : *flick-knife*.
swizzle stick n : stirring rod for drinks.

— t —

table cf v : shelve a meeting item, "table a motion," "table that for later."
tacky adj : shabby, seedy, *naff*.
taco [Mexican] n : hard corn tortilla folded over contents of beans, lettuce, grated cheese, meat, etc.–fish taco, chicken taco . . .
ta da! intj : voilà, but chanted in triumph, syn. *Bob's your uncle*.
taffy (confection) n : like seaside *rock* that's been pulled and worked until it's chewy like toffee.
tag usage n : *label*.
tag line (marketing) n : *strap line*.
tailgate v : to follow too closely in a car, "I have someone tailgating me."
tailpipe n : *exhaust pipe*.
take usage v : *do* (*course*, class).
take a hike imp v : *sod off*.
takeout n : *takeaway, to go*.
taking the fifth expr v : literally, exercising the right specified in the Fifth Amendment to the *Constitution* not to be a witness against oneself. Often used metaphorically to mean not making a comment. No comment, pass, 'I have no response to that.'
tap cf n v : tap on keg (of beer).
tard [contr mentally retarded] sl n : stupid, clumsy person, syn. *retard, spaz, flid*, ignoranus.
tardy adj : late.
Tarheel n : person from N. Carolina, " . . . is an *intern* from UNC (Go Heels!) and will be working on . . ."

tarnation [euph damnation] intj : syn. heck.
tart n : see *poptart* and *bippi tart*.
tater-tots (fast food) n : short cylinder of deep-fried grated potato.
tattle-tale n v : tell-tale (usu. child). (See also *fink*.)
T-bird abbr n : Thunderbird, usu. in reference to the popular classic car.
tea cf n : usu. refers to *hot tea*, or *iced tea* in hot weather or summertime.
tear a new asshole expr v : *bollocking*, chew out, tear into (someone) with a passion, "she tore me a new asshole."
teed off v : *cheesed off*.
teeter-totter n : *see-saw*.
teleprompter [TelePrompTer®] n : *autocue*.
teller, bank teller (also Scot) n : bank cashier.
ten-foot pole n : *barge pole*, in full, I wouldn't touch it with a ten-foot pole.
tennies n : *sneakers*, tennis shoes, *trainers*.
test n : *exam*, "when's your driving test?"
Texas gate n : *cattle grid*, cattle guard, syn. vehicle pass.
Thanksgiving n : think a Christmas feast (turkey, stuffing, pumpkin pie, *corn* (on the cob), etc.) a month before Christmas. Thanksgiving is celebrated on the fourth Thursday in November, towns have parades, and some folks skip work Friday and make a nice long weekend of it, visiting distant relatives (making it the heaviest time for travel). The pilgrims arrived in the Mayflower in 1620 and had quite the miserable first winter. However, the half that survived had an excellent harvest in 1621, with outstanding assistance and friendship from the local Wampanoag tribe, which enabled them to survive well their second winter. They celebrated with a joint three-day harvest festival, which custom spread throughout the colonies,

and is now proclaimed by each new *president*.

theater cf n : *cinema*.

then regional suff adv : a good shibboleth of Minnesotans who turn many a statement into a question suffixed with then, "So, you're planning on visiting us in Minnesota, then?"

third party n : In US politics very little is ever accomplished by anyone without them first joining either the republican or the Democratic Party; if they become powerful they will try to affect their chosen party's agenda rather then go against both parties. Although several other parties have been around for many years, they are usu. considered inconsequential and totally ignored in the news media; so when an exception does occur–usu. in the form of a well-known person running for *president* without major party support–the term "third party" is often used. Or *governor*—the most recent case was Jesse Ventura, a former professional wrestler who was elected governor of Minnesota in 1998. (He did not run again in 2002.)

thread (sewing) n : *cotton*.

three dollar bill expr n : *nine-bob note*, often '*queer* as a three dollar bill'–queer as in strange, but nowadays also *gay*.

Three Musketeers (chocolate bar) n : *Milky bar*.

three sheets to the wind adj : *drunk*.

through prep : to (inclusive), "Monday through Friday."

through v : finished, "are you through with the *ketchup*."

thru inf (sp) prep v : *through*, "drive-thru," "Monday thru Friday," 'A thru Z' /zee/ (rather than A to Z /zed/).

thruway regional n : *expressway*.

thumb tack n : *drawing pin*.

Thunderbirds n : *USAF* exhibition flying team, syn. *Blue Angels*, *Red Arrows*.

ticket, traffic ticket n : receiving a ticket is actually a *summons*, and assuming you are found guilty, then you 'have' a ticket, which counts as a point on your licence, and is equivalent to an *endorsement*, "I got off that ticket by going to traffic school," "remember, three tickets and you're out."

tick off cf v : to irritate.

tic-tac-toe n : *noughts and crosses*.

tidbit sp n : *titbit*.

tiddledywinks sp n : *tiddlywinks*.

tie n : see *railroad tie*.

tight expr adj : *cool*, "that's tight!"

tightie-whities joc n : *Y-fronts*, ant. *boxers*.

tightwad n : miserly person.

time sink [from electronics, allusion to heat sink] n : engaging activity that soaks up time.

timetable n : used only for bus/train timetable–*schedule* used for school timetable.

tire sp n : *tyre*.

toast sl intj n adv : doomed, in big trouble, *history*, "dude, you're toast."

toasty cf adj : toast-like (flavour).

to go (food) v : *take away*, "for here, or to go?"

Togo's /tohgohs/ n : *sandwich* shop chain, syn. *deli* (play on *to go*).

toilet cf n : more usu. brings to mind the toilet bowl rather than the *bathroom*.

toll-free (phone) adj adv : *freefone*, of phone numbers that are free *calls*, such as 800 numbers, 888, 877, 866, (and coming 855, 844, 833, 822, see area code table), "*call* us toll-free."

tomato /təmaydoh/ n : /təmahtoh/.

tongue depressor n : *doctor's spatula*.

tonic n : an old school, general term for any *fizzy drink*, esp. in the *northeast* or *New England* states. See also *coke*, *pop*, and *soda*.

too adv : certainly, indeed, "I do not!" "you do, too!" "do not!" "do, too!" . . .

toolies [Canadian sp and alt. of tules] n : see *tules*.

top (car) n : roof (esp. of a *convertible*, "take off (open) the top"), *hood*.

topping n : any additions on top of food, as in optional pizza toppings, varieties of *icings* and decorations on cakes, *sprinkles*, nuts, fruits, and syrup on ice cream, or even just bran flakes on a bagel.

torch cf v : incinerate, burn.

torpedo n : *hero sandwich*.

tortilla /torteeya/ [Mexican] n : flat round corn or wheat flour bread similar to chapati.

toss cookies v : throw up.

total v : destroy beyond repair [from insurance term 'total loss'], usu. in reference to a car, "my car was totaled," but also even trivial objects, "she totaled the *napkin*," syn. undefuckable.

totally awesome expr adj : means everything from OK to outstanding.

touch base v : to check in with someone, "be sure and touch base with Joe before going home."

tough guy n : *hard case*.

touristas, turistas [Sp] sl n : *vaction*al *diarrhea, Montezuma's revenge*.

toward usage prep : *towards*.

township n : a 6 by 6 miles US surveying unit of 36 *sections*. Most of the US is actually laid out this way, a scheme invented by Jefferson, and in many areas, esp. the *Midwest*, roads can be seen to be laid out on this grid, and it is also behind the square grid layouts in major cities.

tp abbr n v : toilet paper, syn. *loo roll*, "we tp'd the house."

tracks, railroad tracks n : *line, railway line*. See also *from the wrong side of the tracks*.

tractor trailer n : *articulated lorry*.

trade usage v : swap.

traffic circle (road) n : *roundabout*.

trail n : *footpath*.

trailer n : *caravan*.

trailer park n : *caravan site* (same connotations), tornado's favourite striking area, and popular UFO landing site.

trailer trash n adj : *white trash* living in a *trailer park*.

trailer truck n : *articulated lorry*.

train station n : *railway station*.

tramp cf n : slut.

transfer n : bus, train ticket for transfer to another bus, train.

transient n : euph. for homeless person, *tramp*, syn. *cruster, bum*.

transmission n : *gearbox*.

trapezium n : *trapezoid*.

trapezoid n : *trapezium*.

trash n : *rubbish*.

trash bags n : *rubbish bags, dustbin bag*s.

trash can n : *waste paper bin* or *dustbin*.

trash man n : *dustbin man*.

traveling salesperson (or -man or -woman) n : *commercial traveller*.

trick adj : *tricked out*, "that bike is really trick."

tricked out adj : when something (as a bike, car, computer, etc.) has all the latest and hottest accessories or components.

trick or treat /trikətreet/ trad excl v : the cry of children as they scamper from door to door on Hallowe'en gathering *candy*.

trillion cf n : 10^{12}.

trim n : architrave, moulding around doors, windows, etc.

trinity [Cajun, Creole] n : chopped onions, bell peppers, celery, sautéed as the start of any dish, and skipping the divine 'seasoning' is considered a mortal sin.

troll sl n : unattractive older *gay* man.

trolley, trolley car n : *tram, streetcar*.

trot n : old woman.

truck n : *lorry*.

truck n : *pickup* truck.

trucker n : *truck* driver, ***lorry*** driver.

truck flap girl n : *mud flap girl*.

truck stop n : facility near *freeway* or major *highway* including *diner* (see ***transport café***), ***petrol station***, and garage, geared towards *trucks*, syn. ***pull-in***.

trunk (car) n : ***boot***.

tsk /tsk/ intj : cf. ***tut***.

tsk tsk /tsk tsk/ intj : cf. ***tut-tut***.

tub usage n : bath tub.

the tube col n : *TV*, syn ***the box***.

tube (radio) n : ***valve***.

tubular (surfer) sl adj : particularly good, syn. *awesome*.

'tude contr col n : attitude, "he's a *dude* with a 'tude."

tules, tulies /toolees/ [*Scirpus californicus* & spp. a New World bullrush] n : *boondocks*, sticks, "he lives way out in the tules."

tuna melt /toonə/ n : /choonə/ /tyoonə/ see *melt*.

turk usage cf n : often young turk, person keen to implement their new ideas, invariably at odds with preceding ones.

turkey sl n : ***twit***.

turmeric /təməric/ /tooməric/ /tyooməric/ pr n : /terməric/.

turn (business) v : ***make***, as in turn a profit.

turnip n : ***swede***, syn. *rutabaga*.

turnpike n : toll *freeway*.

turn signal n : ***indicator***.

tush, tushie sl n : *butt*.

tux abbr n : *tuxedo*.

tuxedo n : dinner jacket often worn with white frilled shirt, and the young man's choice for formal occasions such as the *high school prom*, or a wedding.

TV n : ***telly***, television.

twat sl n : *vagina*.

tweak sl v : *lose it*, "the *dude*'s tweakin'" [originally from twitching of *crank* or crack withdrawals].

tweaker col n : pubescent who will eventually evolve into a *skater*.

tweaker sl n : unstable person liable to *tweak* out.

twenty-one (card game) n : ***pontoon***, *blackjack*.

Twin Cities n : Minneapolis, St Paul.

twist [and twirl] rsl n : girl, ***bird***.

twister cf n : tornado.

two bits n : quarter, 25¢, reminiscent of ancient days when the Spanish pieces of eight, the precursor to the *dollar*, could be broken into eight pieces.

two-way stop n : see 2-*way stop*.

— U —

ubbie dubbie n : jargon, secret language (like pig-Latin), "if you live in a remote Patagonian Ubbie-Dubbie speaking village . . ." [from kids secret language in 1970s *TV* show *Zoom*].

Udub /yoo dub/ n : University of Washington, north of Seattle.

u-ee, u-ey /yooee/ n : u-turn, "*hang* a u-ee."

uff da /oof dah/ [Norwegian] (Minnesota) intj : disgruntlement, syn. *oy vey*, carumba, good grief.

ukase /yookays/ /ookahz/ n : edict, syn fiat.

ummm . . . intj : a pregnant um, (heavily dependant on intonation or context, but) usu. precedes a more penetrating query, since what previously transpired left something to be desired, "ummm, am I wrong?" "ummm . . . are you naturally stupid, or did you train."

Uncle Sam n : *USA*, the government, or its people, equivalent to ***John Bull***.

underdrapes n : ***net curtains***.

underpass n : see *pedestrian underpass*.

undershirt n : ***singlet***, ***vest***.

under the hood expr prep : behind the scenes, the (inner) workings, the innards.

unglued v : *crazy*.

unhinged adj : unstable, syn. *whacked, unglued,* all *bent out of shape*.

unlisted (phone book) n : *ex-directory,* non-registered.

unsweet tea [Southern] n : *iced tea,* ant. *sweet tea.*

upchuck v : vomit.

upcoming usage adj : *forthcoming*.

up-front adj : direct, unpretentious, open and honest.

Upper Midwest n : includes MN, WI, MI, see *Midwest.*

upscale adj : *upmarket*.

upstairs cf n : (usu.) *first floor*.

uptown n adj : away from *downtown* or *city centre* and towards a suburb or a specific district, 'uptown New York,' also an upscale district, "uptown girl."

US abbr n adj : United States, conventional short form of United States of America, and also regular qualifier, 'US Armed Forces,' 'US-EPA' (Environmental Protection Agency').

US highway (road) n : national numbered *highway* system dating from the 1920s, many superseded by *interstates,* e.g. US 101–the original highway that goes up the *West Coast.*

USA abbr n : United States of America.

USAF abbr n : United States Air Force, syn. *RAF.*

USD abbr n : United States Dollars, used to distinguish it from other currencies. cf. *GBP.*

use usage v : need, "I could use a drink," "he looks like he could use a *vacation.*"

— V —

vacation n : *holiday,* "where are you taking your vacation?"

vacuum usage v : to *hoover.*

vacuum cleaner n : *hoover.*

vagina cf n : syn. *clam, bearded clam, crack, pussy, twat,* twelge, futz, nookie, *muff, snatch,* badger, beaver, "A *plank*ed, split, wet beaver"—John Irving.

valance n : *pelmet* (hides curtain rail).

valedictorian n : highest ranking graduating *high school* student, who gives the class's farewell address at the graduation ceremonies, see *GPA, salutatorian,* cf. *head boy/girl.*

van Gogh /van goh/ n : /van gof/ (Dutch people say /fan khohkh/).

vanilla adj : [the standard US ice cream flavour] ordinary, default, often used in the computer industry to refer to the standard version of some piece of hardware, software or operating system.

vapor, vaporize sp n v : *vapour, vaporise.*

varmint [vermin] n : rascal, pest (person or animal).

varsity n : principal athletic team at university.

vase /vays/ /vayz/ n : /vahz/.

VCR usage n : *video* (the machine).

veep inf n : vice president.

veg col v : vegetate, "I'm gonna veg out in front of the *TV.*"

velveeta [VELVEETA®] n : a toxic orange, pasty, cheese-like product (see *American cheese*) that comes in huge, cheap slabs, snubbed as *trailer trash* food but enjoyed in even the finest homes. Usu. served melted.

vest cf n : *waistcoat.*

vet abbr n : *veteran,* "Vietnam vet," "he's a vet of the Gulf War."

veteran n : experienced, even of only one bout of action, "she's a veteran of three space missions," see *vet.*

veto (politics) n v : legislation, once passed by both houses of *Congress* in the ordinary way, is enacted if either of two things happen: the *president* signs it into law, or the *president* refuses ('vetoes' it) and *Congress* then passes it again ('overrides the veto'), this time with ⅔ of each house voting in favour.

visit vt : chat, spend time with, "It was sure nice visiting with you on the phone," "Let's visit tomorrow."

visiting card n : *calling card*.

vitamin /viedəmin/ n : /vitəmin/.

vo-tech col n : focusing on the vocational aspect of a (non-academic) technical college. (See also *community college*.)

VP inf abbr n : vice president. Vice president is two words in the *Constitution*, although commonly seen in hyphenated form.

— W —

w/ abbr prep : with, a quite common written abbreviation in lists and written instructions, and also office memos and informal notes.

wad n : money, as in a wad of notes, "she blew her wad in *Lost Wages*."

wad sl n : the male groin bulge, syn. *bump*, also sl. semen, cf. *camel toes*.

wagon n : *trolley* for serving food and drinks.

wagon sp n : *waggon*.

wahine /wah heen(a)/ n : surfer *babe*.

wake up and smell the coffee expr v : *get real*.

walk n : partake in the graduation ceremony (*high school* and *college*) and 'walk' down the aisle to the podium and be presented with a diploma, "I'm gonna walk," "He already walked?"

walla /wahlah/ intj : voilà, as pronounced and commonly misspelled.

wall-eyed adj : opposite of cross-eyed.

wall-to-wall (carpet) n : *fitted*.

wannabe [want to be, see *-a*] inf n adj : usu. of a person who wants some unattainable characteristic, "he's just a wannabe" (*loser*), "it's wannabe-wood" (fake-wood plastic paneling), "forever remaining a wannabe."

want ad n : classified ad in newspaper, "check the want ads."

want in, **want out**, **want off**, etc. usage expr v : wish to be included or excluded from some *deal*, "I want in," "she wants out," "If you want *off of* our email list."

wapiti n : *elk*.

wash cloth n : *face flannel*.

wash up cf v : wash your hands, face, etc.

water cooler n : cold water dispenser.

water heater n : *geyser* (gas), *immersion heater* (electric).

wave, **the wave** n : *Mexican wave*, [invented by Krazy George 15 Oct 1981 at an *A's* game, and perhaps independently by *Udub* on 31 Oct 1981].

wax paper n : *grease-proof paper*.

way adj : very, "*way cool*."

way! intj : emphatic response to erroneous 'no way.' "He's way rich." "No way." "Way!"

way cool expr adj : very *cool*.

waymazing col contr adj : *way* amazing.

wazoo expr n : [buttocks] up the wazoo = up the creek without a paddle, out the wazoo = seemingly never ending supply, e.g. "he has bucks out the wazoo" = he's loaded.

weather stripping n : *draught excluder*.

wedding band n : wedding ring.

wedgie n : when your underwear rides up (hungry arse), or gets tugged up, and wedges, "errr! I gave myself a wedgie. I hate that!," *syn. snuggie*.

weed whacker (Weed Whacker™) n : *strimmer*.

wee hours expr n : the *small hours*, the early hours, cf. *oh-dark thirty*.

weenie inf n : subspecies of *nerd*, also *twit*, also ineffectual or weak person.

weenie, wienie, wiener inf n : *penis*.

welcome expr adj : see *you're welcome*.

West Coast n : often refers to things CA, but does include *PNW* (OR and WA), see *out west*, and also *back east*, *the South*, *Midwest*.

wetback [from swimming the Rio Grande] n : illegal immigrant, "I was a wetback for a few years, until I got my *green card*," see *alien*.

wet willie gesture n : getting a freshly licked and slobbered (little) finger thrust in your ear.

whacked [in the head] sl adj : crazy.

whatever intj : gratuitous remark, a filler akin to etc., and used as a conversation continuant, to terminate a question or tall story, or as an expression of disbelief, irritation, or contempt, "whatever," syn. whatsoever (Scot. 'of no use whatsoever').

what's up? cf expr intj : what's going on? what's happening? or even, what's *going down*?

wheat berry n : whole wheat grain, as opposed to split or ground, "wheat berry bread" = bread containing whole wheat grains.

wheezer (Canadian) sl n : syn. *tosser*, *wanker*, *jerk off*.

Where's Waldo n : *Where's Wally*.

whiner usage n : *whinger*, *grizzle*, *grumble*, "He's such a whiner."

whiskey, pl **whiskeys** n : Irish & American kinds, cf. *whisky*, see spelling table.

White House n : the *President*'s home and office, like *10 Downing Street*.

white trash n adj : (usu.) white people at the bottom of the socio-economic scale, syn. *gypo*, "typical white trash living in

a *trailer park*," also white man, syn. *honky*. See *redneck*.

the whole enchilada expr n : the whole thing, syn. 'the whole schmear,' 'the whole ball of wax.'

whoop /wup/ sl v : slap, beat, syn. *dust*.

whoop-ass /wupas/ sl n : a sudden surge of energy, as in the fight of a fight-or-flight response, "there's goin' to be some whoop-ass unless . . .," "*bust out* a can of whoop-ass."

whopper (Hershey chocolate *candy*) n : malteaser.

widget n : gizmo, gadget, see *doodad*, "authorizing the purchase of 1,000 'widgets.'" Although this started life as a term for an unnamed device it now also has the meaning of tool, widgets being understood as a tool set.

wiener, weinerwurst n : shorter frankfurter. Also, sl. for *penis*.

wienie n : *nerd*, but with a bit of the quality of a *wannabe*, "computer wienie."

wifebeater sl n : *vest*.

wig, wig out v : throw a *wobbly*, syn. *flip* out.

wilson n : *wilson burger*, *face plant*, "do a wilson into the [con]crete."

wilson burger [from the Wilson brand of basketball] expr n : basketball blocked and fed back into your face.

wimp n : spineless person, see *ninny*.

wimpy adj : spineless, see *soppy*.

windbreaker n : *windcheater*.

Windex® n : *Windolene*.

windshield n : *windscreen*.

windup adj : *clockwork*, "windup toy," "windup *flashlight*."

the Windy City n : Chicago.

Winnebago n : large *motor home*, popular with retirees, and encountered during your *holiday*s creeping along single lane scenic *highways* three feet in front of your car.

winningest inf adj : most winning, superlative superlative, others include mostest, bestest, *funnest*, ant. *losingest*.

winter squash n : tend to be hard-skinned and orange, like pumpkins.

wipe out col v : to crash, referring to everything from falling off your bicycle to a serious race car crash.

wire n v : telegram, also to send money via a bank.

with usage prep : see *meet with*, *visit*.

with or without v : *black or white*; coffee light & sweet = with milk & sugar (NY).

witness stand n : witness-box.

wolverine n : *Gulo gulo*, basically a giant weasel, getting up to 40 lbs, sightings uncommon.

wonk n : *nerd*, "the [computer] sytem wonks . . ."

woodchuck n : *groundhog*, aka whistle-pig, can get up to 10 lbs and has a life span of about five years.

woodrow inf n : hard on, *woody*, syn. *boner*.

woodwork n : *joinery*.

woody inf n : hard on, syn. boner.

working out v : being in training or maintaining fitness, "I quit working out when I finished school."

workout n : exercise bout.

wow intj : here's a list of syn. from the '70s: *neat*, *keen*, *swell*, groovy, *cool*, super, tough, wild, nifty, swift, stud, *outasight*, fantastic, far out, spiffy, heavy, great, *crazy*, *right on*, *zowie*, boss, outstanding, decent, beautiful.

wreck n : crash, *car wreck*.

wrench n : *spanner*.

wringer usage n : *mangle*.

wumpus n : the monster from the early computer game 'Hunt the Wumpus.'

wuss n : *wimp*, feeble person, chicken, "what a wuss."

— X —

XOXOXO n : postscript of an affectionate letter; the X's are kisses and the O's are hugs.

— y —

yada yada col echoic n : blah blah blah, waffle, nonsense, verbiage, "it says, 'To whom it may concern, yada yada yada,' and then you sign at the bottom," " . . . does not imply endorsement of its products, accuracy of its information, yadda yadda yadda."

y'all, **you-all** [Southern you all] expr n : "hey, y'all! Is there any room up there?" and even, "All y'all git over here!" "All ya'll need ta do is jest wrangle round that there conniction."

yam n : sweet potato.

yank contr n : *Yankee*.

Yankee n : originally a person born in the 'Union or Northern States' of the Civil War, "In Europe, an American. In the Northern States of our Union, a New Englander. In the Southern States the word is unknown."—Ambrose Bierce, *The Devil's Dictionary* 1911.

yard n : *garden*.

yard sale n : *garage sale*, lawn sale, moving sale.

yard sale n : (from skiing and mountain biking) a horrendous crash that leaves all your various "wares"–water bottles, pump, tool bag, *granola bars*, etc.–scattered as if on display for sale.

yawp n : raucous noise, (barbaric yawp : primal yell—Walt Whitman).

yellow jacket n : *wasp*. (In the US there is the bee, yellow jacket, wasp (refers to many kinds of wasps, often wood wasps), hornets, and many kinds of similar insects, cf. *wasp*.)

yellow turnips n : *swedes*, syn. *rutabaga*.

yet usage adv : still, "we have three inches of snow yet" = 'we still have three inches of snow.'

yield (road sign) imp v : *give way*.

you bet! expr intj : you betcha! (MN), another way of saying *you're welcome*.

you're welcome expr intj : a very common response to 'thanks,' similar in usage and meaning to the Italian *prego*, the French *de rien!* (not at all!) or *Il n'ya pas de quoi* (it is nothing, (please) don't mention it!), or the Greek παρακαλώ! /parakaloh/ (don't mention it! please! a pleasure!) in response to ευχαριστώ /efkhareestoh/ (thanks!), "you're most welcome," "you're very welcome."

yowser! excl intj : mild expression of surprise.

yo-yo n : nuisance (person).

yucks n : laughs, "just for yucks."

yugo n : syn. skoda.

— Z —

z /zee/ n : /zed/, used a lot in acronyms: 'E-Z' (easy), '1040EZ' (the easy tax form, see *1040*).

za contr col n : pizza.

Zamboni n : (brand) the ice-smoothing machine at ice rinks [originally a converted farm tractor with a scraper].

zapping v : skipping *adverts* on a *programme* recorded on a video.

zero-dark thirty expr n : *oh-dark thirty*.

zilch n : nothing, syn *sweet FA*.

zine [contr magazine] n : fanzine (magazine for fans), e-zine (electronic magazine), "check out these new zines."

zip code n : *postal code*, but consists of five numbers. There are about 30,000 5-digit zip codes from 01001 in MA to 99950 in AK. 9-digit zip codes (zip+4) of the form 97330–6233 are accurate to the floor of an office building or an apartment complex, and are encouraged by the *postal service*.

zip gun n : homemade one-shot gun from e.g. strong spring (as in prison).

zit n : pimple, spot.

zowie intj : wow!

z's n : nap, *zizz*, "grab some z's."

zucchini n : *courgettes*, *squash*, *marrow*.

zucchini dumping n : You come home to find a bag of *zucchinis* on your porch, left by a well-wishing *green-thumbed* neighbour. This has become so annoying that, during autumn, pranksters delight in sneaking up to a door, leaving a few large *zucchinis*, ringing the door bell and dashing off.

— Differences —

WHEN AN AMERICAN and a British person meet, the first obvious difference is the accent—the pronunciation of words. The next obvious difference is vocabulary—the occasional different word for something, like a foreign language. However, more subtle differences become apparent in syntax (or grammar)—the arrangement of certain words, the position of certain words, or the inclusion or lack of certain words. Not only are these differences reflected in writing, but writing also brings out differences in spelling and punctuation. All these taken together form distinctive American or British English.

To confound the issue, these kinds of differences show up in different regions of the same country. Either way, compared to the main body of English these differences are really quite small. We can read each other's newspapers without too much trouble; only a little of a Monty Python show is lost on an American audience; and the British stomach American soaps and comedies with virtually as much understanding as Americans.

These reflect two of the ways language can be looked at. In the first case, the function of language is to communicate, and this is accomplished by sounds, gestures and symbols. The way the sounds are pronounced create the accent, and the symbols are our writing system, which then invokes spelling and punctuation.

In the second case, the components of language are words, and their arrangement. The words are our vocabulary, which includes idiom, and their arrangement is syntax or grammar.

So now we know where differences can be found, and we find that differences do occur in each of these language facets. These are examined more closely in the following pages.

WHY ARE THERE DIFFERENCES?

Language can also be looked at in a third way, as a process. Steven Pinker draws parallels from evolutionary biology to show that language is subject to three processes which, acting over long periods of time, cause changes. These factors of language change are inheritance, innovation, and isolation. Language as an evolving process is readily apparent when considering how English has changed from Anglo-Saxon to Chaucer to Shakespeare to the present day. It is the effect of these processes over the last 400 years that gave rise to the differences between American and British.

Inheritance—we acquire our language from the society we grow up in, American in America and British in Britain. We don't speak identically to our parents because these particular two cultures are so dynamic. Also, we are affected by exposure to other languages, more as time passes. To give just one example—the Spanish idiom ¡hasta la vista! (/asta/) is so common on the US west coast that it has entered colloquial usage as an idiom, 'hasta la vista, baby!' spawning humorous forms, 'hasta la bye-bye,' but more often just 'hasta!' English is rife with borrowings, which you'll see in the *Brief History of English.*

> The problem with defending the purity of the English language is that English is about as pure as a cribhouse whore. We don't just borrow words; on occasion, English has pursued other languages down alleyways to beat them unconscious and rifle their pockets for new vocabulary.
>
> —JAMES D. NICOLL

Innovation—New activities, which by their nature give rise to new terms, will bring change to the language, especially to those directly involved (see jargon below), and in some cases, for instance technology, this exponentially affects the rest of the population. The verb *morph,* which comes from the computer operation, isn't in any of my regular dictionaries (1993), but is a regular in the press ('Schwarzenegger morphs from bodybuilder to actor to politician'). Younger people experiment more with language, providing slang and jargon, alternative or modified pronunciation, deviant spellings, idiom and expressions, some of which eventually become part of the language. Any social, ethnic, or common interest group, not only develops a particular jargon but also a culture, which becomes more defined over time, and culture holds language change.

Isolation—dialectologists have noticed that some dialects are separated by geographical features that naturally separate peoples, such as hills, rivers, or bogs (which of course extends to mountains, seas, and deserts). So a dialect arises when a group is isolated long enough. Manx, Cornish, and Welsh all started as the same language, but after 1000 years of separation became different languages. And so even though there has always been good communication between America and Britain, via travel, letters, and books, and now radio, movies, TV, phone, fax, email, and most recently the Web, differences have arisen over 400 years. Australian and New Zealand English, which had developed over the last 200 years are also different dialects from British, but not as much as American from British. Social barriers also act to create or maintain separation of groups, and this strengthens language differences, more apparent in the British social classes than American.

Robust communication systems have built-in latency, which in the case of language is known as language redundancy. English is apparently two to four times larger than it needs to be to communicate, which not only allows things to be said or written in myriad different ways, but also allows pieces to be left out. (Consider the British ad—'f u cn rd ths u cd gt a gd jb.' And many folks recently received this in email: Aoccdrnig to a rscheearch at an Elingsh uinervtisy, it deosn't mttaer waht oredr the ltteers in a wrod are, the olny iprmoetnt tihng is taht the frist and lsat ltteer is at the rghit pclae. The rset can be a toatl mses and you can sitll raed it wouthit porbelm. Tihs is bcuseae we do not raed ervey lteter by it slef but the wrod as a wlohe.) These kinds of innovations develop differently in different regions. In the Midwest, for example, you can hear expressions like "The car needs washed" and "These videos need returned," the 'to be' being found redundant. There are more such examples in *Grammar* below.

CULTURE

American and British culture are fundamentally different, based on their history, economics, environment, outlook, and probably anything else you'd care to chew on. Indeed within each country there are strong cultural areas—America's East and West Coast, or the *South,* England's London and the southeast, or the Midlands and the North. As in the language, there are many similarities, but a closer look in virtually any quarter reveals differences. No attempt is made to list these differences. Perhaps a glance at some stereotypes might be revealing enough.

British stereotypes of Americans: Americans are illiterate, have no culture, are immodest and gauche, have a throw away culture (e.g. automobiles) and everything has a price. Churchill called Americans a nation of shopkeepers [Napoleon said the same of the English, *L'Angleterre est une nation de bou-*

tiquiers]. When Clive James visited California in the late 1970s, he reported that restaurants look like car washes, car washes look like art galleries, art galleries look like war memorials, war memorials look like fire stations, fire stations look like churches, and churches look like restaurants.

Americans' stereotypes of themselves: think they are culture free (symptom: culture vultures, no Usenet newsgroup soc.culture.american), think other countries don't like them, think they are the world (world series, international news virtually absent from major news broadcasts and newspapers unless American interests are involved), and are born to shop (for trinkets to show off to each other).

Americans are patriotic, direct and open in conversation, globally naïve, experts at marketing (a studied art: . . . available at finer stores. . . . . . coming to a *theater* near you. . . . . . remember, folks, you heard it here first . . . featured naked woman [imagine your favorite model here] not included, United States of Advertising—Paul Krassner), welcome you into their *store*s, have more shopping malls, and don't have a class structure.

American stereotypes of the British: bad lovers, terrible cooks (food is boiled to within an inch of its flavour, and then some), snotty, pompous, insular, cold, regimented (traditional), do things in their own fashion, make the best 'bad guys' in movies, and speak English correctly. One American at an English college complained, 'The English girls never got my jokes, the brussels sprouts were gray, the drizzle was relentless, and the toilet paper was waxy.'

British stereotypes of themselves: none.

The British despise their own country, pity anyone not British, despise foreigners, talk to themselves (but only after years of acquaintance—Punch Magazine), invented the phrase 'burnt to a turn,' have a class structure (upper middle class, middle class, and lower middle class), and look upon you as you enter their *shop*s as a trespasser. 'The Parliamentarian, Liberal democratic, plutocratic British'—Louis de Bernières.

That previous paragraph about British stereotypes of themselves bothers most people. It is a joke. Here's a clue:

The Scots keep the Sabbath, and anything else they can get their hands on.

The Welsh pray on their knees, and on their neighbours.

The Irish don't know what they want, but will fight to the death for it.

Whereas the English consider themselves a race of self-made men, thereby absolving the almighty of that awesome responsibility.

See also How to Tell If You're American, page 290, and English, page 296.

VOCABULARY

At the basic level, there is a different vocabulary, just like a foreign language. For example, *biro* and *spanner* are strictly British terms, whereas *zip code* and *Realtor* are strictly American terms. *Railroad tie* and *railway sleeper* are different words used in different ways (around the common word rail) to name precisely the same thing. The *bowler* hat in Britain is a *derby* hat in the US. However, unlike a foreign language, these two dialects converge, as the following figure suggests, or perhaps we should say they diverge.

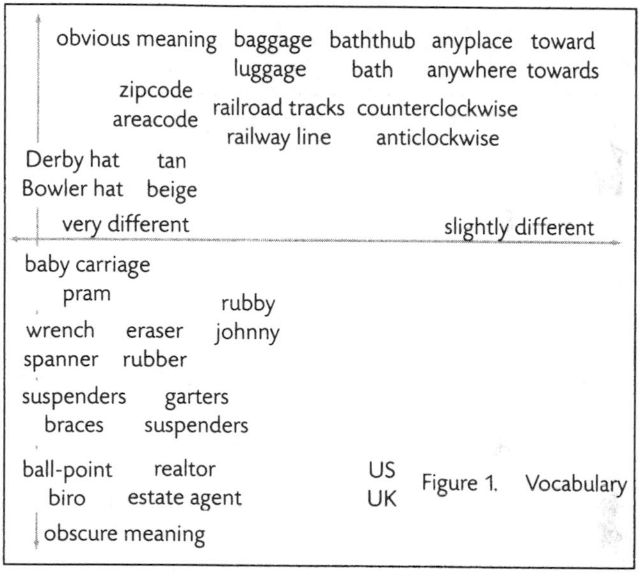

obvious meaning	baggage	baththub	anyplace	toward
	luggage	bath	anywhere	towards
zipcode				
areacode	railroad tracks	counterclockwise		
	railway line	anticlockwise		
Derby hat tan				
Bowler hat beige				
very different			slightly different	

baby carriage
   pram
          rubby
wrench eraser johnny
spanner rubber

suspenders   garters
  braces   suspenders

ball-point   realtor   US
  biro   estate agent   UK
obscure meaning

Figure 1. Vocabulary

Words are completely different at one extreme (to the left in the chart) but converge until they are identical at the other extreme (right). There is also the obvious/obscure aspect; sometimes two different words are used but their meaning is quite apparent (*luggage, baggage*) (at top), and they may often be used interchangeably. In other cases words may be quite obscure (bottom).

Were it so simple. Sometimes a common word may have additional meanings unique to one country. For instance, in Britain a *leader* also means an editorial or the *leading article* in a newspaper. Sometimes the additional meaning becomes the primary meaning, like dumb in the US primarily used of a stupid person, not a mute. In the case of *table*, the secondary meanings are opposite! *Rude* has many shades of meaning, but in the US is often used to mean discourteous, especially when abrupt. Although it has all these meaning in the UK, it has the additional meaning of lewd or indecent, which is how it is usually used.

Some words are used with differing frequency. *Baggage* and *luggage,* or *pole* and *rod*, are interchangeable and are used with only slightly differing frequencies, but if you're used to hearing one (fishing *rod* in the UK), hearing the other will nudge your attention (fishing *pole* in the US). Words like these, where there is a tendency to use certain words over others, add a subtle flavour to the varieties of English. At the other extreme, some words common in one place are rare in the other. I've never heard *soppy* or *row* in America, even though they're listed in American dictionaries just like any other word, but they're quite well known in the UK. Upon encountering ' . . . as computers obsolesce . . . ' one might think it's the American easy-goingness to create forms to fit, but *Webster's Dictionary* has this word as used since 1873.

There are any number of words that have one meaning in the US and another in the UK. Look up *rubber, braces, jumper,* and *jelly* in both sections. These are the kinds of words that cause much confusion, especially when there is a circularity that doesn't seem to end: *garters* are **suspenders**, but *suspenders* are **braces**, but *braces* are orthodontal devices to straighten teeth; a *tramp* is a *bum*, but a *bum* is a *fanny*, but a *fanny* is a *twat*, but a *twat* is a *twit*!

Why are there vocabulary differences? Some words retained in Britain were dropped from American, such as *fortnight* and **constable**, and many no longer used in Britain are retained in American: I *guess, gotten, mad* (angry), *fall* (autumn), sick (ill), *platter* (large plate), *assignment* (job or task), *deck* of cards (pack of cards), *slim* (as in slim chance), *mean* (unpleasant rather than stingy), *trash, hog* (pig), *brunch, chore, skillet, quit* (resign), *sheriff.* Brunch originated as Oxford slang in the late 19th century, and became popular in the US in the 1920s, then made its way back slowly, being considered slang, then informal, until quite recently.

Americans seem freer to use the language to express themselves rather than being constrained by it. For instance, Americans tend more to coin and use

➤ nouns compounded from verbs plus prepositions (fallout, blowout, workout, cookout, know-how, the run-around, the rundown, a stop-over, a try-out),
➤ verbed nouns (to tetris, to text, to author, to vacation, ink-jetted, surveilling, nouned, verbed, -ize words (fetishize), which are often -ise words in Britain, see the spelling list, table 9),
➤ verbed adjectives (more -ize words. I remember **Fleet Street** wincing at ugly Americanisms in the 1960s—why finalize, what's wrong with simply making it final?),
➤ and the reverse (painterly),

➤ nouned verbs (an assist, big push),
➤ nouned adjectives (briefs, hopefuls, special = a sale),
➤ novel superlatives (*winningest*).

Also true of irregular verbs—dove (he dove off the cliff) and snuck (and then snuck off) are well known, and I've even heard fluck (who fluck shit?), but even Americans caution us to watch out for irregular verbs which have crope into our language, perhaps because otherwise good words might get squozen out.

Other reasons for differences are mentioned elsewhere, such as different culture, environment, experiences giving rise to different names for things (*twisters* most frequently occur in the US). Borrowings occur from exposure to different ethnic groups throughout history, and new technologies generate distinct jargons.

IDIOM—OBLIQUE SAYINGS

Idiom is a phrase that captures a unique concept. It is like adding vocabulary to the language. I get the impression that idiom forms because words take on too many meanings, and idiom captures a single concept. (The last time I looked, the word with the highest number of separate meanings in the OED was set with 43. (err . . . update. I just read that set has 158 meanings as a verb, 58 as a noun and 10 as a participal adjective.)) The problem is that there is no logical connection to the words it is composed of (e.g. kick the bucket). The pervasiveness of idiom is apparent from it comprising a large part of ESL classes for foreigners learning conversational English.

Although America and Britain share many idioms, many are obtuse from one to the other. *Go figure*. The *Fourth of July* is celebrated on *July 4th*. **Bob's your Uncle**!

GRAMMAR

All grammars leak.

—EDWARD SAPIR, *Language*, 1921

Some grammar differences are consistent between American and British:

US	UK
write her	write to her
he seems to be an intelligent man	he seems an intelligent man
let's go see a movie	let's go and see a film
look out the window	look out of the window

talk with, meet with	talk to, meet
I [already] ate	I have [already] eaten
different than, different from	different from, different to
I do, I don't	I have, I haven't (In answer to, do you have?)
the house needs painting	the house wants painting
Hudson River, Mississippi River	River Thames, River Avon
came over	came round
to be on a team	to be in a team
to live on a street	to live in a street
to be in a sale	to be on sale
I went	I've gone

Some usages are peculiar to the country. In back of, meaning behind, is only used in the US, and is not known or even generally understood in the UK. 'To visit with' is used in the US, instead of 'to visit,' and has the additional meaning of a virtual meeting, as in visiting with someone on the phone. In the UK 'is John at home' means is he physically there, whereas 'is John home?' means has he returned yet. In the US there is no such distinction, and only the latter is used. In the UK the usage of 'one' is rarely used in the US; one does what one ought. And then there's the classic American—two kids: "I do not!" "you do, too!" "do not!" "do, too!"

There is always a debate about the British being in hospital or going to university whereas Americans are in *the* hospital or going to *a* university (or going to school). In the US 'ten of six' and 'ten after six' mean ten minutes to six and ten past six, and in the UK 'half nine' means half past nine. In the US the 'and' is often dropped from numbers, as a hundred (and) three or two thousand (and) forty six, and even sometimes *2001* (two thousand one) *A Space Odyssey*. In particular cases the 'and' is used to indicate the decimal point: one hundred fifty one (151), one hundred and fifty one (100.51). Americans will as often ask 'have you got' where the British might say 'do you have.' Americans do it over but the British do it again.

In Britain, institutions or any organisation comprising a number of people are often considered plural, for example, 'the company are having their annual picnic.' Count nouns vary: 'I ate too many shrimps,' 'they hunt quail and duck,' 'there's one innings left to play,' 'spending was cut by three millions.'

Some differences are less noticeable because they are interchangeable, but there still is a differing frequency. For instance, Americans part their hair and

Britons have a parting, but sometimes it's the other way around. American is *different than* British in America, but in Britain, American is *different from* British, and sometimes *different to* British.

And then there are endless usages that, although quite obvious, are used only in one variety of English. For instance, Americans might say 'I sure could use a drink' or 'I need to use the bathroom.' The British would say these in any number of different ways ('I really need a drink,' but more likely, 'I'm dying of thirst,' and 'I'm dying to go to the loo'). Some ways of saying things may be unique to the country but only used by a minority, such as 'my dog wants out' in the US, or 'my bank are awful' in the UK.

Perhaps American sounds sloppy to British ears because more variation is allowed, as in new coinages noted above. American often has the adverb before the verb (to boldly go) though both arrangements are found ('they never will agree' and 'they will never agree,' only the latter is allowed in the UK). Perhaps British sounds authoritative because some standard usages (ought) are only encountered in formal US situations, such as legalese.

Grammar considers both syntax—the arrangement of words in a sentence, and morphology—the way a word is built up from pieces. All of the above are examples of differences in syntax. Many of the different word forms result simply in spelling differences (like spelled and spelt) and these can be found in the spelling list, Table 9. Still, many different forms are used. Americans might say shave cream, swim suit, scrub brush, drive test, and cook book rather than shaving cream, swimming costume, scrubbing brush, driving test, and cookery book, and differing informal contractions mean that Americans study math whereas the British study maths. But why do Americans burglarize instead of burgle, obligate instead of oblige, or are complected rather than complexioned?

These kinds of differences are true of regions both in the US and in the UK. For instance, New Yorkers say standing on line instead of standing in line, and some folks in Northern England use mustn't instead of can't, and say 'he gave it me' (he gave it to me). Some Americans use present tense instead of past tense in some irregular verbs (He spit on the *sidewalk*). Regionalisms sometimes spread. In Ireland they say ten till two, as some do in the US and this is not uncommon in Britain. The well known *Southern 'y'all'* (you all) is now heard in informal usage anywhere in the US. See also the notes under *Geography*, below.

See *International English* by Trudgill and Hannah (1994) for a systematic treatment of grammatical differences.

USAGE

Usage is our speech and writing habits. It therefore includes words and idiom, spelling and punctuation, accent, and grammar—pretty much all the pieces of language. The essence of language is that meaning is conveyed by words and phrases. A meaning may be expressed in many ways, or conversely, a number of concepts may be encapsulated in one phrase, but more commonly a cluster of meanings will be expressed by lots of synonymous words and phrases. In the first case, a community will tend to settle on a particular way of expressing an idea or concept, but of course each community (or country) will, over time, gravitate towards a different one, the shifts occurring due to the innovation and isolation processes discussed earlier.

My canonical example from vocabulary is *wrench* and **spanner**, but more well known is the *trunk, hood,* and **boot, bonnet** distinction.

The fun begins at the other end of the spectrum where different ideas or concepts are expressed by one word or phrase. Meanings are easily misconstrued where they are different or even opposite, in words and phrases like *knock up,* **quite**, *table,* and **what's up**.

So, one idea can be expressed in many ways, and, as already mentioned, a number of meanings may be expressed by the same word or phrase. But more commonly, different nuances or senses of something are expressed by the same word or phrase. *Confused* in the US more often means mixed-up, whereas **confused** in Britain more often means disconcerted. And we had already mentioned how **rude** in Britain has the additional meaning of lewd.

Again—the flip side—one idea could be described by more subtle shifts in grammar or word choice. Americans smash a bug, the British crush an insect, but Americans sometimes crush a cigarette butt. *Regular* and **normal**, and tan and beige are virtually interchangeable but are the regular usage of the respective countries.

Which brings us to the finest points where a number of closely related meanings are handled by some words or phrases, but across the **pond** the same meanings and words are matched up differently. For instance a sick American feels ill but an ill Briton feels sick. (However, these words have other related meanings, such as *get sick* in the US, meaning to vomit). Similarly small pebbles are called *rock*s in America and **stone**s in Britain. A stone can be used in America but generally isn't; a rock in Britain brings to mind something larger, like a boulder. These are the sorts of differences between American and British that are so subtle that, even though we can understand them, they still somehow don't sound quite right.

In the dictionary 'usage' is sometimes used to qualify a definition, and it indicates these kinds of hard to classify differences. It also indicates the notion of frequency. A word may be used often in one country and infrequently in the other, and even be familiar in both, such as *caveat* and kudos in the US and decrepit and **grub** in the UK.

Some differences are rarely used but are obvious, if quaint to the ear, such as *gotten* and *auto* in the US, and **whilst**, 'shall' and especially 'shan't' in the UK. Ought is used much more in the UK (you oughtn't to have said that). The differentiation between may and can is virtually absent in the US, and found less and less in the UK.

Clearly, language is complex, but the differences highlighted between two languages as close as American and British might be less obvious in two foreign languages.

The chart is another look at usage differences. It plots word or phrase pairs from distinct on the left to interchangeable or indistinguishable on the right. Pairs whose differences are obvious are towards the top, and those whose differences are obscure are towards the bottom.

It is interesting to see that morphology pairs are in the upper left, slight shifts in meaning are in the upper right, and meaning differences are in the lower left.

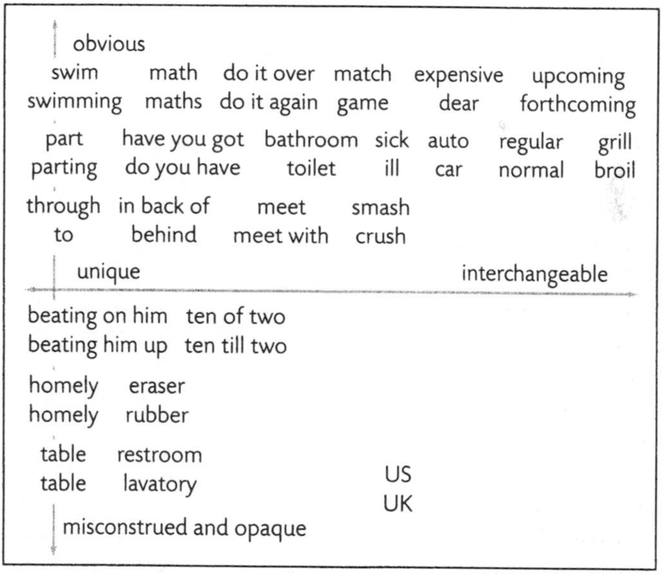

obvious						
swim	math	do it over	match	expensive	upcoming	
swimming	maths	do it again	game	dear	forthcoming	
part	have you got	bathroom	sick	auto	regular	grill
parting	do you have	toilet	ill	car	normal	broil
through	in back of	meet	smash			
to	behind	meet with	crush			
unique				interchangeable		

beating on him   ten of two
beating him up   ten till two

homely   eraser
homely   rubber

table   restroom
table   lavatory

US
UK

misconstrued and opaque

Figure 2. **Usage**

SPELLING

Schoolkid: Is it mirrow or mirror?

Teacher: I'm glad you didn't say mirrer.

Sometimes words are identical in meaning but spelt differently, as in sulfur and sulphur, hemoglobin and haemoglobin (and other oe and ae words). Most words (stolen from the French) in Britain ending in -our end in -or in the US (*colour, humour*, and words like favourite); most words in Britain ending in -tre (*centre, fibre, theatre*) end in -ter in the US. Many of these kinds of changes were passionately extolled by Noah Webster (of the dictionary fame) 200 years ago. The US has a greater tendency to drop silent consonants and vowels, and move to a more phonetic spelling, especially where the old spelling was a French remnant (tyre→tire). This often starts informally (night→nite, light→lite) but eventually becomes mainstream (through→thru, dough-nought→doughnut→donut). The reverse is also true, such as the computer byte, but it is interesting to note that some coinages flounder, such as the politically correct fad, women→wimmin, wimyn, womon, and womyn.

In the US many nouns and adjectives are verbed by adding -ize (standardize). These same words usually end in -ise in Britain, despite the British dictionaries which show -ize as the main form with -ise as an alternative. Sometimes, even American holds a surprize. Makes you realise!

One consistency is the American -yze words (analyze) are all -yse in Britain.

The table of spelling differences, page 201, lists over 500 differently spelled words, grouped into categories (such as the -ize/-ise words, above). Many of the categories are relatively complete, though many may be uncompletable, such as comparing words that are hyphenated (ultrahigh/ultra-high) or spaced (lemongrass/lemon grass) or both (flower-girl/flower girl).

PUNCTUATION & SYMBOLS

➤ quotes (*quotation marks, inverted commas*)

In general, Americans put the trailing punctuation of quoted material inside the quotes (Did you say, "I shot the cat?"), the British put it outside (Did you say, 'I shot the cat'?). Americans exclude the colon and semicolon, but include the *period,* comma, question mark, exclamation mark, and dash, if it is part of the quote. The British take the logical approach—when the punctuation relates to the quoted words it goes inside the *inverted commas*; when it relates to the sentence, it goes outside.

➤ nested quotes

Americans use double quotes, but single quotes for nested quotes, and double again for further nesting.

In 1967, Michigan *governor* George Romney clarified, "I didn't say, 'I didn't say it.' I said, 'I didn't say, "I said it."'"

The British generally recommend the opposite, and that is what's often seen.

➤ abbreviations

Americans indicate abbreviations with a *period* (Mr. Mrs. Dr. Ph.D.) but the British have promulgated the guideline that abbreviations ending in the same letter as the full form drop the *full point* (Mr Mrs Dr St vols) but otherwise leave it (abbr. vol. Ph.D). However, today's British usage, which seems to have been driven by erring on the side of dropping, almost exhorts ever sparser use (eg ie BSc PhD).

The British abbreviation situation seems to have begun in the 1960s as a reaction to overpunctuation (U.S.A. B.B.C). This serves as an excellent example of a linguistic trend that in half a century has swung full cycle.

➤ dashes

Both use long dashes as strong commas or to indicate a sudden shift (eg, anacoluthon), but they are surrounded by spaces in Britain.

Make up your — never mind.

➤ time

Americans use a colon in time designations (6:30 p.m.) but the British tend to use a point (6.30pm).

There are actually few punctuation differences, but they go a long way. Everything else is basically the same, but there are many subtle differences. Perhaps Americans tend to use commas more grammatically (writing oriented) whereas the British more to indicate pauses (reading *orientate*d). The British no longer put an apostrophe in the plurals of abbreviations and dates (*MP*s, 1980s). Note in the time example above how the space disappeared. But these subtle differences are no greater than what you'd find between different magazine or newspaper styles in the same country, or between, say, newsletters and scholarly journals.

Is it the serial comma, the Harvard comma, or the Oxford comma? That last comma before the 'or' (usually an 'and') is apparently left in by Americans whereas standard British usage is to leave it out. Despite fervid arguments that it's:

superfluous: The flag is red, white and blue.

clarifies: My favourite spreads are *marmalade*, nutella, and peanut butter and jelly.

changes meaning: To my parents, Ayn Rand and God.

Many American style manuals urge you to leave it off (not Harvard), whereas British manuals (Oxford) would have you leave it in.

Major publishers are putting their style guides online, which makes fascinating comparative reading (for word nerds). Two extremes might be Wired's style guide and MHRA's (Modern Humanities Research Association). This latter, in addition to using founts, has some rare punctuation examples.

Why does Shakespeare give Malcolm the banal question 'Oh, by whom?'?

I have taken the liberty of punctuating this dictionary according to my whims, following standard British generally, but adopting American convention where it suits me—the former is especially true in my usage of quote marks (which should also please computer types, as I use them like delimiters).

Punctuation is sort of an afterthought in writing. Everyone knows we have twenty-six letters of the alphabet, but ask someone how many punctuation marks we have and you'll get a sort of perplexed indignant look. Most folks know ('":-;–,!.?"' . . .) parentheses, quotation marks (single and double), colon, hyphen, semicolon, dash, comma, exclamation mark (my daughter called it the exciting mark), *period* or *full stop*, question mark, apostrophe, and ellipsis. Symbols are an arcana, and we use an astounding array of them:

➤ [ ] brackets, { } curly braces, <«»> angle brackets, / slashes (virgules), and — & – the em and en dash (because they're the same width as an M and an N),

➤ diacritic marks (àáâãäåāăąǎắầ ạả . . .), [Paul Erdős]

➤ ideograms (0123 . . .), and

➤ logograms ($ ¢ £ @ # % ^ & * . . .), not to mention all those strange symbols used in

➤ documentation (· •• © § ® ¶ ☺ . . .),

➤ science and mathematics ($\int \partial +-\times\div\cap\sqrt{}\infty\equiv\sum\pi°$ . . .),

➤ computerese (⊢⊣⊢ ▨■), and even

➤ linguistics (əɑɛʒɒɐʌɜʔ . . .).

Ancient Egyptians would be challenged. The table of available symbols that comes with any modern word-processor looks like a sheet of inscrutable hieroglyphs, without even squinting. As with the subtler details of punctuation, variation in symbol use is more at the level of groups of users than nations.

Just for fun, here's a few snippets and factoids on some (now) common symbols.

Ray Tomlinson, the inventor of email in 1971, used the @ symbol to construct email addresses primarily because it was an available symbol not found in anyone's name. Prior to that launch into the limelight, it was a little-used symbol outside of accounting and commercial price lists. Recently, the earliest instance of this symbol was found on a 4 May 1536 Italian document, where it represented an amphora—a measure (of wine), and its continued use in that sense eventually gave rise to its meaning of 'at the price of.'

Also in the 16th century, the Oxford mathematician Robert Recorde introduced the equal = sign ("bicause noe 2 thynges can be moare equalle"), and popularised the plus + and minus - signs.

> There be other 2 signes in often use of which the first is made thus + and betokeneth more: the other is made thus - and betokeneth lesse.

(Latter from *A Brief History of Algebra and Computing: An Eclectic Oxonian View*, Jonathan P. Bowen, Oxford University Computing Laboratory, 1994.)

GEOGRAPHY

As mentioned elsewhere, both countries have many pronounced regions, which give rise to local differences, and these further confound the national differences. The regions can be states, counties, cities or small locales. Consider the Bronx, Texas, California, Minnesota /minəsohda/, or London, Liverpool, Newcastle /nookasl/, and Glasgow /gləzge/.

A word may be used heavily in a discreet location and not be typical nationally. For instance a word may be in general use only on the US West Coast. This is a particular problem if also used in a very different sense on the East Coast, and again differently in various parts of Britain.

Many words came to Britain from the colonies, often starting out as army usage (*dekko, bint*). The brief history of English, in a following section, sheds some more light on effects on the language by invasions, migrations and so on.

And America and Britain affect each other. Numerous American words are English stranded in the US by settlers and since dropped in England: fall (Autumn), gotten, flat a's (/bath/ /bahth/), unrounded o's (/not/ /naht/), ate (/ayt/ /et/), mad (angry), I guess. Some words bounce back and forth (brunch), and slang and jargon that arises from new pursuits continues to seep both ways, aided these days by greatly increased communication and connectivity.

TIME
(extinct—obsolete—archaic—current)

Many archaic words are still used, but usually in a semi-humorous and informal way, the humour often due to the ancientness of the word (e.g. *bully*, *cad*, *spiffing*). Some words sound affected or obsolete when used in other areas (reckon). Other words are no longer used but are enshrined in literature and films. Some words are revived or exhumed with new meaning (*radical, rad, heinous,* *brilliant*), and the usage may stay or quietly disappear.

Some obsolete terms will continue to be used (to the bafflement of the listener) by folks who at one time used them regularly. For instance, unless something drastic happens, I will always weigh eleven stone something (rather than 160 odd pounds or 70 some kilos), and if someone gives me their height in centimetres I'll compare it with 183 cm. to see if they are taller or shorter than six feet before it makes intrinsic sense.

Look at the list of groovy American words from the 1970s, under *wow,* check off those that you still use, and compare with how many are dated. A word may be in vogue briefly or for topical reasons and then disappear.

JARGON

Every industry quickly generates jargon as an expedience. Since the practices are so distinct (standards, equipment, regulations, methods, and terminology), so is the language. But the same industry developing in relative isolation has developed distinct jargons.

For example, the *leccy* (electric) systems use different voltages (120V, 240V), different color codes for the wires (including the *earth* wire or *ground*), different shaped plugs and *outlets, sockets*, or *points*, different regulations for installation, and so on. More familiar differences are known for the auto industry and the car itself (*trunk* & *hood, boot* & *bonnet,* etc.).

The computer revolution is a whole nother story. 'Big' publishers (Oxford and such) published their first computer dictionaries in the early 1980s, but technical publishers were putting them out a decade before that. The online

Jargon File gestated around that time, and eventually became *The Hacker's Dictionary* and now *The New Hacker's Dictionary*. The point is that this dynamic and discrete body of computer jargon is so new that most of the lingo was coined by people still living, and it is not only eminently studyable but computers themselves are used to study it.

The Jargon File began in the States but the latest version has many entries of 'Commonwealth hackish,' the only samples in this dictionary being to note the nuances of *kluge* and **kludge**. Perhaps I should include *email,* since my Webster's lists *E-mail* and my College Oxford lists *email* (also *e-mail*). And this is exactly the point. In 1995, Jeff Adams, a scientist from Kurzweil, posted an article about different ways that email is spelt. He examined a 40-million word corpus of online articles, and found that of the over 85 ways people were spelling it, *email* 34% was followed closely by *e-mail* 27%, and then *E-mail* 13% and *Email* 10% led the remainder, on down through many obvious typos (and hyphenation was about 50/50). In other words, a jargon very much in flux.

SWEAR WORDS

Exclusion principle: Although jargon and slang evolve to create words for new ideas, they also serve to exclude any outsider of the particular group, which seems truer as the words become more obscene.

Words have levels of obscenity, crudeness, and strength. So, starting from the formal or 'proper' use of a word there is a kind of scale:

➤ synonyms (words of overlapping scope in meaning or sense),
➤ vernacular (dialect and common speech),
➤ colloquial (informal conversation),
➤ informal (words for some reason not used in a formal setting),
➤ improper (words used in a relaxed manner without regard to grammar),
➤ slang (words used in any manner regardless of prior rules, and often creatively (park the leopard—to throw up) embodying a novel concept, but with a definite consensus meaning), and
➤ vulgar (offensive, crude, derogatory, and by implication bigoted (race, color, religion—all the usual stuff) or taboo).

The bottom of the scale is usually censored by somebody, such as the *FCC* list of censored words, in order: shit, piss, fuck, cunt, cocksucker, motherfucker, tits.

RHYMING SLANG, COCKNEY RHYMING SLANG, AND BACKSLANG

Slang has no country, it owns the world . . . It is the voice of the god that dwells in the people.

—RALCY HUSTED BELL, *The Mystery of Words*

Rhyming slang has been around since the Plio-Pleistocene Era, and the Cockney variant has been around so long that many have become mainstream colloquialisms infecting English as far as it reaches. Bread, meaning money comes from the rhyming slang bread and honey, which rhymes with money. Chew the fat was originally crsl. for have a chat, and brass tacks was originally crsl. for facts. Rhyming Slang is typically a two-word phrase used in place of the word it rhymes with. Sometimes, especially where rhyming slang is used frequently, the end of the phrase gets dropped (as in the above examples) leaving a word seemingly quite unrelated to the word it's standing for. Occasionally nesting occurs, and sometimes quite deeply: bottle (and glass) is rsl. for arse, Aristotle is rsl. for bottle, Aristotle is shortened to aris, plaster of paris becomes rsl. for aris, and so plaster becomes sl. for *arse*. Would you *Adam and Eve* it!

There are many lists of (Cockney) rhyming slang (worth reading at least once if only to realize its surprising breadth), though I have included only those in general use or of some particular interest, including a little strine (Australian pronunciation of Australian), where this practice also flourishes. Apples and Pears (stairs) is well known, often being cited as an example of Cockney rhyming slang. Cockney rhyming slang is a living language with new words being invented all the time (and many becoming obsolete). Some have noted that it gets a boost every *other* generation. My grandparents were well versed, my father silently ignored it, my mother is still trying to hide her Cockney twang, and I am documenting it.

> If there's anything that distinguishes the Cockney, it's his sheer enjoyment of words. He loves to stand them on end and make them jump through hoops and turn circles . . . There's nothing better to a Cockney than to talk—to talk enjoyably, to talk comfortably, to use wonderful phrases. That's Cockney.
>
> —BOB BARLTROP

Whereas this may well be true, it is no less true of all peoples everywhere; pidgins, creoles, valspeak, surfer slang, technobabble—just visit any ghetto, grotto, ethnic area in a big city, the school yard, the beach, the valley, cyberspace . . .

TRANSLATIONS

If it was just a question of translating *diaper* to **nappy**, there would be no problem, but a vast amount of cultural **gubbins** stuck to the bottom of a **welly** is lost from a rubber boot.

> Translation is always a treason, and as a Ming author observes, can at its best be only the reverse side of a brocade—all the threads are there, but not the subtlety of colour or design.
>
> —OKAKURA KAKUZO, *The Book of Tea*

When I read the first Harry Potter, I looked forward to a nice English story, but soon found the tell-tale signs—parking lots and trash cans instead of car parks and dustbins. Resigned, I ploughed on, but felt subtle misgivings at what I was missing, especially when some opaque Briticisms were left in (kip, git, sacked). So, I reread it in the original English, and made some comparisons.

Why they changed the title from Philosopher's Stone to Sorcerer's Stone is inscrutable. Sorcerer conjures up sinister. The Philosopher's Stone has been sought by alchemists for millennia, for turning lead into gold. Interesting. (Why not Hegemon Stone!) Apparently, for the movie, they filmed each part that mentioned the Stone twice, for the separate American and rest-of-the-world audiences.

The translator took it from there. The bulk is spelling (realise → realize, rumours → rumors, maths → math, etc.) and punctuation (Mrs → Mrs., 31 July → July 31, and primary quotes going from 'single' to "double"). Translations are actually few, but they're high profile (ice lolly → ice pop, letterbox → mail slot, packet of crisps → bag of chips). Therefore, it is translations, or partial translations, or lack of translations, that stick out the most. Dudley's new word *shan't!* became *won't!* No complaints, but shan't is just such a lovely word. However, baker's becomes bakery in one sentence, but remains baker's the next. Is this an oversight? 'Dumbledore's barking' becomes 'Dumbledore's off his rocker.' But earlier, barking is left untranslated. Is it because Vernon qualifies it with 'stark raving mad'? A number of other words were left untranslated (headmistress, knickerbocker glory, holidays, ruddy, sprouts, marks) but their meanings would be close enough to be glossed over whilst still leaving a twang of quaintness.

Fiction has to just flow. No pictures, indexes, glossaries, footnotes, or sidebars. One long linear stream of uninterrupted imagination. Therefore, the goal of any translation is to not add any obstructions. There should be no foreign remnant that might cause the reader to stumble.

Everything else has some degree of leeway. An article can have sidebars and the odd footnote. A documentary can have pictures and tables. Nonfiction gets away with appendices, bibliographies, glossaries, and indices. And finally a scientific paper can be riddled with more citations, charts, equations, and inline glosses than words in the text.

In a sense, Harry Potter would be the easiest kind of translation, because it's squarely situated in Britain, unlike something that's set in a present day cosmopolitan location. Even so, much is lost whether translated or not. Even the Dursley's address, 4 Privet Drive, Little *Whing*ing, Surrey, evoking neat privet hedges in tidy drives, reeks of the politely suppressed frustrations of middle class suburbia. You'd never get away with 4600 Prim and Proper *Blvd,* Ostentatia CA 92670 (despite the fact that there probably is such an address!).

In a scientific paper or general non-fiction, translation in either direction is mostly spelling and pronunciation. The editor would catch any jargon or unique vocabulary. In general articles, the same would apply, although a sprinkling of easy foreign terms would add flavour, and where necessary, can be explained. It's fiction that's the trickiest, because a character has to be both authentically ethnic and at the same time understandable. Unlike going from Russian to English or French to Chinese, English to English translation is further confounded by the apparent sameness of the language. Most people are surprised and amused at the extent that translation is even necessary. Ideally, a native would both translate, and have access to the author for finer points of meaning. It seems that there is a greater need to translate from British to American. Was Steinbeck, Hemingway, Twain translated to British?

Creating pieces would also benefit the once-over from a native. In that regard, this dictionary should very much be treated like a thesaurus. Any word should be looked up in a dictionary to make sure the sense is right. For period pieces, research is necessary to do it well. Not only do you not want high tech seeping into a western or Dickensian scene, but you need to capture the right idioms of the time and place.

A SPOT OF LINGUISTICS

Estimates for how many words in the English language vary from half a million to two million. The latter figure perhaps includes all those ungainly chemical names, all the military and other jargon words, all the dialect terms, and slang. The *OED* has about half a million words in it, and the *Webster's Unabridged* almost as many. *Collegiate* and *Concise* dictionaries have about

200,000 words in them (up from 100,000 a few decades ago), but estimates of the average person's vocabulary ranges from 20,000–50,000.

Two thousand words account for three-quarters of the words we use from day-to-day, and another 13,000 make up most of the rest.

Looking at word lengths is a way to get a feel for these large word lists. The tallest histogram in the Word Length chart (dark grey) comes from the Moby list (a public domain list of about half a million words) and is used to approximate the whole English lexicon. The next tallest histogram comes from the bigd list, and represents a collegiate dictionary. The next is the Shorter OED, and the shortest is a Unix spell-check list, which can roughly represent the words we mostly know and use. The shorter the list, the more they contain common words. (Actually, the Unix list contains specially chosen roots from which, along with prefixes and suffixes, spell checking is done by applying rules, thus representing 100,000 words. So as a list it's probably too short and the word length artificially short.)

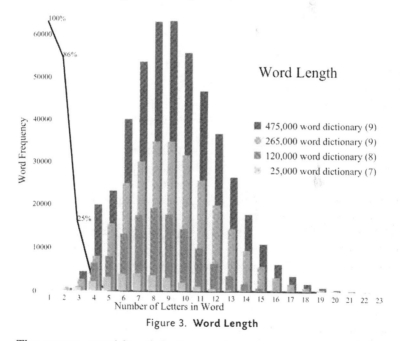

Figure 3. **Word Length**

The average word length in the shorter, more common, word lists is shorter. The average word length in English is over 9 or 10 characters, but of words we commonly use, is only 7.

Of all the ways you could make 2-letter words from 26 letters of the alphabet (26^2), we actually use most of them, but of 3-letter words (26^3) we use only a quarter, 4-letter words (26^4) a twentieth, 5-letter words (26^5) two thousandths, on up to 8-letter words (26^8) where we use a scant three-millionth of the possibilities. For longer words, we have used virtually none of the possibilities. It indicates that we use short words where possible, but that new coinages tend to be longer words. It's easier to combine a couple of existing words (data-base) than make short but awkward new words (*lunk). It also indicates that there are virtually an infinite number of open possibilities for new words using just the 26 letters of the alphabet.

Susie Dent, in her *Language Report* (2003), tells us that over the last 100 years the OED added 90,000 new words. This is two or three new words per day. Most new words (more than half) are indeed coined by combining a couple of existing words. About 15% are simply new meanings added to existing words, 5% are foreign borrowings, and 5% are a blending of word parts (discriminatrix). Less than 1% are actually neologisms, many of those being brand names and technical coinagess. And then there is the smattering of acronyms & abbreviations, suffixes & prefixes, nouned verbs & verbed nouns.

CANADIAN (WORLD ENGLISH)

English now (2000) has 485,000,000 speakers, the second most spoken language in the world behind Chinese (845,000,000). American wields the greatest influence due to the greatest number of speakers and the country's global prominence. For instance, American English is the favoured kind in Asia for ESL learners—a switch from British a generation ago. Although Britain has a quarter of the speakers, compared to American, its historical influence, as the source of English, persists. Here is an apt sample from my (1991) Korean dictionary, and it is telling since there is no entry for spanner:

wrench n. sŭ-p'ae-nŏ 스패너, ren-ch'i 렌치.

By contrast, apart from its regular appearance in the world cup, Nigeria is of little linguistic consequence despite having the third most English speakers. India and the Philippines have many English speakers, but as a lingua franca or non-primary language. (However, there are many Filipinos in the US, and Indians in Britain; English has adopted many Indian words historically (bazaar, bungalow, catamaran, jungle, khaki, pepper, pyjamas, shampoo, shawl, thug, veranda), and more in present day Britain.)

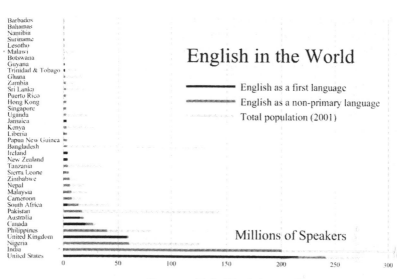

Figure 4. **Global English**

Apart from American and British, the most well-known varieties are Australian, Canadian, South African and New Zealand. Australian and New Zealand are closer to British than American (though when I was a kid, they were the same). For this reason, I have added a few terms to the British side of the dictionary. I was in Australia recently, and found half the lingo quite familiar, but the other half quite alien, albeit delightfully colorful. Canadian, conversely, is very close to American (no surprise), but spelling, and legal and government vocabulary, are strongly influenced by British (US: Department of Defense, UK: Ministry of Defence, Canada: Department of National Defence)

— Accents & Dialects —

Tourist:	*Is it Hawaii or Havaii?*
Benny Hill:	*Havaii.*
Tourist:	*Thank you.*
Benny Hill:	*You're velcome!*

ACCENTS—PRONUNCIATION

Accent is all about pronunciation. Dialect refers to a whole language—grammar and vocabulary, and usually accent. A person's accent is usually the first sign that they're from someplace else. However, although accent is such a strong indicator, differences in accent are difficult to describe, and what accent should we 1

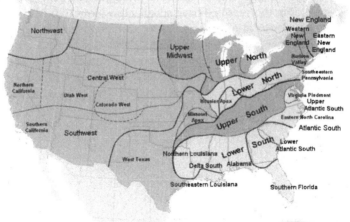

Figure 5. **US Dialects**

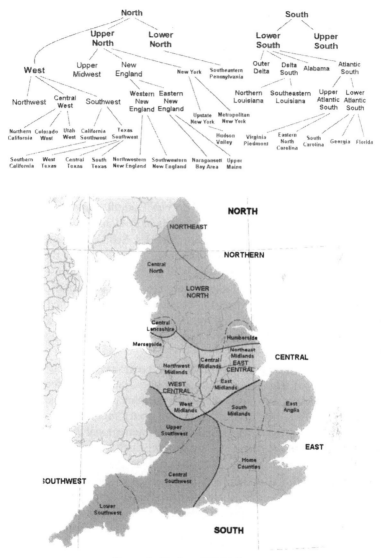

Figure 6. **Modern UK Dialects**

Generally, people speak English with an English accent, and their own regional dialect with the accent of that region—so for instance a Southerner will normally speak with a Southern accent. Accents generally go along with dialects, and so dialect regions generally reflect differing accent regions. But not necessarily. An English person fairly fluent in Spanish or French will speak it with an English accent. An immigrant may speak a good local dialect but in his own accent. Having lived in the States a few decades, I speak American with a British accent—the grammar and vocabulary are mostly American but the pronunciation stuck (along with my driving style).

The next section, Pronunciation, goes into details about each vowel and consonant that sound noticeably different between American and British accents.

DIALECTS

Craig M. Carver shows about two dozen dialect regions in the US, based mainly on vocabulary, in his *American Regional Dialects*. His dialect map and family tree have been reproduced above. Peter Trudgill, in his *Dialects of England,* shows sixteen modern dialect regions in England, based on grammar, vocabulary, and accent (there are more in Wales, Scotland and Ireland), also reproduced above. Trudgill, in *International English,* breaks the US into 8 accent areas, and these coincide well with Carver's delineations.

In both cases there are areas that differ markedly (e.g. North/South in England, Upper North, Lower North, and South in the Eastern United States) and within these areas are discernible subregions. Carver's family tree indicates that the west dialect was derived from the northern dialects, and not the southern.

Carver and Trudgill both stress that dialect regions are merely convenient representations of a language continuum, where language differences grow the farther apart they are, especially across the more distinct boundaries. Studies show that 99% of American is used in pretty much the same way, the remainder flavoring the different regions. The interregional differences in England run much deeper despite its small size, since it has developed over a period about four times as long, and had significant input from other languages (Latin, Norse with the Viking invasions, French with the Norman invasion, and more Latin and Greek with the industrial and scientific revolutions). It is for these reasons that Trudgill highlights traditional dialect areas in England (also reproduced below), which are apparent more in rural and remote areas, and these belie their origins in the Saxon and Norse kingdoms of yore.

Are American and British converging or diverging? By any measure, the difference is greater than 1% and growing. As dialects diverge, they start out mutually intelligible (like American and British), then intelligible with difficulty (like Welsh and Breton), and finally unintelligible (like English and Old

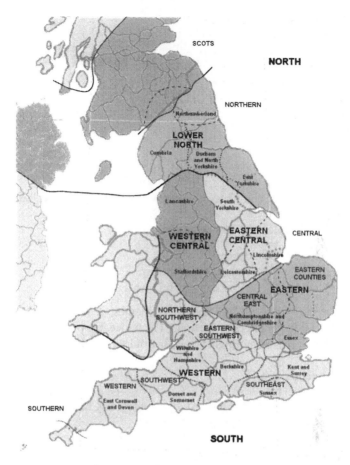

Figure 7. Traditional UK Dialects

English or English and Dutch). However, unlike in the past, today's global communication will probably change, in some unknowable way, the relationship between American and British.

This book exists because American and British are so similar.

— American and British —
Pronunciation Differences

"New Yawkas don't have an axent, da rest of da country does."

Three old ladies sitting in a bus shelter:

    1st lady: "Windy, en'it?"
    2nd lady: "No it's not, it's Thursday."
    3rd lady: "So am I. Let's go and 'ave a drink!"

THIS SECTION FOCUSES on specific phonemes. (Dialects and Accents are discussed in the previous section.) The noticeable pronunciation differences between American English and British English are:

➤ pronunciation of o
➤ the 'or' vowel [ɔ]
➤ pronunciation of 'a' (US has [æ], [ɑ], not [ɒ]; UK has [æ], [ɑ], and [ɒ])
➤ American vowels becoming more neutral
➤ vowel shifts
➤ d'd t's in American; glottal stops in British
➤ rhotic 'r' in American (pronouncing the r in park), non-rhotic 'r' in British (or not)
➤ 'yoo' words losing the y in American (tune: tyoon → toon)
➤ particular words
➤ stress & reductions
➤ other random anomalies

The differences discussed really only apply to 'General American' (most of the west and heartland) and RP ('Received Pronunciation'), which is close to 'BBC English'—the kind spoken by British newscasters. They are not at all universal. For instance, although American is rhotic and English is non-rhotic, there are non-rhotic areas in America and much of Britain is rhotic.

There is a brief description of the cardinal vowel system appended to this section, to provide an additional perspective on the vowel sounds during the following discussions. Also, refer to the Pronunciation Key on page 13—this shows the pronunciation symbols as used throughout this dictionary, alongside the equivalent IPA symbols, which are enclosed in square brackets where used (mostly just in this section).

PRONUNCIATION OF O

In Britain, the 'o' vowel, [ɒ], in words like *dog, hod, pot,* is pronounced with rounded lips and the tongue back in the mouth. Americans do not have this vowel, instead pronouncing the same words using the 'ah' vowel, [ɑ], with the lips unrounded and the tongue back but more relaxed. This is the same vowel in *card* or *bard.* In some cases in the US the 'o' is pronounced using the 'or' vowel in words like *long* (Central East Coast) and *horrid* (especially in the western US).

The 'plummy' quality of some RP speakers is probably due to an exaggeration of this 'o' vowel, and other vowels, by pushing the tongue as far back as possible, accomplished by speaking whilst imagining a mouth full of plums.

THE 'OR' VOWEL [ɔ] (OR THE 'AW' VOWEL)

This is the vowel in *oar, law, Borg, Bork, pork* and so on. If I was American, I would have called it the 'aw' vowel, but I think American 'aw' varies more regionally, and English 'or' is more consistently closer to [ɔ] (as long as you don't pronounce the r).

Many 'or' words in Britain such as *paw, saw, talk, all, bought, launch, taught, port* are pronounced in America using the 'ah' vowel, [ɑ]. I've even heard 'awesome possum' rhyme perfectly [ɑsəm pɑsəm]. But many words in American retain the 'or' vowel, such as *poor,* such that the British homophones *poor paw* are pronounced differently in American. In the Central US East Coast the 'or' vowel occurs in most of the same words as British, but it is slightly shorter, [ɔ] rather than [ɔ:]. In American, 'dawg,' as written in cartoons and such, uses the 'or' vowel, and the spelling emphasizes the pronunciation as unusual. Oddly enough, *quark,* correctly pronounced to rhyme with *quart* by most Americans is often pronounced to rhyme with *dark* by most British people.

PRONUNCIATION OF A

The British have the 'a' vowel, [æ] (cat, hat) and the 'ah' vowel [ɑ], as do Americans, but often in different places. Trudgill notes that words with 'a' followed by [f] [θ] [s] [nt] [ns] [ntʃ] [nd] [mp] (*laugh, path, grass, plant, dance, branch, demand, sample*) have [æ] in American and [ɑ:] in southern British. Northern British bends a's pretty flat in general compared to Southern English, and is generally the same as American, but there are exceptions like *banana, can't, half,* where the a is more like in the south.

In Britain, words like *what* are pronounced using the same vowel [ɒ] as in *dog,* above, and so is phonetically spelled *wot* rather than *wat.* Perhaps this is why *baloney* (nonsense) is so spelled in American dictionaries, but primarily as *boloney* in some British ones.

It should be noted that in America the 'ah' vowel (*father, bard, calm*) is usually shorter and sometimes sounds a little closer to the 'u' vowel in *cup.* So the long, firm [ɑ:] in Britain really stands out in *bath* and *dance* where Americans have the short [æ] mentioned above. Even this southern English accent, with the long 'a' [ɑ:] in words like *father* and *bath,* is not consistent. Only a small group would put a long 'a' in a surveyor's *transit,* as did Hugh Grant in the movie *The Englishman Who Went Up a Hill but Came Down a Mountain.*

AMERICAN VOWELS BECOMING MORE NEUTRAL

Pronunciation can be used to distinguish social class, and social status. In Britain, where class structure is strong, people are more acute to vowel enunciation and, often unconsciously, preserve many pronunciations that would otherwise be unnecessary. Pronunciation of vowels also distinguishes meaning in words, but sometimes the pronunciation is unnecessary. Thus, in American, where nonessentials are more readily dropped, vowels are not always as sharp as in Britain. You get the impression that vowels are closer to neutral (schwa). It might be that in Britain vowels have become sharper (more distinct or enunciated) over the last few hundred years.

The main example of vowels becoming more neutral in American is in words with some vowel in front of an [r] that is also followed by another syllable, such as *marry* or *hurry.*

[æ] in *marry* → [ɛ] in *merry* → [ə]
[ei] in *Mary* → [ɛ] in *merry* → [ə]
[ɪ] in *mirror* and [i:] in *nearer*

[ʌ] in *hurry* → [ə] in *furry*
[ɜ:] in *furry* → [ə] in *furry*

Trudgill's examples give [ei] and [ɛ] merging so that *Mary* and *merry* are pronounced identically, and [æ] and [ɛ] merging so that *marry* and *merry* sound identical. In cases where these both occur, *marry merry Mary* sounds like *merry merry merry*. Since these words are unambiguous in context, it's easy for the [ɛ] to approach schwa [ə]. And where speakers have [æ] or [ei] approaching [ɛ] they all might approach schwa [ə].

The [ɜ:] in *furry* is shorter in the US [ɜ], which is closer to [ə], and in some places the [ʌ] in *hurry* goes towards [ɜ] (or even [ə]) such that *hurry* and *furry* are perfect rhymes.

I overheard a lady saying 'hooking up the equipment' pronouncing *hooking* as [həkən]; the vowels were completely tokens.

VOWEL SHIFTS

Long vowels in Middle English were pronounced as they were in Latin but, during the 15th and 16th centuries, they changed to what we have in general today. This change is called the Great Vowel Shift (described on page 229). In major cities around the Great Lakes area, linguists have noted since the 1970s what they call the Northern Cities Chain Shift. On the West Coast you hear many vowel shifts, notably in younger people, and sometimes words are spelled to match (sense Æ since, pen Æ pin). My daughter growing up pronounced it MickDonalds.

like → lake
cook → kick
pen → pin
petting (pedding) → pədding
thank → think
hot (haht) → hat
jon (jahn) → jen
money → many
racket → rocket (rahket)

D'D T'S IN AMERICAN; GLOTTAL STOPS IN BRITISH

In many areas the American 't,' when not the initial consonant in a word, is pronounced closer to a 'd,' and in some cases can disappear altogether. Thus *latter* and *butter* sounds more like *ladder* and *budder,* and words like *twenty* and *dentist* can sound like *twenny* and *Dennis.*

Why do Americans pronounce t as d? Perhaps because to pronounce the frequent 'r's at the end of words ending in '-er' it is easier to say '-der' than '-ter.'

In Britain, 't' is generally pronounced like a 't,' but there are areas the glottal stop is very well known. This is the sound in between the two vowels in *uh-oh,* or the initial consonant in *honest.* In these two examples, and others like them, the glottal stop occurs as much in America as in Britain. But the glottal stop that replaces the 't' in the Cockney and Glasgow dialects is much stronger; imagine bracing for a punch in the belly when you make the sound. Words like *butter* become [bʌʔə].

As an interesting side note, Americans sometimes replace the 'd' in a British word with a 't,' as if hypercorrecting 'd' back into the more 'correct' 't.' I've heard 'Wimbleton' on American TV, found that spelling in a major American encyclopedia, and whilst looking, even found cases of 'Wimpleton.' This confusion is borne out by Americans trying to imitate a Cockney accent by putting a glottal stop in place of 'd' instead of 't' (*bloody* [blʌʔɪ]), which sounds quite odd to an English person.

In Britain, the glottal stop occurs in informal speech in many areas, although with Estuary English, perhaps not informal anymore. The association of the glottal stop with lower classes or Cockneys typically also includes dropping of 'h's (thus **hooter** becomes [ooʔə]), and dropping the g in -ing words (/woʔ thi el ə yə dooin/ "what the hell are you doing?").

RHOTIC R IN AMERICAN, NON-RHOTIC R IN BRITISH

Rhotic speakers will pronounce the r in *barn, park, cart, fart,* whereas non-rhotic speakers won't, making no distinction between *barn* and *(auto)bahn.* Most of America is rhotic, with the notable exception of the Boston area and New York City. SE Britain is apparently the source of non-rhotic. England is non-rhotic, apart from the SW and some ever-diminishing northern areas. Scotland and Ireland are rhotic. In the movie *The Princess Bride,* the bishop (Peter Cook) over-emphasized the non-rhotic accent by loudly announcing '*mawidge*' (*marriage*), and Americans often joke about eastern New Englanders who 'pahk the cah in Hahvahd yahd.'

In Britain, the non-rhotic accent gives rise to linking 'r's, where an otherwise unpronounced 'r,' in 'clear,' is pronounced if followed by a vowel, 'clear away.' An intrusive 'r' is an 'r' added in such a situation where none actually exists, so 'law and order' becomes 'law ran order.' In some cases, there is even hypercorrection, such as adding an 'r' (Louisa → Louiser), especially when a non-rhotic person moves to a rhotic area. But if Clair hears the 'r' she'll correct you.

In contrast, in the North and Scotland, r's roll stronger. Even d's can be r'd. I've been called a /bluhreeiree?/ (bloody idiot) a few times.

'YOO' WORDS LOSING THE Y IN AMERICAN
(TUNE: TYOON → TOON)

There are many less words in American that pronounce a 'y' in front of a 'u' than in British (as in *mule, mute*). Most American words don't: *assume, new, nude, tune, student, duke, due.* In England most of these words are pronounced with a 'y' in front of the 'u.' Amongst older speakers, this is true for words like *suit* and *lute,* and sometimes even in words like *Susan* and *super.*

I have noticed that my natural (SE English) way of saying *tune, tuna, Tuesday, sand dune* is 'choon, choona, choosday, san June,' and that 'tyoon, tyoona, tyoosday, sand dyoon' sounds a little formal. I imagine this to be regional. Americans generally say 'toon, toona, toosday, san doon.' This also applies to words like perpetual and situation.

PARTICULAR WORDS

Although there are relatively few words pronounced completely differently, many are well known. This list shows some of these, but the examples are not restrictive—*leisure* is pronounced both *leezhure* and *lezhure* in the US, but *leezhure* is prevalent.

word	US	UK
aluminium	aluminum	aluminium
apricot	a-pricot	ay-pricot
ß	bayda	beeta
charade	char-ay-d	char-ah-d
compost	calm-poast	com-post
cordial	corjul	cordee-al
fillet	filay	filit
herb	'erb	herb
leisure	leezhure	lezhure
lever	l-e-ver	leever
privacy	pry-vacy	priv-acy
route	rout	root
schedule	skedule	shedule
scone	scone	skon

semi	sem-eye	sem-ee
strychnine	strich-9	strich-neen
θ	thayta	theeta
tomato	tom-ay-doe	tom-ah-toe
vase	vayz	vahz
vitamin	vie-tamin	vit-amin
yogurt	yo-gurt	yog-ert

STRESS & REDUCTIONS

Stress differences, although minor, stand out. Britons stress the first vowel in *ballet, cafe* (& other borrowed French words), Americans the second, but they often stress the first vowel in *cigarette, police,* and *research.* There are many place names in Britain that also occur in the US, especially on the eastern seaboard. British towns ending in –ham, -wich, -cester, -mouth are fully pronounced in America but reduced in Britain to -[əm] -[ɪdʒ], -[stə], -[məθ] (e.g. *Birmingham, Norwich, Gloucester, Portsmouth*). Similar reductions are found in British personal names, for instance *Raleigh* is *raylee* in the US but *ralee* in Britain.

OTHER RANDOM ANOMALIES

➤ Occasionally Americans add a 't' to *cross* and *across,* and this occasionally shows up in spelling (*accrossed, acrost*).

➤ Some places in the Midwest are famous for pronouncing *wash* 'warsh,' as well as *fish, dish,* as 'feesh,' 'deesh.'

➤ In Bristol some speakers add 'l' to words ending in vowels. Trudgill heard of the three sisters "Evil, Idle, and Normal." When my sister lived there, they asked her about her brother living in a miracle (Americal).

There are other differences, such as American, like southern Irish, being more nasally—many speakers push the sounds through the nose, to some extent. But in all, differences between American and British pronunciation of English can be put into three classes:

Firstly there are many miscellaneous words where one or more syllables are simply different. For instance: *herb*—Americans don't pronounce the h, Britons do; Americans render *tomato* as *tomayto* (or *tomaydo*) rather than the British *tomahto;* both even spell *aluminum/aluminium* differently, as reflected in pronunciation. The list above, under particular words, is in this class.

Then there are classes of words where the vowel used is different. For instance Americans rhyme *pa paw caw,* whereas Britons rhyme *poor paw caw,* and even *Coors cause caws.* In some cases, patterns can be discerned, such as particular vowels following certain kinds of consonants. Most of the differences discussed above fall into this class.

And finally there are vowels and perhaps consonants that are peculiar to each. The British 'o' vowel [ɒ] in *dog,* is not found in America. Perhaps the distinction between schwa [ə] and the 'er' vowel [ɜ], found in British *bird* and *furry,* is lost in America. The British glottal stop is hardly realised in America.

A young man named **Chalmondley** Colquhoun,

Once kept for a pet a babolquhoun,

His aunt said *"Chalmondley!*

Do you think it quite Calmondley

To feed a babolquhoun with a spolquhoun?"

A lively young damsel named Menzies

Inquired: "Do you know what this thenzies?"

Her aunt, with a gasp,

Replied: "It's a wasp,

And you're holding the end where the stenzies."

REFERENCES

Peter Trudgill and Jean Hannah, *International English: A Guide to the Varieties of Standard English,* Third Ed., Routledge, Chapman, and Hall, 1994. Peter Trudgill, *The Dialects of England,* Blackwell, 1990 Craig M. Carver, *American Regional Dialects: A Word Geography.*

THE CARDINAL SYSTEM FOR MAPPING VOWELS

Vowels are made, during voicing, by changing the shape of the vocal tract with the tongue, lip position, and openness of the mouth. The tongue can be close to the roof of the mouth (tongue is high) or flat against the bottom of the mouth (tongue is low) (say "ahh"), or somewhere in between. Also, the tongue can be forward, or pressed back into the mouth, or somewhere in between. So in the following chart "ahh" would be somewhere in the bottom right corner, as the tongue is low and towards the back.

To get a feel for the tongue moving from front to back say 'cat, cut, cot,' 'bed, bird, boat,' 'bee, boo.' (Tongue was low, medium, then high). To get a feel for the tongue moving from high to low, say: 'heed, hid, head, had,' 'boot, boat, bot.' (Tongue was front, then back.) Since we are dealing with only vowels, another way to play with the sounds is to just hum them—instead if 'bee, boo,' hum 'ee-oo.' To determine the difference between [e] and [ɛ] say *bay, eight* ([ei]) and *bed, ten* ([ɛ]) but don't finish the word—extend the first vowel indefinitely. (I don't distinguish these vowels, but the method works great for the others.)

CARDINAL VOWEL SYSTEM

	tongue position			tongue height
front	center	back		
[iː] bead **i**		(**u**) bo̲o̲ed [uː]	**high**	
[ɪ] bi̲d **I**		ʊ bu̲ddhist		
[eɪː] ba̲de **e**	[əʊ] bo̲de **ə**	(**O**) bo̲de [ou]	**medium high**	
be̲d **ɛ**	**3** [ɜː] bi̲rd	**ʌ(ɔ)** bu̲d ba̲wd [ɔː]	**medium low**	
ba̲d **æ**				
[aɪ] bi̲de **a**		**ɑ(ɒ)** [ɑː] ba̲rd bo̲dy	**low**	

[iː] he̲ed **i**		(**u**) sho̲e		[iː] he̲ed **i**		(**u**) sho̲e
[ɪː] hi̲d **I**		ʊ pu̲t		[ɪː] hi̲d **I**		ʊ pu̲t
[eiː] ba̲y **e**		(**O**) bo̲at [ou]		[eiː] ba̲y **e**		(**O**) bo̲at [ou]
	bird **ə**				ago **ə**	
be̲d **ɛ**	3 **ʌ(ɔ)** cu̲t			be̲d **ɛ** bi̲rd **3**	**ʌ(ɔ)** cu̲p sa̲w	
ha̲d **æ**				ha̲d **æ**		
[ai] bu̲y **a**	**ɑ(ɒ)** po̲t			[ai] bu̲y **a**	**ɑ(ɒ)** ha̲rd po̲t	

American (Western)   English (RP)

Figure 8. **Cardinal Vowel System**

American (Western) and British (RP) Vowel Systems

US	UK	US	UK	US	UK
[i]	[i:]			[u]	[u:]
bee	bee			boot	boot
heed	heed			shoe	shoe
very				tour	
[ɪ]				[ʊ]	
bid	bid			put	put
mirror	mirror			[ou]	
wanted				boat	
[ei]				[ʌ]	
bay	bay			cut	cut
eight	eight			hurry	hurry
Mary				[ɔ]	[ɔ:]
pair				port	port
[e]				boring	boring
bed, ten	bed, ten			horrid	paw
merry	merry			hurry	talk
[ɛ:]		[ə]			saw
	pair	about	about	[ɔi]	
	Mary	sofa	sofa	boy	boy
[æ]		butter	butter	[a]	[a:]
bad	bad	bird		balm	balm
cat	cat	furry		calm	calm
khaki	marry	[ɜ:]		bard	bard
banana	Datsun		bird	father	father
path	Milan		furry	pot	dance
dance				top	half
half				bomb	khaki
[ai]				long	hard
ride	buy			cough	banana
night				Datsun	
				Milan	
				paw	
				talk	
				[au]	
				bout	
				loud	
				tower	

BUM BAGS AND FANNY PACKS

US	UK	US	UK	US	UK
					[ɒ]
					cough
					hod
					horrid
					long
					pot
					what

— American and British — Spelling Differences

HERE IS A list of 500 American and British words that are spelt differently.

I (mostly) used two dictionaries to cross check the words, chosen as the best to reflect contemporary usage of generally used words. These are the standard collegiate or desk dictionaries that contain typically up to about 200,000 definitions:

W10 (American): *Merriam-Webster's Collegiate Dictionary*, Tenth Edition, 1993
COD (British): *The Concise Oxford Dictionary*, Eighth Edition, 1990.

I've not included historical words (compleat). I've only included words where there are differences (no compelled) – although I do list what appear to be the same frequency, since you might expect otherwise (encyclopedia, encyclopaedia) – they probably once had a different frequency. I've not listed common spelling errors (*complection*). Not included are differing variants which seem too infrequent or disputable to note (such as advertise or advisor or arguement). And I've not included words like accessorize because although W10 lists -ise as a British variant, the COD doesn't list it. I've ignored hyphenation differences as they vary so much, and include only a token of space, diacritic and punctuation differences.

This list is no way complete – I keep adding words all the time. I originally compiled this from a list of over 180 words sent to me by Dan Tilque, the news:alt.usage.english FAQ, and many other various sources.

I had previously used (WII) Webster's II New Riverside University Dictionary, 1988 (also about 200,000 definitions) for the American side, but revamped the list using W10.

Ideally, there would simply be a unique spelling for each side, but often

---

they both figure to some extent on both sides. Dictionaries list variants in a variety of ways:

➤ word1, or word2
➤ word1, var. word2
➤ word1, also word2

and sometimes word2, however it is designated, is parenthesised. I have inferred from the dictionaries the following two levels of variants, and indicate them as follows:

word1, word2	word1 is the equal or more usual variant
word1 (word2)	word2 is a much less frequent variant than word1

The dictionaries tend to agree generally but sometimes differ in the details. For instance, both COD and WII say spelled or spelt (W10 says spelt is chiefly British). Whereas, COD says oenology, indicating enology is the American, but WII say it's oenology, and that enology is a variant. W10 says enology, and that oenology is a variant.

Many spelling differences are the result of simplifying obsolete spellings that in many cases are vestiges of other languages, such as French, Latin or Greek. This practice, more common in American, was one of Webster's stated aims. American much more readily drops hyphens and spaces in compound words (lemongrass), and in these compounds the variations between American and British seem innumerable. (Does anal-retentive have a hyphen?)

A special note about ize/ise spellings

When I look at UK literature (personal letters, magazines, postings, books, etc.) I find in actuality the -ise form is used.

COD generally lists the -ize form as the regular spelling, with -ise form as the variant. The reason is that the -ize form in the UK is not only accepted but, seemingly in the case of COD, the recommended form.

Since the -ise form is the one used by the natives, I presume that the -ise form is the actually accepted and current spelling in the UK, whereas the -ize word is an acceptable but less often used variant.

Spelling differences in 35 categories

1-5: Greek (classic) & Latin spellings simplified
1. -e-/-oe-
2. -e-/-ae-
3. -r-/-rh-
4. /-ph-
5. -yze/-yse

6-11: Old/Middle English simplified
6. -f-/-ph-
7. -ed/-t
8. other
9. -f-/-gh-
10. -i-/-y-
11. /-st

12-21: French spellings simplified
12. -er/-re
13. -or/-our
14. -o-/-ou-
15. -m/-mme
16. -ck/-que
17. -g/-gue

18. -ction/-xion
19. -ize/-ise
20. -a-/-au-
21. -se/-ce

22-31: Pronunciation simplifications
22. -er/-or
23. -e/-ee
24. -g-/-gg-
25. -ll-/-l-
26. -l-/-ll-
27. -p-/-pp-
28. -s-/-ss-
29. -t-/-tt-
30. -g-/-ge-
31. in-/-en-

32-35: spaces, diacritics, punctuation, miscellaneous
32. spaces
33. diacritics
34. punctuation
35. miscellaneous

(1-5) GREEK (CLASSIC) & LATIN SPELLINGS SIMPLIFIED

American	British
1. -e-/-oe-	
amoeba (ameba)	amoeba
diarrhea	diarrhoea
edema	oedema
enology, oenology	oenology
esophagus (oesophagus)	oesophagus
estrogen (oestrogen)	oestrogen
estrus (oestrus)	oestrus
fetal (foetal)	foetal
fetid, foetid	fetid, foetid

fetor	fetor, foetor
fetus (foetus)	foetus
gonorrhea	gonorrhoea
homeopath	homoeopath
homeostasis	homoeostasis
maneuver, -verability, -vering	manoeuvre, -vrability, -vring (-vreing)
menorrhea	menorrhoea
penology	penology (poenology?)

2. -e-/-ae-

eon, aeon	aeon, eon
aesthete, esthete	aesthete
aesthetic, esthetic	aesthetic
anemia	anaemia
anemic	anaemic
anesthetic, -thesia, -thetist	anaesthetic, -thesia, -thetist
archaeology, archeology	archaeology
cesarean (caesarean) cesarian (caesarian)	caesarean, caesarian
cesium	caesium
diaeresis, dieresis	diaeresis
encyclopedia, encyclopaedia	encyclopedia, encyclopaedia
ether	ether (aether)
fecal (faecal)	faecal
feces (faeces)	faeces
gynecology	gynaecology
hemo-	haemo-
hemoglobin	haemoglobin
hemolysis	haemolysis
hemophilia	haemophilia
hemorrhage	haemorrhage
hemorrhoid	haemorrhoid
leukemia	leukaemia
medieval, mediaeval	medieval, mediaeval
orthopedics, orthopaedics	orthopaedics
paean (pean)	paean
paleobotany	palaeobotany

Paleocene	Palaeocene
paleoclimatology	palaeoclimatology
paleogeography	palaeogeography
paleography	palaeography
paleolithic	palaeolithic
paleomagnetism	palaeomagnetism
paleontology	palaeontology
Paleozoic	Palaeozoic
pedagogy	paedagogy
pederast	pederast, paederast
pediatrician	paediatrician
pediatric	paediatric
pediatrics	paediatrics
pedophile	paedophile
pedophilia	paedophilia
primeval	primeval (primaeval)
syneresis, synaeresis	synaeresis
synesthesia, synaesthesia	synaesthesia

3 -r-/-rh-

eurythmy, eurhythmy	eurhythmy

4. silent -ph-

apothegm	apophthegm

5. -lyze/-lyse

analyze	analyse
autolyze	autolyse
catalyze	catalyse
dialyze	dialyse
electrolyze	electrolyse
hemolyze	haemolyse
hydrolyze	hydrolyse
paralyze	paralyse
photolyze	photolyse
plasmolyze	plasmolyse
psychoanalyze	psychoanalyse
pyrolyze, pyrolize	pyrolyse

(6-11) OLD/MIDDLE ENGLISH SIMPLIFIED

6. -f-/-ph-

bisulfate	bisulphate
disulfide	disulphide
sulfate	sulphate
sulfide	sulphide
sulfur, sulphur	sulphur
sulfurous, sulphurous	sulphurous
trisulfate	trisulphate

7. -ed/-t

burned, burnt	burnt, burned
dreamed, dreamt	dreamt, dreamed
knelt, kneeled	knelt (kneeled)
leaned	leaned, leant
leaped, leapt	leaped, leapt
learned	learned, learnt
skinned	skinned [skint]
smelled, smelt	smelt, smelled
spelled	spelt, spelled
spilled, spilt	spilt, spilled
spoiled, spoilt	spoilt, spoiled

8. other past tense verb forms

alighted (alit)	alighted (alit)
fit	fit, fitted
forecast	forecast, forecasted
gotten, got	got
knit	knitted
lit, lighted	lit, lighted
wed	wedded

9. -f-/-gh- and -ow/-ough

draft, -fty	draught, -ghty (only air current, drawing of liquid)
draftsman	draughtsman, draftsman (one who makes drawings)

plow (plough), -man, -share	plough, -man, -share
snowplow	snowplough

10. -i-/-y-

dryly (drily)	drily (dryly)
gypsy, gipsy	gypsy, gipsy
jibe (gybe)	gybe (nautical)
siphon, syphon	siphon (syphon)
tire	tyre (on vehicles only)
tyke, tike	tyke (tike)
tyro	tiro (tyro)

11. /-st

amid, amidst	amid, amidst
among (amongst)	among, amongst
while	while, whilst

(12-21) FRENCH SPELLINGS SIMPLIFIED

12. -er/-re

accoutre, accouter	accoutre
accouterment, accoutrement	accoutrement
amphitheater	amphitheatre
caliber (calibre)	calibre
center	centre
centerboard	centreboard
centerfold	centrefold
centering	centring, centreing
fiber (fibre)	fibre
fiberboard (fibreboard)	fibreboard
fiberglass (fibreglass)	fibreglass
goiter	goitre
liter (litre)	litre
louver (louvre)	louvre, louver
luster (lustre)	lustre (brilliance)
maneuver, -verability, -vering	manoeuvre, -vrability, -vring (-vreing)
meager (meagre)	meagre

meter	metre (unit of measurement)
miter (mitre)	mitre
niter	nitre
ocher (ochre)	ochre
philter (philtre)	philtre
reconnoiter (reconnoitre)	reconnoitre
saber (sabre)	sabre
saltpeter	saltpetre
scepter	sceptre
sepulchre (sepulcher)	sepulchre
somber (sombre)	sombre
specter (spectre)	spectre
theater (theatre)	theatre
titer (titre)	titre

13. -or/-our

arbor	arbour
ardor	ardour
armor	armour
armorer	armourer
armory	armoury
behavior	behaviour
behavioral	behavioural
candor	candour
clamor	clamour
clangor	clangour
color	colour (and all derivative words)
demeanor	demeanour
dolor	dolour (literary)
enamor	enamour
endeavor	endeavour
favor	favour
favorite	favourite
favoritism	favouritism
fervor	fervour
flavor	flavour
glamor, glamour	glamour
harbor	harbour
honor	honour

humor	humour
labor	labour
misdemeanor	misdemeanour
neighbor	neighbour
neighborhood	neighbourhood
neighborly	neighbourly
odor	odour
parlor	parlour
pavior, paviour	pavior or paviour
rancor	rancour
rigor	rigour
rumor	rumour
savior, saviour	saviour
savor, savour	savour
savory, savoury	savoury
splendor	splendour
succor	succour
tumor	tumour
valor	valour
vapor	vapour
vigor	vigour

14. -o-/-ou-

bolt	bolt (boult) (metal pin)
citrus	citrous (adj)
font	font, fount
mold, mould	mould (rot and form)
molding, moulding	moulding (ornamental wood or stone)
molt (moult)	moult
Romanian, Rumanian, Roumanian	Romanian, Rumanian
ruble, rouble	rouble, ruble
smolder, smoulder	smoulder

15. -m/-mme

gram	gram (gramme)
kilogram	kilogram (kilogramme)
program, programme	programme (verb)
program	programme (noun)
program	program (programme) (computer)

programmed, programed   programmed
programmer, programer   programmer
programming, programing   programming

16. -ck/-que

check   cheque (banking only)
checker   chequer, checker (pattern)

17. -g/-gue

analogue or analog   analogue
catalog, -ged, -ging, catalogue,   catalogue, -gued, -guing
  -gued, -guing
dialogue, dialog   dialogue
demagogue, demagog, -goged,   demagogue, -gogued, -goguing
  -goging
epilogue, epilog   epilogue
homologue, homolog   homologue
monologue, monolog   monologue
pedagogue, pedagog   pedagogue
prologue, prolog   prologue
renege   renege (renegue)
synagogue, synagog   synagogue
travelogue, travelog   travelogue

18. -ction/-xion

connection   connection, connexion
deflection   deflection, deflexion
flexion (flection)   flexion
genuflection   genuflection, genuflexion
inflection   inflection, inflexion
reflection   reflection, reflexion
retroflection   retroflexion

19. -ize/-ise

advertise (-ize listed as Brit.   advertise
  var. in W10)
aggrandize   aggrandize, aggrandise
Americanize   Americanise, Americanize
apologize   apologise, apologize

appetizer, -zing	appetiser, -sing, appetizer, -zing
apprise	apprise (to inform)
apprize	apprize (archaic) (appraise, esteem)
atomize	atomise, atomize
burglarize	burgle, burglarise, burglarize
capitalize	capitalise, capitalize
categorize	categorize, categorise
characterize	characterise, characterize
civilize	civilise, civilize
civilization	civilisation, civilization
colonize	colonize, colonise
computerize	computerise, computerize
criticize	criticize, criticise
dramatize	dramatise, dramatize
economize	economise, economize
empathize (-ise listed as Brit. var. in W10)	empathize
emphasize	emphasize, emphasise
equalize	equalise, equalize
extemporize	extemporize, extemporise
finalize	finalize, finalise
gizmo (gismo)	gismo, gizmo
glamorize, glamourize	glamorise, glamorize, glamourise, glamourize
harmonize	harmonise, harmonize
hospitalize	hospitalise, hospitalize
initialize	initialise, initialize
liberalize	liberalize, liberalise
merchandise (merchandize)	merchandise
memorize	memorise, memorize
memorialize	memorialise, memorialize
mobilize	mobilise, mobilize
monopolize	monopolise, monopolize
motorize	motorise, motorize
naturalize	naturalise, naturalize
normalize	normalize, normalise
organize	organise, organize
oxidize	oxidise, oxidize
parameterize or parametrize	parametrize, parametrise

parenthesize	parenthesize, parenthesise
pasteurize	pasteurise, pasteurize
polarize	polarise, polarize
popularize	popularise, popularize
pulverize	pulverise, pulverize
realize	realise, realize
recognize	recognise, recognize
romanize	romanise, romanize
satirize	satirise, satirize
stabilize	stabilize, stabilise
standardize	standardise, standardize
surprise (surprize)	surprise
symbolize	symbolise, symbolize
sympathize	sympathise, sympathize
tantalize	tantalize, tantalise
utilize	utilise, utilize
vaporize	vaporise, vaporize
	(yep! not vapourise)

20. -a-/-au-

balk	baulk (balk)
cauldron (caldron)	cauldron (caldron)
calk (caulk)	calk, calkin (metal shoe grip)
caulk (calk)	caulk (goop to stop up boat leaks)
gauge (gage)	gauge

21. -se/-ce

defense	defence
license, licence	license (verb)
license, licence	licence (noun)
offense, offence	offence
practice, practise	practise, practice (noun)
practice, practise	practise (verb)
pretense, pretence	pretence
vise	vice (tool for holding work)

(22-31) PRONUNCIATION SIMPLIFICATIONS

22. -er/-or
adapter, adaptor

adviser, advisor

propeller, propellor

adaptor, adapter

adviser (advisor disputed)

propeller

23. -e/-ee
employee, employe

employee

24. -g-/-gg-
fagot, faggot

fagoting, faggoting

wagon

faggot (bundle of sticks)

faggoting (embroidery)

wagon, waggon

25. -ll-/-l-
appall, appal

distill, distil

enroll, enrol

enrollment

enthrall, enthral

fulfill, fulfil

fulfillment

install (instal)

installment, instalment

instill, instil

skillful

thralldom or thraldom

willful, wilful

appal

distil

enrol

enrolment

enthral

fulfil

fulfilment

install, instal

instalment

instil

skilful

thraldom (thralldom)

wilful

26. -l-/-ll-
barreled, -ling, barrelled, -lling

calisthenics

caliper

canceled, -ling or cancelled -lling

chili, chile, chilli

councillor or councilor

counseled, -ling, counselled, -lling

counselor, counsellor

deviled, -ling, devilled, -lling

barrelled, -lling

callisthenics (calisthenics)

calliper

cancelled, -lling

chilli, chili

councillor

counselled, -lling

counsellor

devilled, -lling

disheveled, -ling or dishevelled, -lling	dishevelled, -lling
equaled, -ling, equalled, -lling	equalled, -lling
excelling (exceling)	excelling
fueled, -ling, fuelled, -lling	fuelled, -lling
groveled, -ling, -ler, grovelled, -lling, -ller	grovelled, -lling, -ller
hosteler or hosteller	hosteller
hosteled, -ling or hostelled, -lling	hostelled, -lling
jeweler, jeweller	jeweller
jewelry	jewellery (jewelry) (note -el-, -elle-)
labeled, -ling, labelled, -lling	labelled, -lling
leveled, -ling, levelled, -lling	levelled, -lling
leveler, leveller	leveller
libeled, -ling, libelled, -lling	libelled, -lling
libelous, libellous	libellous
marvelous or marvellous	marvellous
marveled, -ling or marvelled, -lling	marvelled, -lling
medalist, medallist	medallist
metaled, -ling, metalled, -lling	metalled, -lling
modeled, -ling or modelled -lling	modelled, -lling
modeler	modeller
paneled, -ling or panelled, -lling	panelled, -lling
panelist	panellist
propelled (propeled)	propelled
pupilage or pupillage	pupillage (pupilage)
quarreled, -ling, quarrelled, -lling	quarrelled, -lling
quarreler, quarreller	quarreller
rappeled, -ling, rappelled, -lling	rappelled, rappelling
rebelling (rebeling)	rebelling
reveled, -ling, revelled, -lling	revelled, -lling
scalawag (scallywag)	scallywag (scalawag)
signaled, -ling, signalled, -lling	signalled, -lling
traveled, -ling, travelled, -lling	travelled, -lling
traveler, traveller	traveller
troweled, -ling, trowelled, -lling	trowelled, -lling
woolen or woollen	woollen
woolly, wooly	woolly (adj)
woolly, woolie, wooly (pl. -llies, -lies)	woolly (pl. -llies) (noun)

27. -p-/-pp-

kidnapped, kidnaped	kidnapped
kidnapper, -pping, kidnaper, -ping	kidnapper, -pping
worshiped, -ping, worshipped, -pping	worshipped, -pping
worshiper, worshipper	worshipper

28. -s-/-ss-

biased, -sing, biassed, -ssing	biased, -sing, biassed, -ssing
buses, busses	buses (omnibus)
buses, busses	buses, busses (computer)
focused, -sing, focussed, -ssing	focused, -sing or focussed, -ssing

29. -t-/-tt-

benefited, -ting, benefitted ,-tting	benefited, -ting
carburetor	carburettor (carburetter)
cigarette, cigaret	cigarette
clarinetist, clarinettist	clarinettist
garrote, -ted, -ting or garotte, -tted, -tting	garrotte (garotte)
net	net (nett) (of money, result, etc)
omelette, omelet	omelette, omelet
sulfureted	sulphuretted

30. -g-/-ge-

abridgment, abridgement	abridgement (abridgment)
acknowledgment, acknowledgement	acknowledgement (acknowledgment)
aging, ageing	ageing, aging
fledgling	fledgling, fledgeling
judgment, judgement	judgement (judgment)
misjudgment	misjudgement (misjudgment)

31 in-/en-

encase (incase)	encase (incase)
enclose (inclose)	enclose (inclose)
endorse (indorse)	endorse (indorse)
ensure, insure	ensure (make sure)
inquire, enquire	enquire, inquire

inquiry, enquiry

enquiry, inquiry

inure, enure

inure, enure

(32-35) SPACES, DIACRITICS, PUNCTUATION, MISCELLANEOUS

32. spaces

alright	all right
anymore	any more
cooperate	cooperate, co-operate
lemongrass	lemon grass
onto	on to

33. diacritics

café, cafe	café, cafe
elite	élite
entree, entrée	entrée
fete, fête	fête
matinee, matinée	matinée
naive, naïve	naïve, naive
role (rôle)	role, rôle

34. punctuation

B.S.	BSc
Dr.	Dr
jct, junc	jct, jctn, junc
Jr.	Jnr, Jr
M.S.	MSc
Ph.D.	PhD
Sr.	Snr, Sr

35. miscellaneous

adze, adz	adze
airplane	aeroplane
aluminum	aluminium
artifact	artefact, artifact
ass (arse)	arse
ax, axe	axe
bail out	bale out, bail out
baloney (boloney)	boloney, baloney
battle-ax	battleaxe

behoove	behove
boric (boracic)	boracic, boric
borscht or borsch	bortsch (also borsch)
Briticism	Briticism, Britishism
cantaloupe, cantaloup	cantaloup (cantaloupe)
carcass	carcass, carcase
chamomile (camomile)	camomile, chamomile
clerestory, clearstory	clerestory
cozy, cosy	cosy
crayfish, crawfish	crayfish (crawfish)
curb	kerb (edging of road only)
czar, tsar, tzar	tsar, czar
dependent, dependant	dependant (noun)
disc, disk	disc (phono record, CD, CD-ROM, disc harrow, Frisbee)
disk, disc	disk (computing)
disk	disc (other meanings)
dissension, dissention	dissension
doodad	doodah
donut, doughnut	doughnut
flaky (flakey)	flaky
flotation (floatation)	flotation, floatation
furor	furore
gray, grey	grey
jail	jail, gaol
jailbird	jailbird, gaolbird
jailbreak	jailbreak, gaolbreak
jailer	jailer, gaoler
karat (carat)	carat (gold)
ketchup, catsup (catchup)	ketchup (catchup)
kumquat	kumquat (cumquat)
largesse or largess	largesse (largess)
lens, lense	lens
licorice	liquorice (licorice)
meow (miaow)	miaow (meow)
mollusk or mollusc	mollusc
mustache, moustache	moustache
naught, nought	nought (digit 0)
night, nite	night

nursling	nursling, nurseling
pajamas	pyjamas
peddler, pedlar	pedlar
persnickety (pernickety)	pernickety
pickaninny, picaninny	piccaninny
polyethylene	polythene, polyethylene, polyethene
premise, premiss	premise, premiss
propellant, propellent	propellant (n)
propellant, propellent	propellent (adj)
reverie, revery	reverie
Romansh, Romansch	Romansh, Rumansh
routing	routeing (route)
sanatorium, sanitarium or sanitorium	sanatorium
scion (cion)	scion
sissy	sissy (cissy)
skeptic, -al, -ism, sceptic, -al, -ism	sceptic, -al, -ism
specialty	speciality
story, -ries, storey, -reys	storey, -reys (story, -ries) (floor of buildings only)
swab (archaic: swob)	swab, swob
swap	swap, swop
though, tho	though, tho'
through, thru	through
tidbit, titbit	titbit
tonight, tonite	tonight
vial, phial	phial, vial
whiskey, whisky	whisky (generic name)
whiskey	whiskey (Irish & American kinds)
whiskeys, whiskies	whiskeys, whiskies
whisky	whisky (Scottish kinds)

— History —

W HERE DID ENGLISH come from? The Germanic language of the *Angulseaxans* (Anglo-Saxons), who began arriving in the British Isles in the middle of the 5th century AD, developed independently of the original continental *Ealdseaxe* (Old Saxons), becoming what is called both Anglo-Saxon and Old English. English developed from there, more or less as follows:

450–1100	Anglo-Saxon/Old English
1100–1500	Middle English (Chaucer)
1500–1700	Early Modern (Shakespeare)
1700–1900	19th century (Industrial Revolution & Victorians)
1900–2000	Modern (Technology)

But who were these Saxons? Where did they and their language come from, and whom did they find when they arrived in the British Isles?

The Venerable Bede, in his *Historia Ecclesiastica* (written in Latin 735–739 AD) says that there were four peoples (languages) on the island: Scots, Britons, Angles, and Picts. The Scots were Celts who had come from Ireland in the 5th century; the British were the Celts from Manchester; the Angles, a generic term of the time including Angles, Saxons and Jutes, were the Germanic peoples from the continent; and the Picts.

THE CELTS

The Celtic speaking tribes emerged in central Europe around 3000 years ago. They dominated southern Germany and the northern Alps in the 1st millennium BC, and emerged in southern Europe in the 5th century BC (Spain, Celtiberians). They're the Gauls in Europe, and the biblical Galatians in Turkey, as well as in Switzerland/northern Italy (Lepontic) and Britain and Ireland.

The Celts were known to the Greeks as *Keltoi* (barbarians). The first historical account of the Celts by the Romans report how they came out of the Alps (400 BC) and displaced the Etruscans from the fertile Po valley, which eventually led to the decline of the Etruscans (800 BC–100 AD).

The Celts appeared in Britain and Ireland around 2800 years ago, essentially bringing the iron-age to the British Isles. The Irish Celts spoke Goidelic, the language that became Irish (*Gaeilge*), Manx (*Gailck*), and Scottish Gaelic (*Gàidhlig*) (In the late 400s, Gaelic speakers from County Antrim, Ireland invaded the western district of Argyll, Scotland (then Pictland or *Pictavia*). They called their new kingdom Dalriada but they were known as 'scots,' meaning raiders, by their enemies.) Goidelic is also called q-Celtic because it retains the 'kw' sound of proto-Indo-European (below), which survives today in words such as *mac* (son, as in McDonald, son of Donald).

At a later time period, there were more migrations of Celts into England, occurring up until (and possibly even a little after) Julius Caesar's expeditions in 55–54 BC. These Celts spoke Brythonic, which gave rise to Welsh (*Cymraeg*), Cornish, Cumbric (*Cymric*) and Breton (when Cornish folk migrated to Britanny in France in the 5th century AD partially because of the bothersome Irish Celts).

Brythonic is also called p-Celtic because the 'kw' sound had developed into a 'p' (or 'b'). The Welsh for son is *map* or *mab*, the root word of Mabinogion (a well-known collection of ancient Welsh legends including some of King Arthur, although the actual meaning of Mabinogion is unclear, something like 'tales of youth,' 'youthful career,' 'aspirant to bardic honor').

Since Lepontic (northern Italy) is p-Celtic, as is thought Celtiberian, Gaulish, and Galatian, does this mean that Irish (q-Celtic) is the most ancient of Celtic languages, since the p-Celtic diverged from its Indo-European roots?

The Britonnes, so called by the Romans, were one of the many tribes in Britain, and it is this that eventually gives rise to words like (ancient) Briton, British, Britain, and brythonic. Interestingly, the Greeks called the British Isles (300 BC) *Pretaninkai nesoi*, the p-Celtic stem 'pretan' the same as the q-Celtic Crethan, the Irish name for the Picts.

> Tribes typically refer to themselves as the one true people ('the chosen race,' 'all men,' 'the real people') who live in 'the homeland,' but are called by their neighbours usually something disparaging, starting with foreigner (on the other side of the *tracks*), and it is these names that tend to get passed down, becoming that by which they are known today.

| Viking | vik /vik/ originally meant fjord or bay, but also has the connotation landing place, settlement, camp. So vik-ings means people of this camp, or literally townspeople. In Old English, wic means village. |

derogatory terms:

Celt	from the Greek *keltoi* meaning barbarian.
Welsh, Wales	Saxon word *wealas*, meaning foreigner, for the displaced Celts who became the Welsh.
Cornwall	('Cornish Welsh') Cornish foreigners.
Goidelic	Welsh *gwyddel*, meaning savages, for the Irish who briefly colonised in the west. (Goidelic is the language family name, see above.)
Scots	related to an Old Irish word for raider, making Scotland mean the 'Land of the Raiders.'
Gauls	Latin *Gallatae* = barbarians.
barbarian	Greek for foreigner.
Hebrew	derived from a Babylonian word meaning vagrant.

compare:

| gaijin | Japanese term for foreigner |
| gringo | Mexican term for foreigner |

ROMANS

The Romans arrived in Britain in 43 AD and left during the 5th century, completing their withdrawal by 436 AD. They were essentially managers of the land, farmed by the Celts, in return for taxes and protection. (They allowed a small number of Saxons to settle in Britain in those centuries.) They had control of Britain as far as Hadrian's Wall, north of which lived the insurmountable Picts.

GERMANS

Germanic tribes emerged from southern Scandinavia around 3000 years ago and spread into northern areas of Germany. In the ensuing centuries, they expanded, encountering the Celts (4th c. BC), and Romans (1st c. BC). The eastern tribes were the nomadic Goths, the northern groups are the various Scandinavians (which gave rise to the Scandinavian languages), and the western ones in northern Germany were the Angles, Saxons, and Jutes (amongst others). Their languages became German and Dutch, and English began with Angles, Saxons, and Jutes who invaded and settled in Britain in the 5th century AD. (They were initially invited by Celtic King Vortigern to help him fight the Scots and the Picts.)

SOME ANCIENT HISTORY (INDO-EUROPEAN)

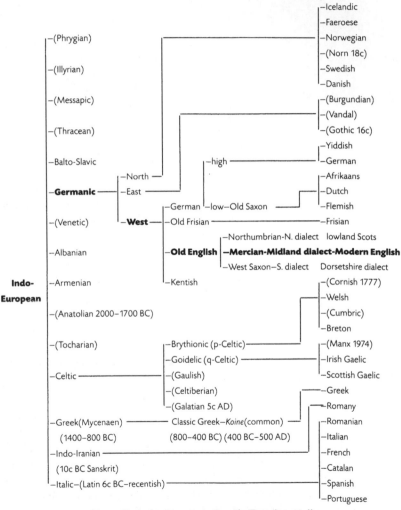

Figure 9. Indo-European Family Tree (partial)

In the same way that Romance languages Spanish, Italian, and Portuguese are obviously related, Germanic languages Dutch and German are related, and the Celtic languages Welsh, Scottish Gaelic, and Irish are related, it was discovered that these language groups are also related, though more distantly. All such related groups are part of the Indo-European language family. As Latin gave rise to the Romance languages, so a proto-Indo-European language is inferred, which gave rise to proto versions of each language group (such as Latin), which then gave rise to most of the languages found today in Europe, Persia, and northern India.

English is a branch of Indo-European, in the Germanic group. The chart shows the Indo-European language family tree, with Celtic and Germanic expanded more than the others. Extinct languages are parenthesised, with prepended dates indicating when a language became unique, and appended dates the language's demise, and a range showing both. Indo-European is one of a score of major language families, such as Austronesian, which includes all the southeast Asian languages, and Amerind which includes most of the native American languages. These language families, deduced linguistically, bear a striking correlation with the major ethnic groups, deduced genetically. One popular theory is that all these languages originated from one language, or at least there were a bunch of coexisting ones, but only one mongrel prevailed (in a similar way to people starting). But when was this, and who were these people?

WHEN DID LANGUAGE START

It all started with a Big Bang about 13.7 billion years ago (± 0.14). After a split second of quark soup, we got radioactive subatomic particle soup which took hundreds of thousands of years of simmering for actual atoms to coalesce. After a few hundred million years, galaxies formed, which promptly started manufacturing stars, and the stars manufactured the chemicals we all know and love, and are made of. Our galaxy formed around that time, about 13 billion years ago, although taking a few billion years to assume its present spiral structure, but our sun formed much later, appearing about 5 billion years ago.

The rightmost scale of the accompanying graph is (almost) linear time. Nothing much was going on in the universe except star formation and aliens going about their usual day-to-day business. The earth formed about 4.6 billion years ago, and after almost another billion years, life finally formed (think wads of bacteria in shallow parts of oceans). After another couple of billion years rolled by, algae formed, and various inexplicable slimy things (Ediacara). Eventually, about half a billion years ago, life as we know it began to

BUM BAGS AND FANNY PACKS

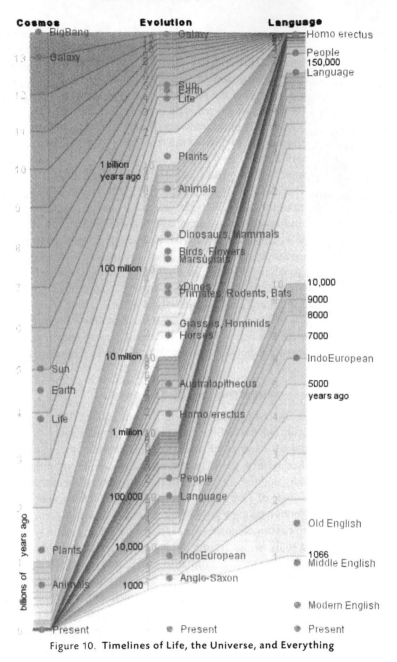

Figure 10. **Timelines of Life, the Universe, and Everything**

proliferate, with lush vegetation and all manner of creepy crawly thingies. Mammals actually appeared about the same time as dinosaurs, but kept well out of the way, until a big meteor nuked all the dinosaurs. The thus-liberated ratty creatures took a mere 5 million years to evolve into primates, but 8 to evolve into real rodents, and 10 for bats. And hominids finally made their appearance, along with grasses, 25 million years ago.

Humans escaped from chimpanzees about 5–7 million years ago, though in modern parlance, we speak of sharing a common ancestor at that time back in the plio-Pleistocene era. The earliest actual *Australopithecus* fossil dates back to about 5 million years ago, and the earliest *Homo erectus* fossils date back to perhaps almost 2 million years ago, and evidence of modern humans *Homo sapiens* date back no earlier than a mere 200,000 years.

Homo erectus (Peking Man, Java Man) survived until 50,000 years ago, and *Homo neanderthalensis* (Neanderthals) survived until 30,000 years ago. But it was *Homo sapiens* (us) who survived solely, until mere moments ago.

Three precipitous things occurred with the advent of modern humans: an astonishingly rapid increase in intelligence or sophistication (your mileage may vary), and along with that, culture and language. The evidence for these comes also from three sources: anthropology, DNA testing, and linguistics. Most of the above comes from stones and bones. DNA testing of people of today has allowed scientists to create a family tree, then by measuring the variation, deduce when there was a common ancestor, and also the relationship between the various ethnic groups. For females, the DNA measured is in the mitochondria, small organelles that pass unchanged, apart from random mutations, from mother to daughter. For males, the DNA measured is on the Y chromosome. Mitochondrial Eve appears in Africa about 130,000 years ago, and Y-chromosome Adam about 59,000 years ago.

Similarly, the linguistic measurement traces the variation in related groups of languages back to a supposed common language, and this language with other so-derived languages back to another common language, all the way back to the original language. All three methods, of thus tracing the original humans and their ultimate dispersal around the planet, produce excellently consistent results, but with enough inconclusivity to keep the raging academic fires burning fiercely.

Migrations out of Africa began possibly as late as 50,000 years ago. Although Europe was thus populated about 40,000 years ago, the Ice Age squoze them out of the main part of Europe until around 16,000 years ago, when they were let back in. Farming was invented around 10,000 years ago in the Middle East area, and these folks spread into Europe around 8000 years ago, when they would have encountered the original people (who did all those cool paintings in France and Spain), still hunting and gathering. God was invented by this time, just in time to create the creationists, 6000 years ago, on Wednesday 23rd October 4004 BC. (This just in—British researchers have just determined that the funniest moment of the year, when people find jokes the funniest, is on 7th October at 6:03 in the evening.)

Some linguists have surmised that language began about 150,000 years ago, and that this language, termed proto-World, diverged as humans spread around the world. So, in this scenario, language appeared with modern humans at around the same time that culture and sophistication suddenly flourished, and culture is seen as a measure of modern consciousness. So the big question is, did consciousness beget language, language beget consciousness, or did they both arise hand in hand?

Which would mean, by the way, that my earlier claim about rhyming slang is patently false, because, Mr Anderson, what good is rhyming if you are unable to speak?

So we've populated Europe and Asia with nattering humans, and history begins about 10,000 years ago when farming was invented in the Middle East. These folks spread east and west, taking farming with them. In this way it entered Europe about 8000 years ago, and was apparently gradually adopted by the indigenous hunter-gatherers in Britain 6000 years ago.

It was previously thought that the Kurgans were the progenitors of Indo-European. They were an agricultural and warlike people from south Russia, as far back as 7000 years ago, spreading to Danube area of Europe and beyond (3500 BC), and arriving in the Adriatic region before 2000 BC. However, the Indo-European proto-language is now thought to have emerged amongst a loose collection of clans in Anatolia (the eastern end of Turkey) 6000 years ago, and from there diffusing many directions, including around the Caspian and Black Seas and into Europe. Over time it diverged to become most of the European languages of today, such as the Celtic, Italic, and Germanic languages.

A BRIEF HISTORY OF ENGLISH

Old English 450–1100   (Germanic)

So the Saxons arrived in 449 AD. As it happens, they were invited to help the various and sundry British tribes defend themselves, now that the Romans were gone, against the ever pillaging Picts, who kept dashing over Hadrian's wall and rushing back again with their loot and booty, occasionally assisted by the Scots from Ireland. Although, it took no time for the Saxons to side with the Picts, chase the British tribes off to the extremities, and use the land for themselves.

The Celts were eventually pushed back to Wales in the west, and Cornwall in the southwest. In the 5th century, some Irish invaded southwestern Scotland, and in the 6th century a large group from South Wales and Cornwall emigrated to Brittany in northern France, where they still speak Breton. This is the Britain as described by Bede.

Today, Scottish Gaelic is spoken in Scotland, Irish Gaelic is spoken in Ireland, and Welsh is spoken in Wales. Manx (Irish Gaelic influenced by Norse) was spoken in the Isle of Man until the middle part of this century (last native speaker was Ned Maddrell who died on 12th December 1974). Cornish was spoken in Cornwall until (inscription on gravestone): "Here lies interred Dorothy Pentreath who died in 1777 said to have been the last person who conversed in the Ancient Cornish the peculiar language of this county from the earliest records till it expired in the eighteenth century in this parish of Saint Paul."

As a result, Old English is predominantly Anglo-Saxon, with very few Celtic words adopted into the language (about a dozen p-Celtic and three or so q-Celtic words).

Picts

Legend has it that Morgaine, King Arthur's lover and petite half-sister, was part Pictish, which explained her mysterious ways, psychic abilities, and dark complexion.

Little is known of the Picts whose language died out in the 10th century, almost without trace, as the people merged with the Scots. Bede says that they were originally Scythians (north of the Black Sea, or Scandanavians?) who sailed to Ireland, picked up wives, and continued to the then fertile shores of Scotland in some remote time.

In the early 1950s, F. T. Wainwright collected everything known about them in *The Problem of the Picts*. The only criticism was that the problem in the title was singular. Many historians wished them away, but were thwarted by sparse but persistent evidence. A mystique continues, despite a recent survey, *The Age of the Picts* by W. A. Cummins, which provides all answers presently knowable.

Old English also borrowed from Church Latin (~450 words) and from Old Norse (~50 words). Seventh century Christian missions to Britain brought learning and literacy, initially entirely in Latin, but an Old English written language did emerge in the northeast and in the West Saxon kingdom of Alfred the Great in the second half of the 9th century.

The first known written English sentence, "This she-wolf is a reward to my kinsman," is an Anglo-Saxon runic inscription on a gold medallion (about the size of a 50¢ piece) found in Suffolk, dated about AD 450–480.

By 750 AD Old English had evolved into a distinct language separate from the original speech of the Angles and Saxons. Of the 1000 most frequently used words today 83% are of Old English origin. Of our remaining vocabulary about 30% are Anglo-Saxon survivals. Tens of thousands of our current words are of French and Latin origin.

From the 8th to the 11th centuries, Vikings plundered lands adjacent to the Baltic and North Seas, including northeast England. The Danish King Cnut conquered Norway and England, usurping the English throne, in the early 11th century. Large numbers of Scandinavians settled in England throughout the Old English period, giving the language several thousand common words.

As well as most alphabetic characters we use today, Old English included ash æ /a/, thorn þ /th/, eth ð /dh/, and (Runic) wynn ᚹ /w/. The þ and ð are still present in Icelandic, and the æ in Danish and Norwegian.

Middle English: 1100–1500   (Germanic + Romance)

With his invading Normans in 1066, William the Conqueror established French domination. They were originally Danes ('Northmen') who had settled the northern coast of France (Normandy) in the 8th and 9th centuries.

All Old English nobility were wiped out. Norman French became the language of the aristocracy and the government (Normanized Latin was used in government, church and learning), and English remained the speech of the masses. So until about 1200 England was bilingual, when many French words were absorbed into English. (English: ox, sheep, swine, calf, and deer. French: beef, mutton, pork, veal, and venison.)

By the mid-1300s, English had reasserted itself, with a statute enacted in Parliament in 1362 that all lawsuits be conducted in English. French became a cultivated rather than a native language. The Hundred Years' War (1337–1453) meant French was the language of the enemy. The Black Death (1349–50), which killed off 30% of the people, increased the economic importance of the labouring classes and with it the importance of their language (not to mention their immune systems).

Geoffrey Chaucer (1340–1400): Chaucer's English (the variety or dialect spoken in London) established itself as the standard. However, from 1250 to 1400, English adopted the greatest number of French words (40%), and of the nearly 10,000, 75% are still in use.

It also changed in fundamental ways, especially in pronunciation and

grammar (becoming simpler), from highly inflected (Germanic) to very analytical (modern). Some dialects retain some of the early pronunciations for a
few words (/doon/ for down in northern England and Scotland).

The Great Vowel Shift

Think of how we say our five vowels (ay, ee, ai, oh, (y)oo) and how we pronounce them phonetically (as in bad, bed, bid, bod, bud). This is an echo of
the shift in pronunciation of vowels from (Old and) Middle English to more
or less what we use now, and it occurred in various stages mainly during the
13th to the 17th centuries. Linguists refer to this change as The Great Vowel
Shift. Spelling of (Old and) Middle English was very phonetic, and was
effectively standardised with the advent of printing (William Caxton 1475).
But after the shift, spelling was no longer consonant with pronunciation, a situation which continues, and exasperates English learners.

Most of the vowels (apparently, 18 out of 20) changed, some completely,
and others just when in relation to certain consonants (/english/ → /inglish/).
The long vowels changed from Middle English to modern, as follows:

VOWEL	EXAMPLE
i: → aɪ	tyme /teem(ə)/ → time
u: → ɑʊ	cou /koo/ → cow
e: → i:	/fet/ → feet
o: → u:	goos /gohs/ → goose
ɛ: → i:	deel, dele /del/ → deal
ɔ: → oʊ, əʊ	ston /storn/ → stone
a: → eɪ	/nam(ə)/ → name

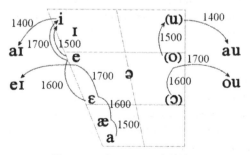

Figure 11. **Great Vowel Shift**

The cardinal vowel chart (see cardinal system at the end of the pronunciation chapter) shows the same changes as the table, and indicates the approximate time when the changes took place. Notice that changes generally started at the top and moved down. Essentially, as changes were occurring, vowels had to remain distinct for clarity, which is why they had to make room for each successive change, and they had to be intelligible across two or three generations, which would modulate the process. In England but not America, noticeable short-vowel changes include the pronunciation of the first vowel in clerk, Derby, and Berkshire to rhyme with star. Some vowels didn't change in all areas. For instance in northern Britain and Canada, the original oo [u] and oh [əʊ] vowel in words like house, down, and about are still pretty much unchanged. In England the or [ɔ] vowel can still be heard in older upper class accents in words like cloth, off, cross, and often.

Early Modern English: 1500–1700
(Elizabethan, Shakespeare, Renaissance)

In 1476, William Caxton (1422–1491) set up the first printing press in Westminster Abbey. By 1640, 20,000 titles had been printed (mostly in London) in English. This pushed English, written and spoken, towards a standard form. The Dictionary was produced, notably Samuel Johnson's in 1755 (which he did on his own time!).

1650–1800: The Age of Reason (Augustan Age), characterized by a strong sense of order and value of standards and regulations. The language of this time is recognizable today. The 'Great Vowel Shift' occurred, along with spelling reform. A strong central government used English as the national language for all purposes, despite the revival of the classics.

Latin and Greek were the most important sources of new words, followed by French, Italian, and Spanish. Most Latin and Greek introductions were deliberate attempts by 16th and early 17th century writers to enrich the language, to elevate 'low' English. Words also came in from 50 other languages, largely due to the expansion of the British Empire.

19th Century English: 1700–1900 (No change—just expansions)

Grammar was standardised, continuing a standardising trend. The Industrial Revolution and the Victorian Age. Words began to come to England from the colonies, especially America. English dialect terms became Standard English.

American English

The first settled English colony was in Jamestown, Virginia in 1607—contemporaries of William Shakespeare (1564–1616), Francis Bacon (1561–1626), Christopher Marlowe (1564–1593) and John Donne (1572–1631). By the 18th century, American was recognized as distinct from British English. The earliest sign is perhaps the absorption of Indian words, almost exclusively the from Algonquian speaking tribes. American also borrowed many words from Africans brought in by the slave trade, and European immigrants, but they tended to be regional: African in the South, French in Louisiana, Spanish in the Southwest, German in Pennsylvania, and Dutch in New York, with Spanish being the most pervasive. Yiddish has contributed differently to both American and British.

Many words and pronunciations died out in England but survive in American. Words adopted new meanings in the new world. Great changes were wrought in 20th century American, with global economic, political, and technological prominence.

The main differences between American and British are vocabulary and pronunciation. There are slighter differences in spelling, pitch and stress. This is borne out in this (not exhaustive) dictionary, where about 60% of the differences are nouns (vocabulary) and 20% are spelling differences. Interestingly, although American is more tolerant of neologisms, written American tends to be stricter in grammar and syntax.

Modern English: 1900–2000

Science and technology, the entertainment industry, the world wars, and the car, have all contributed to the English lexicon. Formations—self-explaining compounds, Greek and Latin compounds, borrowings from other languages, deliberate coinages, extending meaning of current words, slang, and acronyms—are used ever more frequently.

— The Modern English Alphabet's — Evolution from Egyptian Hieroglyphs

About eight symbols from the modern alphabet can be traced back in an unbroken line to Egyptian hieroglyphs. It is surmised that the other symbols were inspired by Egyptian glyphs or newly invented. Most symbols morphed to a greater or lesser degree as they went from alphabet to alphabet, confounded by writing and letters often having no fixed direction. A number of signs were dropped when the new people didn't have a certain sound, and new signs were derived, or an old sign was employed to express a new sound.

The accompanying chart (below) attempts to trace each letter as fully as possible. The following unfolding (really the chart's annotation) is culled from articles, journals, popular books (noted below) and some of their references, which show that many of the theories are still quite contentious, and do change with continuous new archeological discoveries.

EGYPTIAN → PROTO-SINAITIC

In essence, the alphabet was invented by 'Asiatics' in Egypt around 1800 BC, by adopting some of the local hieroglyphs. The Asiatics were the various nomadic tribes occupying the present day Israel-Palestine-Jordan areas between the Babylonian, Hittite (present day Turkey), and Egyptian empires. They were present in Egypt variously as slaves, mercenaries, labour force, and resident aliens.

There were over 700 Egyptian hieroglyphs (at that time) but a subset of over 100 were glyphs that represented one, two, or three consonants. In this sense, the small one-consonant set was alphabetic. For instance, the horizontal zigzag line symbol represented *net* (water), and was therefore used for the letter n. And this is the idea they adopted—one symbol, one sound. It was expedient—learnable in days rather than the lifetime of study abode by Egyptian scribes. The Asiatic word for water was *mayim*. From the chart, we see they adopted the local glyph, and its meaning, but had that glyph represent the first letter in their own language. So the zigzag line glyph was now 'm' (which as the chart shows pretty much maintained its shape and sound till today's m).

Their alphabet spread back to their homelands (Sinai and further north). It had 24 glyphs (some think there were 27 total), which were written in arbitrary directions, and the glyphs were reversible.

PROTO-SINAITIC → PHOENICIAN

The Asiatics' alphabet was adopted by the Phoenicians, the earliest examples from around 1100 BC. Note that since the Phoenicians' language was also Semitic the letter names still had meaning. The modern Hebrew alphabet (shown for reference) descends from Phoenician via the Aramaic, and Arabic is also based on this model. The Phoenician alphabet had 22 glyphs or letters, which were written right to left.

PHOENICIAN → GREEK

The early Greek alphabet (8th century BC) is thought to have been first appropriated from the Phoenician letters by Greeks in Phoenicia (more or less the coastal zone of present day Lebanon), or Cypriots, which then spread over to Greece. They maintained most symbols, sounds, and names, but since the Greek language was different, the new Greek names had no meaning (e.g. alpha from 'aleph (ox head), beta from beth (house)). The Greeks were the first to represent vowels: 'aleph, he, yodh, and 'ayin became the vowels a, e, i, and o, with waw splitting to become both w and the vowel u. It's been noted that most vowel sounds result from the Greeks dropping (or not hearing) the unneeded initial guttural sound: (')aleph → α, (h)e → ε, (h)et → η, 'ayin → o. Other Greek sounds that Phoenicians didn't have were added: φ (f), χ (ch), ψ (ps), and ω (long o). Digamma and qoppa were dropped, and four sounds (zai, semek, sade, sin) that should have become (san, sigma, zeta, xei) became (zeta, xei, san, sigma).

Greek was originally written right-to-left but later changed to left-to-right, with samples of boustrophedon during the intervening period. It has been noted that these changes coincided with the addition of vowels, and that consonantal alphabets are written from right-to-left, and syllabaries and alphabets (with vowels) are written left-to-right. I totted up about 130 scripts and found this to be about 90% true, with notable exceptions being Etruscan and Roman (initially).

The chart shows Classical Greek (5th century BC) and modern, for reference. (Cyrillic is derived from Classical Greek but without the ψ and ω.)

GREEK → ETRUSCAN
(Etruscans referred to themselves as rasna)

The Etruscans were familiar with both the Phoenician and Greek alphabets. In 775 BC Greeks, from their largest island Euboea, settled in Ischia, an island in the Bay of Naples. It is their alphabet, a variant of early Greek, that

Ancient Egyptian 3000 BC			proto-Sinaitic 2000 BC				Phoenician 1100 BC		
word	♫	means	symbol	symbol	♫	word	means	symbol	♫	name
k3		ox		→	/3/	'alep	ox	→	/3/	'aleph
pr	/pr/	house		→	/b/	bayit	house	→	/b/	beth
'm'3t		throw stick		→	/g/	gimel	throw stick	→	/g/	gimel
'3		door (hieratic)		→	/d/	daleth	door	→	/d/	daleth
					/h/	he		→	/h/	he
					/w/	wawwu		→	/v/	waw
					/d/	zain		→	/z/	zayin
ḥct	/h/	wick		→	/h/	heth		→	/ch/	heth
								→	/t/	teth
ni	/ni/	arm. (to push away)		→	/y/	yadu	fist?	→	/y/	yodh
					/k/	kappu		→	/k/	kaph
	/w/				/l/	lamdu	ox goad	→	/l/	lamadh
net	/n/	water		→	/m/	mayim	water	→	/m/	mem
fy	/f/	horned viper		→	/n/	naḥas	snake	→	/n/	nun
									/s/	samekh
irt	/ir/	eye		→	/'/	enu	eye	→	/'/	'ayin
db'		finger		→	/p/			→	/p/	pe
ibḥ	/bḥ/	tooth			/s/	san		→	/ts/	sade
		(elephant 's tusk)			/q/	qoppa		→	/q/	qoph
					/r/	rashu	head	→	/r/	resh
					/sh/	shin		→	/sh/	shin
					/t/	tawwu	cross	→	/t/	taw
nfr	/nfr/	perfect		→	?					
					?					
					?					
					?					

annoying symbols: 3 - alif (glottal stop); ' -- ayin (a pharyngeal consonant);

the Etruscans adopted, but dropped the b, d, g, and o. They used the g sign, which looked like C, for the k sound, giving them three ways to write k: the C before e and i (ce, ci), the k before a (ka), and the q before u (qu). They later added the f, which looked like an 8, for a total of 24 letters, which were written right-to-left.

Hebrew means	early	classic	modern	Greek 800–600 BC early	classic	modern	♪	name	Etruscan symbol	Latin early	modern
ox	א → ΔΑΛ	A	A α				/a/	alpha	→ A	→ ΑΑ	A a
house	ב → ᘯΒΒ	B	B β				/b/	beta	→(ᖰ B)→		B b
throw stick	ג → ΓΛC	Γ	Γ γ				/g/	gamma	→ ⊃ /k/ → G /g/ → C /c/		G g, C c
door	ד → DΔD	Δ	Δ δ				/d/	delta	→(D)	ᘯD	D d
wall	ה → ᖇEE	E	E ε				/e/	e psilon	→ ᘔ	→ᖯE	E e
	ו → FFC						/w/	digamma	→ ᖴ /w/		
		Φ◇Φ	Φ φ				/f/	phi	Φᖰ /ph/	ᖴF	F f
sword?	ז → I⫫I	Z	Z ζ				/dz,sd,zd/	zeta	→ ΙΙ /ts/ →		Z z
	ח → ΒΉΉ	H	H η				/h/	eta	→ ᙆᙅᴓ	→ ᙆ	H h
	ט → ⊗⊕⊙	Θ	Θ θ				/th/	theta	→ ⊗		þ,ð→th
hand	י → ᘔᖶ	I	I ι				/i/	iota	→ I	→ I	I i
	ᘯ										J j
hand?	כ → KK	K	K κ				/k/	kappa	→ᘰ	→ᘰK	K k
	ל → ⅄Λ	Λ	Λ λ				/l/	lamda	→ ᒍ	→ ᒪ	L l
water	מ → ᙏᒼM	M	M μ				/m/	mu	→ᙏ m	→ᙏᒼM	M m
fish?	נ → ᖻN	N	N ν				/n/	nu	→ᖻ𝘯	→	N n
fish?	ס → ᖔᖲ≡		Ξ ξ				/sh, ks/	ksi	→ ⊞ /s/		
eye	ע → O	O	O o				/o/	o mikron	→(O)	O	O o
mouth?	פ → ᒃᒻᒻ	Π	Π π				/p/	pi	→ ᒉ	→ ᒋ	P p
	צ → M						/s/	san	→ M /š/		
monkey	ק → ΦᖿP						/q/	qoppa	→ Q	→ Q	Q q
head	ר → 4PDᖴ	Ρ	Ρ ρ				/r/	rho	→ ᖴD	→ P	R r
tooth?	ש → ᖟᖟᖟ	Σ	Σ σ ς				/s/	sigma	→ ᖟᖹᖹ	→ ᖟ	S s
mark?	ת → ΧΤ		T τ				/t/	tau	→ Τᖷᖲ	→ ᖷ	T t
	→ ᖲΥᐯ	Y	Y u				/u/	u psilon	Υᐯ	Υᐯ	→ U u, V v
							/f/		8 /f/	ᖱ→uu	→ W w
		Χ	X χ				/kh/	chi	Ψↆ /kh/	X	X x
							/š/		X /š/		Y y
	ΥᐯΦ	Y	Ψ ψ				/ps/	psi			
	ᘔᘗ	Ω	Ω ω				/o/	omega			

i – /ee/

ETRUSCAN → ROMAN

The Romans in their rise to power made use of the Etruscan alphabet. They added back the g sound, using the C sign marked with a stroke, forming a G sign. They dropped φ (ph), θ (th), ξ (ks), χ (kh), ψ (ps), ω (long o), and added the f sound back, but used the digamma symbol. They also dropped the Y and Z, but added them back again, which is why they're at the end. This resulted in 23 letters—all the same as our 26—minus J, U, and W.

ROMAN → MODERN

The Anglo-Saxons originally wrote Old English in runes but adopted the prestigious Roman script causing runes to fade away by the Norman conquest. To make up for four sounds not present in Latin, they used the wynn rune ᚹ for their w, which was replaced by uu, and later w, in Middle English. They used the thorn rune þ for the th in theta and later added eth ð for the th in this, both of which were replaced by th in Middle English, and they used æ for the a in cat, named ash after the same sound in runes, but it also faded away. v became u and v, and i became i and j though the full difference wasn't accepted until the 17–19th century. Note that yogh ȝ (like a 3 with a stretched out lower part), which appears in Middle English where we'd now find a y or gh, was until very recently used by some in their handwriting to write z, though probably it was just a version of zeta ζ.

REFERENCES

alpha beta by John Man 2000 Wiley.
The Story of Writing by Andrew Robinson 1995 Thames & Hudson.
Lost Languages by Andrew Robinson 2002 McGraw-Hill.
Hieroglyphics by Maria Carmela Betro 1996 Abbeville Press.
The Egyptian Origin of the Semitic Alphabet Alan H. Gardiner 1916 The Journal of Egyptian Archeology, Vol III.
A History of Writing by Albertine Gaur 1997 Abbeville Press.
The usual random collection of intriguing articles of varying dubiousity found on the web.

Table 1.

Major US and Canadian Holidays and Dates

January 1	*[C] New Year's Day. Observed Friday or Monday if it falls on a weekend. New Year's traditionally brought in with a celebration at midnight; New York Times Square revelry televised and broadcast at the appropriate time, offset for the various time zones.
January 15	+ Martin Luther King, Jr.'s, Birthday. Observed the third Monday in January. This day was signed into law in 1986 by President Reagan, after almost two decades of pressure. The greatness of the tribute can be measured in that the only other nationally observed individual's birthday is George Washington's. In other countries this is also rare: (apart from Christ, Buddha, and Muhammad), Simón Bolívar (July 24) in Ecuador and Venezuela, Mahatma Gandhi (October 2) in India, Benito Pablo Juárez (March 21) in Mexico, Quaid-i-Azam (December 25) in Pakistan, and Victoria Day in Canada (Monday preceding May 25th).
January 19	[L] Robert E. Lee's Birthday. Observed on the third Monday in January in some Southern States.
January 20	Inauguration Day.
February 2	*Groundhog Day.*
February 12	[L] Abraham Lincoln's Birthday. Observed on the first Monday in February in some states.
February 14	Valentine's Day.
February 22	George Washington's Birthday.
February	+ President's Day, celebrates Lincoln and Washington's birthdays, observed on the third Monday in February.
March 17	St. Patrick's Day.
March 21	Spring begins around March 21.
March/April	~ [Canada only] Good Friday
March/April	~ Easter Sunday.
March/April	~ [Canada only] Easter Monday.
April 1	April Fools Day.
April	daylight saving time, starts at 2 a.m. (is 3 a.m.) local time on first Sunday in April—'Spring forward' (not in Arizona, Hawaii, parts of southern Indiana, most of Saskatchewan).
April 13	Jefferson Davis Day. His birthday observed in some Southern States, particularly Alabama.
April 14	Pan American Day.
April 15	Federal Income Taxes due (16th if 15th is a Sunday).
April 22	Earth Day.
April 30	[Canada] Federal Income Taxes due.
May 1	May Day.
May 5	*Cinco de Mayo* (which see). Holiday informally celebrated in many parts of the US.

May	Mother's Day. Second Sunday in May.
May	+ Armed Forces Day. Third Saturday in May.
May	[Canada only] Victoria Day. Monday before May 25th.
May 30	* Memorial Day. Observed the last Monday in May. Created in 1948 as a "prayer for peace" day.
June 3	L Jefferson Davis's Birthday. First Monday in June. Observed in many Southern States.
June 14	Flag Day.
June	Father's Day. Third Sunday in June.
June 21	Summer begins.
July 1	[Canada only] Canada Day.
July 4	* Independence Day. Observed Friday or Monday if it falls on a weekend, although all celebrations (fireworks, etc.) occur on the 4th.
August/September	Burning Man, the week prior to Labor Day. The Man burns the Saturday night before Labor Day.
September	+ C Labor Day. Observed first Monday in September.
September 17	Citizenship Day.
September 21	Autumn begins around September 22.
September	Native American Day. Fourth Friday in September.
October 12	* Columbus Day. Observed second Monday in October.
October	[Canada only] Thanksgiving Day. Second Monday in October.
October 24	United Nations Day.
October	daylight saving time ends 2 a.m. (is 1 a.m.) local time on last Sunday in October- 'Fall back' (not in Arizona, Hawaii, parts of southern Indiana, most of Saskatchewan).
October 31	Halloween.
November	L Election Day, Tuesday after the first Monday in November.
November 11	* Veteran's Day. Observed Monday or Friday if it falls on a weekend. Created as Armistice Day in 1926 to honor those who died in World War I. [C Remembrance Day in Canada.]
November	* Thanksgiving. Observed on the fourth Thursday in November. (First Monday in October in Canada.)
November	Saturday after Thanksgiving—busiest shopping day of the year
December 21	Winter begins.
December 25	* C Christmas Day. Observed Monday or Friday if it falls on a weekend.
December 26	[Canada only] Boxing Day.

* Officially designated national holidays.
+ Usually observed by federal workers.
~ Moveable days in reference to Easter.
C Major holiday in Canada as well as the US.
L Legal holiday for the mentioned region; the national and federal holidays are all legal nationally.

Table 2.

Main UK Public and Bank Holidays and Dates

January 1	†(Bank Holiday since 1974) New Year's Day. Observed following Monday if it falls on a weekend.
January 2	[Scotland only] Bank Holiday.
January 13	Hilary festival.
February 1	Imbolc (Celtic festival, goddess Brigit).
March 1	St. David (Wales), (Mad March Hare Day).
March	~ Pancake Day (Shrove Tuesday)
March	Commonwealth Day (formerly Empire Day), second Monday in March
March/April	~ Maundy Thursday, Thursday before Easter.
March/April	~* Good Friday.
March/April	Easter.
March/April	~+ Easter Monday [not Scotland].
March 17	[Northern Ireland only] St. Patrick's Day.
March	Simnel Sunday
March 25	(¼) Lady Day (Feast of the Annunciation).
March	~ Mothering Sunday [Mother's Day]. Fourth Sunday in Lent.
March	summer time, starts at 1 a.m. (is 2 a.m.) UTC on last Sunday in March.
April 23	St. George (England).
May 1	May Day [not Scotland]. Beltane (Celtic festival, 'bright fire,' beginning of the light half of the year).
May	†(since 1978) May Day Bank Holiday, observed first Monday in May.
May 9	[Channel Islands only] Liberation Day
May/June	~ Whitsuntide (Whit Sunday and Whit Monday). Seventh Sunday after Easter.
May	+ Spring Bank Holiday, also known as Whitsun Holiday (last Monday in May, early May in Scotland).
May	[Scotland only] May bank holiday (late May).
May	Commonwealth Day (formally called Empire Day).
June 21	(¼) Midsummer's Day
July	Orangemans' Day–Northern Ireland only (second Monday in July).
July 12	[Northern Ireland only] Anniversary of the Battle of the Boyne.
July 15	St. Swithin's Day.
August 1	Lammas [Lughnasadh] (Celtic festival, harvest, god Lugh).
August	+ Late Summer Bank Holiday (last Monday in August, early August in Scotland).
September 29	(¼) Michaelmas Day (Feast of St. Michael)
October	winter time, starts 1 a.m. (is 12 a.m.) UTC on last Sunday in October.

November 1	All Saint's Day. Samhain (Celtic festival, beginning of the dark half of the year).
December 24	Christmas Eve.
December 25	(¼)* Christmas Day. Observed following Monday if it falls on a weekend.
December 26	+ Boxing Day (St. Stephen's Day), observed the day after Christmas (or Monday or even Tuesday to avoid weekend collisions).
December 31	New Year's Eve.

~ Moveable days in reference to Easter
(¼) Quarter Days—traditionally when quarter payments are due.
* Common Law or Public holiday
+ Bank (Statutory) holiday
† Holiday by Royal proclamation.

Sittings (law):   Hilary (Jan-Mar), Easter (Apr-May), Trinity (May-Jul), Michaelmas (Oct-Dec).
terms (Oxford):   Hilary (Jan-Mar), Trinity (Apr-Jun), Michaelmas (Oct-Dec).
terms (Cambridge): Lent (Jan-Mar), Easter (Apr-Jun), Michaelmas (Oct-Dec).

The UK has no national day (like July 4th in US).

Table 3.

American Coins

Monetary System:
5 cents = 1 nickel
10 cents = 1 dime
25 cents = 1 quarter
50 cents = half dollar
100 cents = 1 dollar

(width & dia. in mm)

VALUE	NAME	WIDTH	DIA.	SUBSTANCE	DATES	NOTES
½¢	half cent	1.5	23.0	copper	1840–1857	
1¢	cent	1.9	28.5	copper	1816–1857	
		1.8	19.0	cupro-nickel	1856–1864	
		1.2	19.0	bronze	1864–1982	1943 steel
		1.2	19.0	copper-clad zinc	1982-date	0.75 inches dia.
2¢	two cent	1.7	23.0	bronze	1864–1873	
3¢	three cent	0.5	14.0	silver	1851–1873	
		0.9	17.9	cupro-nickel	1865–1889	
5¢	half dime	0.7	15.5	silver	1829–1873	
5¢	nickel	1.7	20.5	cupro-nickel	1866–1883	
		1.6	21.2	cupro-nickel	1883-date	0.835 inches dia.
10¢	dime	0.9	18.8	silver	1809–1837	
		1.0	17.9	silver	1837–1964	
		1.0	17.9	CuNi-clad Cu	1965-date	0.705 inches dia.
20¢	twenty cents	1.3	22.0	silver	1875–1878	
25¢	quarter	1.4	24.3	silver	1831–1964	
		1.4	24.3	CuNi-clad Cu	1965-date	0.955 inches dia.
50¢	half dollar	1.8	30.0	silver	1836–1839	
		1.8	30.6	silver	1839–1964	
		1.6	30.6	40% silver	1965–1970	
		1.7	30.6	CuNi-clad Cu	1971-date	1.205 inches dia.
$1	dollar	2.3	38.1	silver	1840–1935	
		2.2	38.1	cupro-nickel	1971–1978	
Susan B. Anthony		1.6	26.5	cupro-nickel	1979–1981	
	Sacagawea	1.6	26.4	cupro-nickel	2000	
	gold dollar	0.7	13.0	gold	1849–1854	
		0.5	15.0	gold	1854–1889	
$2.50	quarter eagle	0.9	18.2	gold	1834–1839	
$3	three dollar	0.8	20.5	gold	1854–1889	
$4	stella	0.8	20.5	gold	1879–1880	

BUM BAGS AND FANNY PACKS

VALUE	NAME	WIDTH	DIA.	SUBSTANCE	DATES	NOTES
$5	half eagle	1.2	22.5	gold	1829–1838	
$5	half eagle	1.2	21.6	gold	1839–1908	
$10	eagle	1.6	27.0	gold	1838–1933	
$20	double eagle	2.0	34.0	gold	1849–1933	

Table 4.

British Money

Monetary System (pre-decimalization):
4 farthings = 1 penny
12 pence   = 1 shilling
2 shillings   = 1 florin
5 shillings   = 1 crown
20 shillings = 1 pound (sovereign)
21 shillings = 1 guinea

VALUE	NAME	TH.	DIA.	SUBSTANCE	DATES	NOTES
1/16d	1/4 farthing	—	14.0	copper	1839, 1851–1853	for Ceylon
1/12d	1/3 farthing	—	14.5	copper	1835, 1844	for Malta
1/12d	1/3 farthing	—	14.5	bronze	1866, 1868, 1876, 1878, 1881, 1884–1885, 1902, 1913	for Malta
1/8d	1/2 farthing	—	15.5	copper	1839, 1842–1844, 1847, 1851–1854, 1856	for Ceylon
1/4d	farthing	—	—	silver	1279–1672	
	—		21.5	copper	1672–1860	
	—		20.1	bronze	1860–1956	
1/2d	halfpenny	—	—	silver	1280–1672	
	—		28.0	copper	1672–1859	
		1.2	25.4	bronze	1860–1970	exactly 1" dia.
1d	penny	—	—	silver	8th c.–1797	
				gold	1257	
	—		33.0	copper	1797–1860	
		1.6	30.8	bronze	1860–1970	
		0.5	10.8	silver	1660–present	Maundy money
1 1/2d		0.6	11.9	silver	1834–1862	Ceylon & Jamaica
2d	twopence	0.7	13.0	silver	1660–present	Maundy money
3d	threepence	—	15.0	silver	1551–1944	
		3.0	21.5	nickel-brass	1937–1970	12 sided
		0.7	16.0	silver	1660–present	Maundy money
4d	groat	—	16.3	silver	1279–1662, 1838–1855	1831–1855, 1888 for British Guiana
		0.7	17.9	silver	1660–present	Maundy money
6d	sixpence	0.9	19.3	silver	1551–1920	

VALUE	NAME	TH.	DIA.	SUBSTANCE	DATES	NOTES
		0.9	19.8	half silver	1920–1946	
		1.1	19.0	cupro-nickel	1947–1970	legal tender –1980
1/-	shilling	1.3	23.3	silver	1504–1919	
		1.3	24.3	half silver	1920–1946	
		1.2	23.5	cupro-nickel	1947–1970	legal tender –1990
2/-	florin			gold	1344, 1526–1625	value: 6/-, not 2/-
		1.8	28.0	silver	1849–1919	
		2.0	27.5	half silver	1920–1946	
		1.9	28.1	cupro-nickel	1947–1970	legal tender –1993
2/6d	half-crown	–	–	gold	1470–1551	
		1.7	32.0	silver	1551–1850, 1874–1919	
		1.8	32.4	half silver	1927–1937	
		–	32.6	cupro-nickel	1947–1967	
4/-	double florin	2.1	36.0	silver	1887–1890	
5/-	crown	–	–	gold	1526–1551	never popular in general use, often commemorative
		2.3	38.9	silver	1551–1902	
		2.6	38.0	half silver	1927–1937	
		–	38.0	cupro-nickel	1951, 1953, 1960, 1965, 1981	commemorative
5/-	quarter guinea	–	–	gold	1718, 1762	
$1	dollar	2.2	39.0	silver	1895–1934	trade coinage for trade in Orient
80d	noble	–	–	gold	1344–1634	
6/8d	third guinea	–	–	gold	1797	
10/-	ten shillings			note	1914–1971	
10/-	half sovereign	0.8	19.0	gold	1831–1915, 1980–present	
10/6d	half guinea	–	–	gold	1625–1760	
160d	mark	–	–	[value]	till the 18th c.	
13/6d	merk (thistle half dollar)			silver	1580–1660	also ½, 2 & 4 merk
£1	sovereign	1.1	22.7	gold	1489–1660, 1831–1925, 1957–present	
20/-		–	–	silver	1642	
	–			gold	1660–1685	
£1	pound	–	–	note	1914–1983	
21/-	guinea	–	–	gold	1663–1799, 1813	fixed at 21/- in 1717

VALUE	NAME	TH.	DIA.	SUBSTANCE	DATES	NOTES
£2	two pound	1.4	28.2	gold	1831, 1887, 1893, 1902, 1911, 1937, 1980, 1982–1983	
£2-2s	two guineas	–	–	gold	1625–1760	
£5	five pound	2.4	34.0	gold	1839, 1887, 1893, 1902, 1911, 1937, 1980–1982, 1984–1985, 1990	
£5-5s	five guineas	–	–	gold	1625–1760	
£5				note		
£10				note		
£20				note		

Notes:

20 (troy) pennyweights (of silver) = 1 oz, 12oz = 1 pound, which is possibly the origin of the old monetary system.

16th c. European silver coin and its imitators: crown, daler, dollar, écu (écu á la couronne (crown)), peso, piastre, seudo, tallero, thaler (taler).

Merk (17th c.) was originally a mark of pure of silver (20 sterling pennies), and were struck as coins in Scotland with a value of 160d = 1¾d.

Pound *sterling*, meaning 'of the fixed authorized national value' (sterling applied to any small silver coin of fine quality in previous centuries, especially pennies).

Monetary System (post-decimalization):
100p (pence) = 1 Pound

Decimal Money

VALUE	NAME	WIDTH	DIA.	SUBSTANCE	DATES	NOTES
½p	½ new penny	0.9	17.0	bronze	1971–1981	
½p	half penny	0.9	17.0	bronze	1982–1984	
1p	new penny	1.3	20.0	bronze	1971–1981	
1p	one penny	1.3	20.0	bronze	1982–date	
2p	2 new pence	1.6	26.5	bronze	1971–1981	
2p	two pence	1.6	26.5	bronze	1972–date	
5p	5 new pence	1.4	24.0	cupro-nickel	1968–1981	
5p	five pence	1.4	24.0	cupro-nickel	1982–1990	
5p	five pence	1.3	17.2	cupro-nickel	1990–date	
10p	10 new pence	2.0	28.0	cupro-nickel	1968–1981	
10p	ten pence	2.0	28.0	cupro-nickel	1982–1991	
10p	ten pence	1.4	24.0	cupro-nickel	1992–date	
20p	twenty pence	—	20.5	cupro-nickel	1982–date	5 sided
25p	25 new pence	2.3	39.1	cupro-nickel	1972, 1977, 1980	commemorative
25p	25 new pence	2.3	39.1	silver	1972, 1977, 1980	commemorative
50p	50 new pence	2.2	29.2	cupro-nickel	1969–1981	7 sided
50p	fifty pence	2.2	29.2	cupro-nickel	1973, 1982–date	7 sided
£1	one pound	3.0	22.9	nickel-brass	1983–date	
£1	one pound	2.2	22.9	silver	1983, 1985	commemorative
£2	two pounds	2.5	28.0	nickel-brass	1986, 1989	commemorative
£5	five pounds	2.5	37.5	cupro-nickel	1990	commemorative

£1 coin designs: plain shield with coat of arms, Scottish thistle, Welsh leek, Northern Ireland blooming flax, English oak tree, and British royal coat of arms.

Table 5.

Presidents of the United States

#	NAME	POLITICAL PARTY	TERM	NOTES
1	George Washington	Federalist	1789–1797	$1, *quarter*, Mt. Rushmore
2	John Adams	Federalist	1797–1801	
3	Thomas Jefferson	Democratic Republican (now called Democratic party)	1801–1809	*nickel*, $2, Mt. Rushmore
4	James Madison	Democratic Republican	1809–1817	$5000
5	James Monroe	Democratic Republican	1817–1825	
6	John Quincy Adams	Democratic Republican	1825–1829	
7	Andrew Jackson	Democrat	1829–1837	$20
8	Martin Van Buren	Democrat	1837–1841	
9	William H. Harrison	Whig	1841	(died after a few weeks)
10	John Tyler	Whig	1841–1845	
11	James K. Polk	Democrat	1845–1849	
12	Zachary Taylor	Whig	1849–1850	
13	Millard Fillmore	Whig	1850–1853	
14	Franklin Pierce	Democrat	1853–1857	
15	James Buchanan	Democrat	1857–1861	
16	Abraham Lincoln	Republican	1861–1865	assassinated, $5, 1¢, Mt. Rushmore
17	Andrew Johnson	Union Democrat	1865–1869	impeached by the *House* but not convicted
18	Ulysses Simpson Grant	Republican	1869–1877	$50
19	Rutherford B. Hayes	Republican	1877–1881	stole election
20	James A. Garfield	Republican	1881	assassinated
21	Chester A. Arthur	Republican	1881–1885	
22	Grover Cleveland	Democrat	1885–1889	$1000
23	Benjamin Harrison	Republican	1889–1893	
24	Grover Cleveland	Democrat	1893–1897	$1000
25	William M⸢Kinley	Republican	1897–1901	assassinated, $500
26	Theodore Roosevelt	Republican	1901–1909	Mt. Rushmore
27	William Howard Taft	Republican	1909–1913	

#	NAME	POLITICAL PARTY	TERM	NOTES
28	Woodrow Wilson	Democrat	1913–1921	$100,000
29	Warren Gamaliel Harding	Republican	1921–1923	
30	Calvin Coolidge	Republican	1923–1929	
31	Herbert C. Hoover	Republican	1929–1933	
32	Franklin Delano Roosevelt	Democrat	1933–1945	FDR, died in office, *dime,* Eleanor—the First Lady of the world
33	Harry S. Truman	Democrat	1945–1953	"The buck stops here."
34	Dwight D. Eisenhower	Republican	1953–1961	'Ike'
35	John Fitzgerald Kennedy	Democrat	1961–1963	JFK, assassinated, *half dollar*
36	Lyndon Baines Johnson	Democrat	1963–1969	
37	Richard Millhouse Nixon	Republican	1969–1974	resigned, 'Tricky Dick'
38	Gerald R. Ford	Republican	1974–1977	not elected—appointed *VP* by Nixon, then assumed presidency
39	Jimmy Carter	Democrat	1977–1981	
40	Ronald Wilson Reagan	Republican	1981–1989	'The Gipper'
41	George Herbert Walker Bush	Republican	1989–1993	
42	William Jefferson Clinton	Democrat	1993–2001	impeached but not convicted, 'Slick Willy'
43	George Walker Bush	Republican	2001–	'dubya,' stole election, Wanker
44				

Table 6.

Kings and Queens

Kings of All England

KING	REIGN	AGE DURING REIGN
Egbert	829–839	27–37
Ethylwulf, son of Egbert	839–858	
Ethylbald, son of Ethylwulf	858–860	
Ethylbert, 2nd son of Ethylwulf	860–866	
Ethylred I, 3rd son of Ethylwulf	866–871	
Alfred The Great, 4th son of Ethylwulf	871–899	
Edward the elder, son of Alfred	899–924	
Athelstan the Glorious, son of Edward	924–939	25–40
Edmund, 3rd son of Edward	939–946	
Edred	946–955	
Edwy	955–959	14–18
Edgar	959–975	16–32
Edward the Martyr	975–978	13–16
Ethelred the Unready	979–1013	10–45
Swegn Forkbeard	1013–1014	
Edmund Ironside	1016	24
Cnut	1016–1035	21–40
Harold Harefoot	1036–1040	20–24
Harthacnut	1040–1042	22–24
Edward the Confessor	1043–1066	39–62±2
Harold Godwinson	1066	46
(Edgar Etheling	1066)	

Kings and Queens of England, 1066–1603

KING/QUEEN	REIGN	ROYAL HOUSE	
William I	1066–1087	Normandy	'The Conqueror'
William II	1087–1100	Normandy	'Rufus'
Henry I	1100–1135	Normandy	'Beauclerc'
Stephen	1135–1141, 1141–1154	Blois	
Matilda	1141 (April–Nov)	Normandy	'Empress Maud'
Henry II	1154–1189	Anjou	
Richard I	1189–1199	Anjou	'Coeur de Lion'
John	1199–1216	Anjou	'Lackland'
(Louis	1216–1217)		
Henry III	1216–1272	Anjou	

KING/QUEEN	REIGN	ROYAL HOUSE	
Edward I	1272–1307	Anjou	'Longshanks'
Edward II	1307–1327	Anjou	'of Caernarfon'
Edward III	1327–1377	Anjou	
Richard II	1377–1399	Anjou	
Henry IV	1399–1413	Anjou	
Henry V	1413–1422	Anjou	(Prince Hal)
Henry VI	1422–1461, 1470–1471	Anjou	
Edward IV	1461–1470, 1471–1483	Anjou	
Edward V	1483 (April–June)	Anjou	
Richard III	1483–1485	Anjou	
Henry VII	1485–1509	Tudor	
Henry VIII	1509–1547	Tudor	
Edward VI	1547–1553	Tudor	
Jane	1553 (9 days in July)	Grey or Suffolk	
Mary I	1553–1558	Tudor	
Elizabeth I	1558–1603	Tudor	

Kings and Queens of England and Scotland, 1603–1707

KING/QUEEN	REIGN	ROYAL HOUSE
James I (VI Scotland)	1603–1625	Stuart
Charles I	1625–1649	Stuart
[Oliver Cromwell	1649–1658	Commonwealth]
[Richard Cromwell	1658–1660	Commonwealth]
Charles II	1660–1685	Stuart
James II	1685–1688	Stuart
William III	1689–1702	Stuart and Orange, with …
Mary II	1689–1694	Stuart

Kings and Queens of Great Britain, 1707–1801

KING/QUEEN	REIGN	ROYAL HOUSE
Anne	1702–1714	Stuart
George I	1714–1727	Hanover & Brunswick Lüneburg
George II	1727–1760	Hanover & Brunswick Lüneburg

Kings and Queens of the United Kingdom, 1801–present

KING/QUEEN	REIGN	ROYAL HOUSE
George III	1760–1820	Hanover & Brunswick-Lüneburg
George IV	1820–1830	Hanover & Brunswick-Lüneburg
William IV	1830–1837	Hanover & Brunswick-Lüneburg
Victoria	1837–1901	Hanover & Brunswick-Lüneburg

KING/QUEEN	REIGN	ROYAL HOUSE
Edward VII	1901–1910	Saxe-Coburg & Gotha(Tum tum)
George V	1910–1936	Saxe-Coburg & Gotha/Windsor
Edward VIII	1936 (Jan–Dec)	Windsor
George VI	1936–1952	Windsor
Elizabeth II	1952–	Windsor (The Boss)

Table 7.

Prime Ministers

#	NAME	POLITICAL PARTY	MINISTRY
1	Robert Walpole	Whig	1721–1742
2	Spencer Compton, Earl of Wilmington	Whig	1742–1743
3	Henry Pelham	Whig	1743–1754
	William Pulteney	Whig	(1746)
4	Thomas Pelham-Holles, Duke of Newcastle	Whig	1754–1756, 1757–1762
5	William Cavendish, Duke of Devonshire	Whig	1756–1757
	James Waldegrave		(1757)
6	John Stuart, Earl of Bute	Tory	1762–1763
7	George Grenville	Whig	1763–1765
8	Charles Watson Wentworth, Marquess of Rockingham	Whig	1765–1766, 1782
9	William Pitt 'The Elder', Earl of Chatham	Whig	1766–1768
10	Augustus Henry Fitzroy, Duke of Grafton	Whig	1767–1770
11	Frederick North, Lord North	Tory	1770–1782
12	William Petty, Earl of Shelburne	Whig	1782–1783
13	William Henry Cavendish Bentink, Duke of Portland	Coalition Tory	1783 1807–1809
14	William Pitt, "The Younger"	Tory	1783–1801, 1804–1806
15	Henry Addington	Tory	1801–1804
16	William Wyndham Grenville, Lord Grenville	Whig	1806–1807
17	Spencer Perceval	Tory	1809–1812
18	Robert Banks Jenkinson, Earl of Liverpool	Tory	1812–1827
19	George Canning	Tory	1827
20	Frederick John Robinson, Viscount Goderich	Tory	1827–1828
21	Arthur Wellesley, Duke of Wellington	Tory	1828–1830
22	Charles Grey, Earl Grey	Whig	1830–1834
23	William Lamb, Viscount Melbourne	Whig	1834, 1835–1841
24	Robert Peel	Conservative - Tory	1834–1835, 1841–1846
25	John Russel, Earl Russel	Whig Liberal	1846–1851 1865–1866
26	Edward Geoffrey Smith-Stanley, The Earl of Derby	Tory & Conservative	1852, 1858–1859, 1866–1868
27	George Hamilton Gordon, Earl of Aberdeen	Peelite - Tory	1852–1855
28	Henry John Temple, Viscount Palmerston	Liberal	1855–1858, 1859–1865

#	NAME	POLITICAL PARTY	MINISTRY
29	Benjamin Disraeli	Conservative	1868, 1874–1880
30	William Ewart Gladstone	Liberal	1868–1874, 1880–1885, 1886, 1892–1894
31	Robert Arthur Talbot Gascoyne-Cecil, Marquess of Salisbury	Conservative	1885–1886, 1886–1892, 1895–1902
32	Archibald Philip Primrose, Earl of Rosebery	Liberal	1894–1895
33	Arthur James Balfour	Conservative	1902–1905
34	Henry Campbell Bannerman	Liberal	1905–1908
35	Herbert Henry Asquith	Liberal	1908–1916
36	David Lloyd George	Liberal-led Coalition	1916–1922
37	Andrew Bonar Law	Conservative	1922–1923
38	Stanley Baldwin	Conservative	1923, 1924–1929, 1935–1937
39	James Ramsey MacDonald	Labour	1924–1927, 1929–1935
40	Neville Chamberlain	National Government - Conservative	1937–1940
41	Winston Churchill	Coalition Conservative	1940–1945 1951–1955
42	Clement Attlee	Labour	1945–1951
43	Anthony Eden	Conservative	1955–1957
44	Harold MacMillan	Conservative	1957–1963
45	Alec Douglas-Home	Conservative	1963–1964
46	Harold Wilson	Labour	1964–1970, 1974–1976
47	Edward Heath	Conservative	1970–1974
48	James Callaghan	Labour	1976–1979
49	Margaret Thatcher 'Iron Lady', 'Attila the Hen'	Conservative	1979–1990
50	John Major	Conservative	1990–1997
51	Tony Blair 'Poodle'	Labour	1997–

Table 8.

Comparative Measures

US Measures

liquid:		
(0.062 ml)	1 minim	
(3.7 ml)	1 fluidram	= 60 minims
(4.9 ml)	1 teaspoon	= 4/3 fluidrams 98 tears of joy (Rob Brezsny) 121 tears of sadness (Tom Waites)
(14.8 ml)	1 tablespoon	= 3 teaspoons
(29.6 ml)	1 fluid oz.	= 2 tablespoons, 8 fluidrams
(118.3 ml)	1 gill	= 4 fluid oz.
(236.6 ml)	1 cup (½ pint)	= 8 fluid oz.
(473.2 ml)	1 pint	= 16 fluid oz.
(3.79 l)	1 gallon	= 8 pints (231.00 cu. in.)
dry:		
(550.6 ml)	1 pint	(33.60 cu. in.)
(1.10 l)	1 quart	= 2 pints (67.20 cu. in.)
(8.81 l)	1 peck	= 8 quarts (537.60 cu. in.)
(35.24 l)	1 bushel	= 4 pecks (2,150.42 cu. in.)

Comparative Measures

UK Measures

(0.059 ml)	1 minim (a drop)	
(3.6 ml)	1 drachm	= 60 minims
(3.6 ml)	1 teaspoon	= 1 drachm
(7.1 ml)	1 dessertspoon	= 2 teaspoons
(14.2 ml)	1 tablespoon	= 4 teaspoons
(28.4 ml)	1 fluid oz.	= 2 tablespoons, 8 teaspoons, 8 drachms
(71.0 ml)	1 wine (sherry) glass	= 5 tablespoons, 2½ fluid oz.
(142.1 ml)	1 gill (ghyll), 1 teacup	= ¼ pint, 2 wineglassfuls, 5 fluid oz.
(284.1 ml)	1 tumbler	= ½ pint, 2 teacups, 10 fluid oz.
(568.3 ml)	1 pint	= 20 fluid oz. (34.68 cu. in.)
(4.55 l)	1 gallon	= 8 pints (277.42 cu. in.)
(9.09 l)	1 peck	= 2 gallons (554.84 cu. in.)
(36.37 l)	1 bushel	= 4 pecks (2,219.36 cu. in.)
(290.95 l)	1 quarter	= 8 bushels (17,754.85 cu. in.)

Reference:
1 gallon US   = 3.785411784 litres
1 gallon Canada   = 4.54609 litres
1 gallon UK   = 4.546092 litres

Note: culinary measures (cups, spoons, glasses) are designated as above, and are included for comparisons, but are not volumetrically 'defined' as such in the way gallons and pints are.

Table 9.

Musical Notes

US	UK
one hundred twenty-eighth note	quasihemidemisemiquaver
sixty-fourth note	hemidemisemiquaver
thirty-second note	demisemiquaver
sixteenth note	semiquaver
eighth note	quaver
quarter note	crotchet
half note	minim
whole note	semi-breve
double note, 2 whole notes, 4 half notes	breve, double whole note
4 whole notes	lunga

Table 10.

Old Number Denominations

X	XILLION	US: $10^{3(X+1)}$	UK: 10^{6X}
1	**mil**lion	1,000,000	1,000,000
	milliard		1,000,000,000
2	**bil**lion	1,000,000,000	1,000,000,000,000
3	**tril**lion	1,000,000,000,000	1,000,000,000,000,000,000
4	**quad**rillion	1,000,000,000,000,000	1,000,000,000,000,000,000,000,000
5	**quint**illion	1,000,000,000,000,000,000	1,000,000,000,000,000,000,000,000,000,000

The table depicts the denominations of big numbers as they are used in the US, and as they used to be used in the UK. British Academia went to the SI system a long time ago, and the British press mostly uses the US denominations these days. However, in reading British publications, any unqualified mention of billion or trillion should be double-checked, if it matters. Quadrillion and above occur so infrequently that they're barely worth mentioning, but if you saw an old text informing you that there were a vigintillion electrons in the known universe, Americans would be under by about a quintillion times, the British over by a septillion times.

Table 11.

Legal Age of Independence

	US	UK	
driver's permit	15 (14–17)	16	***provisional licence***
driver's license	16 (14–18)	17	***driving licence***
R rated movies	17	18	(R18)
age of consent	16 (14–18)	16	17 in Northern Ireland
age of consent—homosexual	16–18	16	17 in Northern Ireland
marriage with parental consent	16 (12–18)	16	
marriage	18 (18–21)	18	
porn star	18	18	
cigarettes	18	16	
draft (males, registration required)	18	16	no draft, but can enlist
vote	18	18	
tattoos	18	18	
body piercings	18	(no law)	
drink	21	18	can be in ***lounge bar*** at 14, though can't drink
buy glue and solvents	16		
buy knives	16		
handguns	21		handguns are banned
rifles, shotguns	18	16	
gaming (lotteries, scratch cards …)	18	16	
gambling		18	
casino	21	21	
credit cards, borrowing money	18	18	

In the US, the age of independence is under state jurisdiction. The above ages are medians, with ranges shown in parentheses.

Table 12.

Gestures

A quick note about gestures as indicated in writing. As per usual there is no standard for indicating a gesture, but many ad hoc ones have arisen by necessity, such as emoticons or smileys, and abbreviations for often-used phrases (btw = by the way, rotfl = rolling on the floor laughing, etc.) especially in electronic communications (email, IRC, blogs, etc.), and various flavours have gravitated towards a particular usage. These few examples should give an idea:

➤ [soap box mode on] (used to precede a brief missive.)
➤ So, this <ethnic> walks into a bar . . .
➤ "But the car's ok?"
 ::nods::
 "ok then"
➤ I was all <shrug>, and then she went away.
➤ One of the practical exams I did <mumble> years ago . . .

US	UK	MEANING
"I hate rabbits"		This invocation causes smoke from a campfire to not blow in your face
"tut"	/t!/	(see **tut** in the UK section)
	aye aye	I agree (at meetings, etc.)
	aye	yes ('the ayes have it')
forefinger and thumb extended (making an 'L')—emphasised by slapping to forehead		'loser,' meaning failure, can be self-referential but usually directed at someone, usu. ironically or sarcastically
extended forefinger and thumb on both hands, thumb tips touching, and then held up to form a W		'whatever' (see entry in US section)
make circle with finger & thumb, other fingers straight		OK sign
someone (typically male) asks you (typically a child) to pull their finger		they then fart
grasp an imaginary object in front of the face with the first two fingers of both hands		air quotes—during speech, "quotes" the word so indicated
middle finger, see the finger	first two fingers, see **V sign**	the 'fuck off' hand gesture
clapping	hear hear	I agree (at meetings, etc.)

US	UK	MEANING
saying "knock on wood" along with actually knocking on wood	saying "touch wood" along with actually touching wood	gesture performed to ensure continued luck
left arm out	left arm out (bicycle), or right arm out and moving in a circular motion	car and bicycle left hand turn signal
right arm out (bicycle) or left arm out with forearm pointing up	right arm out	car and bicycle right hand turn signal
left arm out with forearm pointing (hanging) down	right arm out and moving up and down	car slowing down hand signal
switch up	switch down	electric (light) switch on
switch down	switch up	electric (light) switch off
110v	240v (220v in **Europe**)	electricity (see **mains**)
black cat crossing path	white cat crossing path	unlucky omen
	black cat crossing path	lucky omen
drive on right	drive on left As well as Great Britain and Ireland, many Commonwealth countries drive on the left—Australia and New Zealand; India including Pakistan, Bangladesh, and Sri Lanka; Somaliland and East African countries from Kenya all the way down to, and including South Africa. Also Malaysia and Indonesia, including Singapore and Papua New Guinea; Thailand; Japan; Guyana and Surinam in South America, and numerous Island countries and territories	According to population numbers and miles of roadway, he world is split about $\frac{1}{3}$ left and $\frac{2}{3}$ right
China	Australia	This is where kids expect to come out when they dig a hole so deep it comes out on the other side of the earth

Table 13.

American States

The United Kingdom and its constituent countries (England, Wales, Scotland, and Northern Ireland) are included for comparison in the first two tables of States.

The data is compiled from various sources, but mostly from the 2000 US census (www.census.gov), and the 2001 UK census.

Each state has a slew of symbols, mottoes and slogans. For instance, in Ohio, the state insect is the *ladybug* (1975), the state beverage is tomato juice (1965), and the state rock song is Hang on Sloopy (1985), and in Nevada the state artifact is the Tule Duck Decoy (1995). The dates in the table show when they were instigated.

The following tables show state nicknames. Most of them are historical, many echoing the War of Independence or the Civil War. Some are funny, for instance, puke state (Missouri 1827) and bug-eating state (Nebraska). Some states have officially adopted a slogan (**bolded**), and often a slogan appears on the state's *license plate* (*italicized*).

Occasionally you see bumper stickers with impromptu slogans, such as state tree of North Dakota: telegraph pole, Oregon: land of wet dreams, Michigan state bird: mosquito, and Wisconsin state vegetable: the state legislature. Also, upon hearing a car alarm you might announce 'that's the state bird of California' (or whichever state you're in).

These nicknames came from www.netstate.com, who include an explanation for each nickname, and also list every state, their symbols, almanacs, flags and various demographics.

The following map is of the contiguous United States and excludes Alaska and Hawaii.

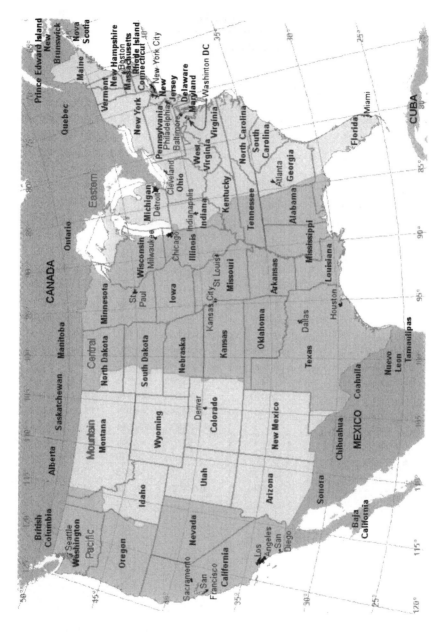

Figure 12. American States

American States
(sorted by size — square miles)

AB.	STATE	JOIN DATE	#	POPULATION	LAND	WATER	TOTAL
DC	District of Columbia	2-27-1801		572,059	61	6	67
RI	Rhode Island	5-29-1790	13	1,048,319	1,045	500	1,545
DE	Delaware	12-7-1787	1	783,600	1,955	535	2,489
	Northern Ireland			**1,685,267**	**5,252**	**200**	**5,452**
CT	Connecticut	1-9-1788	5	3,405,565	4,845	698	5,544
	Wales			**2,903,085**	**80,14**	**5**	**8,019**
NJ	New Jersey	12-18-1787	3	8,414,350	7,419	1,303	8,722
NH	New Hampshire	6-21-1788	9	1,235,786	8,969	382	9,351
VT	Vermont	3-4-1791	14	608,827	9,249	366	9,615
MA	Massachusetts	2-6-1788	6	6,349,097	7,838	2,717	10,555
HI	Hawaii	8-21-1959	50	1,211,537	6,423	4,508	10,932
MD	Maryland	4-28-1788	7	5,296,486	9,775	2,633	12,407
WV	West Virginia	6-20-1863	35	1,808,344	24,087	145	24,231
	Scotland			**5,062,011**	**30,276**	**139**	**30,415**
SC	South Carolina	5-23-1788	8	4,012,012	30,111	1,896	32,007
ME	Maine	3-15-1820	23	1,274,923	30,865	4,523	33,387
IN	Indiana	12-11-1816	19	6,080,485	35,870	550	36,420
KY	Kentucky	6-1-1792	15	4,041,769	39,732	679	40,411
TN	Tennessee	6-1-1796	16	5,689,283	41,220	926	42,146
VA	Virginia	6-26-1788	10	7,078,515	39,598	3,171	42,769
OH	Ohio	3-1-1803	17	11,353,140	40,953	3,875	44,828
PA	Pennsylvania	12-12-1787	2	12,281,054	44,820	1,239	46,058
MS	Mississippi	12-10-1817	20	2,697,243	46,914	1,520	48,434
	England			**49,138,831**	**50,344**	**19**	**50,363**
LA	Louisiana	4-30-1812	18	4,468,976	43,566	8,277	51,843
AL	Alabama	12-14-1819	22	4,447,100	50,750	1673	52,423
AR	Arkansas	6-15-1836	25	2,673,400	52,075	1107	53,182
NC	North Carolina	11-21-1789	12	8,049,313	48,708	5,103	53,821
NY	New York	7-26-1788	11	18,976,457	47,224	7,251	54,475
IA	Iowa	12-28-1846	29	2,926,324	55,875	401	56,276
IL	Illinois	12-3-1818	21	12,419,293	55,593	2,325	57,918
GA	Georgia	1-2-1788	4	8,186,453	57,919	1,522	59,441
WI	Wisconsin	5-29-1848	30	5,363,675	54,314	11,190	65,503
FL	Florida	3-3-1845	27	15,982,378	52,997	11,761	65,758
MO	Missouri	8-10-1821	24	5,595,211	68,898	811	69,709
OK	Oklahoma	11-16-1907	46	3,450,654	68,679	1,224	69,903
ND	North Dakota	11-2-1889	39	642,200	68,994	1,710	70,704

AB.	STATE	JOIN DATE	#	POPULATION	LAND	WATER	TOTAL
WA	Washington	11-11-1889	42	5,894,121	66,582	4,721	71,303
SD	South Dakota	11-2-1889	40	754,844	75,898	1,224	77,121
NE	Nebraska	3-1-1867	37	1,711,263	76,878	481	77,358
KS	Kansas	1-29-1861	34	2,688,418	81,823	459	82,282
ID	Idaho	7-3-1890	43	1,293,953	82,751	823	83,574
UT	Utah	1-4-1896	45	2,233,169	82,168	2,736	84,904
MN	Minnesota	5-11-1858	32	4,919,479	79,617	7,326	86,943
UK	**United Kingdom**			**58,789,194**	**94,035**	**214**	**94,249**
MI	Michigan	1-26-1837	26	9,938,444	56,809	40,001	96,810
WY	Wyoming	7-10-1890	44	493,782	97,105	714	97,818
OR	Oregon	2-14-1859	33	3,421,399	96,003	2,383	98,386
CO	Colorado	8-1-1876	38	4,301,261	103,730	371	104,100
NV	Nevada	10-31-1864	36	1,998,257	109,806	761	110,567
AZ	Arizona	2-14-1912	48	5,130,632	113,642	364	114,006
NM	New Mexico	1-6-1912	47	1,819,046	121,365	234	121,598
MT	Montana	11-8-1889	41	902,195	145,556	1,490	147,046
CA	California	9-9-1850	31	33,871,648	155,973	7,734	163,707
TX	Texas	12-29-1845	28	20,851,820	261,914	6,687	268,601
AK	Alaska	1-3-1959	49	626,932	570,374	86,051	656,424
	US Total			**280,702,432**	**3,353,335**	**251,087**	**3,785,422**

American States
(sorted alphabetically)

AB.	STATE	POPULATION	CAPITAL CITY	POP	LARGEST CITY	POP
AK	Alaska	626,932	Juneau	30,711	Anchorage	260,283
AL	Alabama	4,447,100	Montgomery	201,568	Birmingham	242,820
AR	Arkansas	2,673,400	Little Rock	183,133	Fort Smith	80,268
AZ	Arizona	5,130,632	Phoenix	1,321,045	Tucson	486,699
CA	California	33,871,648	Sacramento	407,018	Los Angeles	3,694,820
CO	Colorado	4,301,261	Denver	554,636	Colorado Springs	360,890
CT	Connecticut	3,405,565	Hartford	121,578	Bridgeport	139,529
DC	District of Columbia	572,059	Washington	572,059		
DE	Delaware	783,600	Dover	32,135	Wilmington	72,664
	England	**49,138,831**	**London**	**7,680,000**		
FL	Florida	15,982,378	Tallahassee	150,624	Jacksonville	735,617
GA	Georgia	8,186,453	Atlanta	416,474	Augusta	199,775
HI	Hawaii	1,211,537	Honolulu	371,657	Hilo	40,759
IA	Iowa	2,926,324	Des Moines	198,682	Cedar Rapids	120,758
ID	Idaho	1,293,953	Boise	185,787	Nampa	51,867
IL	Illinois	12,419,293	Springfield	111,454	Chicago	2,896,016
IN	Indiana	6,080,485	Indianapolis	791,926	Fort Wayne	205,727
KS	Kansas	2,688,418	Topeka	122,377	Wichita	344,284
KY	Kentucky	4,041,769	Frankfort	27,741	Lexington-Fayette	260,512
LA	Louisiana	4,468,976	Baton Rouge	227,818	New Orleans	484,674
MA	Massachusetts	6,349,097	Boston	589,141	Worcester	172,648
MD	Maryland	5,296,486	Annapolis	35,838	Baltimore	651,154
ME	Maine	1,274,923	Augusta	18,560	Portland	64,249
MI	Michigan	9,938,444	Lansing	119,128	Detroit	951,270
MN	Minnesota	4,919,479	St Paul	287,151	Minneapolis	382,618
MO	Missouri	5,595,211	Jefferson City	39,636	Kansas City	441,545
MS	Mississippi	2,697,243	Jackson	184,256	Gulfport	71,127
MT	Montana	902,195	Helena	25,780	Billings	89,847
NC	North Carolina	8,049,313	Raleigh	276,093	Charlotte	540,828
ND	North Dakota	642,200	Bismarck	55,532	Fargo	90,599
	Northern Ireland	**1,685,267**	**Belfast**	**435,000**		
NE	Nebraska	1,711,263	Lincoln	225,581	Omaha	390,007
NH	New Hampshire	1,235,786	Concord	40,687	Manchester	107,006
NJ	New Jersey	8,414,350	Trenton	85,403	Newark	273,546
NM	New Mexico	1,819,046	Santa Fe	62,203	Albuquerque	448,607
NV	Nevada	1,998,257	Carson City	52,457	Las Vegas	478,434
NY	New York	18,976,457	Albany	95,658	New York	8,008,278

AB.	STATE	POPULATION	CAPITAL CITY	POP	LARGEST CITY	POP
OH	Ohio	11,353,140	Columbus	711,470	Cleveland	478,403
OK	Oklahoma	3,450,654	Oklahoma City	506,132	Tulsa	393,049
OR	Oregon	3,421,399	Salem	136,924	Portland	529,121
PA	Pennsylvania	12,281,054	Harrisburg	48,950	Philadelphia	1,517,550
RI	Rhode Island	1,048,319	Providence	173,618	Warwick	85,808
	Scotland	**5,062,011**	**Edinburgh**	**460,000**	**Glasgow**	**654,542**
SC	South Carolina	4,012,012	Columbia	116,278	Charleston	96,650
SD	South Dakota	754,844	Pierre	13,876	Sioux Falls	123,975
TN	Tennessee	5,689,283	Nashville	569,891	Memphis	650,100
TX	Texas	20,851,820	Austin	656,562	Houston	1,953,631
UK	**United Kingdom**	**58,789,194**				
UT	Utah	2,233,169	Salt Lake City	181,743	West Valley City	108,896
VA	Virginia	7,078,515	Richmond	197,790	Virginia Beach	425,257
VT	Vermont	608,827	Montpelier	8,035	Burlington	38,889
	Wales	**2,903,085**	**Cardiff**	**284,000**		
WA	Washington	5,894,121	Olympia	42,514	Seattle	563,374
WI	Wisconsin	5,363,675	Madison	208,054	Milwaukee	596,974
WV	West Virginia	1,808,344	Charleston	53,421	Huntingdon	51,475
WY	Wyoming	493,782	Cheyenne	53,011	Casper	49,644
	US Total	**280,702,432**				

ABBR	STATE	(OFFICIAL) NICKNAMES (APPEARS ON *LICENCE PLATE*)
AL	Alabama	*Heart of Dixie*, Yellowhammer State, Cotton Plantation State, Cotton State, Lizard State
AK	Alaska	*Last Frontier*, Land of the Midnight Sun, Seward's Folly, Seward's Ice Box
AZ	Arizona	*Grand Canyon State*, Copper State, Apache State, Aztec State, Baby State, Valentine State, Italy of America, Sand Hill State, Sunset Land
AR	Arkansas	**Natural State**, *Land of Opportunity*, Wonder State, Razorback State, Hot Springs State, Bowie State, Toothpick State, Bear /bar/ State
CA	California	**Golden State**, Land of Milk and Honey, Grape State, El Dorado State
CO	Colorado	*Centennial State*, Silver State, Lead State, Buffalo Plains State, Switzerland of America, Highest State
CT	Connecticut	**Constitution State**, Nutmeg State, Blue Law State, Brownstone State, Freestone State, Provisions State, Land of Steady Habits
DE	Delaware	**First State**, Diamond State, Blue Hen State, Peach State, New Sweden, Uncle Sam's Pocket Handkerchief, Corporate Capital, Small Wonder, Chemical Capital, Home of Tax Free Shopping
DC	District of Columbia	
FL	Florida	*Sunshine State*, Alligator State, Everglade State, Orange State, Land of Flower, Peninsula State, Gulf State
GA	Georgia	*Peach State*, Empire State of the South, Yankee-land of the South, Goober State, Cracker State, Buzzard State
HI	Hawaii	*Aloha State*, Pineapple State, Paradise of the Pacific, Youngest State
ID	Idaho	*Famous Potatoes*, Gem State, Gem of the Mountains, Little Ida
IL	Illinois	**Land of Lincoln,** Prairie State, Corn State, Garden of the West, Sucker State, Egypt
IN	Indiana	*Hoosier State*, **Crossroads of America**
IA	Iowa	*Corn State*, Hawkeye State, Land of the Rolling Prairie
KS	Kansas	Sunflower State, *Wheat State*, *Midway U.S*, Central State, Cyclone State, Grasshopper State, Garden of the West, Squatter State, Bleeding Kansas, Battleground of Freedom, Jayhawk State
KY	Kentucky	*Bluegrass State*, Hemp State, Tobacco State, Corn-cracker State, Dark and Bloody Ground State
LA	Louisiana	Pelican State, *Bayou State*, Sugar State, Child of the Mississippi, Creole State, *Sportsman's Paradise*, Fisherman's Paradise, Holland of America
ME	Maine	Pine Tree State, Lumber State, Border State, Old Dirigo State, Switzerland of America, Polar Star State
MD	Maryland	Old Line State, Free State, Cockade State, Monumental State, Oyster State, Queen State

ABBR	STATE	(OFFICIAL) **NICKNAMES** (APPEARS ON *LICENCE PLATE*)
MA	Massachusetts	Bay State, Baked Bean State, Old Colony State, Pilgrim State, Puritan State
MI	Michigan	Wolverine State, *Great Lake State*, *Water Wonderland*, Lady of the Lake, Auto State
MN	Minnesota	North Star State, *Land of 10,000 Lakes*, Bread and Butter State, Wheat State, Gopher State, New England of the West
MS	Mississippi	Magnolia State, Bayou State, Eagle State, Border-eagle State, Mud-cat State, Mud-waddler State, Ground-hog State
MO	Missouri	*Show Me State*, Cave State, Lead State, Bullion State, Ozark State, Mother of the West, Iron Mountain State, Puke State, Pennsylvania of the West
MT	Montana	*Big Sky* Country, *Treasure State*, Bonanza State, Land of Shining Mountains, Mountain State, Stubtoe State
NE	Nebraska	**Cornhusker State**, Tree Planters State, *Beef State*, Antelope State, Bug-eating State, Blackwater State
NV	Nevada	Battle Born State, *Silver State*, Mining State, Sagebrush State, Sage-hen State
NH	New Hampshire	Granite State, Mother of Rivers, White Mountain State, Switzerland of America
NJ	New Jersey	*Garden State*, Clam State, Camden & Amboy State, Jersey Blue State, Pathway of Revolution, Switzerland of America, Mosquito State, New Spain, Foreigner State
NM	New Mexico	**Land of Enchantment**, Cactus State, Spanish State, Land of Sunshine, *Sunshine State*, Land of the Delight Makers, Land of Opportunity, Land of the Heart's Desire
NY	New York	*Empire State*, Excelsior State, Knickerbocker State
NC	North Carolina	Tarheel State, Land of the Sky, Old North State, Turpentine State, Rip Van Winkle State
ND	North Dakota	**Peace Garden State**, Land of the Dakotas, Sioux State, Roughrider State, Flickertail State, Great Central State
OH	Ohio	**Buckeye State**, Mother of Presidents, Yankee State
OK	Oklahoma	Sooner State, Boomer's Paradise
OR	Oregon	Beaver State, Web-foot State, Hard-case State, Sunset State, Land of Wet Dreams
PA	Pennsylvania	*Keystone State*, Quaker State, Oil State, Coal State, Steel State
RI	Rhode Island	**Ocean State**, Little Rhody, Plantation State, Smallest State, Land of Roger Williams, Southern Gateway of New England
SC	South Carolina	Palmetto State, Rice State, Swamp State, Keystone of the South Atlantic Seaboard, *Iodine State*, Sand-lapper State
SD	South Dakota	**Mount Rushmore State**, Sunshine State, Coyote State, Artesian State, Blizzard State, Land of Plenty, Land of Infinite Variety
TN	Tennessee	*Volunteer State*, Big Bend State, Mother of Southwestern Statesmen, Hog and Hominy State, Lion's Den State

ABBR	STATE	(OFFICIAL) **NICKNAMES** (APPEARS ON *LICENCE PLATE*)
TX	Texas	*Lone Star State*, Beef State, Banner State, Blizzard State, Jumbo State
UT	Utah	Beehive State, Desert State, Mormon State, Land of the Saints, Land of the Mormons, Salt Lake State
VT	Vermont	Green Mountain State
VA	Virginia	Old Dominion, Mother of Presidents, Mother of Statesmen, Mother of States, Cavalier State, Down Where the South Begins
WA	Washington	*Evergreen State*, Green Tree State, Chinook State
WV	West Virginia	*Mountain State*, Switzerland of America, Panhandle State
WI	Wisconsin	Badger State, Dairy State, *America's Dairyland*, Cheese State, Copper State
WY	Wyoming	Equality State, Suffrage State, Sagebrush State, Cowboy State, Big Wyoming, Wonderland of America

ABBR	STATE	LICENSE PLATE SLOGAN
AL	Alabama	♥ Heart of Dixie (1955–present)
AK	Alaska	North to the Future (1966–1975), The Greatland (1968), The Last Frontier (1981–present)
AZ	Arizona	Marcos De Niza (1939), Grand Canyon State (1940–present)
AR	Arkansas	Centennial Celebration (1935), Opportunity Land (1941, 1948), Land of Opportunity (1950–1967, 1975–1986), The Natural State (1989–present)
CA	California	California Worlds Fair (1939), The Golden State (1984–present)
CO	Colorado	Colorful (1950–1955, 1958–1959, 1973–1974), Centennial (1975–1976)
CT	Connecticut	Constitution State (1974–present)
DE	Delaware	The First State (1963–present)
DC	District of Columbia	Nation's Capital (1954–1974, 1979–1990), Bicentennial (1976), A Capital City (1985–present), Celebrate and Discover (1991–present), Taxation without representation
FL	Florida	Sunshine State (1949–1976), Keep Florida Green (1951), 400th Anniversary (1965)
GA	Georgia	Peach State (1940–1941, 1947–1980)
HI	Hawaii	Aloha (1957–1960), Aloha State (1961–present)
ID	Idaho	Potatoes (1928), 50 Years Statehood (1940), Scenic (1941–1946), Vacation Wonderland (1947), World Famous Potatoes (1948), World Famous Potato (1943, 1956), Famous Potatoes (1957–present)
IL	Illinois	Land of Lincoln (1954–present)
IN	Indiana	Drive Safely (1956–1958), Lincoln's Year (1959), Safety Pays (1960–1962), 150th Statehood (1966), The Heritage State (1976), George Rogers Clark (1980), Hoosier State (1982), Wander (1985), Back Home Again (1988), Hoosier Hospitality (1991–present), Amber Waves of Grain (1994)
IA	Iowa	The Corn State (1953–1956)
KS	Kansas	The Wheat State (1949–1959), Centennial (1960–1961), Midway USA (1965–1970), Wheat Centennial (1975)
KY	Kentucky	For Progress (1929–1930), Tour (1951–1957), The Bluegrass State (1988–present)
LA	LoUiSiAna	Yams (1954), Sportsmen's Paradise (1958–1959, 1961–1973, 1980–1984, 1989, 1993–present), LSU Centennial (1960), Bayou State (1974, 1977)
ME	Maine	Vacationland (1936–present)
MD	Maryland	Tercentenary (1934), Drive Carefully (1942–1947)
MA	Massachusetts	The Spirit of America (1988)
MI	Michigan	Water Wonderland (1954–1964), Water Winter Wonderland (1965–1967), Great Lakes State (1968–1975, 1979–1983), Great Lakes (1983–present)

ABBR	STATE	LICENSE PLATE SLOGAN
MN	Minnesota	1849–Centennial–1949 (1949), 10,000 Lakes (1950–present), Explore (1987–present)
MS	Mississippi	Hospitality State (1977–1981)
MO	Missouri	200 Years (1976), Show Me State (1980–present)
MT	Montana	The Treasure State (1950–1956, 1963), Big Sky Country (1967–1975), Big Sky (1976–present), 100 Years (1987)
NE	Nebraska	The Beef State (1956–1965), Cornhusker (1969–1975), Centennial (1966–1968), 1776–Bicentennial–1976 (1969–1984)
NV	Nevada	1864–Nevada–1964/Centennial (1964), The Silver State (1983–present)
NH	New Hampshire	Scenic (1957–1970), Photoscenic (1964), Live Free or Die (1971–present)
NJ	New Jersey	The Garden State (1959–present)
NM	New Mexico	Sunshine State (1932), Coronado Quarto Centennial/1540–1940 (1940), The Land of Enchantment (1941–1951), Land of Enchantment (1952–present)
NY	New York	New York World's Fair (1938–1940), Empire State (1951-1963), World's Fair (1964-1965)
NC	North Carolina	Drive Safely (1954, 1956-1963), First in Freedom (1975-1984), First in Flight (1981-present)
ND	North Dakota	Peace Garden State (1956-present), Centennial (1987)
OH	Ohio	150 Anniv. N.W. Terr. (1938), 1803-Ohio-1953 (1953), Seat Belts Fastened? (1973-1975), The Heart of it All (1991-present)
OK	Oklahoma	Visit (1955-1962), Is OK (1967-1975, 1978-1979, 81-present), 1776 Bicentennial 1976 (1976), OK! (1989-present)
OR	Oregon	Pacific Wonderland (1961-1990)
PA	Pennsylvania	Bicentennial State (1971-1976), Keystone State (1977-present), You've Got a Friend (1983-present)
RI	Rhode Island	1636-Rhode Island-1936/300th Year (1936), Discover (1967–1981), Ocean State (1972–present)
SC	South Carolina	Iodine (1930), The Iodine State (1931–1932), The Iodine Products State (1933), 1670 300 Years 1970 (1970), Bicentennial (1976)
SD	South Dakota	Rushmore Memorial (1939), 1889–1989 (1987–1988), Celebrate the Century/1889–1989 (1989), Great Faces, Great Places (1991–present)
TN	Tennessee	The Volunteer State (1977–1989)
TX	Texas	Centennial (1936), Hemisfair (1968), Sesquicentennial (1985), The Lone Star State (1994)
UT	Utah	Center Scenic America (1942, 1945–1946), This is the Place (1947), The Friendly State (1948), Ski Utah!/Greatest Snow on Earth (1983–present)

ABBR	STATE	LICENSE PLATE SLOGAN
VT	Vermont	Green Mountains (1948–1950, 1977–1990), See (1957–1966, 1969–1976), Green Mountain State (1985–present)
VA	Virginia	Independence Bicentennial 1776–1976 (1976)
WA	Washington	1839–Golden Jubilee–1939 (1939), Centennial Celebration (1989–present), Evergreen State
WV	West Virginia	1863 Centennial 1963 (1963–1964), Mountain State (1965–1976), Wild, Wonderful (1976–present)
WI	Wisconsin	America's Dairyland (1940–present)
WY	Wyoming	The Spirit of 76–In the American West (1975–1977), 1890 Centennial 1990 (1988–1992)

English, Welsh, and Scottish Counties

Figure 13. Map of Traditional English and Welsh Counties

ENGLISH COUNTIES TABLE 14.

COUNTY (ABBREVIATION) (PRE-1974 DIVISION, E.G. THE THREE RIDINGS OF YORKSHIRE)

PRE-1974 (40)	1974-1996 (46)	POST-1998 (47)
Bedfordshire (Beds)	Avon	Bedfordshire (Beds)
Berkshire (Berks)	Bedfordshire (Beds)	Berkshire (Berks)
Buckinghamshire (Bucks)	Berkshire (Berks)	Bristol
Cambridgeshire (Cambs) (Isle of Ely)	Buckinghamshire (Bucks)	Buckinghamshire (Bucks)
Cheshire (Ches)	Cambridgeshire (Cambs)	Cambridgeshire (Cambs)
Cornwall (Corn)	Cheshire (Ches)	Cheshire
Cumberland (Cumb)	Cleveland	Cornwall
Derbyshire	Cornwall (Corn)	Cumbria
Devon	Cumbria	Derbyshire
Dorset	Derbyshire (Derby)	Devon
Durham	Devon	Dorset
Essex	Dorset	Durham
Gloucestershire (Glos)	Durham	East Riding of Yorkshire
Hampshire (Hants)	East Sussex	East Sussex (E Sussex)
Herefordshire	Essex	Essex
Hertfordshire (Herts)	Gloucestershire (Glos)	Gloucestershire (Glos)
Huntingdonshire (Hunts)	Greater London	Greater London
Kent	Greater Manchester	Greater Manchester
Lancashire (Lancs)	Hampshire (Hants)	Hampshire (Hants)
Leicestershire (Leics)	Hereford and Worcester	Herefordshire
Lincolnshire (Lincs) (Holland, Kesteven, Lindsey)	Hertfordshire (Herts)	Hertfordshire (Herts)
London	Humberside	Isle of Wight
Middlesex	Isle of Wight (IOW)	Kent
Norfolk	Kent	Lancashire (Lancs)
Northamptonshire (Northants) (Soke of Peterborough)	Lancashire (Lancs)	Leicestershire (Leics)
Northumberland (Northumb)	Leicestershire (Leics)	Lincolnshire (Lincs)
Nottinghamshire (Notts)	Lincolnshire (Lincs)	Merseyside
Oxfordshire (Oxon)	Merseyside	Norfolk
Rutland	Norfolk	North Yorkshire (N Yorkshire)
Shropshire (Northants)	North Yorkshire	Northamptonshire
Somerset (Som)	Northamptonshire (Northants)	Northumberland (Northd)
Staffordshire (Staffs)	Northumberland (Northumb)	Nottinghamshire (Notts)

PRE-1974 (40)	1974-1996 (46)	POST-1998 (47)
Suffolk (East & West)	Nottinghamshire (Notts)	Oxfordshire (Oxon)
Surrey	Oxfordshire (Oxon)	Rutland
Sussex	Shropshire	Shropshire
Warwickshire (War)	Somerset (Som)	Somerset
Westmorland	South Yorkshire	South Yorkshire (S Yorkshire)
Wiltshire (Wilts)	Staffordshire (Staffs)	Staffordshire (Staffs)
Worcestershire (Worcs)	Suffolk	Suffolk
Yorkshire (Yorks) (East Riding, North Riding, West Riding)	Surrey	Surrey
	Tyne and Wear	Tyne and Wear (Tyne & Wear)
	Warwickshire (War)	Warwickshire (Warks)
	West Midlands	West Midlands (W Midlands)
	West Sussex	West Sussex (W Sussex)
	West Yorkshire	West Yorkshire (W Yorkshire)
	Wiltshire (Wilts)	Wiltshire (Wilts)
		Worcestershire (Worcs)

WELSH COUNTIES

PRE-1974 (11)	1974-1996 (8)	POST-1998 (22)
Anglesey	Clwyd	Anglesey
Caernarvonshire	Dyfed	Blaenau Gwent
Cardiganshire	Gwent	Bridgend
Carmarthenshire	Gwynedd	Caerphilly
Denbighshire	Mid Glamorgan	Cardiff
Flintshire	Powys	Carmarthenshire
Glamorgan	South Glamorgan	Ceredigion
Merionethshire	West Glamorgan	Conwy
Monmouthshire		Denbighshire
Montgomeryshire		Flintshire
Pembrokeshire		Gwynedd
		Merthyr Tydfil
		Monmouthshire
		Neath Port Talbot

PRE-1974 (11)	1974-1996 (8)	POST-1998 (22)
		Newport
		Pembrokeshire
		Powys
		Rhondda Cynon Taff
		Swansea
		Torfaen
		Vale of Glamorgan
		Wrexham

SCOTTISH COUNTIES

PRE-1974 (35)	1974-1996 (12)	POST-1998 (32)
Aberdeenshire	Borders	Aberdeen
Angus	Central	Aberdeenshire
Argyllshire	Dumfries and Galloway	Angus
Ayrshire	Fife	Argyll and Bute
Banffshire	Grampian	Clackmannanshire
Berwickshire	Highland	Dumfries and Galloway
Brecknockshire	Lothian	Dundee
Buteshire	Orkney Islands	East Ayrshire
Caithness	Shetland Islands	East Dunbartonshire
Clackmannanshire	Strathclyde	East Lothian
Dumfriesshire	Tayside	East Renfrewshire
Dunbartonshire	Western Isles	Edinburgh
East Lothian		Falkirk
Fife		Fife
Inverness-shire		Glasgow
Kincardineshire		Highland
Kinross-shire		Inverclyde
Kirkcudbrightshire		Midlothian
Lanarkshire		Moray
Midlothian		North Ayrshire
Morayshire		North Lanarkshire
Nairnshire		Orkney Islands
Orkney Islands		Perth and Kinross
Peeblesshire		Renfrewshire
Perthshire		Scottish Borders
Radnorshire		Shetland Islands

PRE-1974 (35)	1974-1996 (12)	POST-1998 (32)
Renfrewshire		South Ayrshire
Ross and Cromarty		South Lanarkshire
Roxburghshire		Stirling
Selkirkshire		West Dunbartonshire
Shetland Islands		West Lothian
Stirlingshire		Western Isles
Sutherland		
West Lothian		
Wigtownshire		

County information from Jonathan Rawle's Counties of Great Britain.
http://jonathan.rawle.org/counties/

Table 15.

Telephone Area Codes
(sorted by state)

− 600	− 800	CA 424	IA 563	MD249	NC704	OK405	TX 903
− 911	AB 780	CA 747	IA 641	MD969	ND701	ON705	TX 806
− 456	AB 403	CA 818	IA 712	MD240	NE 402	ON289	TX 737
− 700	AK 907	CA 858	ID 208	MD301	NE 308	ON905	TX 512
− 211	AL 205	CA 935	IL 217	ME207	NF 709	ON647	TX 361
− 511	AL 256	CA 619	IL 872	MI 517	NH603	ON416	TX 210
− 999	AL 334	CA 805	IL 312	MI 810	NJ 908	ON613	TX 936
− 880	AL 251	CA 369	IL 773	MI 278	NJ 848	ON519	TX 409
− 881	AR 870	CO 720	IL 464	MI 313	NJ 732	ON807	TX 979
− 882	AR 501	CO 303	IL 708	MI 586	NJ 551	OR 503	TX 972
− 976	AR 479	CO 970	IL 815	MI 248	NJ 201	OR 971	TX 469
− 500	AZ 480	CO 719	IL 224	MI 734	NJ 862	OR 541	TX 214
− 311	AZ 623	CT 203	IL 847	MI 269	NJ 973	PA 814	TX 682
− 411	AZ 928	CT 959	IL 618	MI 906	NJ 609	PA 717	TX 832
− 611	AZ 602	CT 475	IL 309	MI 989	NJ 856	PA 570	TX 281
− 811	AZ 520	CT 860	IL 331	MI 616	NM505	PA 878	TX 830
− 711	BC 250	DC 202	IL 630	MI 231	NM957	PA 835	TX 956
− 684	BC 778	DE 302	IN 765	MI 679	NS 902	PA 484	TX 432
− 264	BC 604	FL 689	IN 574	MI 947	NV702	PA 610	TX 915
− 268	CA 628	FL 407	IN 260	MN612	NV775	PA 267	UT 435
− 246	CA 341	FL 239	IN 219	MN320	NY 315	PA 215	UT 801
− 441	CA 764	FL 727	IN 317	MN651	NY 518	PA 724	UT 385
− 284	CA 925	FL 321	IN 812	MN763	NY 716	PA 412	VA 434
− 767	CA 909	FL 754	KS 913	MN952	NY 585	PR 939	VA 804
− 809	CA 562	FL 954	KS 785	MN218	NY646	PR 787	VA 757
− 473	CA 661	FL 352	KS 316	MN507	NY347	QC438	VA 703
− 664	CA 657	FL 863	KS 620	MO636	NY 718	QC514	VA 571
− 869	CA 510	FL 904	KY 502	MO660	NY 212	QC819	VA 540
− 758	CA 650	FL 386	KY 859	MO975	NY 516	QC418	VA 276
− 784	CA 949	FL 561	KY 606	MO816	NY 917	QC450	VA 236
− 868	CA 760	FL 772	KY 270	MO314	NY845	RI 401	VT 802
− 340	CA 415	FL 786	LA 504	MO557	NY 631	SC 843	WA509
− 242	CA 951	FL 305	LA 985	MO573	NY607	SC 864	WA360
− 345	CA 831	FL 941	LA 225	MO417	NY 914	SC 803	WA564
− 876	CA 209	FL 813	LA 318	MP670	OH216	SD 605	WA206
− 649	CA 669	FL 850	LA 337	MS601	OH330	SK 306	WA425

–							
– 555	CA 408	GA 478	MA774	MS662	OH234	TN 423	WA253
– 710	CA 559	GA770	MA508	MS769	OH567	TN 865	WI 715
– 900	CA 626	GA 470	MA781	MS228	OH419	TN 931	WI 920
– 866	CA 442	GA 404	MA339	MT406	OH380	TN 615	WI 414
– 877	CA 530	GA706	MA857	NB 506	OH440	TN 901	WI 262
– 888	CA 916	GA 678	MA617	NC336	OH740	TN 731	WI 608
– 898	CA 707	GA 912	MA978	NC252	OH614	TX 254	WV304
– 822	CA 627	GA 229	MA351	NC984	OH283	TX 325	WY307
– 829	CA 714	GU 671	MA413	NC 919	OH513	TX 713	YT 867
– 833	CA 310	HI 808	MB204	NC980	OH937	TX 940	
– 844	CA 323	IA 515	MD443	NC 910	OK 918	TX 817	
– 855	CA 213	IA 319	MD410	NC828	OK580	TX 430	

Telephone Area Codes
(sorted by area code)

AC	REG	UTC	DESCRIPTION
201	NJ	-5	N New Jersey: Jersey City, Hackensack
202	DC	-5	Washington, D.C.
203	CT	-5	Connecticut: Fairfield County and New Haven County; Bridgeport, New Haven
204	MB	-6	Canada: Manitoba
205	AL	-6	Central Alabama (including Birmingham; excludes the southeastern corner of Alabama and the deep South)
206	WA	-8	W Washington state: Seattle and Bainbridge Island
207	ME	-5	Maine
208	ID	-7/-8	Idaho
209	CA	-8	Central California: Stockton
210	TX	-6	S Texas: San Antonio
211	–	–	Local community info / referral services
212	NY	-5	New York City, New York (Manhattan)
213	CA	-8	S California: Los Angeles
214	TX	-6	Texas: Dallas Metro
215	PA	-5	SE Pennsylvania: Philadelphia
216	OH	-5	Cleveland
217	IL	-6	Central Illinois: Springfield
218	MN	-6	N Minnesota: Duluth
219	IN	-5	NW Indiana: Gary
224	IL	-6	Northern NE Illinois: Evanston, Waukegan, Northbrook
225	LA	-6	Louisiana: Baton Rouge, New Roads, Donaldsonville, Albany, Gonzales, Greensburg, Plaquemine, Vacherie
228	MS	-6	S Mississippi (coastal areas, Biloxi, Gulfport)
229	GA	-5	SW Georgia: Albany
231	MI	-5	W Michigan: Northwestern portion of lower Peninsula; Traverse City, Muskegon, Cheboyhan, Alanson
234	OH	-5	NE Ohio: Canton, Akron
236	VA	-5	Virginia
239	FL	-5	Florida (Lee, Collier, and Monroe Counties, excl the Keys)
240	MD	-5	W Maryland: Silver Spring, Frederick, Gaithersburg
242	–	-5	Bahamas
246	–	-4	Barbados
248	MI	-5	Michigan: Oakland County, Pontiac
249	MD	-5	Maryland: Gaithersburg area
250	BC	-8	Canada: British Columbia

AC	REG	UTC	DESCRIPTION
251	AL	-6	S Alabama: Mobile and coastal areas, Jackson, Evergreen, Monroeville
252	NC	-5	E North Carolina (Rocky Mount)
253	WA	-8	Washington: South Tier—Tacoma, Federal Way
254	TX	-6	Central Texas (Waco, Stephenville)
256	AL	-6	E and N Alabama (Huntsville, Florence, Gadsden)
260	IN	-5	NE Indiana: Fort Wayne
262	WI	-6	SE Wisconsin: counties of Kenosha, Ozaukee, Racine, Walworth, Washington, Waukesha
264	–	-4	Anguilla
267	PA	-5	SE Pennsylvania: Philadelphia
268	–	-4	Antigua and Barbuda
269	MI	-5	SW Michigan: Kalamazoo, Saugatuck, Hastings, Battle Creek, Sturgis to Lake Michigan
270	KY	-6	W Kentucky: Bowling Green, Paducah
276	VA	-5	S and SW Virginia: Bristol, Stuart, Martinsville
278	MI	-5	Michigan
281	TX	-6	Texas: Houston Metro
283	OH	-5	SW Ohio: Cincinnati
284	–	-4	British Virgin Islands
289	ON	-5	Canada: S Central Ontario: Greater Toronto Area—Durham, Halton, Hamilton-Wentworth, Niagara, Peel, York, and southern Simcoe County
301	MD	-5	W Maryland: Silver Spring, Frederick, Camp Springs, Prince George's County
302	DE	-5	Delaware
303	CO	-7	Central Colorado: Denver
304	WV	-5	West Virginia
305	FL	-5	SE Florida: Miami, the Keys
306	SK	-6/-7	Canada: Saskatchewan
307	WY	-7	Wyoming
308	NE	-6/-7	W Nebraska: North Platte
309	IL	-6	W Central Illinois: Peoria
310	CA	-8	S California: Beverly Hills, West Hollywood, West Los Angeles
311	–	–	Reserved for special applications
312	IL	-6	Illinois: Chicago (downtown only—in the Loop)
313	MI	-5	Michigan: Detroit and suburbs
314	MO	-6	SE Missouri: St Louis city and parts of the Metro area only
315	NY	-5	N Central New York: Syracuse
316	KS	-6	S Kansas: Wichita
317	IN	-6	Central Indiana: Indianapolis
318	LA	-6	N Louisiana: Shreveport, Ruston, Monroe, Alexandria

AC	REG	UTC	DESCRIPTION
319	IA	-6	E Iowa: Cedar Rapids
320	MN	-6	Central Minnesota: Saint Cloud (rural Minn, excl St. Paul/Minneapolis)
321	FL	-5	Florida: Brevard County, Cape Canaveral area; Metro Orlando
323	CA	-8	S California: Los Angeles (outside downtown: Hollywood)
325	TX	-6	Central Texas: Abilene, Sweetwater, Snyder, San Angelo
330	OH	-5	NE Ohio: Akron, Canton, Youngstown; Mahoning County, parts of Trumbull/Warren counties
331	IL	-6	W NE Illinois, western suburbs of Chicago
334	AL	-6	S Alabama: Auburn/Opelika, Montgomery and coastal areas
336	NC	-5	Central North Carolina: Greensboro
337	LA	-6	SW Louisiana: Lake Charles, Lafayette
339	MA	-5	Massachusetts: Boston suburbs, to the south and west
340	–	-4	US Virgin Islands
341	CA	-8	
345	–	-5	Cayman Islands
347	NY	-5	New York (NYC area, except Manhattan)
351	MA	-5	Massachusetts: north of Boston to NH, 508, and 781
352	FL	-5	Florida: Gainesville area, Ocala, Crystal River
360	WA	-8	W Washington State: Olympia, Bellingham (except Seattle area)
361	TX	-6	S Texas: Corpus Christi
369	CA	-8	Solano County
380	OH	-5	Ohio: Columbus
385	UT	-7	Utah: Salt Lake City Metro
386	FL	-5	N central Florida: Lake City
401	RI	-5	Rhode Island
402	NE	-6	E Nebraska: Omaha, Lincoln
403	AB	-7	Canada: Southern Alberta
404	GA	-5	N Georgia: Atlanta and suburbs
405	OK	-6	W Oklahoma: Oklahoma City
406	MT	-7	Montana
407	FL	-5	Central Florida: Metro Orlando
408	CA	-8	Cent. Coastal California: San Jose
409	TX	-6	SE Texas: Galveston, Port Arthur
410	MD	-5	E Maryland: Baltimore, Annapolis, Chesapeake Bay area, Ocean City
411	–	–	Reserved for special applications
412	PA	-5	W Pennsylvania: Pittsburgh
413	MA	-5	W Massachusetts: Springfield
414	WI	-6	SE Wisconsin: Milwaukee County
415	CA	-8	California: San Francisco County and Marin County on the north side of the Golden Gate Bridge, extending north to Sonoma County

AC	REG	UTC	DESCRIPTION
416	ON	-5	Canada: S Cent. Ontario: Toronto
417	MO	-6	SW Missouri: Springfield
418	QC	-5/-4	Canada: NE Quebec: Quebec
419	OH	-5	NW Ohio: Toledo
423	TN	-5	E Tennessee, except Knoxville metro area: Chattanooga, Bristol, Johnson City, Kingsport, Greeneville
424	CA	-8	S California: Los Angeles
425	WA	-8	Washington: North Tier—Everett, Bellevue
430	TX	-6	NE Texas: Tyler
432	TX	-7/-6	W Texas: Big Spring, Midland, Odessa
434	VA	-5	E Virginia: Charlottesville, Lynchburg, Danville, South Boston, and Emporia
435	UT	-7	Rural Utah outside Salt Lake City Metro
438	QC	-5	Canada: SW Quebec: Montreal city
440	OH	-5	Ohio: Cleveland Metro area, excluding Cleveland
441	–	-4	Bermuda
442	CA	-8	Far north suburbs of San Diego (Oceanside, Escondido)
443	MD	-5	E Maryland: Baltimore, Annapolis, Chesapeake Bay area, Ocean City
450	QC	-5/-4	Canada: Southeastern Quebec; suburbs outside Metro Montreal
456	–	–	Inbound International
464	IL	-6	Illinois: south suburbs of Chicago
469	TX	-6	Texas: Dallas Metro
470	GA	-5	Georgia: Greater Atlanta Metropolitan Area
473	–	-4	Grenada
475	CT	-5	Connecticut: New Haven, Greenwich, southwestern
478	GA	-5	Central Georgia: Macon
479	AR	-6	NW Arkansas: Fayetteville, Springdale, Bentonville
480	AZ	-7	Arizona: East Phoenix
484	PA	-5	SE Pennsylvania: Allentown, Bethlehem, Reading, West Chester, Norristown
500	–	–	Personal Communication Service
501	AR	-6	Central Arkansas: Little Rock, Hot Srpings, Conway
502	KY	-5	N Central Kentucky: Louisville
503	OR	-8	Oregon: Portland area
504	LA	-6	E Louisiana: New Orleans metro area
505	NM	-7	New Mexico
506	NB	-4	Canada: New Brunswick
507	MN	-6	S Minnesota: Rochester, Mankato, Worthington
508	MA	-5	Cent. Massachusetts: Framingham; Cape Cod
509	WA	-8	E Washington state: Spokane

AC	REG	UTC	DESCRIPTION
510	CA	-8	California: Oakland, East Bay
511	–	–	Nationwide travel information
512	TX	-6	S Texas: Austin
513	OH	-5	SW Ohio: Cincinnati
514	QC	-5	Canada: SW Quebec: Montreal city
515	IA	-6	Central Iowa: Des Moines
516	NY	-5	New York: Nassau County, Long Island; Hempstead
517	MI	-5	Cent. Michigan: Lansing
518	NY	-5	NE New York: Albany
519	ON	-5	Canada: SW Ontario: Windsor
520	AZ	-8	SE Arizona: Flagstaff, Tucson area
530	CA	-8	NE California: Eldorado County area, excluding Eldorado Hills itself: includes Auburn, Chico, Redding, So. Lake Tahoe, Marysville, Nevada City/Grass Valley
540	VA	-5	Western and Southwest Virginia: Shenandoah and Roanoke valleys: Fredericksburg, Harrisonburg, Roanoke, Salem, Lexington and nearby areas
541	OR	-8/-7	Oregon: (apart from NW parts of Portland/Salem)
551	NJ	-5	N New Jersey: Jersey City, Hackensack
555	–	?	Reserved for directory assistance applications
557	MO	-6	SE Missouri: St Louis Metro area only
559	CA	-8	Central California: Fresno
561	FL	-5	S. Central Florida: Palm Beach County (West Palm Beach, Boca Raton, Vero Beach)
562	CA	-8	California: Long Beach
563	IA	-6	E Iowa: Davenport, Dubuque
564	WA	-8	W Washington State: Olympia, Bellingham
567	OH	-5	NW Ohio: Toledo
570	PA	-5	NE and N Central Pennsylvania: Wilkes-Barre, Scranton
571	VA	-5	Northern Virginia: Arlington, McLean, Tysons Corner
573	MO	-6	SE Missouri: excluding St Louis Metro area, includes Central/East Missouri, area between St. Louis and Kansas City
574	IN	-5	N Indiana: Elkhart, South Bend
580	OK	-6	W Oklahoma (rural areas outside Oklahoma City)
585	NY	-5	NW New York: Rochester
586	MI	-5	Michigan: Macomb County
600	–	–	Canadian Services
601	MS	-6	Mississippi: Meridian, Jackson area
602	AZ	-8	Arizona: Phoenix
603	NH	-5	New Hampshire
604	BC	-8	Canada: British Columbia: Greater Vancouver

AC	REG	UTC	DESCRIPTION
605	SD	-6/-7	South Dakota
606	KY	-5/-6	E Kentucky: area east of Frankfort: Ashland
607	NY	-5	S Central New York: Ithaca, Binghamton; Catskills
608	WI	-6	SW Wisconsin: Madison
609	NJ	-5	S New Jersey: Trenton
610	PA	-5	SE Pennsylvania: Allentown, Bethlehem, Reading, West Chester, Norristown
611	–	–	Reserved for special applications
612	MN	-6	Central Minnesota: Minneapolis
613	ON	-5	Canada: SE Ontario: Ottawa
614	OH	-5	SE Ohio: Columbus
615	TN	-6	Northern Middle Tennessee: Nashville Metro area
616	MI	-5	W Michigan: Holland, Grand Haven, Greenville, Grand Rapids, Ionia
617	MA	-5	Massachusetts: greater Boston
618	IL	-6	S Illinois: Centralia
619	CA	-8	S California: San Diego
620	KS	-6	S Kansas: Wichita
623	AZ	-7	Arizona: West Phoenix
626	CA	-8	SW California: Pasadena
627	CA	-8	Napa, Sonoma counties
628	CA	-8	
630	IL	-6	W NE Illinois, western suburbs of Chicago
631	NY	-5	New York: Suffolk County, Long Island; Huntington, Riverhead
636	MO	-6	Missouri: W St. Louis Metro area of St. Louis county, St. Charles County, Jefferson County area south
641	IA	-6	Iowa: Mason City, Marshalltown, Creston, Ottumwa
646	NY	-5	New York NYC: Manhattan only
647	ON	-5	Canada: S Central Ontario: Toronto
649	–	-5	Turks & Caicos Islands
650	CA	-8	California: Peninsula south of San Francisco—San Mateo County, parts of Santa Clara County
651	MN	-6	Central Minnesota: St. Paul
657	CA	-8	California: North and Central Orange County
660	MO	-6	N Missouri
661	CA	-8	California: N Los Angeles, Mckittrick, Mojave, Newhall, Oildale, Palmdale, Taft, Tehachapi, Bakersfield, Earlimart, Lancaster
662	MS	-6	N Mississippi: Tupelo, Grenada
664	–	-4	Montserrat
669	CA	-8	Central Coastal California: San Jose
670	MP	+10	Commonwealth of the Northern Mariana Islands (CNMI, US Commonwealth)

AC	REG	UTC	DESCRIPTION
671	GU	+10	Guam
678	GA	-5	N Georgia: Metropolitan Atlanta
679	MI	-5/-6	Michigan: Dearborn area
682	TX	-6	Texas: Fort Worth areas
684	–	-11	American Samoa
689	FL	-5	Central Florida: Metro Orlando
700	–	–	Interexchange Carrier Services
701	ND	-6	North Dakota
702	NV	-8	Nevada: Clark County, incl Las Vegas
703	VA	-5	Northern Virginia: Arlington, McLean, Tysons Corner
704	NC	-5	W North Carolina: Charlotte
705	ON	-5	Canada: NW Ontario: Sault Ste. Marie/N Ontario: N Bay, Sudbury
706	GA	-5	N Georgia: Columbus, Augusta
707	CA	-8	NW California: Santa Rosa, Napa, Vallejo, American Canyon, Fairfield
708	IL	-6	Illinois: south suburbs of Chicago
709	NF	-4/-3.5	Canada: Newfoundland
710	–	?	US Government
711	–	–	Telecommunications Relay Services
712	IA	-6	W Iowa: Council Bluffs
713	TX	-6	Mid SE Texas: central Houston
714	CA	-8	North and Central Orange County
715	WI	-6	N Wisconsin: Eau Claire, Wausau, Superior
716	NY	-5	NW New York: Buffalo
717	PA	-5	E Pennsylvania: Harrisburg
718	NY	-5	New York City Metro Area, New York (Queens, Staten Island, the Bronx, and Brooklyn)
719	CO	-7	SE Colorado: Pueblo, Colorado Springs
720	CO	-7	Central Colorado: Denver
724	PA	-5	SW Pennsylvania (areas outside Metro Pittsburgh)
727	FL	-5	Florida Tampa Metro: Saint Petersburg, Clearwater (Pinellas and parts of Pasco County)
731	TN	-6	W Tennessee: outside Memphis Metro area
732	NJ	-5	Central New Jersey: Toms River, New Brunswick, Bound Brook
734	MI	-5	SE Michigan: west and south of Detroit—Ann Arbor, Monroe
737	TX	-6	S Texas: Austin
740	OH	-5	SE Ohio (rural areas outside Columbus)
747	CA	-8	S California: Los Angeles, Agoura Hills, Calabasas, Hidden Hills, and Westlake Village
754	FL	-5	Florida: Broward County area, incl Ft. Lauderdale
757	VA	-5	E Virginia: Tidewater / Hampton Roads area—Norfolk, Virginia Beach, Chesapeake, Portsmouth, Hampton, Newport News, Suffolk

AC	REG	UTC	DESCRIPTION
758	—	-4	St. Lucia
760	CA	-8	California: San Diego North County to Sierra Nevada
763	MN	-6	Minnesota: Minneapolis Metro area
764	CA	-8	
765	IN	-5	Indiana: outside Indianapolis
767	—	-4	Dominica
769	MS	-6	Mississippi: Meridian, Jackson area
770	GA	-5	Georgia: Atlanta suburbs: outside of I-285 ring road
772	FL	-5	S. Central Florida: St. Lucie, Martin, and Indian River counties
773	IL	-6	Illinois: city of Chicago, outside the Loop
774	MA	-5	Central Massachusetts: Framingham; Cape Cod
775	NV	-8	Nevada: Reno (all of NV except Clark County area)
778	BC	-8	Canada: British Columbia: Greater Vancouver
780	AB	-7	Canada: Northern Alberta, north of Lacombe
781	MA	-5	Massachusetts: Boston surburbs, to the north and west
784	—	-4	St. Vincent & Grenadines
785	KS	-6	N & W Kansas: Topeka
786	FL	-5	SE Florida, Monroe County (Miami)
787	PR	-4	Puerto Rico
800	—	?	US/Canada toll free
801	UT	-7	Utah: Salt Lake City Metro
802	VT	-5	Vermont
803	SC	-5	South Carolina: Columbia, Aiken, Sumter
804	VA	-5	E Virginia: Richmond
805	CA	-8	S Central and Central Coastal California: Ventura County, Santa Barbara County: San Luis Obispo, Thousand Oaks, Carpinteria, Santa Barbara, Santa Maria, Lompoc, Santa Ynez Valley / Solvang
806	TX	-6	Panhandle Texas: Amarillo, Lubbock
807	ON	-5/-6	Canada: W Ontario: Thunder Bay region to Manitoba border
808	HI	-10	Hawaii
809	—	-4	Dominican Republic
810	MI	-5	E Michigan: Flint, Pontiac
811	—	—	Reserved for special applications
812	IN	-6	S Indiana: Evansville, Cincinnati outskirts in IN, Columbus, Bloomington
813	FL	-5	SW Florida: Tampa Metro
814	PA	-5	Central Pennsylvania: Erie
815	IL	-6	NW Illinois: Rockford, Kankakee
816	MO	-6	N Missouri: Kansas City
817	TX	-6	N Central Texas: Fort Worth area

AC	REG	UTC	DESCRIPTION
818	CA	-8	S California: Los Angeles: San Fernando Valley
819	QC	-5	NW Quebec: Trois Rivieres, Outaouais (Gatineau, Hull), and the Laurentians (up to St Jovite / Tremblant)
822	–	?	US/Canada toll free
828	NC	-5	W North Carolina: Asheville
829	–	-4	Dominican Republic
830	TX	-6	Texas: region surrounding San Antonio
831	CA	-8	California: central coast area from Santa Cruz through Monterey County
832	TX	-6	Texas: Houston
833	–	?	US/Canada toll free
835	PA	-5	SE Pennsylvania: Allentown, Bethlehem, Reading, West Chester, Norristown
843	SC	-5	South Carolina, coastal area: Charleston, Beaufort, Myrtle Beach
844	–	?	US/Canada toll free
845	NY	-5	New York: Poughkeepsie; Nyack, Nanuet, Valley Cottage, New City, Putnam, Dutchess, Rockland, Orange, Ulster and parts of Sullivan counties in New York's lower Hudson Valley and Delaware County in the Catskills
847	IL	-6	Northern NE Illinois: northwestern suburbs of Chicago (Evanston, Waukegan, Northbrook)
848	NJ	-5	Central New Jersey: Toms River, New Brunswick, Bound Brook
850	FL	-6	Florida Panhandle, from east of Tallahassee to Pensacola
855	–	?	US/Canada toll free
856	NJ	-5	SW New Jersey: greater Camden area, Mt Laurel
857	MA	-5	Massachusetts: greater Boston
858	CA	-8	S California: San Diego
859	KY	-5	N and Central Kentucky: Lexington; suburban KY counties of Cincinnati OH metro area; Covington, Newport, Ft. Thomas, Ft. Wright, Florence
860	CT	-5	Connecticut: areas outside of Fairfield and New Haven Counties
862	NJ	-5	N New Jersey: Newark, Paterson, Morristown
863	FL	-5	Florida: Polk County
864	SC	-5	South Carolina, upstate area: Greenville, Spartanburg
865	TN	-5	E Tennessee: Knoxville, Knox and adjacent counties
866	–	?	US/Canada toll free
867	YT	-8/-9	Canada: Yukon, Northwest Territories, Nunavut
868	–	-4	Trinidad and Tobago
869	–	-4	St. Kitts & Nevis
870	AR	-6	Arkansas: areas outside of west/central AR: Jonesboro, etc
872	IL	-6	Illinois: Chicago (downtown only—in the Loop)

AC	REG	UTC	DESCRIPTION
876	–	-5	Jamaica
877	–	?	US/Canada toll free
878	PA	-5	Pittsburgh, New Castle
880	–	–	Paid Toll-Free Service
881	–	–	Paid Toll-Free Service
882	–	–	Paid Toll-Free Service
888	–	?	US/Canada toll free
898	–	–	VoIP service
900	–	?	US toll calls—prices vary with the number called
901	TN	-6	W Tennessee: Memphis Metro area
902	NS	-4	Canada: Nova Scotia, Prince Edward Island
903	TX	-6	NE Texas: Tyler
904	FL	-5	N Florida: Jacksonville
905	ON	-5	Canada: S Cent. Ontario: Greater Toronto Area—Durham, Halton, Hamilton-Wentworth, Niagara, Peel, York, and southern Simcoe County (excluding Toronto)
906	MI	-5	Upper Peninsula Michigan: Sault Ste. Marie, Escanaba, Marquette
907	AK	-9	Alaska
908	NJ	-5	Central New Jersey: Elizabeth, Basking Ridge, Somerville, Bridgewater
909	CA	-8	California: Inland empire: San Bernardino, Riverside
910	NC	-5	S Central North Carolina: Fayetteville, Wilmington
911	–	–	Emergency
912	GA	-5	SE Georgia: Savannah
913	KS	-6	Kansas: Kansas City area
914	NY	-5	S New York: Westchester County
915	TX	-7/-6	W Texas: El Paso
916	CA	-8	NE California: Sacramento, Walnut Grove, Lincoln, Newcastle and El Dorado Hills
917	NY	-5	New York: New York City
918	OK	-6	E Oklahoma: Tulsa
919	NC	-5	E North Carolina: Raleigh
920	WI	-6	NE Wisconsin: Appleton, Green Bay, Sheboygan, Fond du Lac (from Beaver Dam NE to Oshkosh, Appleton, and Door County)
925	CA	-8	California: Contra Costa area: Antioch, Concord, Pleasanton, Walnut Creek
928	AZ	-7	Central and Northern Arizona: Prescott, Flagstaff, Yuma
931	TN	-6	Middle Tennessee: semi-circular ring around Nashville
935	CA	-8	S California: San Diego
936	TX	-6	SE Texas: Conroe, Lufkin, Nacogdoches, Crockett
937	OH	-5	SW Ohio: Dayton
939	PR	-4	Puerto Rico

AC	REG	UTC	DESCRIPTION
940	TX	-6	N Central Texas: Denton, Wichita Falls
941	FL	-5	SW Florida: Sarasota and Manatee counties
947	MI	-5/-6	Michigan: Oakland County
949	CA	-8	California: S Coastal Orange County
951	CA	-8	California: W Riverside County
952	MN	-6	Minnesota: Minneapolis Metro area, Bloomington
954	FL	-5	Florida: Broward County area, incl Ft. Lauderdale
956	TX	-6	Texas: Valley of Texas area; Harlingen, Laredo
957	NM	-7	New Mexico
959	CT	-5	Connecticut: Hartford, New London
969	MD	-5	Maryland: Severn area
970	CO	-7	N and W Colorado
971	OR	-8	Oregon: Metropolitan Portland, Salem/Keizer area, incl Cricket Wireless
972	TX	-6	Texas: Dallas Metro
973	NJ	-5	N New Jersey: Newark, Paterson, Morristown
975	MO	-6	N Missouri: Kansas City
976	–	–	Pay services
978	MA	-5	Massachusetts: north of Boston to NH
979	TX	-6	SE Texas: Galveston, Port Arthur, Bryan, College Station
980	NC	-5	North Carolina: Kingston, Charlotte
984	NC	-5	E North Carolina: Raleigh
985	LA	-6	E Louisiana: SE/N shore of Lake Pontchartrain: Hammond, Slidell, Covington, Amite, Kentwood, area SW of New Orleans, Houma, Thibodaux, Morgan City
989	MI	-5	Upper central Michigan: Mt Pleasant, Saginaw
999	–	–	Often used by carriers to indicate that the area code information is unavailable for CNID, even though the rest of the number is present

Source: http://www.bennetyee.org/ucsd-pages/area.html

— How to Tell If You're American —

by Mark Rosenfelder

N OT LONG AGO, one of those earnest-freshman puppydogs on the Net declared that there was "no such thing as American culture." Right. Fish have also been known to doubt the existence of water.

The following is a first crack at an ostensive definition of 'American culture'—things shared by the vast majority (let's say 90%) of native-born Americans. Many of these won't sound 'cultural' at all to Americans; they'll sound like just descriptions of the way things are. But each one of them would be contested in one or more non-American cultures.

IF YOU'RE AMERICAN...

➤ You believe deep down in the First Amendment, guaranteed by the government and perhaps by God.

➤ You're familiar with David Letterman, Mary Tyler Moore, *Saturday Night Live*, *Bewitched*, the *Flintstones*, *Sesame Street*, Mr. Rogers, Bob Newhart, Bill Cosby, Bugs Bunny, Road Runner, Donald Duck, the Fonz, Archie Bunker, *Star Trek*, the *Honeymooners*, the *Addams Family*, the Three Stooges, and Beetle Bailey.

➤ You know how baseball, basketball, and American football are played. If you're male, you can argue intricate points about their rules. On the other hand (and unless you're under about 20), you don't care that much for soccer.

➤ You count yourself fortunate if you get three weeks of vacation a year.

If you died tonight...

➤ You're fairly likely to believe in God; if not, you've certainly been approached by people asking whether you know that you're going to Heaven.

➤ You think of McDonald's, Burger King, KFC etc. as cheap food.

➤ You probably own a telephone and a TV. Your place is heated in the winter and has its own bathroom. You do your laundry in a machine. You don't kill your own food. You don't have a dirt floor. You eat at a table, sitting on chairs.

➤ You don't consider insects, dogs, cats, monkeys, or guinea pigs to be food.

➤ A bathroom may not have a bathtub in it, but it certainly has a toilet.

➤ It seems natural to you that the telephone system, railroads, auto manufacturers, airlines, and power companies are privately run; indeed, you can hardly picture things working differently.

➤ You expect, as a matter of course, that the phones will work. Getting a new phone is routine.

➤ The train system, by contrast, isn't very good. Trains don't go any faster than cars; you're better off taking a plane.

➤ You find a two-party system natural. You expect the politicians of both parties to be responsive to business, strong on defense, and concerned with the middle class. You find parliamentary systems (such as Italy's) inefficient and comic.

➤ You don't expect to hear socialism seriously defended. Communism, fuhgeddaboudit.

➤ Between "black" and "white" there are no other races. Someone with one black and one white parent looks black to you.

➤ You think most problems could be solved if only people would put aside their prejudices and work together.

➤ You take a strong court system for granted, even if you don't use it. You know that if you went into business and had problems with a customer, partner, or supplier, you could take them to court.

➤ You'd respect someone who speaks French, German, or Japanese— but you very likely don't yourself speak them well enough to communicate with a monolingual foreigner. You're a bit more ambivalent about Spanish; you think the schools should teach kids English.

➤ It's not all that necessary to learn foreign languages anyway. You can travel the continent using nothing but English – and get by pretty well in the rest of the world, too.

➤ You think a tax level of 30% is scandalously high.

➤ School is free through high school (at least, it's an option, even if you went to private school); college isn't, unless you get a scholarship.

➤ College is (normally, and excluding graduate study) four years long.

Everybody knows that

➤ Mustard comes in jars. Shaving cream comes in cans. Milk comes in plastic jugs or cardboard boxes, and occasionally in bottles.

➤ The day's date comes second: 11/22/63. (And you know what happened on that date.)

➤ The decimal point is a dot. Certainly not a comma.

➤ A billion is a thousand times a million.

➤ World War II was a just war, and (granted all the suffering of course) ended all right. It was a time when the country came together and did what was right. And instead of insisting on vengeance, the US very generously rebuilt Europe instead, with the Marshall Plan.

➤ You expect marriages to be made for love, not arranged by third parties. Getting married by a judge is an option, but not a requirement; most marriages happen in church. You have a best man and a maid or matron of honor at the wedding – a friend or a sibling. And, naturally, a man gets only one wife at a time.

➤ If a man has sex with another man, he's a homosexual.

➤ Once you're introduced to someone (well, besides the President and other lofty figures), you can call them by their first name.

➤ If you're a woman, you don't go to the beach topless.

➤ A hotel room has a private bath.

➤ You'd rather a film be subtitled than dubbed (if you go to foreign films at all).

➤ You seriously expect to be able to transact business, or deal with the government, without paying bribes.

➤ If a politician has been cheating on his wife, you would question his ability to govern.

➤ Just about any store will take your credit card.

➤ A company can fire just about anybody it wants, unless it discriminates by doing so.

➤ You like your bacon crisp (unless it's Canadian bacon, of course).

➤ Labor Day is in the fall.

Contributions to world civilization

➤ You've probably seen *Star Wars*, *ET*, *Home Alone*, *Casablanca*, and *Snow White*. If you're under forty, add *Blazing Saddles*, *Terminator*, *Jaws*, and *2001: A Space Odyssey*; otherwise, add *Gone with the Wind*, *A Night at the Opera*, *Psycho*, and *Citizen Kane*.

➤ You know the Beatles, the Rolling Stones, Bob Dylan, Elvis, Chuck Berry, Michael Jackson, Simon & Garfunkel, Linda Ronstadt. If not, you know Frank Sinatra, Al Jolson, Duke Ellington, Louis Armstrong, Tony Bennett, and Kate Smith.

➤ You count on excellent medical treatment. You know you're not going to die of cholera or other Third World diseases. You expect very strong measures to be taken to save very ill babies or people in their eighties. You think dying at 65 would be a tragedy.

➤ You went over US history, and some European, in school. Not much Russian, Chinese, or Latin American. You couldn't name ten US interventions in Latin America.

➤ You expect the military to fight wars, not get involved in politics. You may not be able to name the head of the Joint Chiefs of Staff.

➤ Your country has never been conquered by a foreign nation.

➤ You're used to a wide variety of choices for almost anything you buy.

➤ You still measure things in feet, pounds, and gallons.

➤ You are not a farmer.

➤ Comics basically come in two varieties: newspaper comics and magazines; the latter pretty much all feature superheroes.

➤ The people who appear on the most popular talk shows are mostly entertainers, politicians, or rather strange individuals. Certainly not, say, authors.

➤ You drive on the right side of the road. You stop at red lights even if nobody's around. If you're a pedestrian and cars are stopped at a red light, you will fearlessly cross the street in front of them.

➤ You think of Canada as a pleasant, peaceful, but rather dull country, which has suddenly developed an inexplicable problem in Québec. You probably couldn't explain why the Canadians didn't join the other British colonies in rebelling against King George.

➤ You consider the Volkswagen Beetle to be a small car.

➤ The police are armed, but not with submachine guns.

➤ If a woman is plumper than the average, it doesn't improve her looks.

➤ The biggest meal of the day is in the evening.

➤ The nationality people most often make jokes about is the Poles.

➤ There's parts of the city you definitely want to avoid at night.

Outside the Beltway

➤ You feel that your kind of people aren't being listened to enough in Washington.

➤ You wouldn't expect both inflation and unemployment to be very high (say, over 15%) at the same time.

➤ You don't care very much what family someone comes from.

➤ The normal thing, when a couple dies, is for their estate to be divided equally between their children.

➤ You think of opera and ballet as rather elite entertainments. It's likely you don't see that many plays, either.

➤ Christmas is in the winter. Unless you're Jewish, you spend it with your family, give presents, and put up a tree.

➤ You may think the church is too powerful, or the state is; but you are used to not having a state church and don't think that it would be a good idea.

➤ You'd be hard pressed to name the capitals or the leaders of all the nations of Europe.

➤ You aren't familiar with Mafalda, Lucky Luke, Corto Maltese, Milo Manara, Guido Crepax, Gotlib, or Moebius.

➤ You've left a message at the beep.

➤ Taxis are generally operated by foreigners, who are often deplorably ignorant about the city.

➤ You are distrustful of welfare and unemployment payments – you think people should earn a living and not take handouts. But you would not be in favor of eliminating Social Security and Medicare.

➤ If you want to be a doctor, you need to get a bachelor's first.

➤ There sure are a lot of lawyers.

Space and time

➤ If you have an appointment, you'll mutter an excuse if you're five minutes late, and apologize profusely if it's ten minutes. An hour late is almost inexcusable.

➤ If you're talking to someone, you get uncomfortable if they approach closer than about two feet.

➤ About the only things you expect to bargain for are houses, cars, and antiques. Haggling is largely a matter of finding the hidden point that's the buyer's minimum.

➤ Once you're past college, you very rarely simply show up at someone's place. People have to invite each other over – especially if a meal is involved.

➤ When you negotiate, you are polite, of course, but it's only good business to 'play hardball'. Some foreigners pay excessive attention to status, or don't say what they mean, and that's exasperating.

➤ If you have a business appointment or interview with someone, you expect to have that person to yourself, and the business shouldn't take more than an hour or so.

Reprinted with kind permission from Mark Rosenfelder.
http://www.zompist.com/amercult.html

— How to Tell If You're English —

by Graham John Francis de Sales Wheeler

RAHAM IS A *classicist based at Cambridge University who does an odd bit of singing and other things musical on the side. He believes he is the only person in England who actually likes the French.*

IF YOU'RE ENGLISH...

➤ You're not a card-carrying republican. You may or may not particularly like the present Royal Family, but you're dimly aware that the royals have always been there and probably always will.

➤ You're familiar with *Eastenders, Coronation Street, Who Want to Be a Millionaire?, The Generation Game* and *Panorama*, as well as the classic comedies which are to be worshipped like minor deities: *Blackadder, Fawlty Towers, Only Fools and Horses* and *Monty Python's Flying Circus*.

➤ If middle-aged, you may be slightly sniffy about American TV, but your greatest contempt is reserved for Australian shows like Neighbours.

➤ You're not all that interested in baseball, basketball, or American football. If male, on the other hand, you know everything there is to know about soccer, which you call simply 'football', and perhaps cricket as well. Middle-aged men can add snooker and golf.

➤ You count yourself fortunate if you get four weeks of vacation a year.

Where do you find these blokes?

➤ You probably have a vague belief in God, but you think it's bad manners to talk (or think) very much about religion, at least in public. You'd probably be turned off by a zealously Christian politician, and you laugh your socks off at the American Christian Right whenever they're on the news.

➤ You think of McDonald's, Burger King, KFC etc. as cheap food.

➤ You probably own a telephone and a TV. Your place is heated in the winter and has its own bathroom. You do your laundry in a machine. You don't kill your own food. You don't have a dirt floor. You eat at a table, sitting on chairs.

➤ You don't consider insects, dogs, cats, monkeys, or guinea pigs to be food, though if you're an older northerner you may have a strange taste for tripe and onions.

➤ You usually refer to the smallest room as 'the toilet', or (if socially aspirant) 'the loo'. Cockneys (speakers of the famous/notorious London dialect) call it the 'khazi' for some reason, and 'bog' is a common colloquialism. You'll be understood if you call it the 'bathroom', but some people like to use that for the room (possibly separate) where you take a bath.

➤ It is beginning to seem natural to you that the telephone system, railroads, auto manufacturers, airlines, and power companies are privately run; you can remember back to the pre-Thatcher era when things were different, but you can't see things changing and don't have very strong feelings on the subject anyway.

➤ You expect, as a matter of course, that the phones will work. Getting a new phone is routine.

➤ The train system, by contrast, is dreadful. Trains go much faster than cars, but never run on time, especially Virgin Trains.

Tories and Whigs . . . or is that Tories in wigs?

➤ You find a three-party system natural. You think that the Conservatives are too weak and divided to vote for. You vote Labour, either because (if middle-class) they've moved far enough to the right to be safe; or because (if working-class) your parents did and you somehow feel that you ought to. If you're middle-class, you may vote for the Liberal Democrats if you think of yourself as socially concerned.

➤ You don't expect to hear socialism seriously defended, except by ageing eccentrics like Arthur Scargill and Tony Benn. You can't think of any British Communists off hand (except Philby and the other MI5 spies).

➤ You think most problems could be solved if only people would put aside their prejudices, work together and (if foreign) know their place.

➤ You take a strong court system for granted, even if you don't use it. You know that if you went into business and had problems with a customer, partner, or supplier, you could take them to court.

➤ You'd respect someone who speaks French, German, or Spanish. You probably learnt a bit of French at school, but everyone speaks English nowadays, so what's the point of learning foreign languages? Best of all, the advance of English has gloriously succeeded in really annoying the French, a major ambition for any red-blooded Englishman. If privately educated, you may have been forced to study Latin for a year or two.

➤ You think a tax level of over 50% for high earners is rather high.

The old school tie

➤ School is free through high school (at least, it's an option, even if you went to public (that is, private) school); college is heavily subsidised—at the moment.

➤ College is (normally, and excluding graduate study) three years long.

➤ Mustard comes in jars. Shaving cream comes in cans. Milk comes in bottles or in cardboard boxes.

➤ The last appliances you've bought came with plugs, but until a few years ago you had to hunt through the house for a plug whenever you got a new TV or something similar.

➤ The day's date comes first: 03.09.39. (And you know what happened on that date.)

➤ The decimal point is a dot. Certainly not a comma.

➤ A billion is a thousand times a million. But it used to be a million times a million.

➤ World War II was a just war, and (granted all the suffering of course) ended all right, if slightly belatedly because of the traditional American dithering (cf. World War I). It was a time when the country came together and did what was right. You still have your (grand)father's North African medals, and you had an aunty who was bombed out in the East End (of London) and knows lots of stories about the blitz.

➤ You expect marriages to be made for love, not arranged by third parties. Getting married by a registrar is an option, but not a requirement; many marriages happen in church, but mainly for the photos. You have a best man and several bridesmaids. And, naturally, a man gets only one wife at a time.

➤ If a man has sex with another man, he's a homosexual.

No burned bacon, please

➤ Once you're introduced to someone (up to and including the Prime Minister), you can nowadays call them by their first name, unless you're in an officers' mess or the Garrick Club.

➤ If you're a woman, you might go to the beach topless.

➤ You seriously expect to be able to transact business, or deal with the government, without paying bribes.

➤ If a politician has been cheating on his wife, you would be overcome with a mixture of horror and glee. You would probably expect a British minister to 'do the decent thing' and resign, but you thought that the Yanks went a bit over the top on Clinton.

➤ Just about any store will take your credit card.

➤ A company can mostly fire who it wants, but there is a reasonable amount of employment legislation and unions do exist and often take their role seriously.

➤ You've never come across crispy bacon.

➤ Labour Day is (technically) the first Monday in May, but everyone's always called it 'May Day Bank Holiday.'

Contributions to world culture

➤ You have a slightly chauvinistic pride in the success of British films like *Four Weddings*, *The Full Monty* and the Nick Park animations. You disapprove of Hollywood distortions of history, a la Private Ryan. You've seen and enjoyed all the old American movies like *Casablanca*, *Citizen Kane*, *Psycho*, *The Great Escape* and (for the grandmothers) *Gone with the Wind*, but you thought that *Titanic* was pathetic.

➤ You know the Beatles, the Rolling Stones, Bob Dylan, Elvis, Chuck Berry, Michael Jackson, Simon & Garfinkel, Linda Ronstadt. If not, you know Frank Sinatra, Al Joplin, Duke Ellington, Louis Armstrong, Tony Bennett, and Kate Smith.

➤ Privatization of the National Health Service is absolutely unthinkable. You can count on excellent medical treatment — in an emergency. If you've just got something minor but painful, you expect a long, long wait for NHS treatment. You know you're not going to die of cholera or other Third World diseases. You think dying at 65 would be a tragedy.

➤ You went over British history, and some European, in school, not much American, Asian, or anything else. You did Hitler and Stalin in particular because they're memorable and easy to teach, or else the Reformation years for similar reasons.

➤ You expect the military to fight wars, not get involved in politics. You couldn't name any serving soldier, sailor or airman (except Andy McNab, the SAS men who started the flood of army books, and Gulf veteran Sir Peter de la Billiere).

➤ Your country has never been conquered by a foreign nation, at any rate since 1066. (William of Orange (1688) doesn't count – he was invited.)

➤ You're used to a wide variety of choices for almost anything you buy.

➤ You still mentally measure things in feet, pounds, and gallons, though the European Union has made metric measures mandatory for most things.

➤ You are not a farmer. Farmers are grumpy old curmudgeons who grow rich and fat on subsidies (unless they've been ruined by BSE and committed suicide).

➤ The people who appear on the most popular talk shows are mostly entertainers, authors, or rather strange individuals. Certainly not, say, politicians.

➤ You drive on the left and often wonder why foreigners drive on the wrong side. You stop at red lights even if nobody's around. If you're a pedestrian and cars are stopped at a red light, you will fearlessly cross the street in front of them.

Sending Johnny Foreigner to an early grave

➤ You think of the French as the ancient tribal enemy, people who are (in the words of Edmund Blackadder) into 'cruelty to animals and urinating in the street'. The Germans are little better, and memories of the Wars and of Germany's defeat in the 1966 football World Cup final are still quite vivid. If you're middle-class, you may often holiday in France; if working-class, you'll probably prefer Spain or the Spanish islands.

➤ The Scots are tight-fisted, humourless, savage, and wear skirts which they insist on calling 'kilts.' They play ridiculous musical instruments (badly) and eat stuffed sheep's stomachs.

➤ The Welsh are all excellent singers, eat leeks, all the time and start speaking Welsh whenever an Englishman (detected by some kind of telepathic radar system) walks into the shop. If they come from the 'valleys,' they are probably hopelessly inbred.

➤ The Irish drink lots and lots of Guinness, are all devout Catholics, and set off bombs in Belfast every so often. They are also irremediably stupid.

➤ All Americans are terribly wealthy, so an American accent acts on a shopkeeper or stallholder just like the sound of the feeding-bell did on Pavlov's dogs.

➤ You consider the Volkswagen Beetle to be a reasonably small car.

➤ The police are certainly not armed. This is England, for God's sake, not 1930s Chicago!

➤ If a woman is plumper than the average, it doesn't improve her looks.

> The biggest meal of the day is in the evening.
> The nationality people most often make jokes about is the Irish (and occasionally the Scottish, on account of their meanness or national dress).
> There's parts of the city you definitely want to avoid at night.

Outside the M25

> You feel that your kind of people aren't being listened to enough in Westminster (where Parliament sits) or Whitehall (where the Civil Service works).
> You wouldn't expect both inflation and unemployment to be very high (say, over 10%) at the same time.
> You don't care very much what family someone comes from, unless they're in Burke's or Debrett's (directories of the aristocracy).
> The normal thing, when a couple dies, is for their estate to be divided equally between their children.
> You think of opera and ballet as rather elite entertainments. It's likely you don't see that many plays, either (unless, perhaps, if you're a Londoner).
> Christmas is in the winter. Unless you're Jewish, you spend it with your family, give presents, and put up a tree.
> You dimly remember hearing about a time when the established Church of England had some political influence.
> You'd be hard pressed to name the leaders of all the nations of Europe. The capitals you could probably do.
> If over 50, you still haven't got used to answering machines.
> Taxis, particularly in London, are generally operated by fascists who entertain you with their quirky views on immigration and penal policy. They do know the city, though.
> You think that the Welfare State is a necessary part of a civilized society.
> If you want to be a doctor, you need to get a master's first.
> Being a lawyer is still (just about) an honourable profession. Barristers still wear gowns and wigs.

Reprinted with kind permission from Mark Rosenfelder.
http://www.zompist.com/pomcult.html

— References —
and Further Reading

LANGUAGE HAS ALWAYS held great fascination (in the beginning was the word), and a dialog continues between scholars and the rest of us, via books, newspapers, magazines, internet newsgroups, and the media. This curiosity covers language in general, English in particular, and the American/British issue because American is ever more prevalent, and British the once prevalent source. Part of the impetus behind this dictionary was to accumulate answers to some of these latter questions. But over the last decade or so, a number of books and documentaries have satisfied that curiosity.

I have an annotated list of such books below under general language reference. I enthusiastically encourage readers to at least pop down to the local library and leaf through these books, or check out the videos.

I also list some books about American, some books about British, and a special class, dictionaries or word lists that go both from American to British and British to American, to which this dictionary belongs.

Finally, alphabetically sorted by author, is an inclusive list of books and articles that I used in researching for the various chapters in this dictionary, everything from contemporary slang to ancient linguistics.

Web links to a similar set of resources are maintained separately online, since they have a shorter half-life — http://www.peak.org/~jeremy/dictionary/links/.

General Language References:

***The Story of English**, A companion to the PBS television series*, Robert McCrum, William Cran, Robert McNeil, Viking Press 1986, ISBN 0-670-80467-3.

> This book accompanies nine hours of documentary of the English language. The language is not only traced to its source, but also shown how it is evolving in the most surprising places. There are highlights of English in

many areas including Australia, previously Celtic regions, the colonies, and of course the USA and Britain. I found it most enlightening and absolutely worth viewing.

The Cambridge Encyclopedia of The English Language, David Crystal, Cambridge University Press, 1995, ISBN 0-521-40179-8.

This is **the** general reference of the English Language. It's the ultimate English Language FAQ. And for an overview of all the world's languages, see David Crystal's *The Cambridge Encyclopedia of Language*.

Steven Pinker, *The Language Instinct*, William Morrow, 1994.

This delightful book brings our thinking about language into the 21st century. I found it clarifies all the language issues, and provides a context for exploring any particular aspect.

American References:

American Slang, Robert L. Chapman, 2nd edition, HarperPerennial, 1995.
Lonely Planet USA Phrasebook: Understanding Americans & Their Culture, Colleen Cotter (Editor), Sally Steward, 2nd edition, Lonely Planet, August 2001.

British References:

British English A to Zed, Norman W. Schur, revised by Eugene Ehrlich, Checkmark, Books 2001. (This is the latest, and posthumous, revision of Schur's 1973 *British Self Taught*.)
British English for American Readers: A Dictionary of the Language, Customs, and Places of British Life and Literature, David Grote, Greenwood Press, 1992.
Lonely Planet British Phrasebook, Elizabeth Bartsch-Parker, Dr Roibeard O'Maolalaigh, Stephen Burger, Lonely Planet, August 1999.
English for Americans with a sense of humour, M Tracey, White-Boucke.
NTC's Dictionary of British Slang and Colloquial Expressions, Ewart James, Editor, NTC Publishing Group, November 1996.
The Very Best of British, Mike Etherington, Effingpot Productions, September 2000.
Understanding British English, Margaret Moore, Citadel Press, 1989.

American—British Cross-References:

The American-British British-American Dictionary with Helpful Hints to Travelers, William Quinby de Funiak, A.S. Barnes & Co, 1963, 1978.

American English English American, E J Perkins, A Domino Book, (1997) 1998.

Anglo-American American-Anglo, William N. Gallard & L. Amanda Smith, Water Lane Publishing Co, 1984.

An Anglo-American Interpreter A Vocabulary and Phrase Book, H. W. Horwill, The Folcroft Press, 1939 (1970).

British & American English Since 1900, John W. Clark, Eric Partridge, Greenwood Press, NY 1951, 1968.

British and American English, Peter Streven, Collier-Macmillan, 1972 .

British/American Language Dictionary, Norman Moss, Passport Books, (1973) 1984.

British: British-American American-British, Catherine McCormick, Hippocrene Books, (1996) 2001.

A Common Language, British & American English, BBC & Voice of America, 1964.

Divided by a Common Language, Christopher Davies, Jason Murphy, Mayflower Press, January 1998.

Mighty Fine Words and Smashing Expressions: Making Sense of Transatlantic English, Orin Hargraves, Oxford University Press, November 2002.

Particular Dialect Studies:

The Dialects of England, Peter Trudgill, Blackwell, 1990, ISBN 0-631-13917-6.

A most elucidating book on modern and traditional dialects of England.

The Muvver Tongue, Robert Barltrop & Jim Wolveridge, The Journeyman Press, 1980.

An excellent, personal account of Cockney, the language, as the means of expression of the people and their culture. It elucidates what Cockney is, as much by showing us what it is not, and emphasizes the livingness of the language as opposed to the static renditions often portrayed in stories, shows and movies.

My favourite story from the book (concerning the Cockney silent h): "One Sunday morning some years ago I sat in a bus behind a man who had a little boy of about four in his lap. The child had a picture-alphabet book, and the father was explaining it carefully; when they came to h, the picture was of a hedgehog. The man said: 'that's an edgeog. It's really two words, edge and og. They both start with h.' "

A Personal Kiwi-Yankee Slanguage Dictionary, Louis S. Leland Jr., John McIndoe Ltd, 51 Crawford Street, Dunedin, New Zealand 1980, 1987.

This explains NZ words and phrases. Designed to amuse and enlighten. It does the latter, and the difference between the two languages does the former anyway. This book is thorough and includes many explanatory details. Since a lot of NZ jargon comes from GB it complements the above, though it must be noted that it is mostly their own (and the Maori's).

The New Hacker's Dictionary, Eric S. Raymond, The MIT Press 1991.

The definitive dictionary of the hacker culture jargon. Because of the particular peculiarities of the subject, namely computers, communications, and its self-containedness (until the 1990s), the compiled list of jargon terms has been subjected to real-time feedback and updating by the many thousands of computer folks. It has become a self-sustaining, real-time record of its own evolution which, again, by its nature (namely, new, unique, and very rapid), is also a glimpse of the process of language itself evolving.

References (alphabetical by author)

Ed. R. E. Allen, *The Concise Oxford Dictionary*, Eighth Edition, Clarendon OUP, 1990.

Christine Ammer, *The American Heritage Dictionary of Idioms*, Houghton Mifflin Company, 1997.

Lars Andersson & Peter Trudgill, *Bad Language*, Blackwell, 1990, ISBN 0-631-17872-4.

Robert Barltrop & Jim Wolveridge, *The Muvver Tongue*, The Journeyman Press, 1980 ISBN 0-904526-63-1.

Elizabeth Bartsch-Parker, Dr Roibeard O'Maolalaigh, Stephen Burger, *Lonely Planet British Phrasebook*, Lonely Planet, August 1999.

Henry Beard, Christopher Cerf, *The Official Politically Correct Dictionary and Handbook*, Villard Books, October 1993.

Maria Carmela Betro, *Hieroglyphics*, Abbeville Press, 1996.

Anthea Bickerton, *American English · English American,* Abson Books 1997.

Georges Bourcier, *An Introduction to the History of the English Language*, Stanley Thornes, 1981.

Gyles Brandreth, *The Joy of Lex*, William Morrow & Co, April 1983.

G. V. Carey, *Mind the Stop: A Brief Guide to Punctuation*, Penguin, (1939, 1958) 1976.

Craig M. Carver, *American Regional Dialects, A Word Geography*, The University of Michigan Press, 1990, ISBN 0-472-10076-9 & 0-472-08103-9 pbk.

J. C. Catford, *A Practical Introduction to Phonetics*, Clarendon Press, 1994.

Robert L. Chapman, *American Slang*, 2nd edition, HarperPerennial, 1995.

John W. Clark, Eric Partridge, *British & American English Since 1900*, Greenwood Press, NY 1951, 1968.

Collins Cobuild Dictionary of Idioms, HarperCollins, 1998.

Collins Cobuild English Dictionary, HarperCollins, 1998.

A Common Language, British & American English, BBC & Voice of America 1964.

Michael C. Corballis, *The Gestural Origins of Language*, American Scientist, March-April 1999 <u>87</u> 2.

Colleen Cotter (Editor), Sally Steward, *Lonely Planet USA Phrasebook: Understanding Americans & Their Culture*, 2nd edition, Lonely Planet, August 2001.

David Crystal, *The Cambridge Encyclopedia of The English Language*, Cambridge University Press, 1995, ISBN 0-521-40179-8.

David Crystal, *The Cambridge Encyclopedia of Language*, Cambridge University Press, 1987, ISBN 0-521-42443-7.

David Crystal, *The English Language: A guided tour of the language by the presenter of BBC Radio 4's English Now*, Penguin, 1990, ISBN 0-14-013532-4.

Christopher Davies, Jason Murphy, *Divided by a Common Language*, Mayflower Press, January 1998.

Susie Dent, *The Language Report*, Oxford University Press, 2003.

Mike Etherington, *The Very Best of British*, Effingpot Productions, September 2000.

William Quinby de Funiak, *The American-British British-American Dictionary with Helpful Hints to Travelers*, A.S. Barnes & Co, 1963, 1978.

William N. Gallard & L. Amanda Smith, *Anglo-American American-Anglo*, Water Lane Publishing Co, 1984.

Alan H. Gardiner, *The Egyptian Origin of the Semitic Alphabet*, The Journal of Egyptian Archeology, Vol III, 1916.

Albertine Gaur, *A History of Writing*, Abbeville Press, 1997.

Jonathon Green, *The Cassell Dictionary of Slang*, Cassell, 1998,

John Grimond, *The Economist Style Guide*, The Economist, 1997.

David Grote, *British English for American Readers. A Dictionary of the Language, Customs, and Places of British Life and Literature*, Greenwood Press, 1992, ISBN 0-313-27851-2.

Orin Hargraves, *Mighty Fine Words and Smashing Expressions: Making Sense of Transatlantic English*, Oxford University Press, November 2002.

H. W. Horwill, *An Anglo-American Interpreter A Vocabulary and Phrase book*, The Folcroft Press 1939 (1970).

Ewart James, Editor, *NTC's Dictionary of British Slang and Colloquial Expressions*, NTC Publishing Group, November 1996.

Gordon Jarvie, *Good Punctuation Guide*, Chambers, 1992.

Elizabeth Knowles, *The Oxford Dictionary of New Words*, Oxford University Press, 1998.

Chester L. Krause & Clifford Mishler, Colin R. Bruce II, Editor, *1993 Standard Catalog of World Coins*, Krause Publications, 1993, ISBN 0-87341-187-0.

Louis S. Leland Jr., *A Personal Kiwi-Yankee Slanguage Dictionary*, John McIndoe Ltd, 51 Crawford Street, Dunedin, New Zealand 1980, 1987.

John Man, *alpha beta*, Wiley, 2000.

Ed. A. S. Maney & R. L. Smallwood, *MHRA Style Book*, Modern Humanities Research Association, 1971.

Ed. Tom McArthur, *The Oxford Companion to the English Language*, Oxford University Press, 1992.

Catherine McCormick, *British: British-American American-British*, Hippocrene Books, 1996.

Robert McCrum, William Cran, Robert McNeil, *The Story of English, A companion to the PBS television series*, Viking Press 1986, ISBN 0-670-80467-3.

Roger Mellie, *Roger's Profanisaurus*, Viz, 2002.

Margaret Moore, *Understanding British English*, Citadel Press 1989.

Norman Moss, *British/American Language Dictionary*, Passport Books (1973) 1984.

Eric Partridge, *A Dictionary of Historical Slang*, Penguin, 1972.

Eric Partridge, *Origins*, Greenwich House, 1983. [My first stop for etymology.]

E J Perkins, *American English English American*, A Domino Book, (1997) 1998.

Steven Pinker, *The Language Instinct*, William Morrow, 1994.

Eric S. Raymond, *The New Hacker's Dictionary*, The MIT Press 1991, ISBN 0-262-68069-6.

Andrew Robinson, *Lost Languages*, McGraw-Hill, 2002.

Andrew Robinson, *The Story of Writing*, Thames & Hudson, 1995.

Norman W. Schur, *British Self Taught: with Comments in American*, Macmillan Company 1973.

Norman W. Schur, revised by Eugene Ehrlich, *British English A to Zed*, Checkmark Books, 2001.

John Seely, *The Oxford Guide to Writing and Speaking*, Oxford University Press, 1998.

Roger W. Shuy, *Discovering American Dialects*, National Council of Teachers of English, 1967.

Peter Streven, *British and American English*, Collier-Macmillan, 1972 .

M Tracey, *English for Americans with a Sense of Humour*, White-Boucke.

Peter Trudgill, *The Dialects of England*, Blackwell, 1990, ISBN 0-631-13917-6.

Peter Trudgill & Jean Hannah, *International English*, 3rd edition, Routledge, Chapman, Hall, 1994.

Peter Trudgill, *Language in the British Isles*, Cambridge University Press, June 1984.

Webster's Collegiate Dictionary, Tenth Edition, Merriam-Webster, 1993.

Welcome to Britain, Whitehall Press, 1971.

— The Author —

J EREMY SMITH, REPUTED to be someone else of the same name, was born at an early age, supposedly on his birthday, in a suburb of London in the Western Hemisphere (just). He lived there and various of the *Home Counties* for 24 years. On impulse he came over to the USA spending 6 years in Southern California, 2 years in the San Francisco Bay Area, and 16 years in Oregon. He has an American ex-wife, 6 English nephews and nieces, 7 American nieces and nephews, and a daughter who is *half and half*/hahf n haf/. He continues to maintain the dictionary's online presence at www.peak.org/~jeremy/dictionary. He has been touched by His Noodly Appendage.

> Time flies like an arrow
> Fruit flies like a banana
> —Groucho Marx

Επεα πτεροευτα—Homer, *Illiad.*

plus floribus unum

(Oh, and I'm the half full guy. No! Wait! What was the question?)

Printed in Great Britain
by Amazon